D0603764

English
At Your Command!

HAMPTON-BROWN

Hampton – Brown
P.O. Box 223220
Carmel, California 93922
800-333-3510
www.hampton-brown.com

Printed in the United States of America

ISBN 0-7362-1972-2 Softcover
ISBN 0-7362-1973-0 Hardcover

04 05 06 07 08 09 10 11 12 9 8 7 6 5 4 3 2

Hampton-Brown extends special thanks to the following consultants who contributed to the development of *English At Your Command!*

Nancy Alexander
ESL Teacher, Grades 6, 7, 8
Nichols Middle School
Community Consolidated SD 65
Evanston, Illinois

Kristi M. Lichtenberg
Bilingual 3rd Grade Teacher
Williams Elementary School
Garland ISD
Garland, Texas

Ellie Paiewonsky
Director, Nassau BOCES BETAC
Bilingual/ESL Technical
Assistance Center
Seaford, New York

Elizabeth M. Buckley
ESL Teacher, Grades K–8
Lincoln, Emerson, Whittier,
Mann Schools
Oak Park SD 97
Oak Park, Illinois

Lourdes A. Lopez
ESOL Grade 3 Teacher
Citrus Grove Elementary School
Miami-Dade County Public Schools
Miami, Florida

Wilma Ramírez
Instructional Coach for
Curriculum-Based ELD
Alisal Community and Chavez
Elementary Schools/Alisal USD
Salinas, California

ACKNOWLEDGMENTS
Every effort has been made to secure permission, but if any omissions have been made, please let us know. We gratefully acknowledge permission to reprint the following material:

ZB Font Method Copyright © 1996 Zaner-Bloser.

P52, **p292**, **p294**, **pp312-315:** From MARS. Copyright © 1991 Elaine Landau. All rights reserved. Used by permission of Grolier Publishing Company. Cover photo courtesy of NASA.

P79: from CINDER-ELLY by Frances Minters. Copyright © 1994 by Frances Minters, text. Used by permission of Viking Penguin, a division of Penguin Putnam Inc.

P80: RICHIE'S ROCKET by Joan Anderson. Illustrations by George Ancona. Text Copyright © 1993 by Joan Anderson. Illustrations Copyright © 1993 by George Ancona. Used by permission of Morrow Jr. Books, a division of William Morrow & Company, Inc.

P81: Cover illustration from SUBWAY SPARROW by Leyla Torres. Copyright © 1993 by Leyla Torres. Reprinted by permission of Farrar, Straus & Giroux, Inc.

P83: Illustration from "The Clever Wife," Shirley Felts, SWEET AND SOUR TALES FROM CHINA, Carol Kendall and Yao-wen Li. Used by permission of The Random House Group Limited.

P93: Cover from THE AMERICAN HERITAGE® CHILDREN'S DICTIONARY. Copyright © 1998 by Houghton Mifflin Company. All rights reserved. Used by permission of the publisher.

P93, **p295** and **pp322-325:** Reprinted with the permission of Simon & Schuster Books for Young Readers, an imprint of Simon & Schuster Children's Publishing Division from MACMILLAN DICTIONARY FOR CHILDREN, Revised by Robert B. Costello, Editor in Chief. Copyright © 1997 Simon & Schuster. Photos pp322-323 and p325 courtesy of NASA. Photo of Pennybacker Bridge, p323, courtesy of Texas Department of Transportation.

P93: Cover from RANDOM HOUSE JAPANESE-ENGLISH/ENGLISH-JAPANESE DICTIONARY. © Copyright The British Museum.

P93: From THE NEW WORLD SPANISH/ENGLISH-ENGLISH/SPANISH DICTIONARY. Copyright © Penguin Putnam Inc., 1969, 1996. Used by permission of publisher.

P93: Cover from THE AMERICAN HERITAGE® CHILDREN'S THESAURUS by Paul Hellweg. Copyright © 1997 by Paul Hellweg. All rights reserved. Used by permission of Houghton Mifflin Company.

P93: Cover from SCHOLASTIC CHILDREN'S THESAURUS. Copyright © 1998 by Scholastic Inc. Reprinted by permission of Scholastic Inc.

P112: "Help! From You" courtesy of American Girl Magazine, Pleasant Company Publications.

P115: "Circus Ponies" by María Izquierdo. Used by permission of Galeria de ArteMexicano.

P116: Cover from THE LOST LAKE by Allen Say. Copyright © 1989 by Allen Say. Reprinted by permission of Houghton Mifflin Co. All rights reserved.

P117: "The Born Loser" by Art Sansom. Extensive unsuccessful attempts were made to contact the copyright holder of this work.

P117 and **p157:** Comic strip by Betty Woods, p117, and "Oak," p157, Copyright © 1997 by Highlights for Children, Inc., Columbus, Ohio.

Pp152-153: ANNIE photos courtesy of the Fredericksburg Theatre Company, Mary Washington College, Dept. of Theatre and Dance, Fredericksburg, VA.

P158: "Matriarch" from SNAKE POEMS by Francisco Alarcón. © 1992. Published by Chronicle Books, San Francisco.

P159: "Today is Very Boring" from THE NEW KID ON THE BLOCK by Jack Prelutsky. Copyright © 1984 by Jack Prelutsky. By permission of Greenwillow Books, a division of William Morrow & Company, Inc.

P160: "There Was an Old Man" limerick and art by Edward Lear, from THE COMPLETE NONSENSE OF EDWARD LEAR. Copyright © 1951, Dover Publications, Inc. Used by permission of the publisher.

Acknowledgments continued on pages 414-416.

Welcome!

In this book, you'll find all kinds of ways to communicate what you're thinking, feeling, and imagining. You can use this book to find out just what you want to know about words and writing. You'll learn how to organize and present ideas and how English works. You can also learn how to do research—not just in the library, but on the Internet, too! At the back, you'll find fascinating facts about life in the U.S.A.

Whenever you have a question about English, you can look here first. This book will put **English At Your Command!**

Table of Contents

Chapter 2

Picture It!

Chapter 3

Put It in Writing!

The Good Writer Guide

Chapter 4

Present It!

Chapter 5

Grammar Made Graphic . . . 230

Chapter 6

Look It Up!

Chapter 1

Just the Right Word

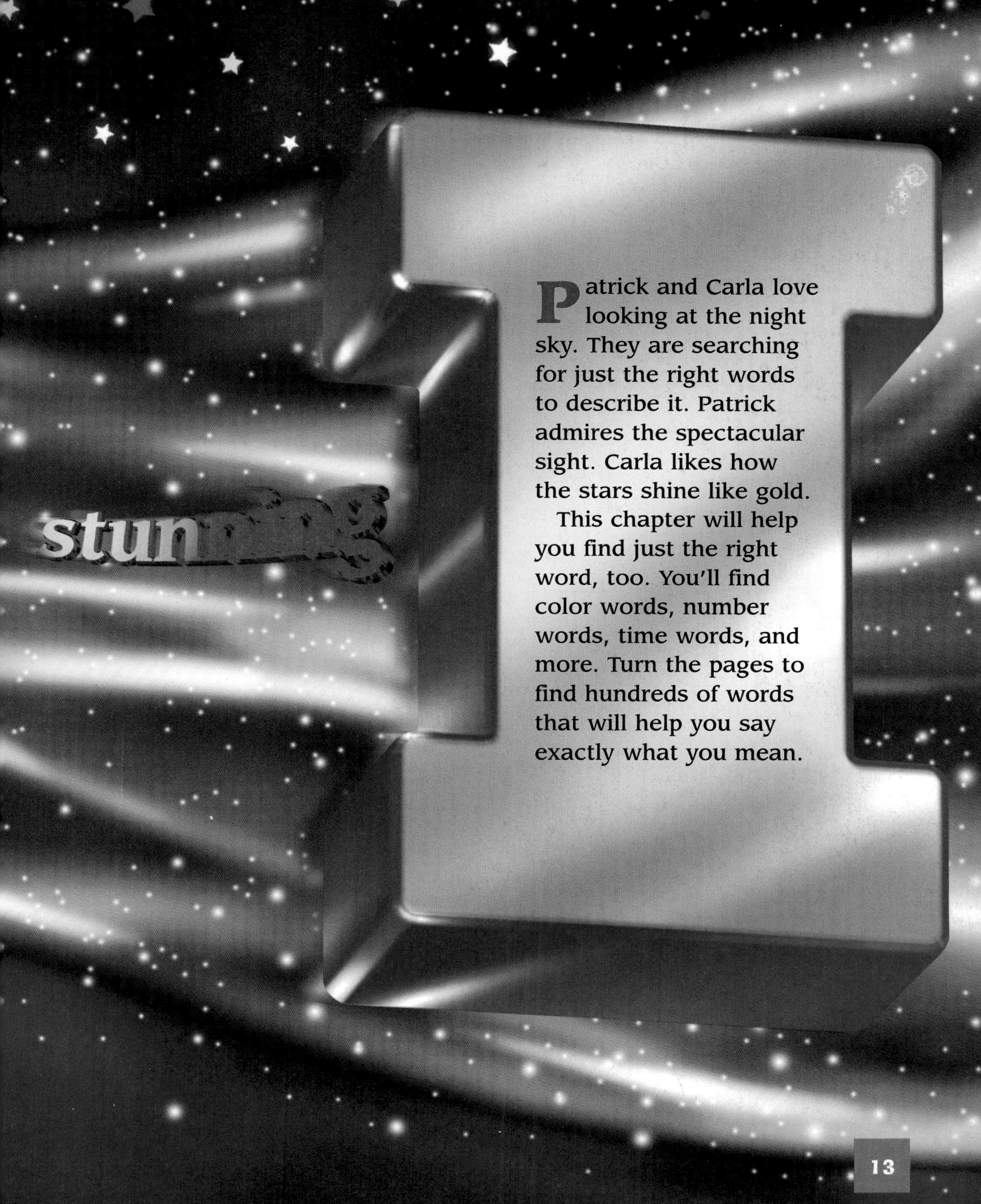

Patrick and Carla love looking at the night sky. They are searching for just the right words to describe it. Patrick admires the spectacular sight. Carla likes how the stars shine like gold.

This chapter will help you find just the right word, too. You'll find color words, number words, time words, and more. Turn the pages to find hundreds of words that will help you say exactly what you mean.

Describing Words

Some **describing words** tell what something is like. Others tell how many, how you or someone else feels, or where something is.

Color Words

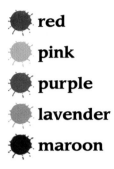

- red
- pink
- purple
- lavender
- maroon

This cat mask has **red** lips and **green** eyes.

- blue
- turquoise
- royal blue
- sky blue
- navy blue
- green
- lime green
- forest green
- yellow
- gold
- orange
- brown
- tan
- black
- gray
- silver
- white

Size Words

small

medium

large

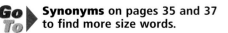

Go To **Synonyms** on pages 35 and 37 to find more size words.

Shape Words

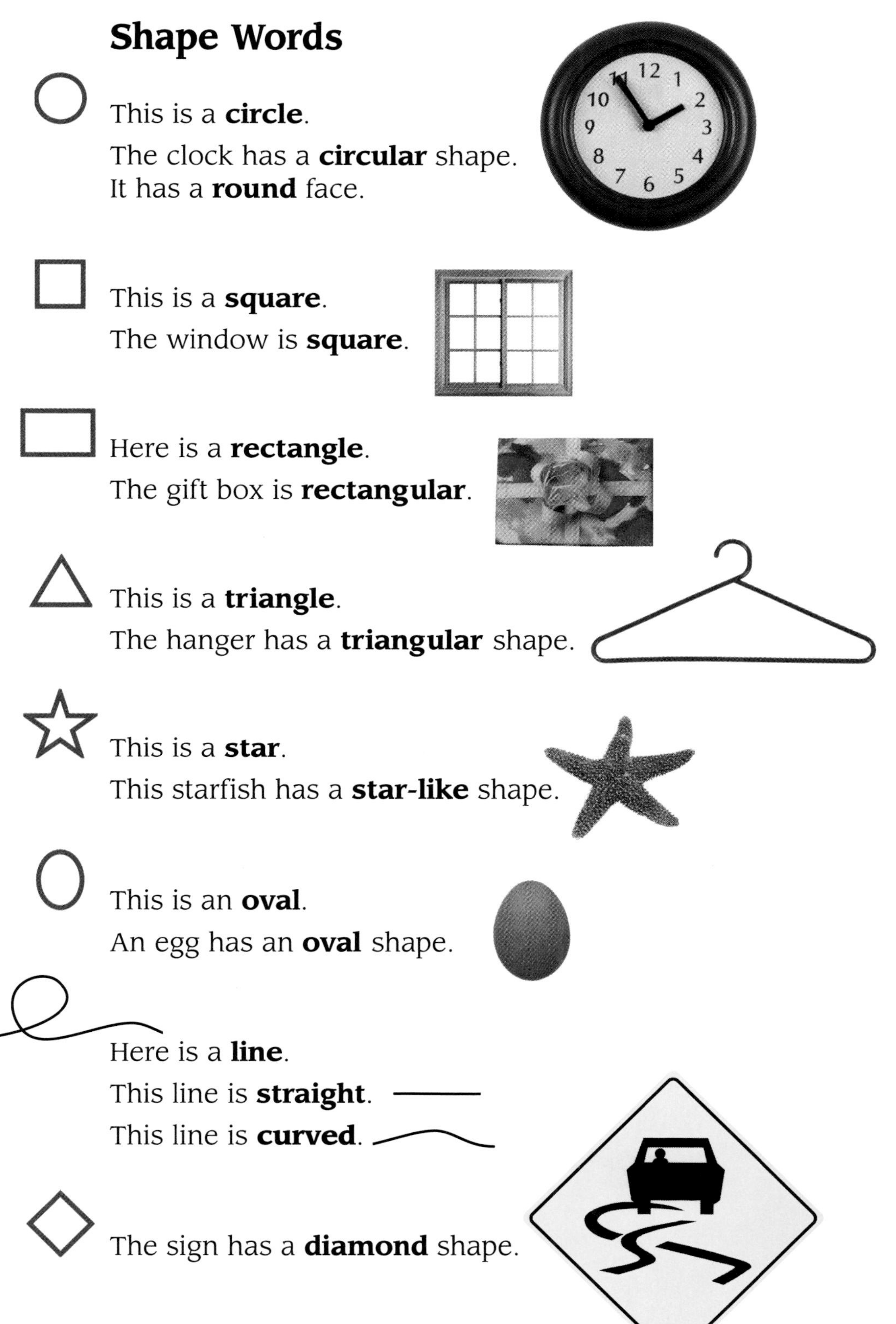

This is a **circle**.

The clock has a **circular** shape.
It has a **round** face.

This is a **square**.

The window is **square**.

Here is a **rectangle**.

The gift box is **rectangular**.

This is a **triangle**.

The hanger has a **triangular** shape.

This is a **star**.

This starfish has a **star-like** shape.

This is an **oval**.

An egg has an **oval** shape.

Here is a **line**.

This line is **straight**.

This line is **curved**.

The sign has a **diamond** shape.

Number Words

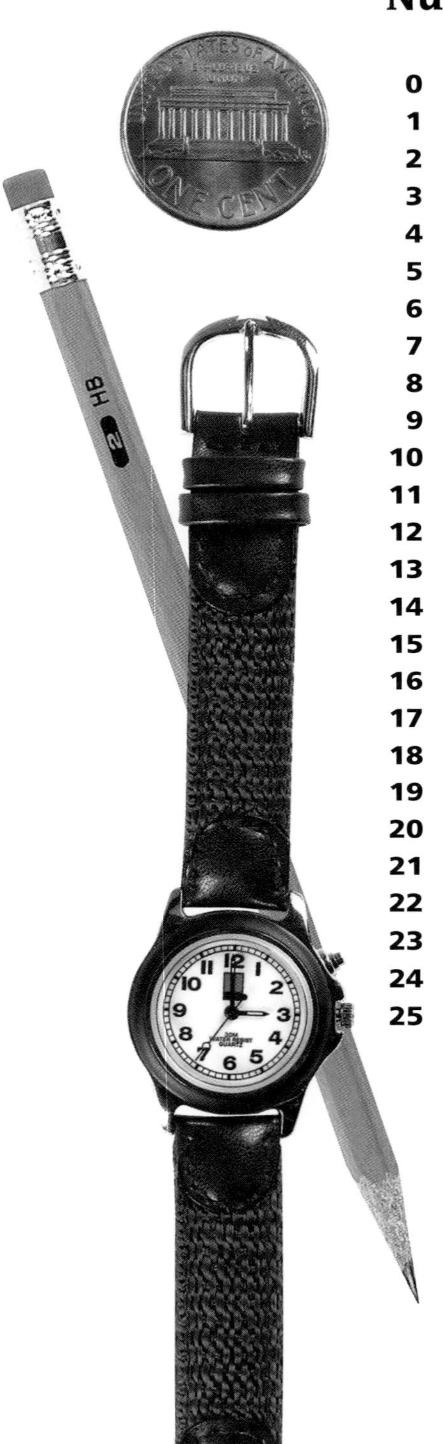

0	zero
1	one
2	two
3	three
4	four
5	five
6	six
7	seven
8	eight
9	nine
10	ten
11	eleven
12	twelve
13	thirteen
14	fourteen
15	fifteen
16	sixteen
17	seventeen
18	eighteen
19	nineteen
20	twenty
21	twenty-one
22	twenty-two
23	twenty-three
24	twenty-four
25	twenty-five
26	twenty-six
27	twenty-seven
28	twenty-eight
29	twenty-nine
30	thirty
40	forty
50	fifty
60	sixty
70	seventy
80	eighty
90	ninety
100	one hundred
500	five hundred
1,000	one thousand
5,000	five thousand
10,000	ten thousand
100,000	one hundred thousand
500,000	five hundred thousand
1,000,000	one million

Order Words

1st	first
2nd	second
3rd	third
4th	fourth
5th	fifth
6th	sixth
7th	seventh
8th	eighth
9th	ninth
10th	tenth
11th	eleventh
12th	twelfth
13th	thirteenth
14th	fourteenth
15th	fifteenth
16th	sixteenth
17th	seventeenth
18th	eighteenth
19th	nineteenth
20th	twentieth
21st	twenty-first
22nd	twenty-second
23rd	twenty-third
24th	twenty-fourth
25th	twenty-fifth
26th	twenty-sixth
27th	twenty-seventh
28th	twenty-eighth
29th	twenty-ninth
30th	thirtieth
40th	fortieth
50th	fiftieth
60th	sixtieth
70th	seventieth
80th	eightieth
90th	ninetieth
100th	one hundredth

More Words That Tell How Many

a **couple** of eggs

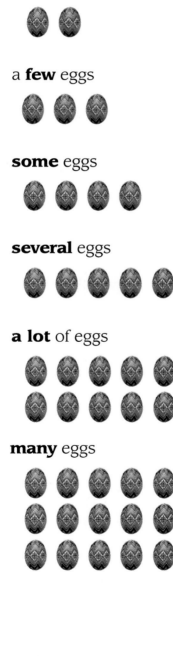

The red egg is **first**.
The blue egg is **second**.

a **pair** of eggs

a **few** eggs

some eggs

several eggs

a lot of eggs

many eggs

all the eggs

Sensory Words

Look at the **red** apples.

An apple has **smooth** skin.

How it looks:

beautiful sunset 

dark shadow

fluffy clouds 

gloomy day

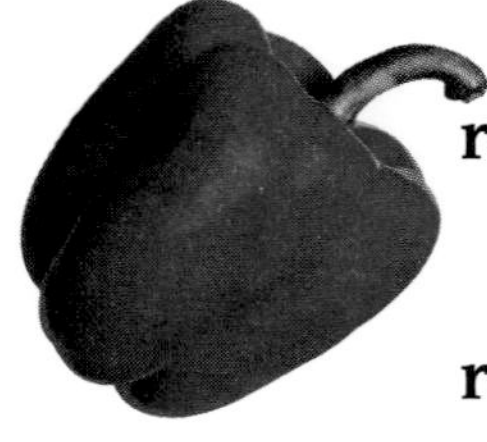

red pepper

round ball 

shiny medal 

tiny ants 

How it feels:

bumpy road

dry chalk

hard rock

hot soup 

rough wood

slimy worm

smooth grapes 

soft cotton 

It has a **fresh** smell.

It sounds **crisp**.

The apple tastes **delicious**!

How it smells:

fragrant rose

fresh pepper

rotten garbage

musty closet

sweet perfume

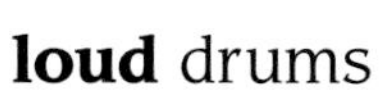

How it sounds:

blaring siren

crisp celery

crunchy carrot

loud drums

noisy music

quiet footsteps

soft whisper

How it tastes:

bitter herb

delicious food

fresh vegetables

salty pretzel

sour lemon

spicy mustard

sweet cake

tangy orange

Feeling Words

Jason is **afraid** of the bee.

Is Jason **bored**?

Jason is **sad**.

Jason is **angry**.

What is Jason **happy** about?

He's **puzzled**.

Jason is **surprised**.

Words That Tell Where

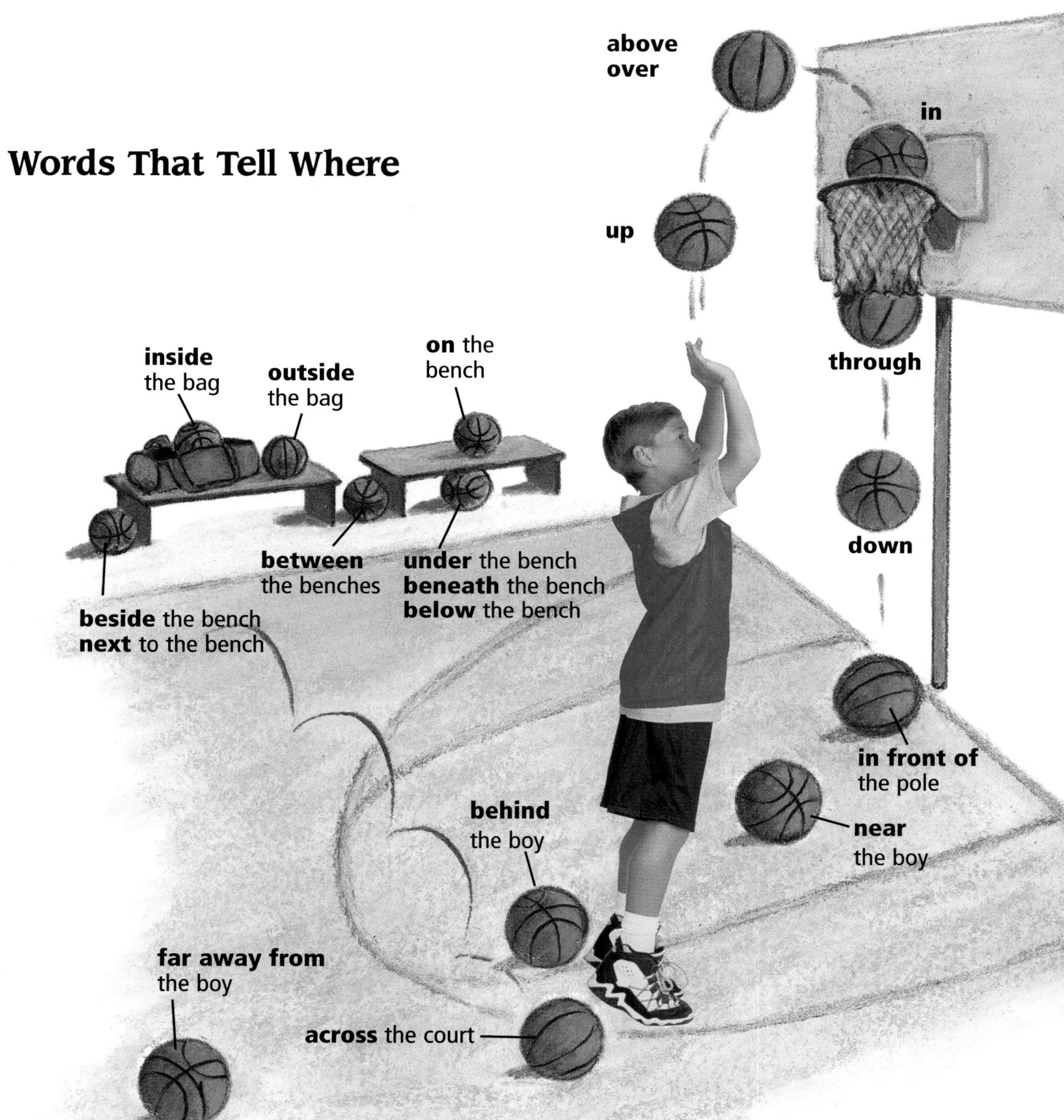
above
over
in
up
through
down
inside
the bag
outside
the bag
on the
bench
between
the benches
under the bench
beneath the bench
below the bench
beside the bench
next to the bench
in front of
the pole
behind
the boy
near
the boy
far away from
the boy
across the court

Greetings and Good-byes

There are many ways to say **hello** and **good-bye**. When you say hello and good-bye to your friends, you can be **informal**. When you say hello and good-bye to teachers and other adults, you need to be **formal**.

Informal

Hello

Hi!
Hi, there!
Hello, there!
Hey!
Howdy!
How's it going?
What's up?
What's new?
What's happening?

Good-bye

Bye!
Bye-bye!
See you later!
See ya!
So long!
Take care!
Take it easy!

Formal

Hello

Good morning!
Good afternoon!
Good evening!
How are you?
It's nice to see you.

Good-bye

It was nice talking to you.
Good night!
Good-bye!
Have a good day.
I hope you have a good afternoon.
It was good to see you.

Multiple-Meaning Words

Multiple-meaning words look the same but have different meanings. They can have two or more different meanings.

address

noun
1. My **address** is 231 South Elm Street.

verb
2. The speaker will give a report today. He will **address** the group.

bark

noun
1. A dog makes a short, loud sound called a **bark**.

noun
2. **Bark** covers the outside of a tree trunk.

bat

noun
1. Use a **bat** to hit a baseball.

noun
2. A **bat** is a small, flying animal.

country

noun
1. The United States of America is a big **country**.

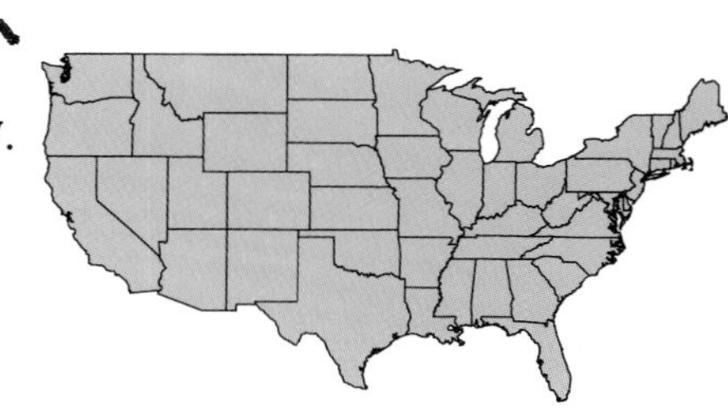

noun
2. Farms are found in the **country**.

Multiple-Meaning Words, continued

current

adjective

1. When something is **current**, it is happening now.

noun

2. Strong winds and the ocean **current** moved the sailboat farther out to sea.

directions

noun

1. The **directions** on a test tell you what to do to answer the questions.

> ***Directions:***
> Please fill in the space next to the correct answer.

noun

2. The **directions** on a map are north, south, east, and west.

fair

noun

1. A **fair** is a place that has rides and games.

adjective

2. You're being **fair** if you treat everyone the same way.

adjective

3. When the weather is clear and sunny, it's **fair**.

fan

noun

1. They love sports. They are sports **fans**.

noun

2. Turn on the **fan** to make the air move.

float

noun
1. Our **float** for the parade was colorful.

verb
2. An inner tube can **float** in water.

foot

noun
1. Put the shoe on your **foot**.

noun
2. A **foot** is 12 inches long.

ground

noun
1. The corn is growing in the **ground**.

adjective
2. Use **ground** corn to make tortillas.

jam

noun
1. Jam is a sweet food. It is made with fruit and sugar.

verb
2. I tried to **jam** too many clothes into my small suitcase.

key

noun
1. Press the delete **key** to erase a word.

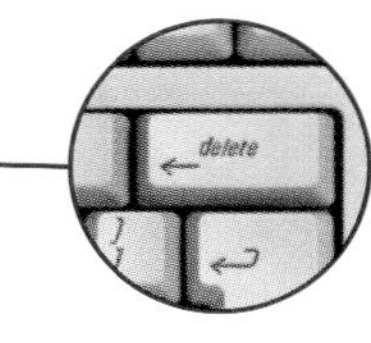

noun
2. You need a **key** to open the lock.

Multiple-Meaning Words, continued

last

adjective
1. The person at the end of the line is **last**.

verb
2. If you take good care of something, it will **last** a long time.

left

verb
1. He is not here. He has **left** the room.

adjective
2. Part of the cookie is **left**.

adjective
3. She wore a ring on her **left** hand.

letter

noun
1. My friend wrote me a **letter**.

noun
2. The first **letter** in the English alphabet is A.

Aa Bb Cc

light

adjective
1. Something that is not heavy is **light**.

noun
2. Turn on the **light** so you can see.

miss

verb
1. When my mother is gone, I **miss** her.

verb
2. When you don't hit your target, you **miss** it.

noun
3. She is called **Miss** Kratky because she is not married.

pen

noun
1. A **pen** is a fenced-in area for animals.

noun
2. You can write a letter with a **pen**.

pitcher

noun
1. The **pitcher** is a baseball player who throws the ball to a catcher.

noun
2. Mix the juice in a **pitcher**. Then pour some into a glass.

plant

noun
1. My dad works at the **plant**.

noun
2. A tree is one kind of green **plant**.

verb
3. **Plant** tomato seeds two inches apart.

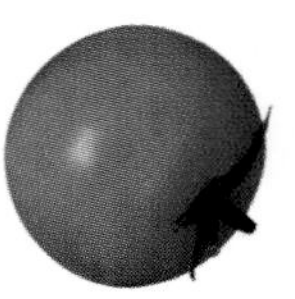

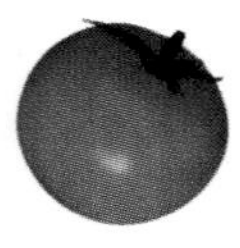

point

verb
1. Point to the place on the map.

noun
2. A **point** is a dot on a line.

noun
3. She made a good **point** in the debate.

pound

noun
1. The vegetables weigh one **pound**.

verb
2. Use a hammer to **pound** a nail into wood.

pupil

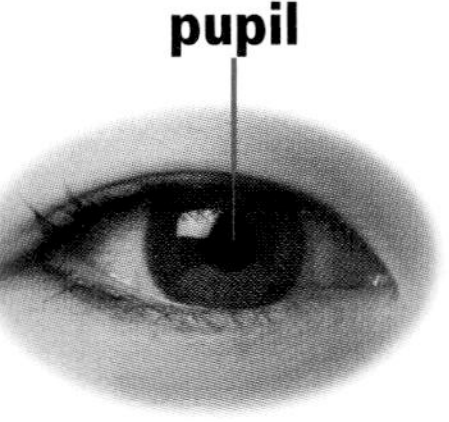

noun
1. The **pupil** is the center part of the eye.

noun
2. Another word for *student* is **pupil**.

ring

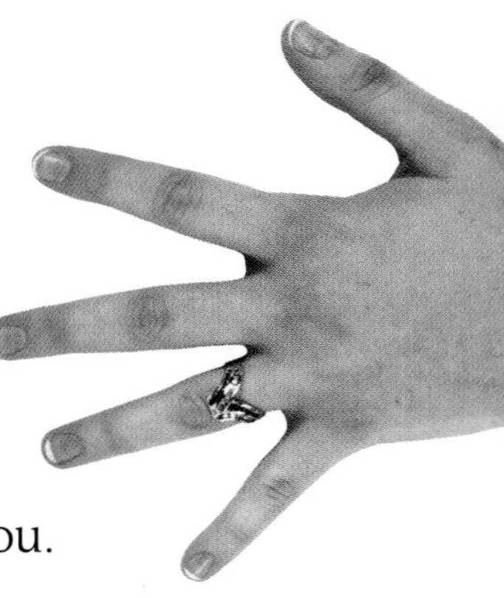

noun
1. A **ring** is a piece of jewelry. You wear it on your finger.

verb
2. When you hear the telephone **ring**, someone is calling you.

noun
3. Draw a **ring**, or a circle, around the answer.

scale

noun
1. You can use a **scale** to find out how much something weighs.

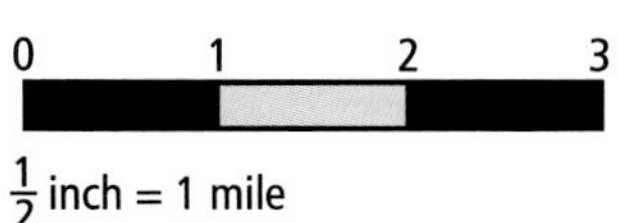

noun
2. A map **scale** shows how many inches on the map are equal to real miles.

noun
3. Each **scale** on a fish's body is thin and flat.

space

noun
1. Words in a sentence are separated by a blank **space**.

noun
2. An astronaut works in outer **space**.

state

noun
1. Illinois is a **state** in the United States.

verb
2. I heard him **state** that he wanted to go to Illinois.

table

noun
1. I use a multiplication **table** in math class.

3 x 1 = 3
3 x 2 = 6

noun
2. We put our food on the **table**.

Similes

A **simile** compares one thing to another. Sometimes it uses the word *as*. Other times it uses the word *like*.

1. His hands were **as cold as ice**.

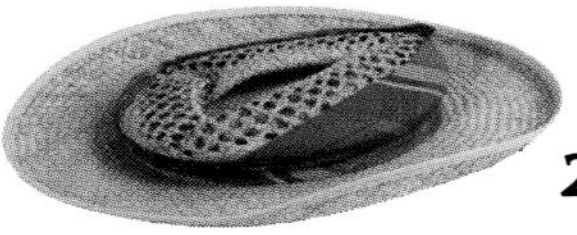

2. Dad's hat is **as flat as a pancake**.

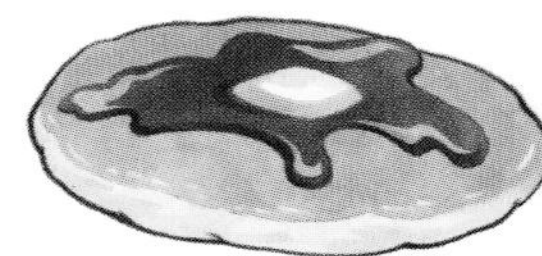

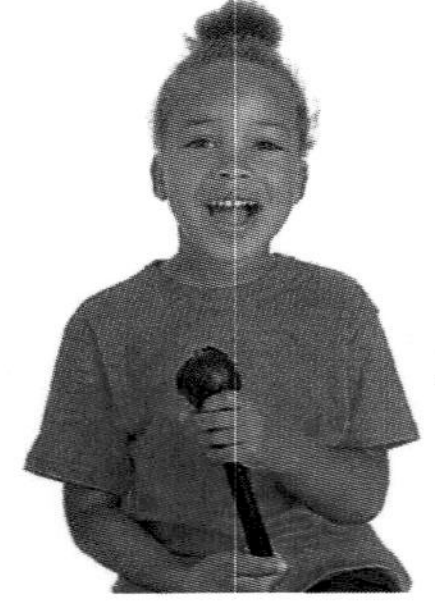

3. My sister can sing **like a bird**.

4. That balloon is **as light as a feather**.

5. Her hair shines **like gold**.

6. Cora and Tara are **like two peas in a pod**.

Sound Words

How does a bee sound? What sound do you hear when a person sneezes? To name those sounds, you can use **sound words**.

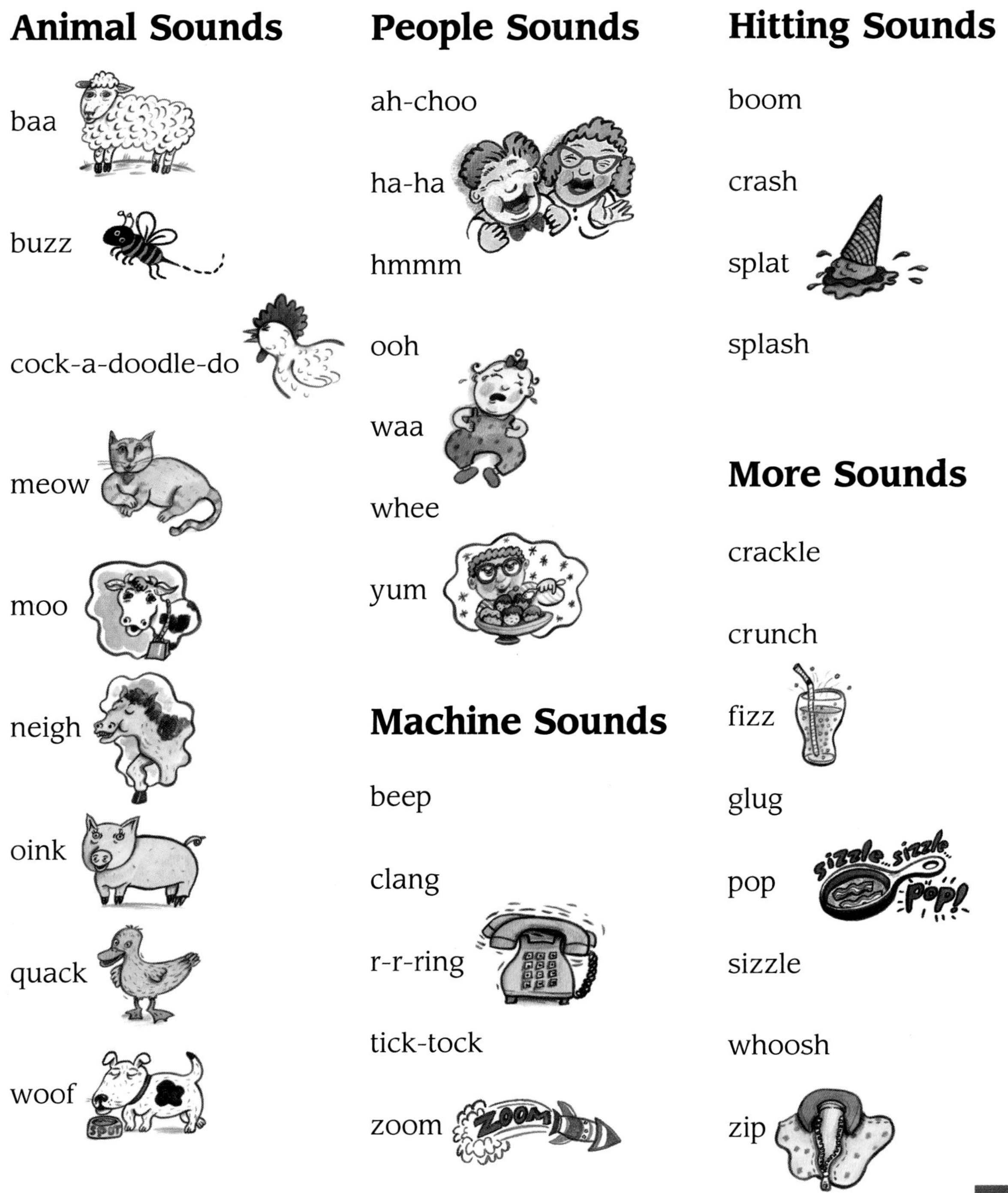

Animal Sounds

baa

buzz

cock-a-doodle-do

meow

moo

neigh

oink

quack

woof

People Sounds

ah-choo

ha-ha

hmmm

ooh

waa

whee

yum

Machine Sounds

beep

clang

r-r-ring

tick-tock

zoom

Hitting Sounds

boom

crash

splat

splash

More Sounds

crackle

crunch

fizz

glug

pop

sizzle

whoosh

zip

Sound-Alike Words

Many words like *flour* and *flower* sound alike but have different spellings and different meanings. Be sure to choose the right meaning for the word you want to use.

flour

flower

ant *noun*
An **ant** is a tiny insect.

aunt *noun*
My **aunt** is my mother's sister.

ate *verb*
I **ate** a sandwich.

eight *noun*
The number **eight** comes after seven.

be *verb*
What time will you **be** there?

bee *noun*
A **bee** is an insect that makes honey.

blew *verb*
The girl **blew** out the candles.

blue *noun*
Her shirt is **blue**.

buy *verb*
When you **buy** something, you pay money for it.

by *preposition*
The ball is **by** the paddle.

cent *noun*
A penny is one **cent**.

scent *noun*
When something smells, it has a **scent**.

sent *verb*
She **sent** a letter to her cousin in Peru.

for *preposition*
What's **for** dinner?

four *noun*
The number **four** comes after three.

hear *verb*
You **hear** with your ears.

here *adverb*
Please come **here**.

hour *noun*
One **hour** is sixty minutes.

our *adjective*
She took **our** picture.

one *noun*
The number **one** comes before two.

won *verb*
The fifth grade **won** the geography contest!

Sound-Alike Words, continued

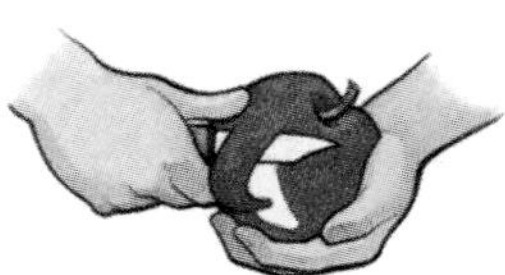

pair — *noun*
A **pair** is two of something.

pare — *verb*
When you **pare** an apple, you peel it.

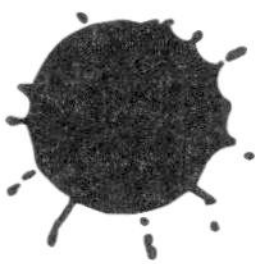

pear — *noun*
A **pear** is a kind of fruit.

read — *verb*
We **read** that book last year.

red — *noun*
Red is a bright color.

right — *adjective*
Right is the opposite of left. It also means *correct*.

write — *verb*
Write your name on the paper.

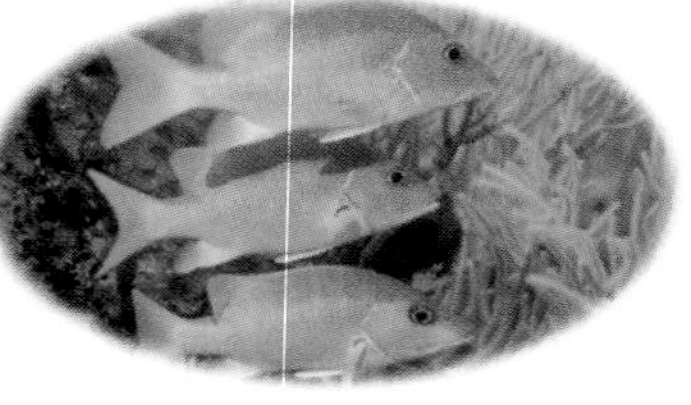

sea — *noun*
The **sea** is home for lots of fish.

see — *verb*
Glasses help you **see** better.

threw — *verb*
She **threw** a ball across the field.

through — *preposition*
I like to walk **through** the woods.

Synonyms and Antonyms

Synonyms

A **synonym** is a word that has almost the same meaning as another word.

afraid

The cat is **afraid** of the dog.

frightened
scared
fearful
alarmed
terrified

big

What a **big** dinosaur!

large
huge
enormous
gigantic
colossal

cold

It's **cold** today.

cool
chilly
brisk
frosty
icy
freezing

bad

That monster is **bad**!

mean
naughty
unkind
awful
terrible
horrible
rotten

brave

The **brave** dog saved its puppy from drowning.

unafraid
courageous
fearless
heroic

cry

Don't **cry**. You'll be okay.

weep
whimper
whine
sob
bawl
wail

Synonyms, continued

eat

How many cookies did you **eat**?

nibble on
bite into
chew up
dine on
consume
gobble up
feast on
devour
swallow

go

Come on! Let's **go**!

Ways to go fast:
run
scamper
scurry
gallop
jog
hurry
rush
dash
race
scramble
sprint

Ways to go slowly:
walk
meander
stroll
ramble
trudge
hobble

Other ways to go:
crawl
hop
jump
leap
march
skip

good

That was **good**!

fine
pleasing
enjoyable
delightful
agreeable
wonderful
great
super
excellent
marvelous
terrific
awesome
splendid
top-notch
perfect
tremendous
spectacular
fabulous

happy

We're so **happy**! We won!

glad
pleased
cheerful
joyful
delighted
thrilled

like

They **like** their grandmother.

enjoy
appreciate
admire
adore
love
cherish
treasure

mad

Why is he **mad**?

annoyed
cranky
irritated
cross
upset
angry
furious
enraged

laugh

My little brother likes to **laugh** when he's happy.

giggle
chuckle
cackle
howl

little

The flea is **little**.

small
slight
tiny
wee
miniature
minute
microscopic

noisy

Oh! That's too **noisy**!

loud
clamorous
shrill
booming
blaring
thunderous

pretty

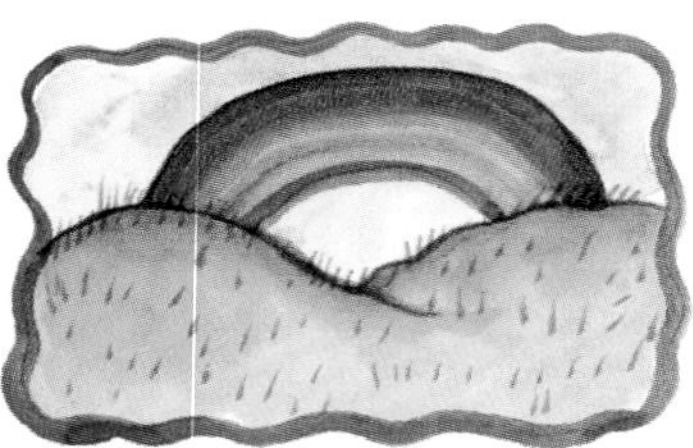

What a **pretty** rainbow.

attractive
lovely
beautiful
gorgeous
stunning

sad

He's **sad**. His toy is broken.

unhappy
blue
down
cheerless
disappointed
gloomy
miserable

quiet

This is such a **quiet** place.
I can't hear a thing.

still
hushed
tranquil
silent
soundless

strong

The elephant is **strong**.

sturdy
tough
powerful
mighty
brawny

talk

Everyone's **talking**!

Ways to talk loudly:
cheering
calling out
crying out
shouting
hollering
yelling
screaming

Ways to talk softly:
murmuring
whispering
mumbling

Ways to say *said*:
added
answered
asked
blurted
declared
exclaimed
explained
inquired
replied
reported
responded
stated
suggested
told

ugly

Ugh! All the trash on the beach is **ugly**!

homely
unattractive
unappealing
unsightly
disgusting

warm

Wow! It's **warm** today!

hot
roasting
steaming
scorching
sweltering
sizzling
boiling

wet

My shoes are **wet**.

damp
moist
soggy
soaked
drenched

worried

You're late.
I was **worried**.

uneasy
concerned
upset
troubled
fretful
anxious
disturbed
distressed

Antonyms

Antonyms are words that have opposite meanings. All kinds of words can have antonyms.

Nouns

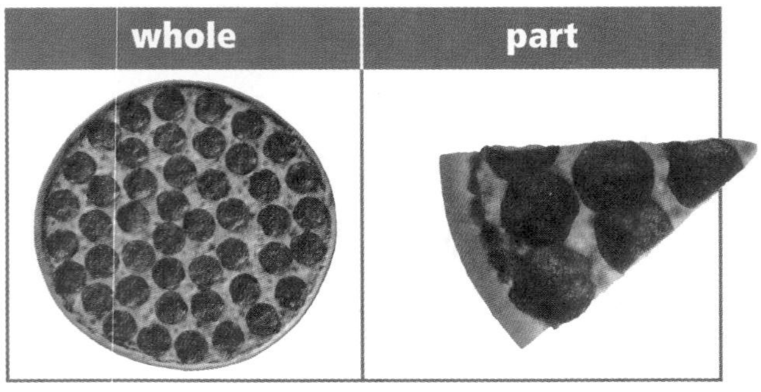

Verbs

add	subtract
$2 + 1 = 3$	$3 - 2 = 1$

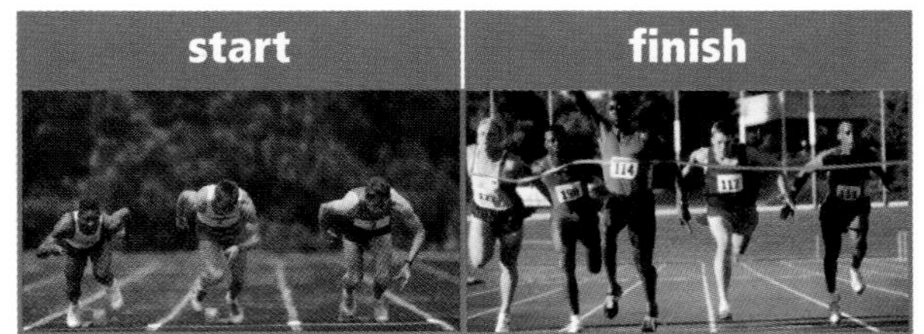

Adjectives

wild
tame

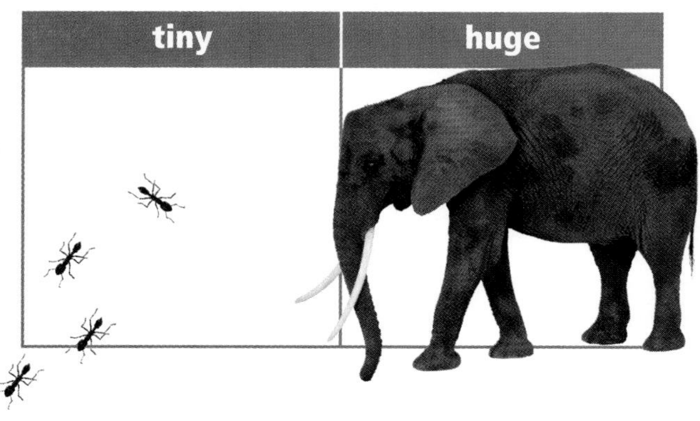
tiny
huge

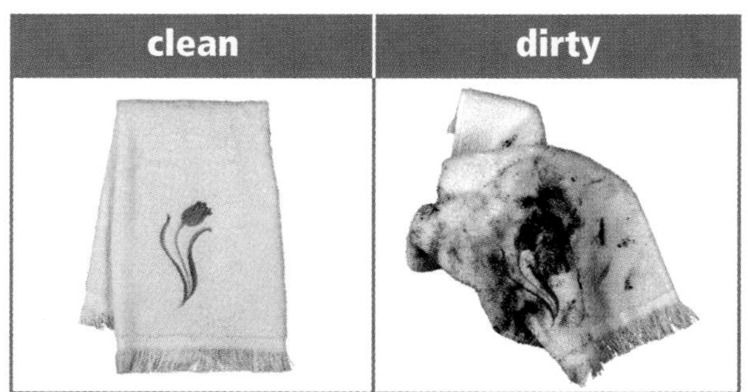
clean
dirty

empty
full

broken
fixed

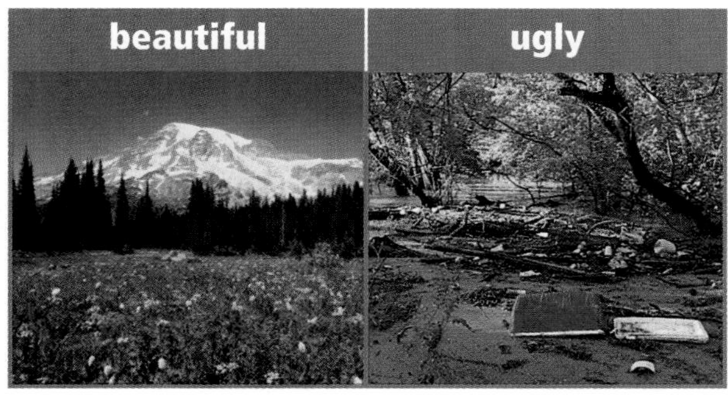
beautiful
ugly

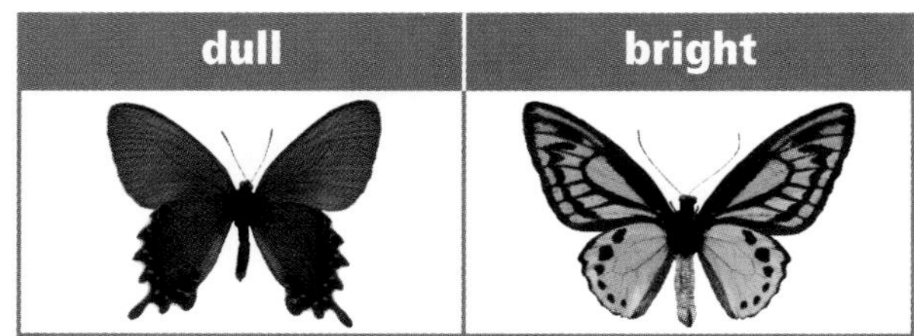
dull
bright

Time and Measurement Words

Time words tell you when things happen.
Measurement words tell how much of something you have.

calendar

Instruments for Measuring Time

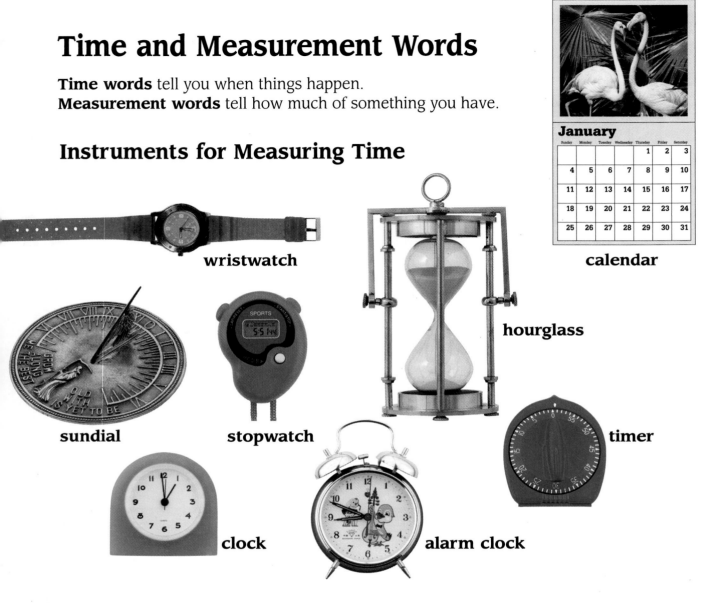

wristwatch

hourglass

sundial

stopwatch

timer

clock

alarm clock

Words for Telling Time

o'clock

second

minute

hour

half hour
half past

quarter hour
quarter past

Short Periods of Time

instant moment second nanosecond split-second

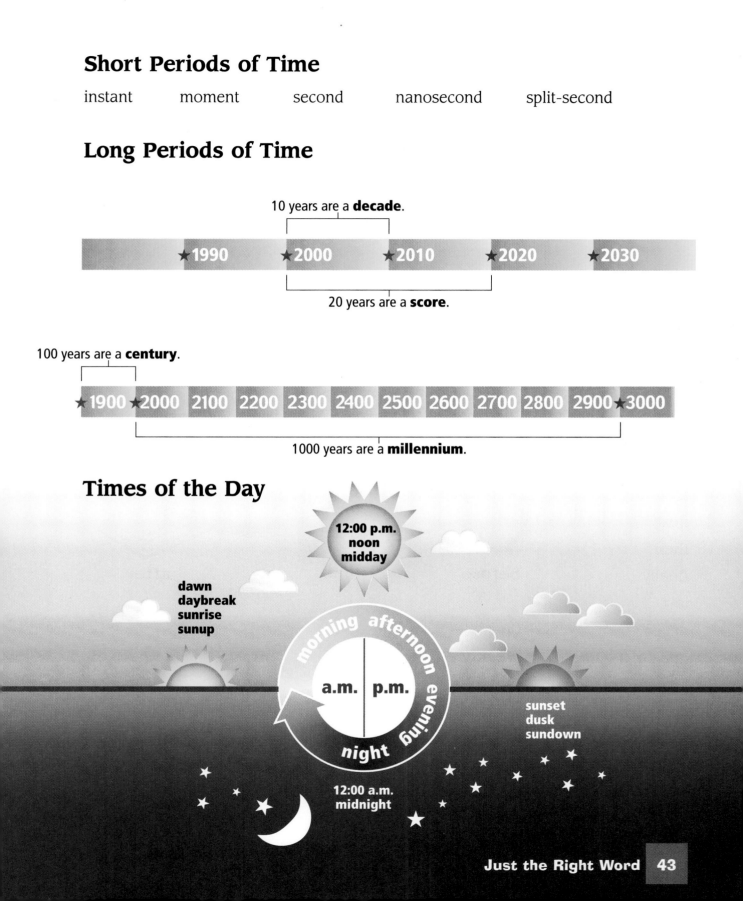

Long Periods of Time

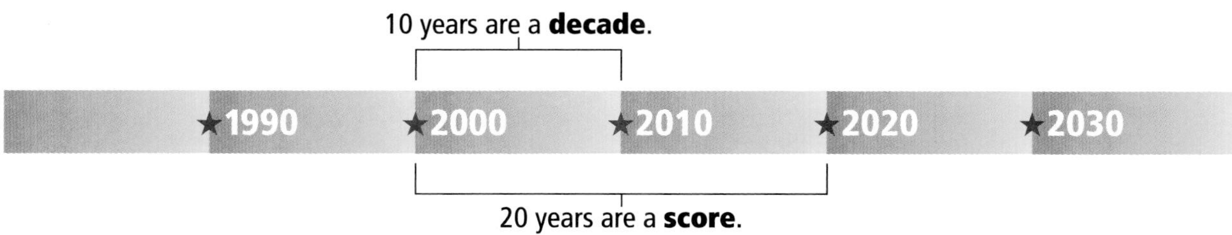

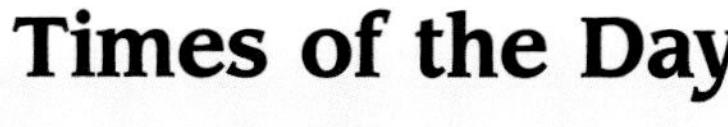

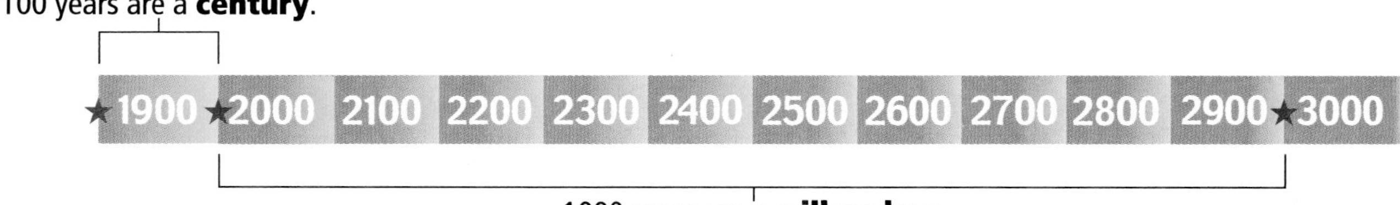

Times of the Day

12:00 p.m.
noon
midday

dawn
daybreak
sunrise
sunup

morning afternoon evening night

a.m. p.m.

sunset
dusk
sundown

12:00 a.m.
midnight

Seasons and Months of the Year

fall or **autumn**

September
October
November

winter

December
January
February

spring

March
April
May

summer

June
July
August

Days of the Week

Sunday Monday Tuesday Wednesday Thursday Friday Saturday

More Words That Tell When

first
next
then
finally
last
never
once in a while
sometimes
occasionally
frequently
always

before **after**

daily — every day
weekly — every week
biweekly — every two weeks
monthly — every month
quarterly — four times in a year
semiannually — two times in a year
annually — one time in a year

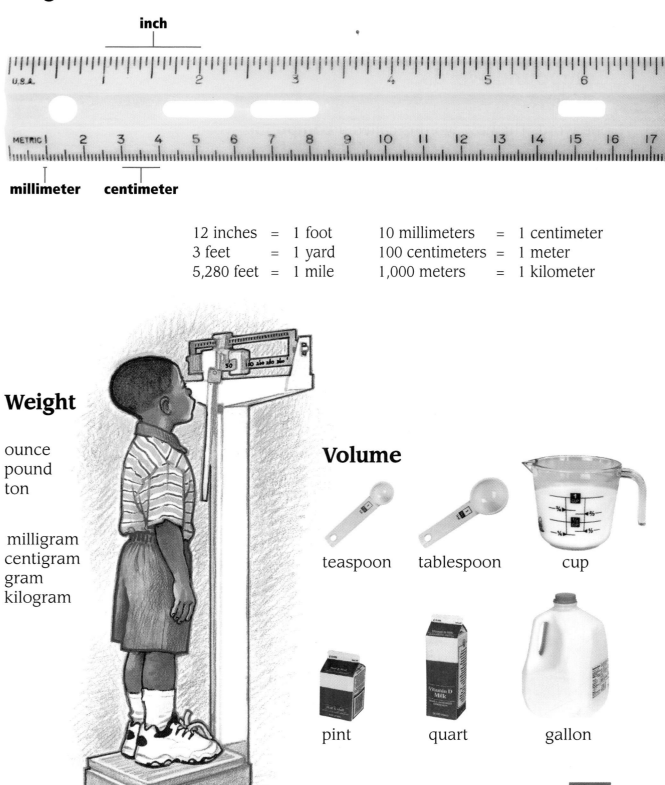

Length

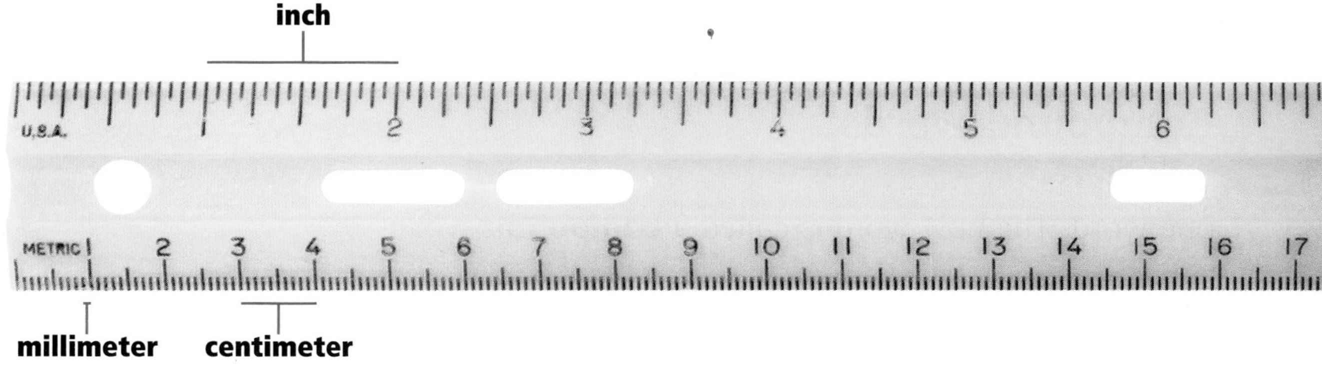

12 inches	=	1 foot	10 millimeters	=	1 centimeter
3 feet	=	1 yard	100 centimeters	=	1 meter
5,280 feet	=	1 mile	1,000 meters	=	1 kilometer

Weight

ounce
pound
ton

milligram
centigram
gram
kilogram

Volume

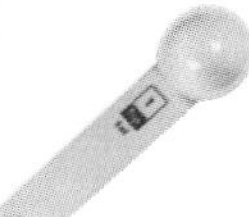

teaspoon

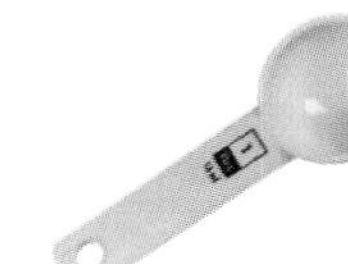
tablespoon

cup

pint

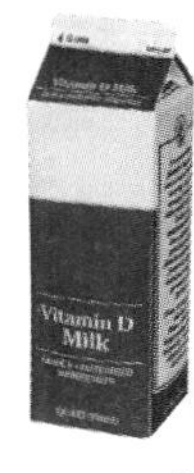
quart

gallon

Word Building

Word building is what you do when you make new words.

Compound Words

You can put two or more small words together to make one word. The new word is called a **compound word**.

backpack =
back + pack

backyard =
back + yard

basketball =
basket + ball

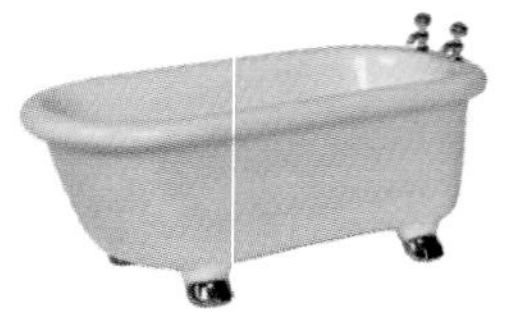

bathtub =
bath + tub

bookshelf =
book + shelf

fingernail =
finger + nail

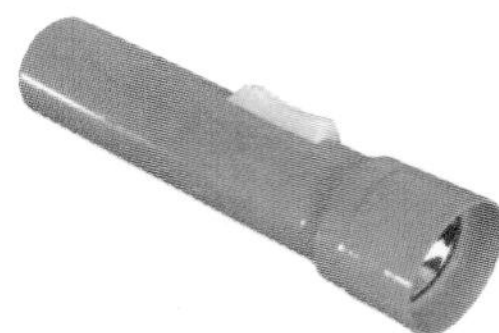

flashlight =
flash + light

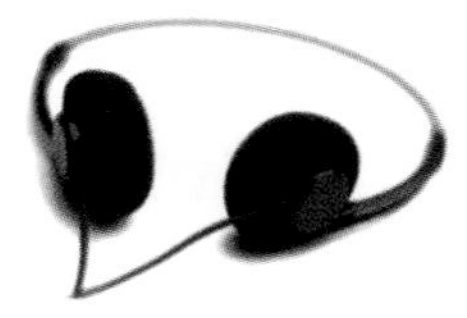

headphones =
head + phones

houseboat =
house + boat

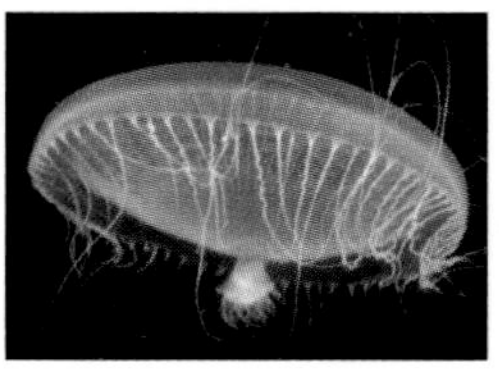

jellyfish =
jelly + fish

keyboard =
key + board

lighthouse =
light + house

motorcycle =
motor + cycle

pineapple =
pine + apple

popcorn =
pop + corn

rainbow =
rain + bow

seashells =
sea + shells

shoelaces =
shoe + laces

sunflower =
sun + flower

sweatshirt =
sweat + shirt

toothbrush =
tooth + brush

videocassette =
video + cassette

Suffixes

A **suffix** is a word part that comes at the end of a word. When you add a suffix, you change the word's meaning.

-able, -ible mean "can be"

A **breakable** vase can be broken.

A **reversible** coat can be reversed, or turned inside out.

-en means "to make" or "made of"

She **sharpens** the pencil to make the point sharp.

Is the mask made of wood? Yes, it is **wooden**.

-er means "a person who"

A **runner** is a person who runs in a race.

A **baker** is a person who bakes.

-ful means "full of"

Some spider bites can be **harmful**.

An umbrella can be **useful**.

-less means "without"

A butterfly is **harmless**.

A broken umbrella is **useless**.

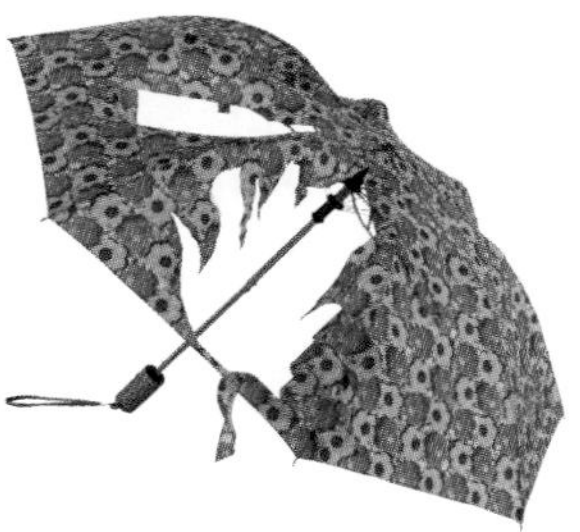

-ward means "in the direction of"

To go **forward** means to go in the direction in front of you.

To go **backward** means to go in the direction in back of you.

More Suffixes

Some suffixes turn words into nouns.

-ion, -sion, -tion

Put an **i** here. It makes the word easier to say.

add + tion = addition
Can you **add** the numbers?
Your **addition** is correct!

Drop the **e** before you add the suffix.

confuse + ion = confusion
These directions **confuse** me!
They cause **confusion**.

-ment

agree + ment = agreement
We **agree** on the color.
We have an **agreement**.

-ness

kind + ness = kindness
A **kind** person helped me.
I appreciated her **kindness**.

Prefixes

A **prefix** is a word part that comes at the beginning of a word. When you add a prefix, you change the word's meaning.

auto- means "self"

An **automobile** does not need to be pulled or pushed. It moves by itself.

bi- means "two" or "twice"

A **bicycle** has two wheels.

co- means "together"

A team **cooperates**, or works together.

dis- means "the opposite of"

First she connected the cars. Then she **disconnected** them.

More Prefixes

il-, im-, in-, non-, un- mean "not"

Driving too fast is **illegal**, or not legal. It is against the law.

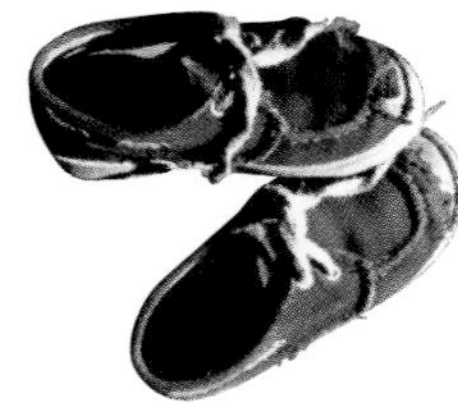

Imperfect clothes are not completely right. These sneakers have holes in them.

Inexpensive items are ones that do not cost a lot.

A **nonfiction** book is about facts, not fiction.

Oh, no! She is really **unhappy** now!

mini- means "small" or "little"

The little globe is called a **miniglobe**.

pre- means "before"

You can buy **precut** vegetables at the store.

re- means "again" or "back"

When you use something again, you **reuse** it.

When you put something back in its place, you **replace** it.

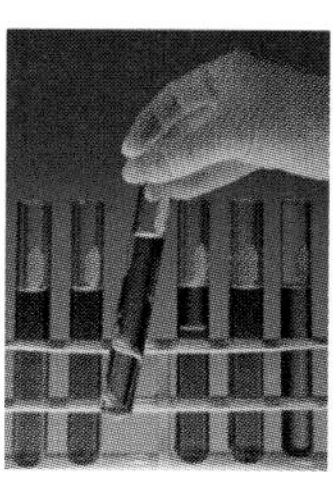

semi- means "half"

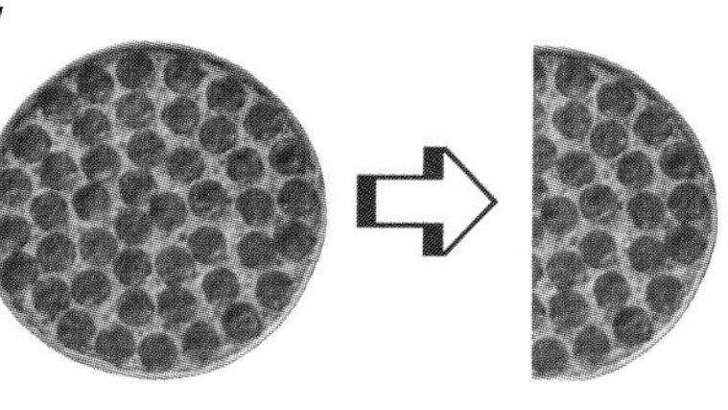

A **semicircle** is half of a circle.

Word Families

Some groups of words have the same smaller word in them. Use the meaning of the smaller word, which is called the **root word**, to figure out the meaning of the other words.

correct

adjective
She uses a dictionary to find the **correct** spelling of a word.

verb
She will **correct** the misspelling.

incorrect

adjective
The answer is not right. It is **incorrect**.

9 + 3 = ~~11~~

correction

noun
Write your **corrections** neatly.

My first day of school in the United States was very scary ~~and~~ because I didn't speak English ~~and~~.

govern

verb
Congress and the President **govern**, or rule, the United States.

governor

noun
Who is the **governor** of your state?

government

noun
We elect the leaders of our **government**.

grow

verb
Babies **grow** quickly.

outgrow

verb
I always **outgrow** my clothes!

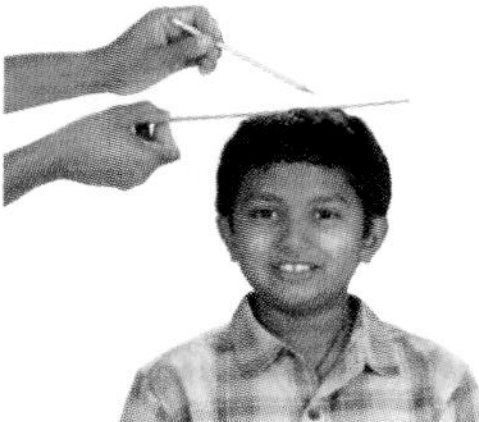

growth

noun
My **growth** is marked every year.

grown-up

noun
There are two children and one **grown-up**.

nation

noun
Another word for *country* is **nation**.

national

adjective
A country's official song is called its **national** anthem.

international

adjective
The United Nations is an **international** organization. It represents many different countries.

Words from Around the U.S.

Some things are called by different names in different parts of the United States. Which word do *you* use?

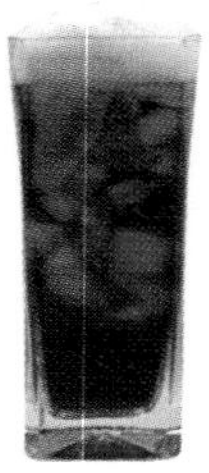

soda
pop
tonic
soft drink

My friend from California ordered a **soda** to go with his hamburger.

sub
hoagie
grinder
hero
poor boy

A **poor boy**, or "po' boy," is a popular kind of sandwich in Louisiana.

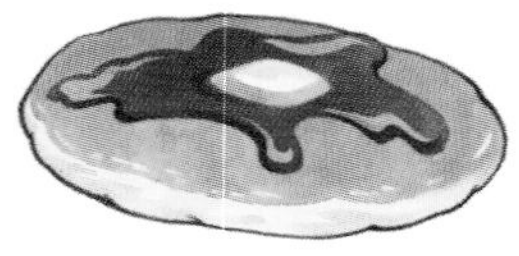

pancakes
flannel cakes
griddle cakes
flapjacks

I read about a **flapjack**-eating contest held in Virginia.

peanut
goober
ground pea

Most Southerners know that a **goober** is a peanut.

firebug
firefly
glowworm
lightning bug

Do you call an insect that flashes in the dark a **firefly** or a **lightning bug**?

green beans
snap beans
string beans

Many restaurants along the East Coast serve **snap beans**.

faucet
spigot
tap

The word **faucet** comes from the North, but the word is now used all over the country.

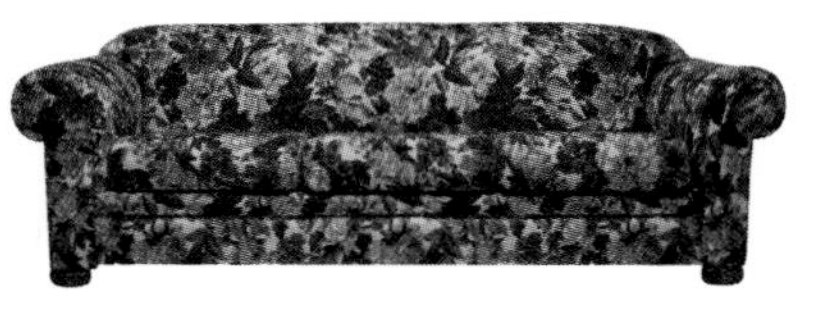

couch
sofa
davenport

A furniture store in North Dakota sells **davenports**.

drinking fountain
water fountain
bubbler

In Wisconsin, people drink water from a **bubbler**.

Words Used in Special Ways

Idioms

Idioms are colorful ways to say something. Usually, a few words combine, or go together, to make up an idiom. In combination, these words mean something different than what the words mean by themselves.

What you say:	What you mean:
Skating is **a piece of cake**.	Skating is easy.
I'm **all thumbs**.	I'm clumsy.
Stop **beating around the bush**.	Stop avoiding the main subject.

Pam always **bends over backwards**.

Pam always does whatever she can to help.

What you say:	What you mean:
Don't **blow your top**.	Don't get angry.
Break a leg!	Good luck!
Juan is **as cool as a cucumber**.	Juan is very calm.
That car **costs an arm and a leg**.	That car is very expensive.
Cut it out.	Stop what you're doing.
My friend is **down in the dumps**.	My friend is feeling very sad.
Mr. Meyers is **down to earth**.	Mr. Meyers is easy to talk to.
I'll **drop you a line**.	I'll write you a letter.
It's **as easy as pie**.	It's very simple.

What you say:	What you mean:
I had to **eat my words**.	I had to say, "I'm sorry."
My **eyes were bigger than my stomach**.	I took more food than I could eat.
Now you have to **face the music**.	Now you have to take responsibility for what you did.
She **gave him the cold shoulder**.	She didn't pay any attention to him.
I'll **give it my best shot**.	I'll try my hardest.
Give me a break!	That's ridiculous!
Go fly a kite!	Go away!
I **got cold feet**.	I became unsure about doing something.
Tim **got up on the wrong side of the bed** today.	Tim is in a bad mood today.
Mom has **a green thumb**.	Mom is a good gardener.
Hang on.	Wait.

Daniel has **a heart of gold**.

Daniel is kind and generous.

I need to **hit the books**.	I need to study.
My mom **hit the ceiling**.	My mom got mad.

Idioms, continued

What you say:	What you mean:
Hold your horses.	Wait a minute.
I am walking around **in a fog**.	I am confused.
I'm **in a jam**.	I'm in trouble.
My brother's **in hot water**.	My brother's in trouble.
Don't **jump down my throat**.	Don't yell at me.
Keep your shirt on.	Wait a minute. Be patient.
Knock it off!	Stop it!

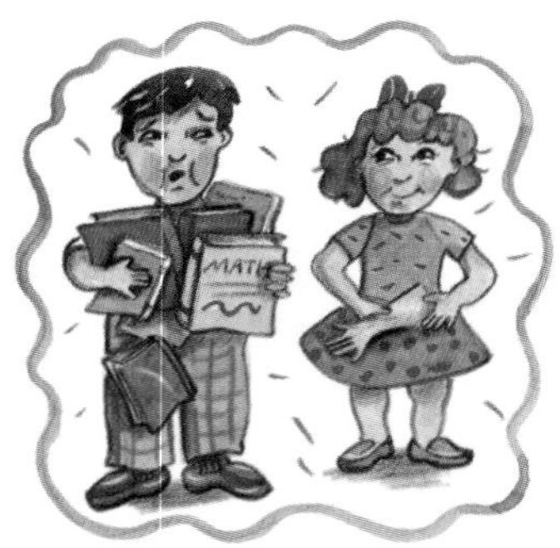

Will you **lend me a hand**?

Will you help me?

Her car runs **like clockwork**.	Her car runs smoothly.
We'd better **make tracks**.	We'd better hurry.
You're **off the hook**.	You're out of trouble.
My dad is **out of shape**.	My dad needs to exercise.
You're **out of the woods**.	You're safe.
Don't be **a pain in the neck**.	Don't bother me.
Pat yourself on the back.	Tell yourself you did a good job.

What you say:	What you mean:
He's **playing with fire**.	He's doing something dangerous.
Stop **pulling my leg**.	Stop kidding me.
I always **put my best foot forward**.	I always do my best.
Let's **put our heads together**.	Let's work together.
We don't **see eye to eye**.	We don't agree with each other.
My dog is **as smart as a whip**.	My dog is very clever.
Please don't **spill the beans**.	Please don't tell my secret.
Don't **spread yourself too thin**.	Don't try to do too much.
That car can **stop on a dime**.	That car can stop quickly.
I **turned the room upside down**.	I looked everywhere in the room.
Jasmine is **under the weather**.	Jasmine is not feeling well.
You bet!	Yes, I agree!

Zip your lips!

Be quiet!

Two-Word Verbs

Sometimes a little word like *in*, *up*, or *out* can make a big difference in meaning. A **two-word verb** often includes one of these little words. Look at how they change a verb's meaning.

break

1. **break** — *to split into pieces*
   Don't drop the plate! It will **break**.

2. **break down** — *to stop working*
   My old car **breaks down** every week.

3. **break up** — *to come apart*
   The ice on the lake will **break up** in the spring.

bring

1. **bring** — *to take or carry something with you*
   Bring a salad to the picnic.

2. **bring out** — *to take out things you have in another place*
   She **brings out** the pies.

3. **bring up** — *to suggest*
   She **brings up** the idea to her friends.

check

1. check — *to make sure what you did is right*

Always **check** your work.

2. check in — *to stay in touch with someone*

My grandmother phones to **check in** with me every week.

3. check off — *to mark off a list*

Tom **checked off** the chores he had done.

4. check up — *to see if everything is okay*

The cowboy **checks up** on the cattle.

fill

1. fill — *to put as much as possible into a container or space*

Fill the pail with water.

2. fill in — *to color or shade in a space*

Please **fill in** the circle.

3. fill out — *to complete*

Marcos **fills out** a form to order a book.

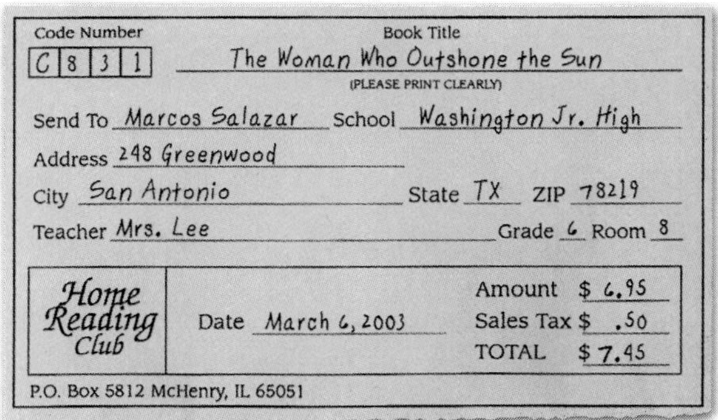

Code Number: C 8 3 1

Book Title: The Woman Who Outshone the Sun

(PLEASE PRINT CLEARLY)

Send To: Marcos Salazar School: Washington Jr. High

Address: 248 Greenwood

City: San Antonio State: TX ZIP: 78219

Teacher: Mrs. Lee Grade: 6 Room: 8

Home Reading Club

Date: March 6, 2003

Amount $ 6.95

Sales Tax $ .50

TOTAL $ 7.45

P.O. Box 5812 McHenry, IL 65051

get

1. get — *to go after something*
Get the keys, please.

2. get through — *to finish*
I can **get through** this book tonight.

3. get ahead — *to go beyond what is expected of you*
She worked hard to **get ahead** in her math class.

4. get out — *to leave*
The students **get out** at the bus stop.

5. get over — *to feel better*
She'll **get over** her cold soon.

give

1. give — *to hand someone something*
I will **give** you some cake.

2. give back — *to return*
She **gives back** the CD she borrowed.

3. give up — *to quit*
Never **give up**!
Practice until you get it right!

go

1. **go** — *to move from one place to another*
   I will **go** to the movies on Saturday.

2. **go away** — *to leave*
   Tomorrow the rain will **go away**.

3. **go back** — *to return*
   Every spring, the geese **go back** north.

4. **go on** — *to keep happening*
   I hope the music will **go on** forever.

5. **go out** — *to go someplace special*
   They like to **go out** to breakfast.

look

1. **look** — *to see or watch*
   Look at the stars.

2. **look forward** — *to be excited about something that will happen*
   I **look forward** to the parade every year.

3. **look out** — *to watch for danger*
   Look out! The ball is coming right at you!

4. **look over** — *to review*
   He needs to **look over** his test.

5. **look up** — *to hunt for and find*
   You can **look up** a word in the dictionary.

pick

1. pick — *to choose*
I always **pick** red clothes.

2. pick on — *to bother or tease*
If you **pick on** someone, you're being mean.

3. pick out — *to choose*
I always **pick out** red clothes.

4. pick up — *to gather*
My class project is to **pick up** trash.

5. pick up — *to go faster*
When the wind **picks up**, you'll need your jacket.

run

1. run — *to move quickly on foot*
He had to **run** to catch the bus.

2. run into — *to see someone you know when you weren't expecting it*
Sometimes I **run into** my neighbor on the street.

3. run out — *to suddenly have nothing left*
If you use all of the milk, we'll **run out**.

stand

1. **stand** — *to be in a straight up and down position*
   We **stand** in line to buy movie tickets.

2. **stand for** — *to represent*
   The stars on the U.S. flag **stand for** the 50 states.

3. **stand in** — *to take the place of*
   While our team pitcher is gone, Jerry will **stand in** for him.

4. **stand out** — *to be easier to see*
   Highlight the words so they **stand out**.

My words really
stand out.

turn

1. **turn** — *to change direction*
   Turn right at the next corner.

BOOK RETUR

2. **turn in** — *to give or return*
   He has to **turn in** his library book before it is due.

3. **turn off** — *to make something stop working*
   Please **turn off** the lights when you leave.

4. **turn up** — *to appear*
   I lost my favorite socks. I hope they **turn up**.

5. **turn over** — *put something on its opposite side*
   He **turns over** the pot.

Chapter 2
Picture It!

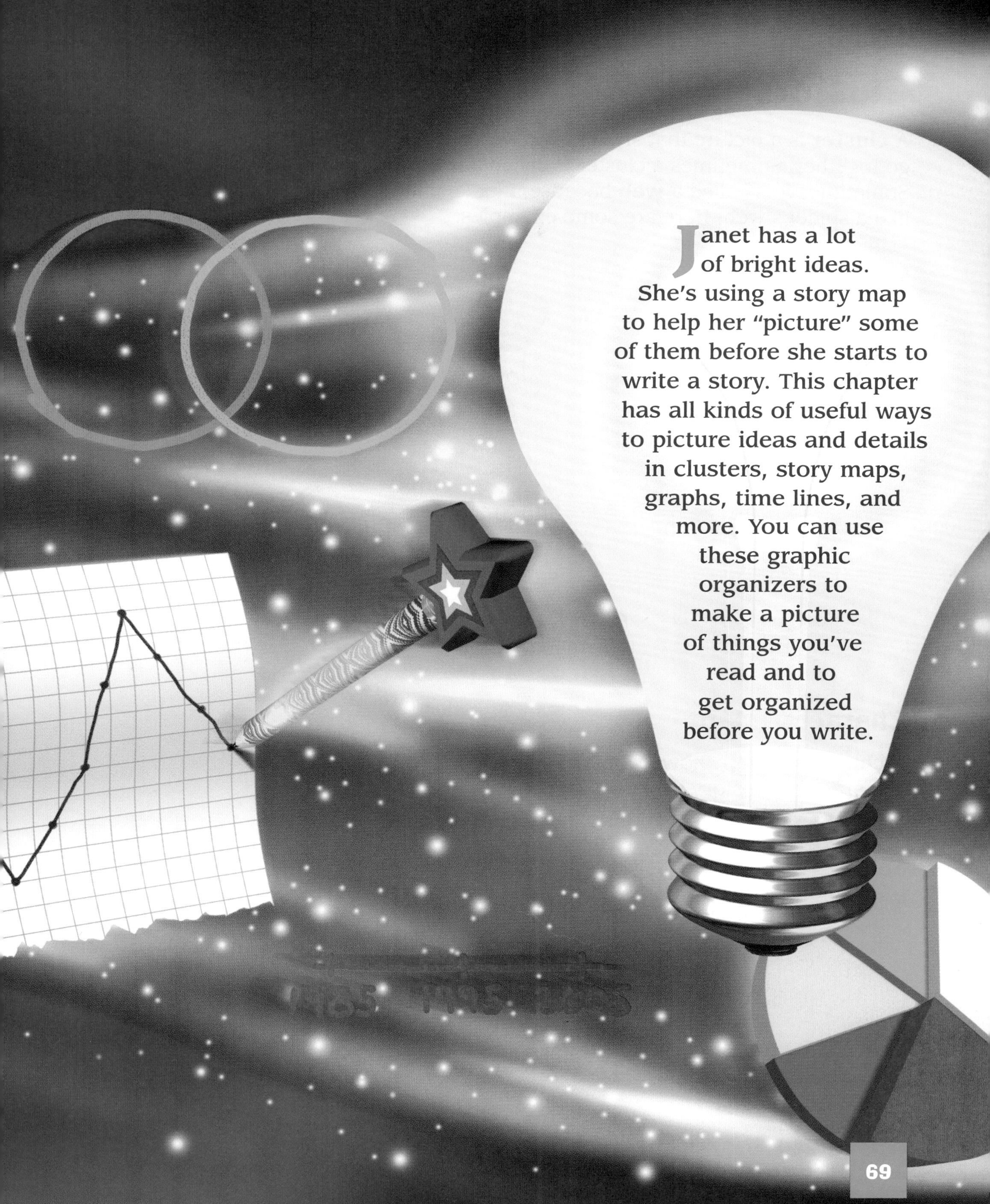

Janet has a lot of bright ideas. She's using a story map to help her "picture" some of them before she starts to write a story. This chapter has all kinds of useful ways to picture ideas and details in clusters, story maps, graphs, time lines, and more. You can use these graphic organizers to make a picture of things you've read and to get organized before you write.

Clusters

A **cluster** is a picture that shows how words or ideas go together. Sometimes a cluster is called a **map**. Sometimes it is called a **web** because it looks a little like a spider's web! Here are some examples.

Word Web

This **word web** groups words related to baseball.

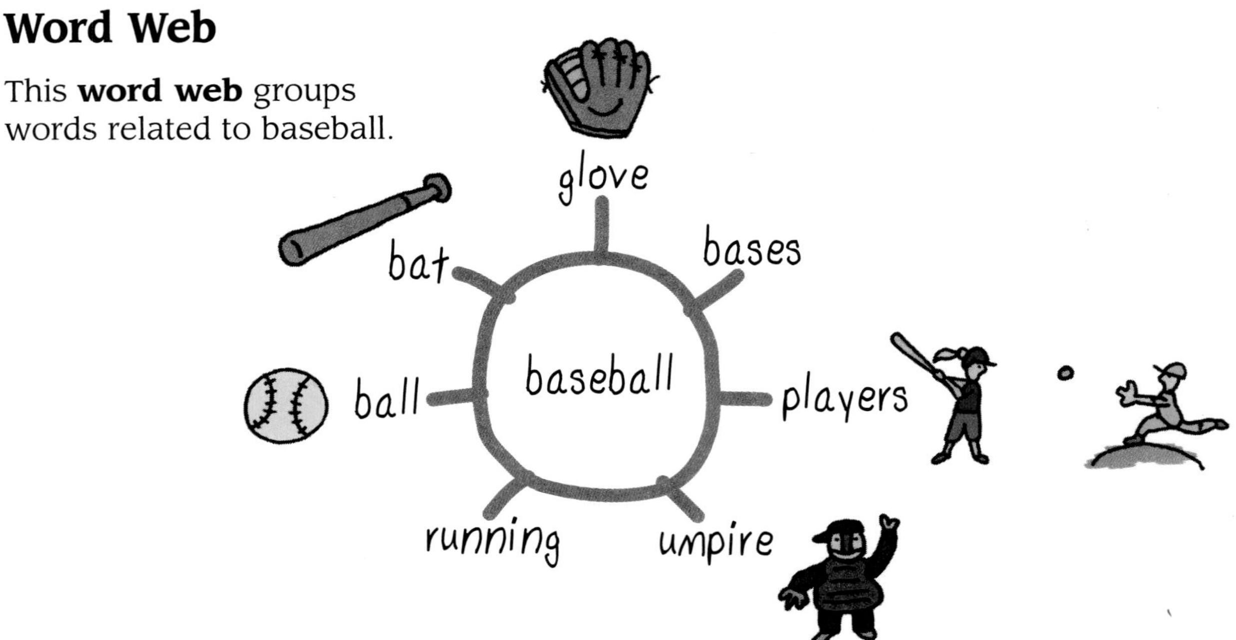

Character Map

A **character map** shows what a character in a story is like.

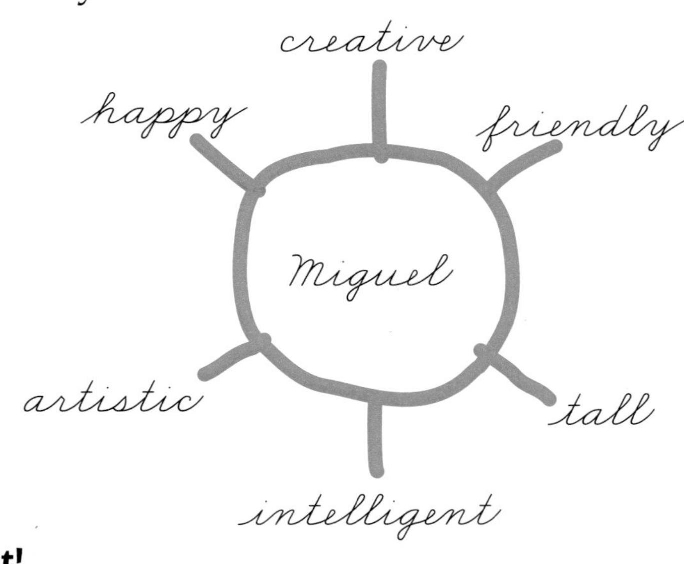

Event Cluster

The girl who made this **event cluster** was getting ready to write about a special celebration. She organized her ideas so she could tell what happened.

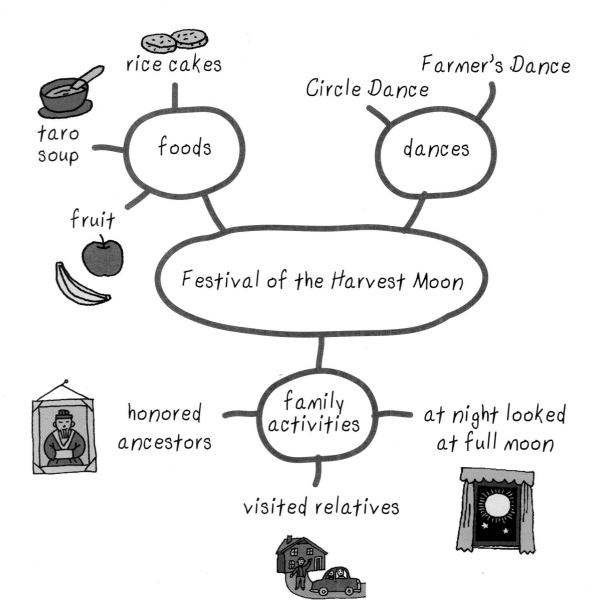

rice cakes

taro soup

foods

fruit

Circle Dance

Farmer's Dance

dances

Festival of the Harvest Moon

family activities

honored ancestors

visited relatives

at night looked at full moon

Diagrams

A **diagram** is a drawing that shows where things are, how something works, or when something happens. Most diagrams have words, or **labels**, that tell more about the drawing. Look at these examples.

Floor Plan

A **floor plan** is a diagram that shows where things are in a building. It shows what a room looks like from above. Here is the floor plan for a room in a museum.

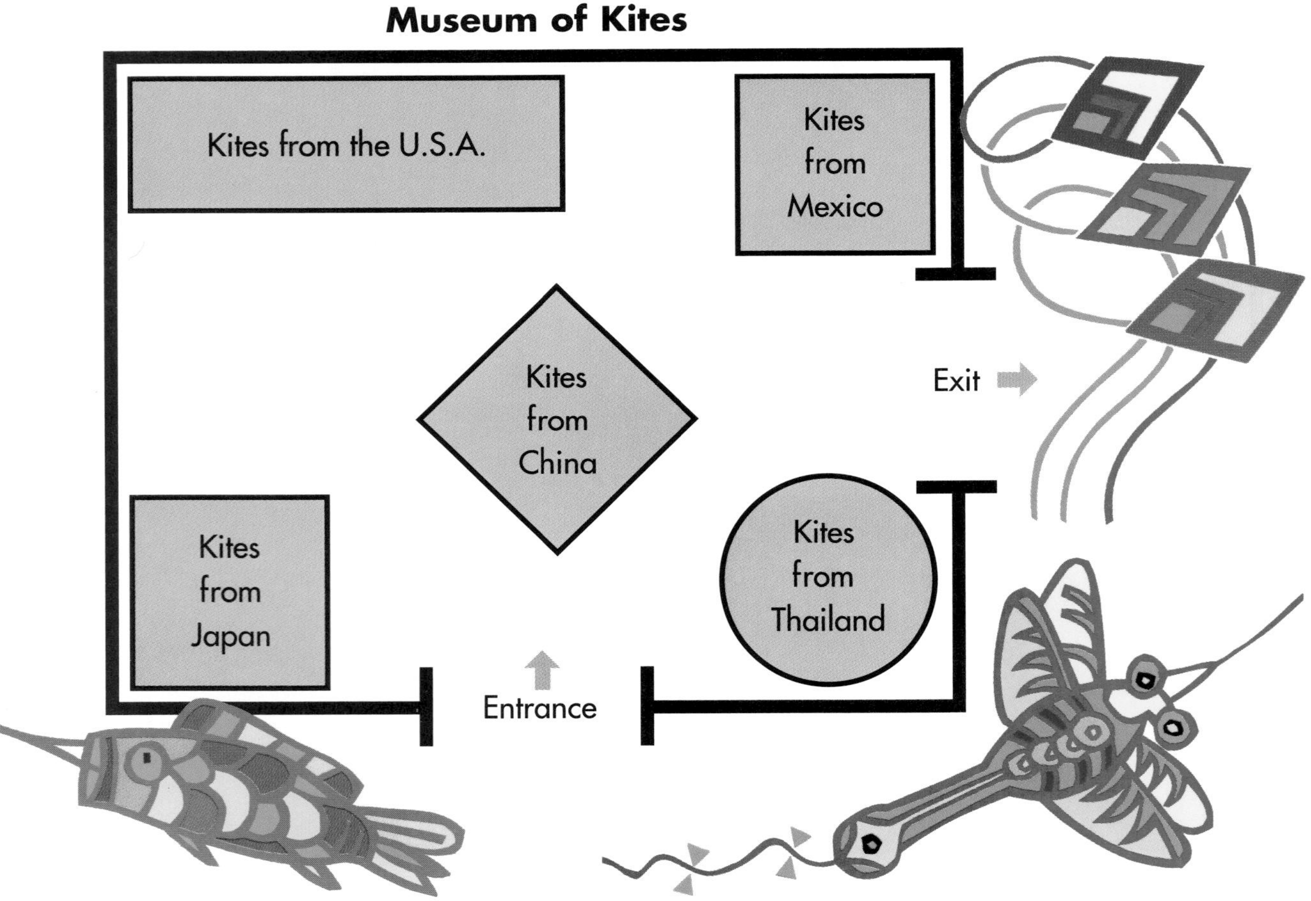

Parts Diagram

This diagram tells you the parts of a guitar.

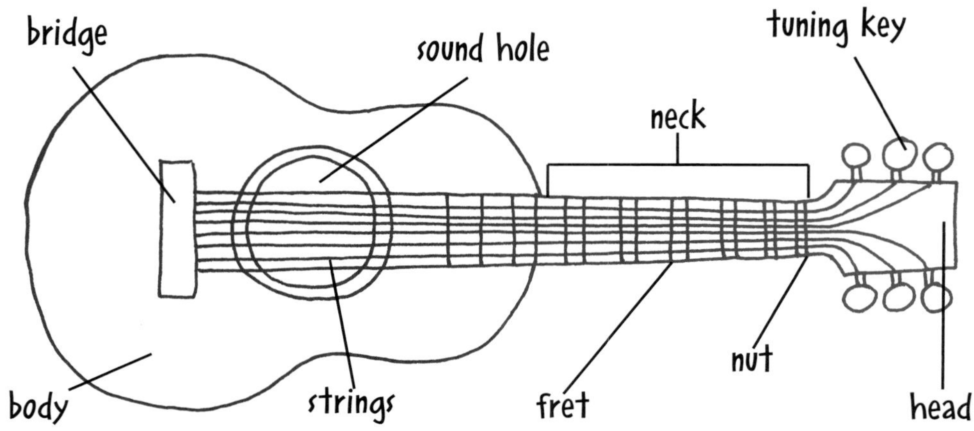

Scientific Diagram

Follow the arrows in this diagram to see how a beetle grows and changes over time.

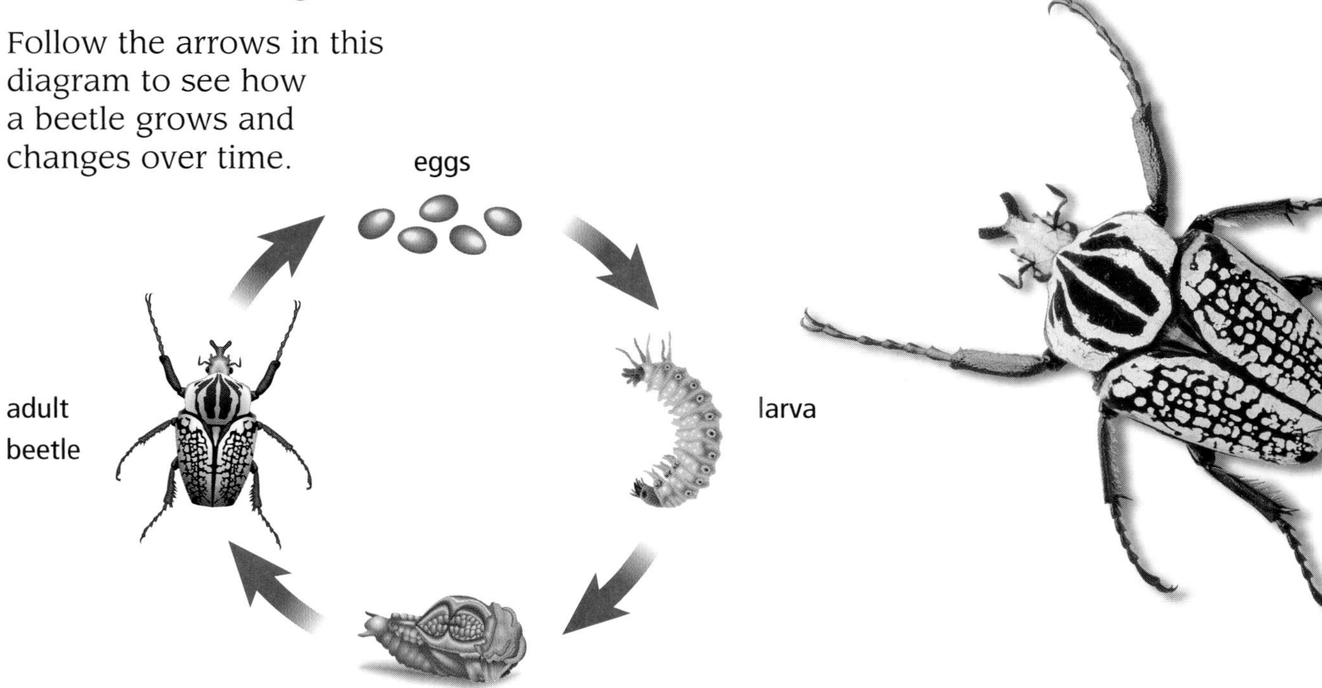

Main Idea Diagrams

These diagrams show how **details** are related to a **main idea**.

Main Idea

My family likes to celebrate the Fourth of July.

Details

Dad gets out the flag.	Mom makes star-shaped cookies.	I put up red, white, and blue decorations.

Main Idea

There are many ways to celebrate the Fourth of July.

Details

- Cities and towns have firework displays.
- Families and friends have picnics together.
- Many communities have parades.

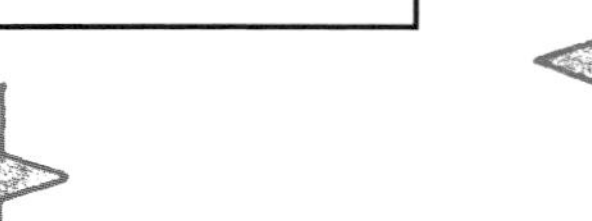

Venn Diagram

A **Venn diagram** compares and contrasts two things. It shows how two things are the same and how they are different.

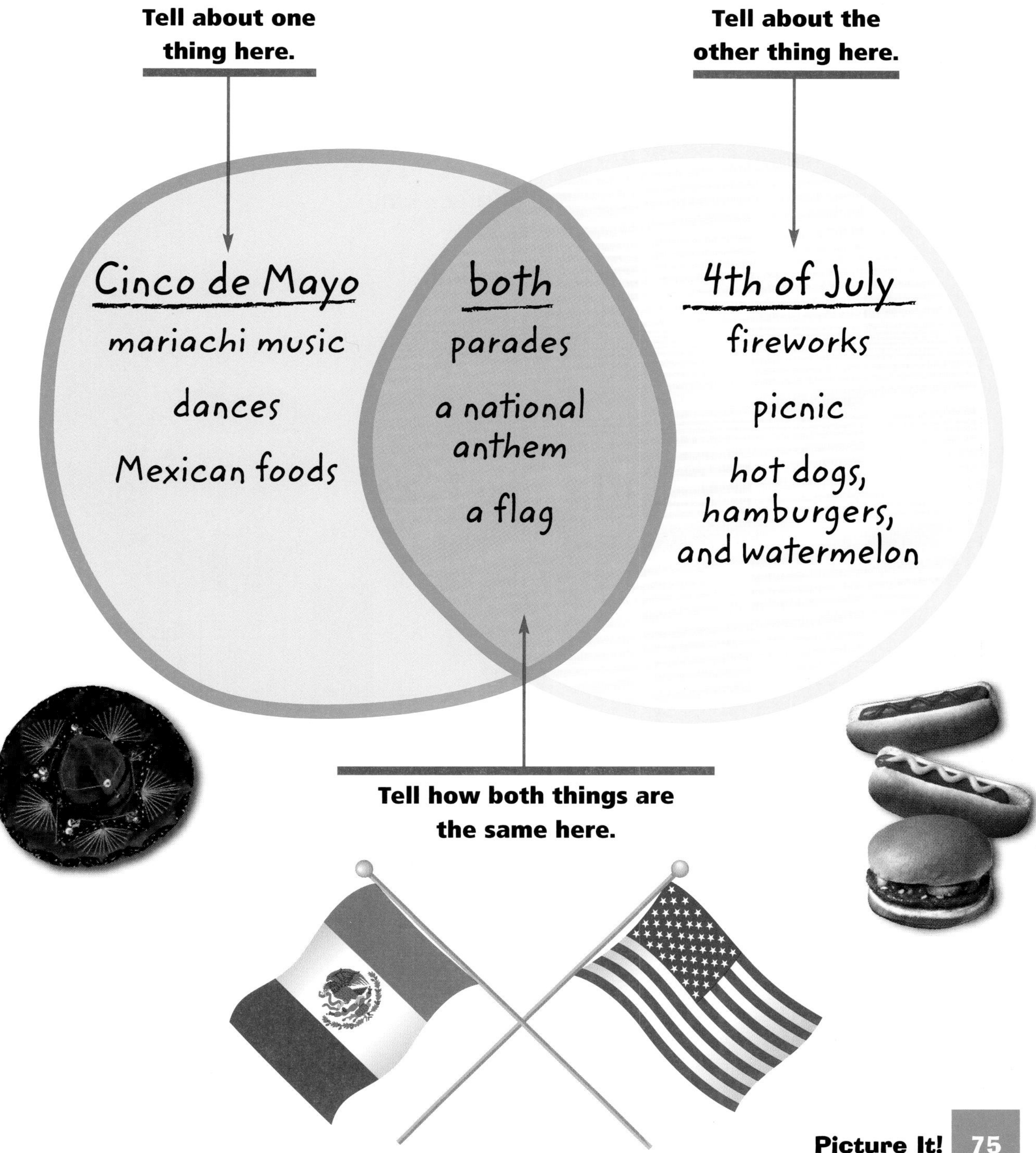

Graphs

A **graph** is a picture that compares mathematical information, or **data**.

Bar Graph

One kind of graph has bars that go either up and down or from left to right to give information. That's why it's called a **bar graph**.

- Each bar shows one kind of information.
- The height or length of the bar shows another kind of information.

In this graph, look at the bars to see which family sold the most tickets.

This is the **vertical axis**. It shows how many tickets were sold.

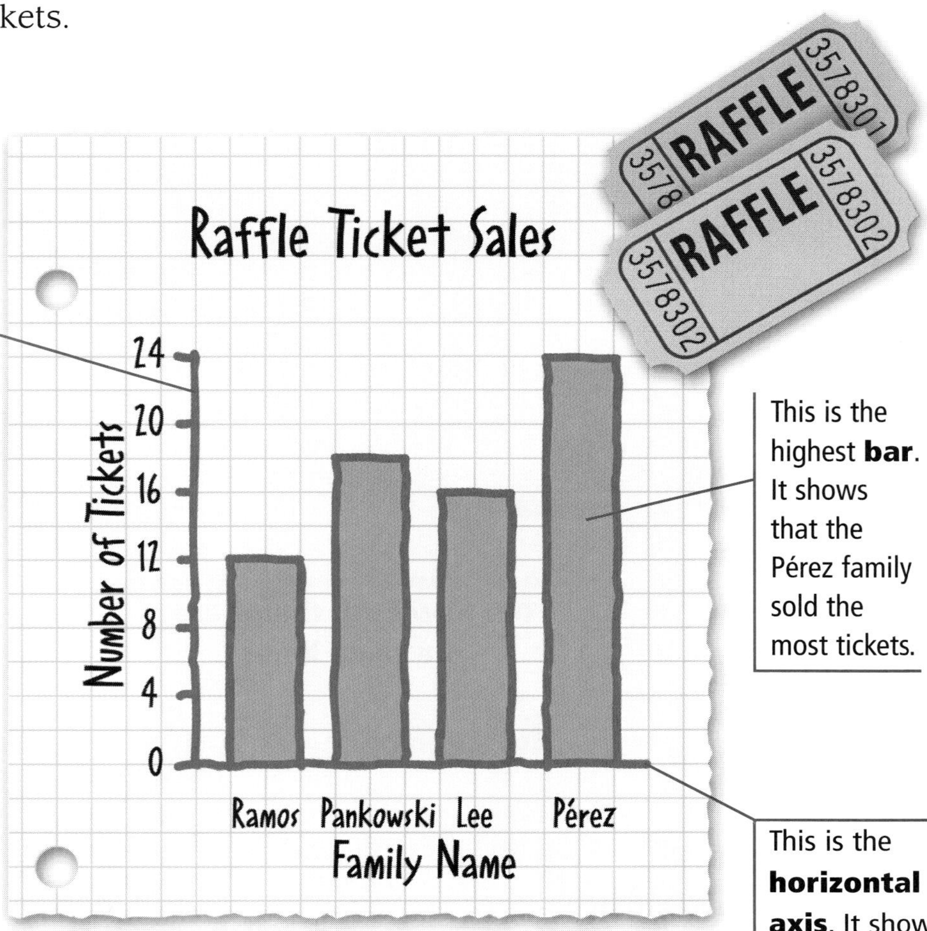

This is the highest **bar**. It shows that the Pérez family sold the most tickets.

This is the **horizontal axis**. It shows which families sold tickets.

Line Graph

This kind of graph has points, or dots, that show the data. It's called a **line graph** because lines are used to connect the points.

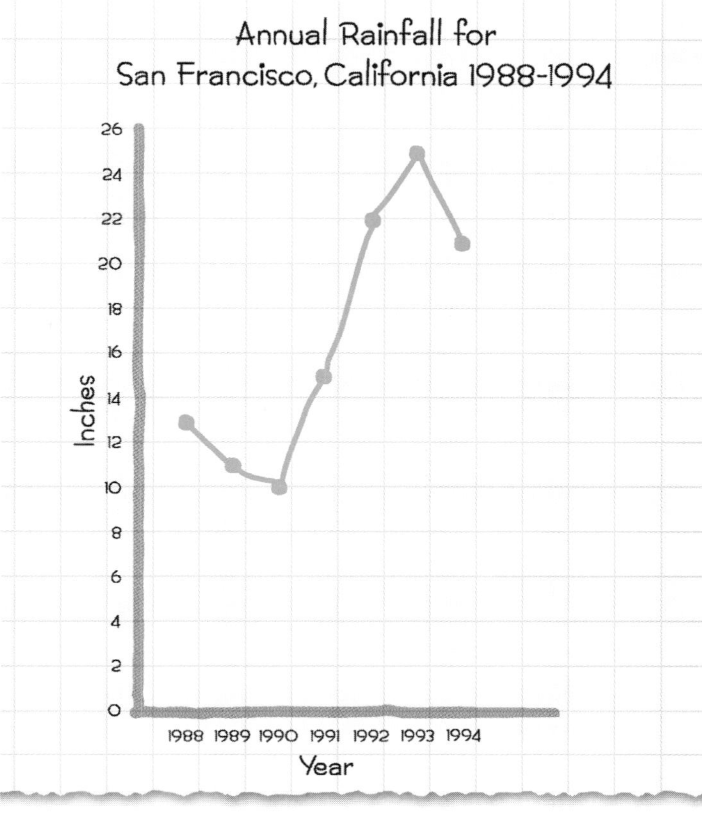

Pie Graph

A **pie graph** looks a lot like a pie! It has a circular shape and is divided into parts. Each part of a pie graph is a percentage of the whole circle. All parts added together equal 100 percent.

Medals Won by Each Country in the 2002 Winter Olympics

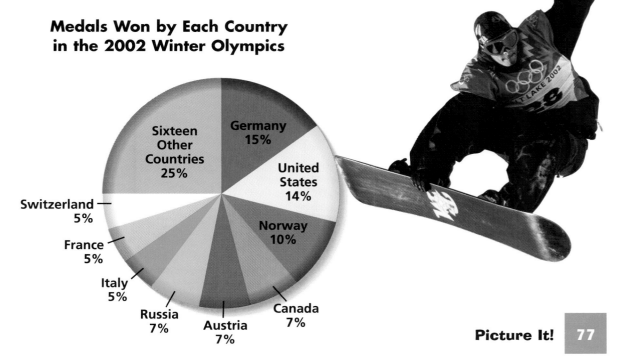

Germany 15%
United States 14%
Norway 10%
Canada 7%
Austria 7%
Russia 7%
Italy 5%
France 5%
Switzerland 5%
Sixteen Other Countries 25%

Outlines

An **outline** uses words to show the most important information about a topic. It groups the main ideas and details related to the topic.

Topic

Main Idea

Details

Related Details

Ways to Get Exercise

I. Everyday activities
   A. Ride a bike or walk to places
   B. Walk the neighbors' dogs
   C. Play outside
      1. Play jump rope
      2. Ride a skateboard
      3. Roller-skate
      4. Play hopscotch

II. Group sports or lessons
   A. Join a team
      1. Basketball
      2. Soccer
      3. Baseball
   B. Take dance lessons
   C. Take karate or other martial arts

III. Special exercises
   A. Build muscles
      1. Push-ups and pull-ups for arms
      2. Sit-ups for stomach
   B. Stretch

Story Maps

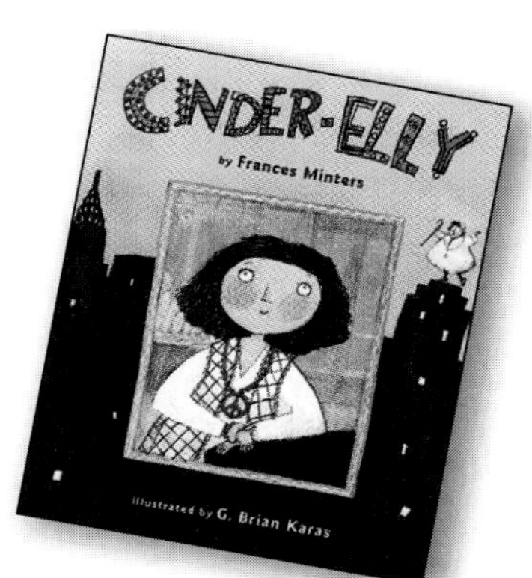

A **story map** is a picture that tells what happens in a story. There are many different kinds of story maps because there are so many different kinds of stories. You can use a story map to plan a story you will write or to show what happened in a story you read.

Beginning, Middle, and End

This kind of story map tells what happens in each main part of a story.

Title: Cinder-Elly

Author: Frances Minters

Beginning

Cinder-Elly and her sisters win free tickets to a basketball game. Elly's mean sisters and her mother won't let her go.

↓

Middle

1. Elly's godmother helps Elly. She uses a magic cane to give Elly glass shoes, new clothes, and a bike.
2. Elly goes to the basketball game and meets Prince Charming.
3. Elly stays too late so her new clothes and bike disappear. She loses a glass shoe.
4. Prince Charming tries to find Elly, but he only finds her shoe.
5. Prince Charming writes a note asking the shoe's owner to call him.

↓

End

Elly's mean sisters try on the glass shoe, but it doesn't fit.
It only fits Elly.
The sisters say they are sorry for being mean.
Cinder-Elly and Prince Charming live happily ever after.

Circular Story Map

Sometimes a story ends at the same place it begins. Use a **circular story map** for this kind of story.

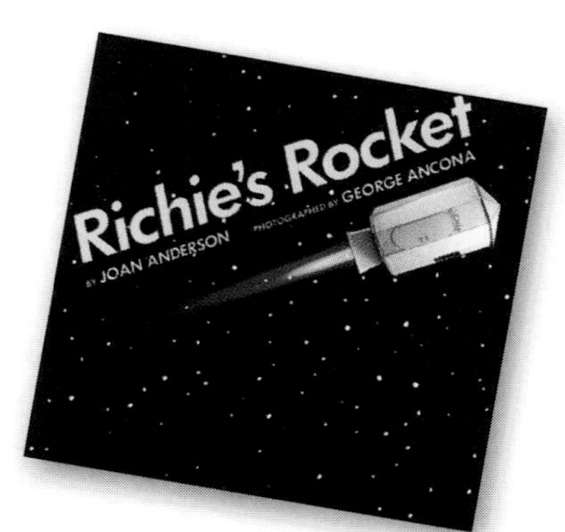

Richie's Rocket
Author: Joan Anderson

Event 1
Richie is in his homemade rocket on the roof when it blasts off into outer space.

Event 2
Richie meets some astronauts from another spacecraft. They tow his rocket to the moon.

Event 3
The rocket lands on the moon. Richie walks on the moon and writes his name in moon dust.

Event 4
The astronauts come back. Their spacecraft lifts Richie's rocket off the moon.

Event 5
The rocket soars back through space toward Earth.

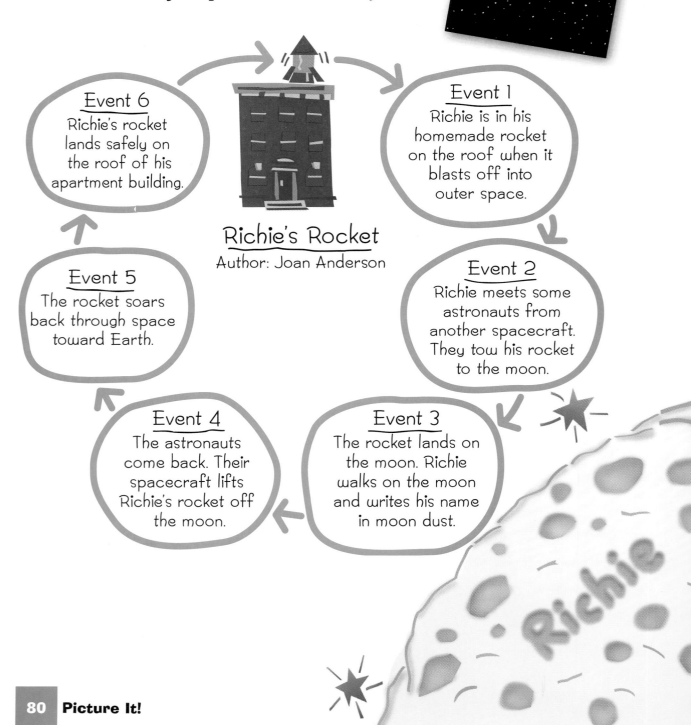

Event 6
Richie's rocket lands safely on the roof of his apartment building.

Problem-and-Solution Map

In some stories, there is a problem that has to be solved. A **problem-and-solution map** will help you show the problem, the ways the characters try to solve it, and the solution.

The **problem** gets the story started.

The **events** tell what happens.

The **solution** tells how the problem is solved.

Title: Subway Sparrow

Author: Leyla Torres

Characters: Four passengers on a subway train

Setting: Atlantic Avenue subway station in Brooklyn, New York

↓

Problem: A sparrow flies inside a subway car. The doors close and the bird can't get out.

↓

Event 1: A girl tries to catch the sparrow, but it flies away from her.

Event 2: A man tries to help by catching the sparrow with his hat, but he misses.

Event 3: A boy wants to help, too, but he's afraid that he might hurt the sparrow.

Event 4: The man starts to use an umbrella to catch the bird, but a woman stops him. She's afraid the umbrella will hurt the bird.

Event 5: Finally, the sparrow lands on the floor of the train and the woman covers it gently with her scarf.

↓

Solution: The girl picks up the sparrow and takes it out of the subway car. Outside the station, the four passengers watch the bird fly away.

Goal-and-Outcome Map

Some stories tell what characters do to get what they want, or to **reach their goals**. Use a **goal-and-outcome map** for these stories.

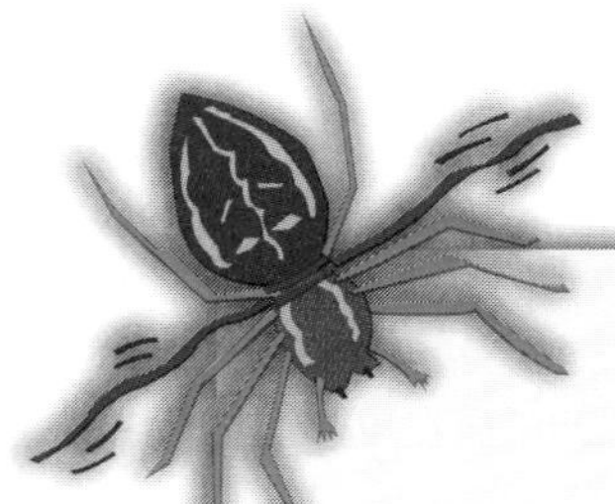

The **goal** tells what the character in a story wants.

The **events** tell what happens.

The **outcome** tells if the character gets what he or she wants.

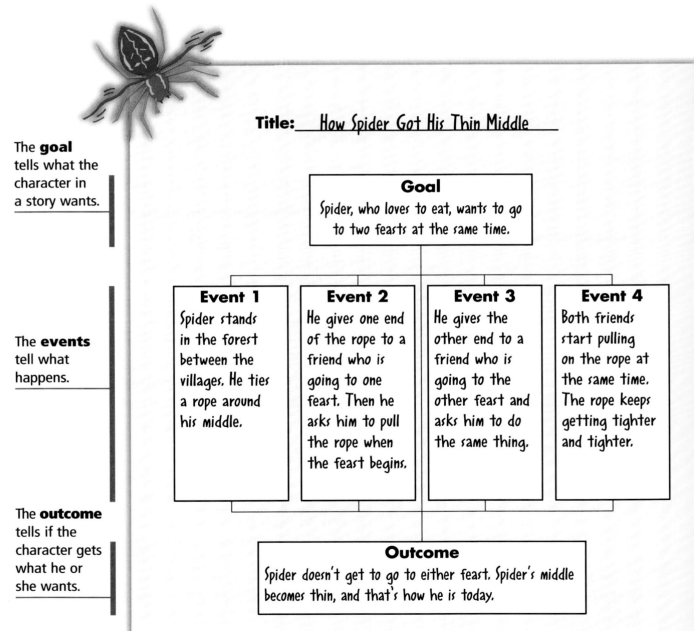

Title: How Spider Got His Thin Middle

Goal
Spider, who loves to eat, wants to go to two feasts at the same time.

Event 1	Event 2	Event 3	Event 4
Spider stands in the forest between the villages. He ties a rope around his middle.	He gives one end of the rope to a friend who is going to one feast. Then he asks him to pull the rope when the feast begins.	He gives the other end to a friend who is going to the other feast and asks him to do the same thing.	Both friends start pulling on the rope at the same time. The rope keeps getting tighter and tighter.

Outcome
Spider doesn't get to go to either feast. Spider's middle becomes thin, and that's how he is today.

Map for Rising and Falling Action

This kind of story map looks like a mountain. The most important part of the story, the **climax**, is at the top. The action that builds up to it tells about a **conflict**, or struggle between a character and someone or something. The action after the climax leads down to the **resolution** at the end.

The Clever Wife

a Chinese folk tale

Climax:

5. Fu-hsing carries out his wife's plan.

4. Fu-hsing tells his wife. She thinks of a plan to outsmart the law officer.

3. The law officer gives Fu-hsing three impossible tasks. Fu-hsing is afraid.

Conflict:

2. The law officer sees the signs and becomes angry. He thinks Fu-hsing is boasting about himself.

1. Fu-hsing is proud of his clever wife. He hangs signs praising her.

Rising Action

6. The law officer is impressed with Fu-hsing's cleverness. He doesn't realize that Fu-hsing's wife is the clever one.

Falling Action

Setting

Ancient China

Characters

Fu-hsing, his wife, and the law officer

Resolution:

7. The law officer lets Fu-hsing go and never bothers him again.

Tables and Charts

Tables and **charts** present information in rows and columns. Read across the rows and down the columns to compare information.

Number of Books Read During the October Read-a-thon

The **rows** go from left to right (➡).

The **columns** go from top to bottom (⬇).

	Class 1	Class 2	Class 3
Grade 1	47	35	62
Grade 2	33	85	102
Grade 3	75	95	88
Grade 4	78	93	82
Grade 5	96	96	95
Grade 6	102	107	65

Comparison Table

Some tables show how two things are the same and how they're different.

Life in the United States and Russia

These rows tell how the U.S. and Russia are the same.

Life in the U. S.	Life in Russia
go to school Monday through Friday	go to school Monday through Friday
participate in many different sports	participate in many different sports
don't learn to swim at school	learn to swim at school in kindergarten
cable or satellite television with many channels	television with only a few channels
can learn another language	must learn another language

These rows tell how the U.S. and Russia are different.

Cause-and-Effect Chart

This chart shows how one event causes another event to happen. That's why it's called a **cause-and-effect chart**.

How a Volcano Erupts

Cause	Effect
The temperature is very hot below the earth's surface.	The rock melts to form a pool of magma in a magma chamber.
Solid rock around the magma chamber puts pressure on the magma.	The hot magma makes a conduit, or tunnel, up through the earth.
The magma forces its way out of the conduit.	The volcano erupts!

KWLQ Chart

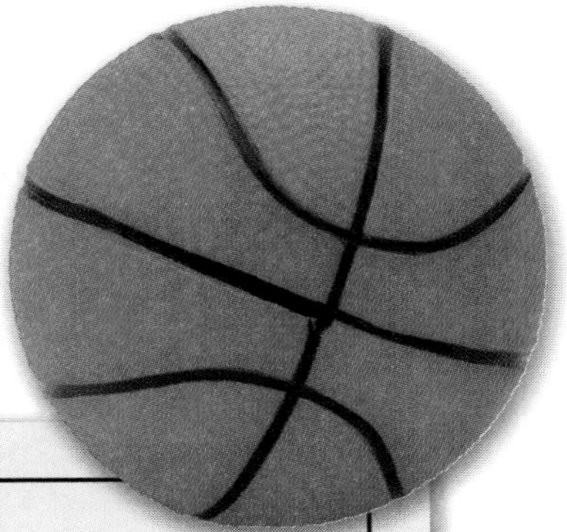

A **KWLQ chart** helps you think about something you are studying. Read the question at the top of each column. It tells you how to complete the chart.

Topic: Basketball

K What Do I Know?	W What Do I Want to Learn?	L What Did I Learn?	Q What Questions Do I Still Have?
It takes two teams to play a game. Each team tries to throw the ball into the basket. The team that makes the most baskets wins.	How many players are on each team? How many points are given for a basket? How long does the game last?	There are 5 players on a team. A basket can count as 1, 2, or 3 points. A game is 32 minutes long. The game is played in two parts. Each part takes 16 minutes.	What does each player do? What happens if there's a tie after 32 minutes? When was basketball invented?

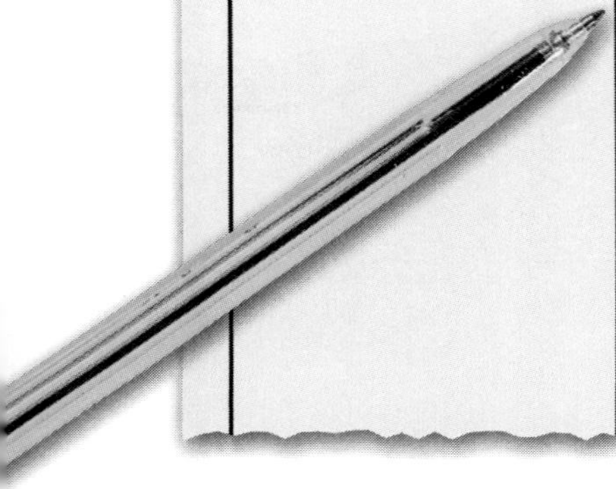

Flow Chart

A **flow chart** shows the steps in a process. Arrows show the order of the steps.

How Jeans Are Made

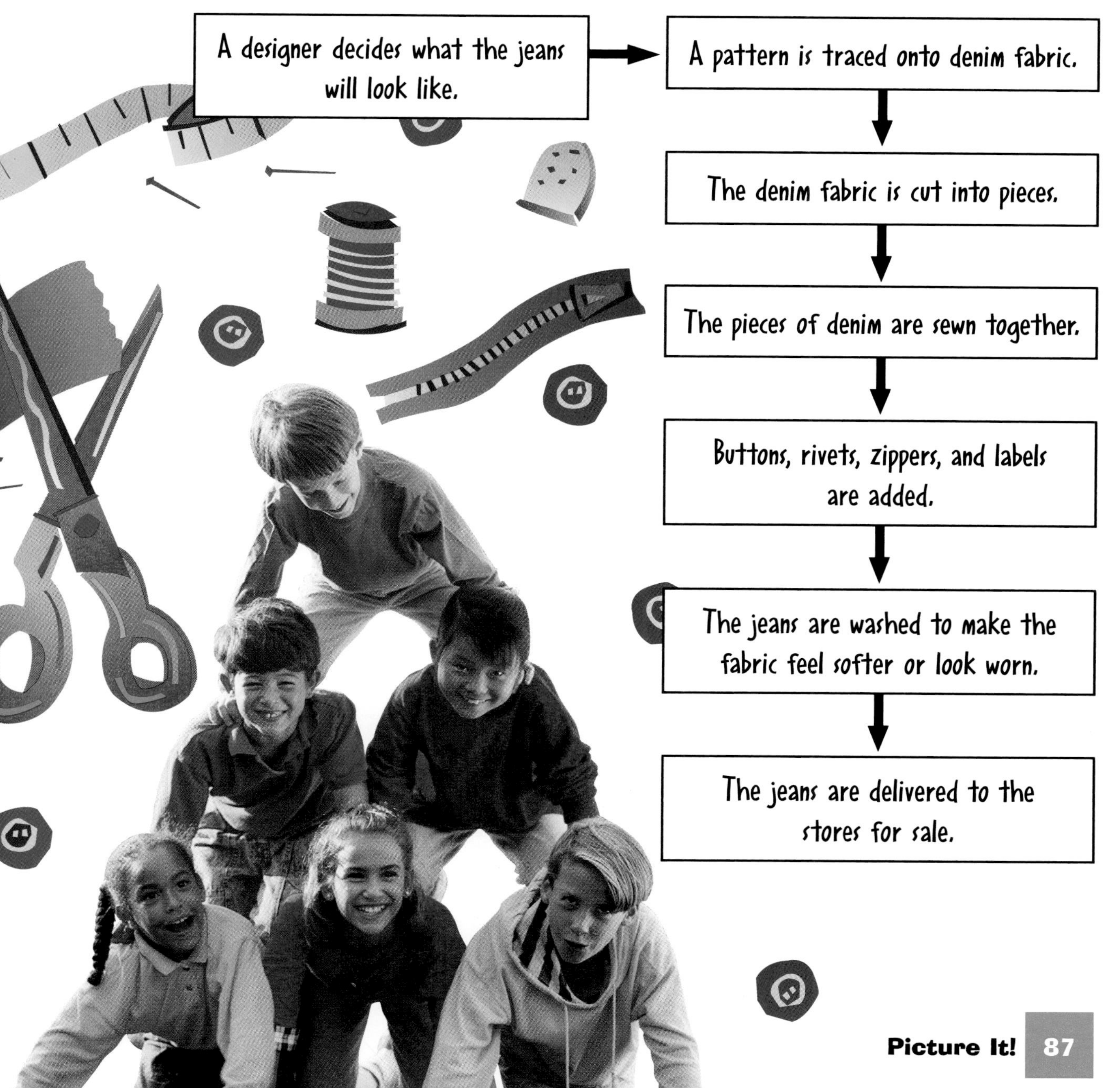

A designer decides what the jeans will look like.
→ A pattern is traced onto denim fabric.
↓ The denim fabric is cut into pieces.
↓ The pieces of denim are sewn together.
↓ Buttons, rivets, zippers, and labels are added.
↓ The jeans are washed to make the fabric feel softer or look worn.
↓ The jeans are delivered to the stores for sale.

Time Lines

A **time line** shows a series of important events. It tells about each event and when it happened.

Horizontal Time Line

This time line tells about special events in a person's life. It's called a **horizontal time line** because the line goes from left to right (➡).

U.S.A
SCHOOL
Restaurant
FOOD
1st Place National Spelling Bee
Age 3
My family leaves the Philippines and moves to the United States.
Age 5
I start kindergarten at a school in Los Angeles, California.
Age 7
My family opens a restaurant.
Age 9
We go back to the Philippines to visit relatives.
Age 12
I win 1st place at the National Spelling Bee.

1st
PLACE
NATIONAL SPELLING BEE

Vertical Time Line

This time line goes from top to bottom (⬇). That's why it's called a **vertical time line**.

Dr. Franklin Chang-Díaz has spent over 1,600 hours in space.

Dr. Chang-Díaz: Astronaut

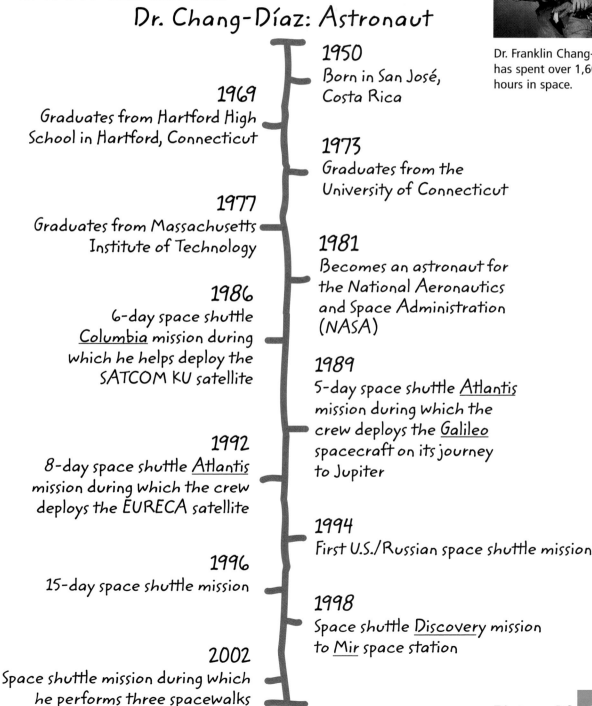

1950
Born in San José, Costa Rica

1969
Graduates from Hartford High School in Hartford, Connecticut

1973
Graduates from the University of Connecticut

1977
Graduates from Massachusetts Institute of Technology

1981
Becomes an astronaut for the National Aeronautics and Space Administration (NASA)

1986
6-day space shuttle *Columbia* mission during which he helps deploy the SATCOM KU satellite

1989
5-day space shuttle *Atlantis* mission during which the crew deploys the *Galileo* spacecraft on its journey to Jupiter

1992
8-day space shuttle *Atlantis* mission during which the crew deploys the EURECA satellite

1994
First U.S./Russian space shuttle mission

1996
15-day space shuttle mission

1998
Space shuttle *Discovery* mission to *Mir* space station

2002
Space shuttle mission during which he performs three spacewalks

Chapter 3
Put It in Writing!

Danny and Aisha love to write! They know that writing is a good way to share ideas with others and to express their own personal thoughts and feelings.

How can you be a spectacular writer? Just look in this chapter and you'll find out! You'll learn how to put your own ideas in writing and how to write everything from letters and reports to stories and even tongue twisters!

Writer's Resources

Every writer needs tools to work with. Here are some you will use often.

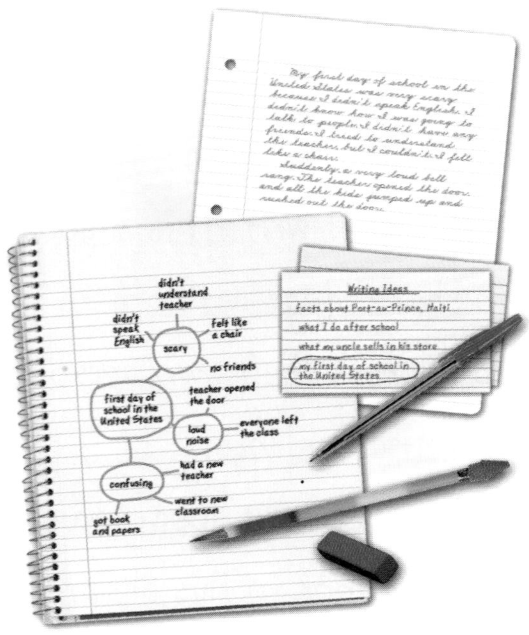

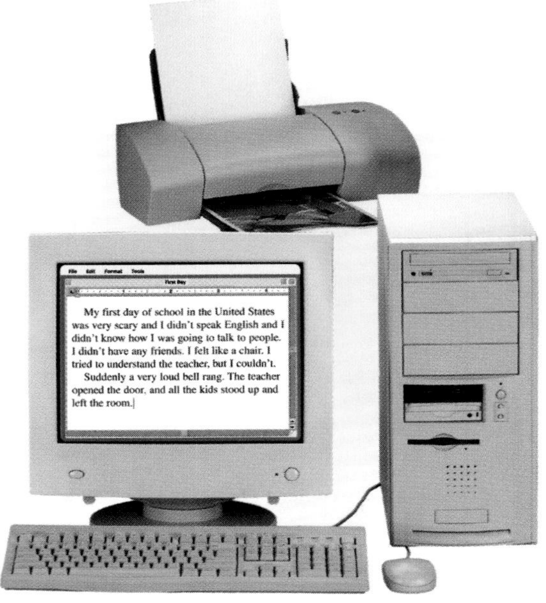

- Use **notecards** to gather information and organize your ideas.
- Use **paper** and **pencil** to plan, draft, and revise your writing.
- Write in **pen** when you're ready to write your final version.
- If you have a **computer**, you can write in a **word processing program**.
- **Save** a copy of each draft so you can look back at what you wrote.
- When you edit and proofread, **print out** your writing instead of trying to read on the screen.
- Most programs can show and help you fix **spelling and grammar** mistakes.

Look in a **dictionary** to find meanings and spellings of words.

Use a **bilingual dictionary** to find the English word for a word you know in your home language.

Use a **thesaurus** to find more precise or interesting words for words that you use too often or words that aren't quite right.

You can use a **handbook** like this one for help with each step of the Writing Process.

- Look in Chapter 2 for ways to **plan and organize** your writing.
- See pages 112–171 of Chapter 3 for different **writing forms**. Use pages 174–177 of The Good Writer Guide to learn how to write for a specific **audience and purpose**.
- Use pages 178–188 of The Good Writer Guide to **revise** your draft.
- Use the **spelling tips** in Chapter 4 and the **grammar, capitalization, and punctuation** rules in Chapter 5 to polish your writing.
- Use Chapter 4 to get ideas for **presenting** your final work.

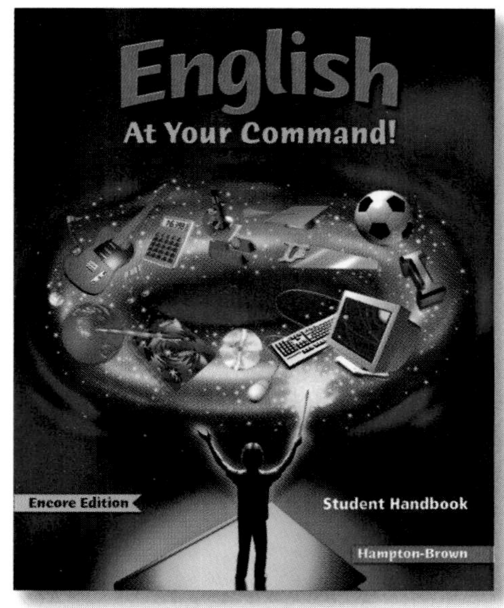

The Writing Process

Writing is a great way to express yourself! The **Writing Process** will help you plan, create, improve, and publish your writing.

STEP 1 Prewriting

Prewriting is what you do before you write. That's when you decide what to write about and you organize your ideas.

Brainstorm Ideas and Choose a Topic

An idea is all you need to get started! Collect ideas in a writing file. Every time you think of an idea, add it to your file. Then, when it's time to write, look in your file for ideas.

Think about your ideas. Which one do you know the most about? Which one means something special to you? Circle one. That will be your **topic**.

Writing Ideas

facts about Port-au-Prince, Haiti

what I do after school

what my uncle sells in his store

my first day of school in the United States

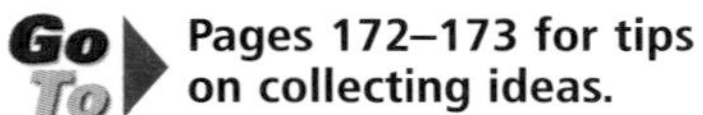
Go To Pages 172–173 for tips on collecting ideas.

Plan Your Writing

Before you start writing, think about these important questions. Record your answers in an **FATP** chart.

1. **Why** are you writing? This is your **purpose**. For example, you might want to express your feelings or give information.
2. **Who** will read your writing? This is your **audience**. Are you writing for your classmates, a teacher, family, or friends?
3. **What** will you write? Choose a **writing form** that fits your purpose and audience.

Form:	personal narrative
Audience:	my classmates
Topic:	first day of school in United States
Purpose:	to describe my experience

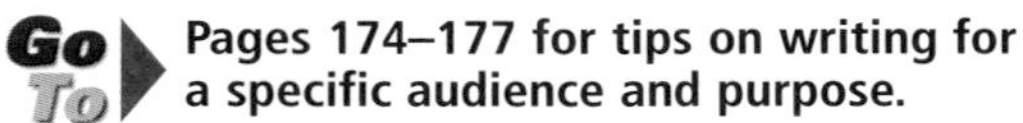
Go To Pages 174–177 for tips on writing for a specific audience and purpose.

Think About What You Know

Collect details about your topic. List what you already know about it. Talk about it with others. They might help you remember more details. Here are some ways to show your details.

Make a cluster.

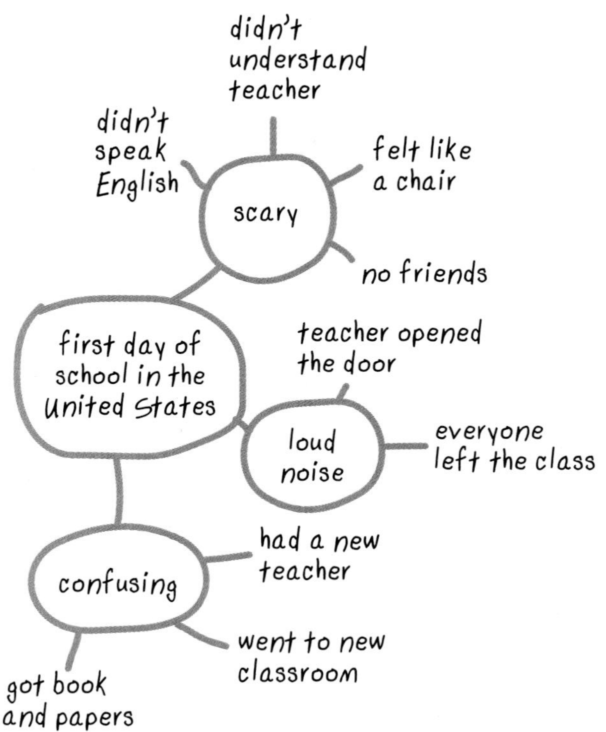

Make a list.

Topic: my first day of school in the United States

lots of different teachers

everything is strange

moving classes—confusing

didn't know how to speak English

didn't know anyone

felt like a chair

Draw and label pictures.

I didn't understand the teacher.

A really loud bell rang. Everyone got up and left.

Then we had a different teacher.

Organize Details

Are the details about your topic in order? Sometimes you can organize the details as you write them down. Other times, you may need to go back and put your details in order. One way to do this is to add numbers to show the order.

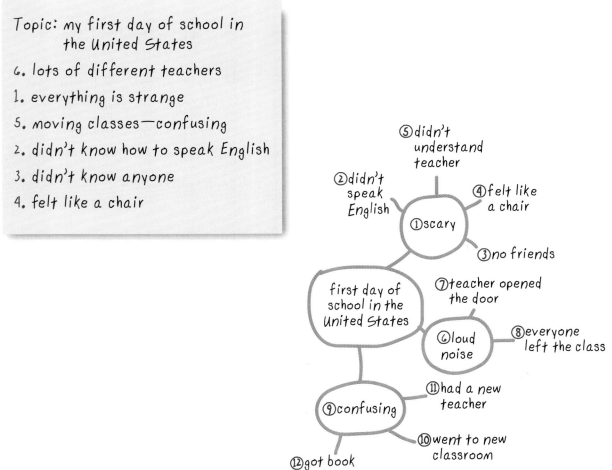

Topic: my first day of school in the United States

6. lots of different teachers
1. everything is strange
5. moving classes—confusing
2. didn't know how to speak English
3. didn't know anyone
4. felt like a chair

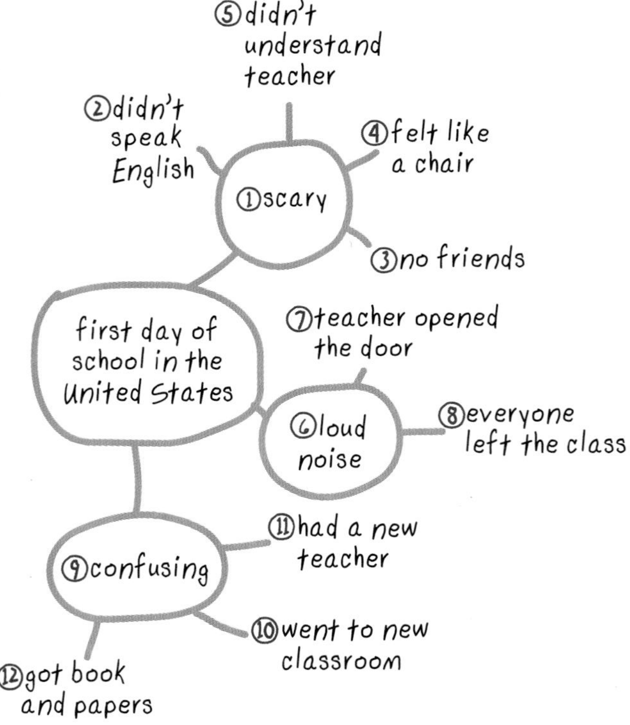

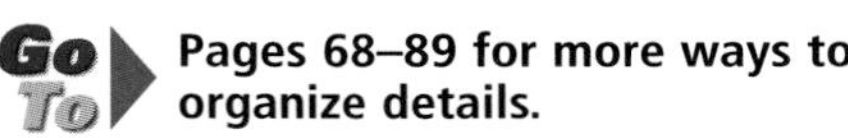
Go To Pages 68–89 for more ways to organize details.

STEP

2 Drafting

Now you're ready to write your **first draft**. That's when you turn your ideas into sentences and paragraphs. Write quickly and don't worry about mistakes. You can correct them later.

Write a Topic Sentence

The **topic sentence** tells the main idea of a paragraph. In the first paragraph, the topic sentence should tell your audience the main idea of your writing.

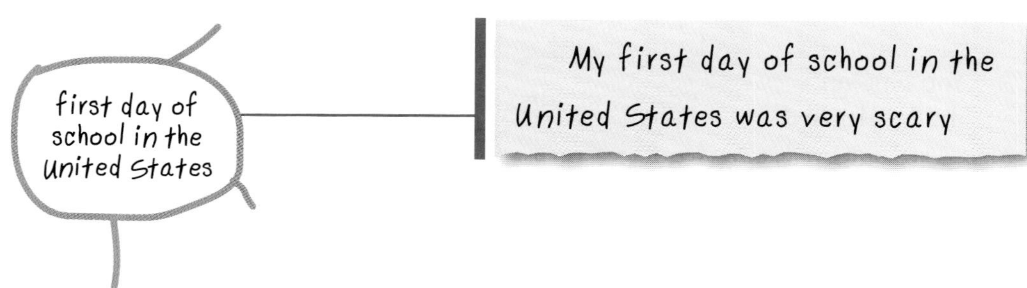

Add Details

Add sentences to give more **details** about the main idea. Start a new paragraph when you have a new main idea, or when the action or setting changes.

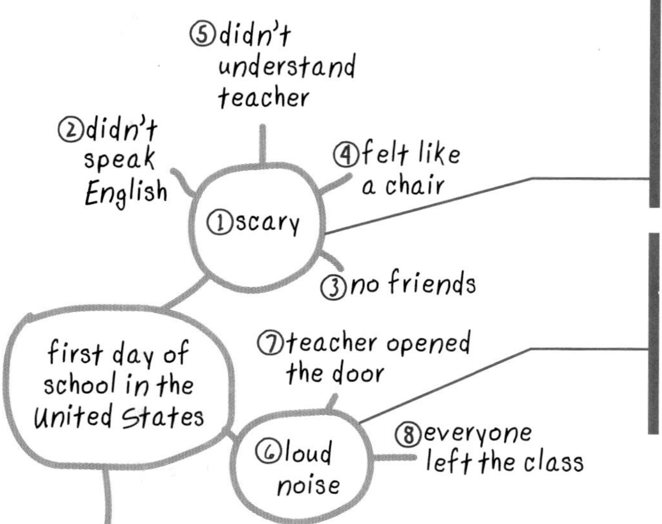

My first day of school in the United States was ①very scary and ②I didn't speak English and I didn't know how I was going to talk to people. ③I didn't have any friends. ④I felt like a chair. ⑤I tried to understand the teacher, but I couldn't.

⑥Suddenly, a very loud bell rang. ⑦The teacher opened the door, and ⑧all the kids stood up and left the room.

Keys to the Computer

If you want to write your draft on the computer, you will need to use a **word processing program**. Here's how to get started.

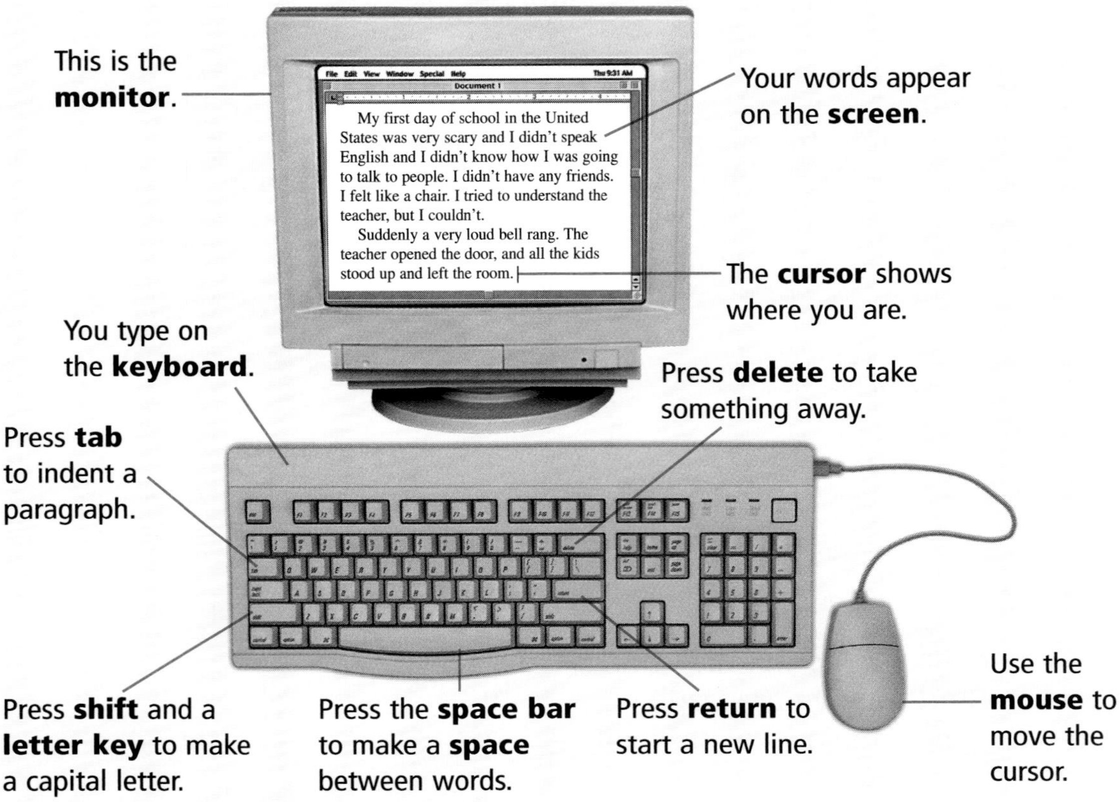
This is the **monitor**.
Your words appear on the **screen**.
My first day of school in the United States was very scary and I didn't speak English and I didn't know how I was going to talk to people. I didn't have any friends. I felt like a chair. I tried to understand the teacher, but I couldn't.
Suddenly a very loud bell rang. The teacher opened the door, and all the kids stood up and left the room.
The **cursor** shows where you are.
You type on the **keyboard**.
Press **delete** to take something away.
Press **tab** to indent a paragraph.
Press **shift** and a **letter key** to make a capital letter.
Press the **space bar** to make a **space** between words.
Press **return** to start a new line.
Use the **mouse** to move the cursor.

Set Up a File

To make a new document, or **file**:

1. Click on **File** in the menu bar.
2. Click on **New Blank Document** in the **File** menu. A blank file will appear.

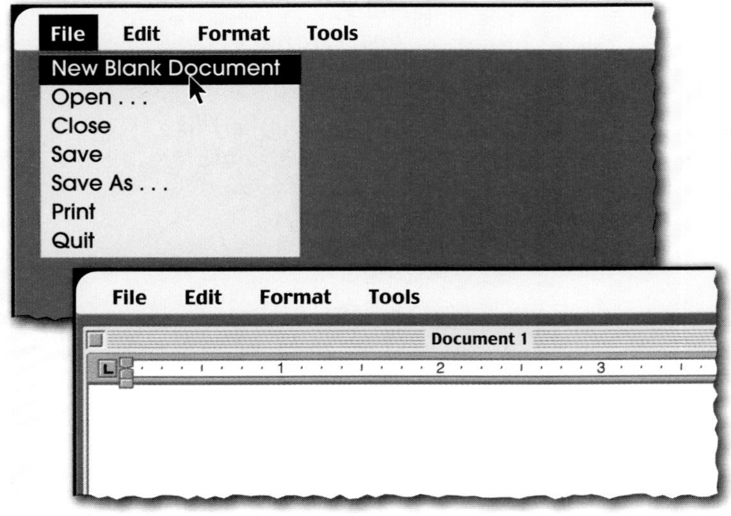
File
Edit
Format
Tools
New Blank Document
Open . . .
Close
Save
Save As . . .
Print
Quit
File
Edit
Format
Tools
Document 1

Save Your File

The first time you save your file, you will need to name it.

1. Go to the **File** menu and click **Save As**.

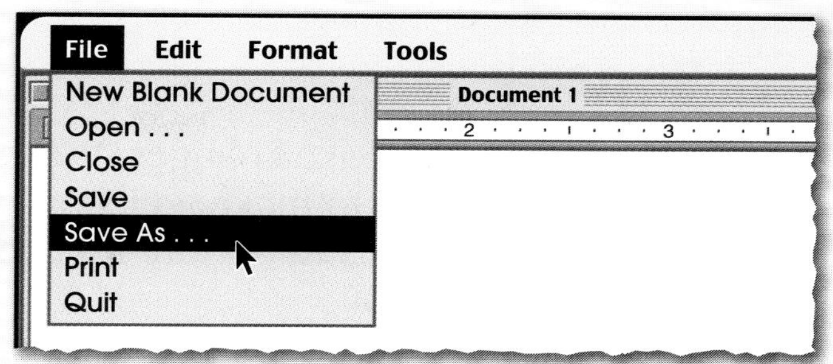

2. Type a name for your **file**.
3. Choose the **folder** where you want your file to be saved.
4. Click **Save**.

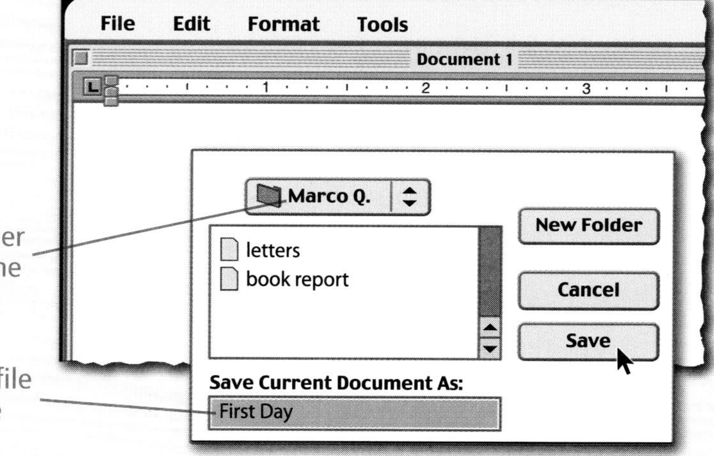

Start Typing

Move the mouse and click it to put the cursor where you want to type. Use the **arrows** on the **scroll bar** to move up and down in your file.

Remember to save regularly. You don't want lose your hard work! Click on **Save** in the **File** menu:

- every 10 minutes
- before you leave the computer
- before you print
- before you quit.

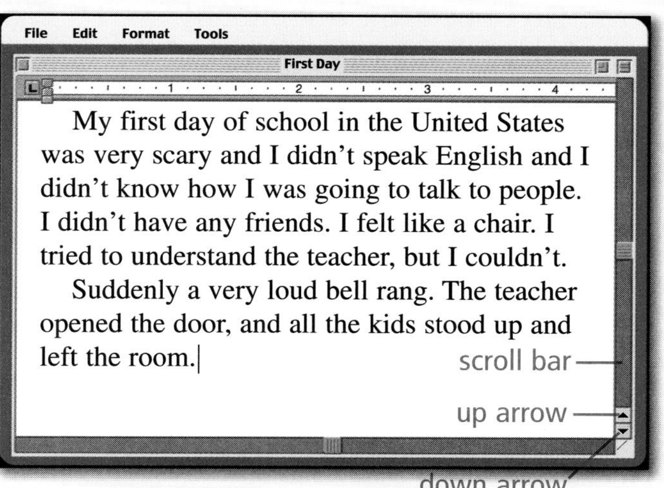

STEP
3 Revising

To **revise** means to make changes. When you revise your writing, you change it to make it clearer or more interesting. You also make changes to be sure that your writing says what you want it to say.

Read Your Draft

Ask yourself these questions about your writing.

- ❑ Is my writing interesting?
- ❑ Did I achieve my purpose? Did I say what I wanted to say?
- ❑ Did I include all the details? Should I take any out? Should I add some?
- ❑ Did I stick to the topic?
- ❑ Is my writing clear? Are there any words I need to change to make it clearer?
- ❑ Does my writing make sense? Are the events, sentences, and details in the best order?
- ❑ Do I need to combine any short sentences? Do I need to break up any long ones?

Have Someone Else Read Your Draft

Have the person who reads your draft follow these steps to give you ideas for making your writing better. This is called a **peer conference**.

The Reader's Role in a Peer Conference

1. **Read the writing at least two times.**
2. **Try summarizing it in one sentence. What is the main idea?**

   This story (report) is all about ____.
3. **Tell which part you liked best. Why?**

   I really liked how you ____. The beginning (ending) is really good because ____.
4. **Tell which part you liked least. Why?**

   The beginning (ending) didn't get my attention because ____. I didn't like ____ because ____.
5. **Tell if any parts confused you.**

   I didn't understand the part where ____.

   I was surprised to read that ____.
6. **Tell how to make it better. Be specific.**

   This would be better if ____.

   You might try adding (or taking out) ____.

Revising, continued

Mark Your Changes

Now mark your changes using the **revising marks**.

Revising Marks	Meaning
^	**Add.**
	Move to here.
	Replace with this.
	Take out.
⊙	**Add a period.**

I used "and" too many times in this sentence.

My first day of school in the United States was very scary ~~and~~ [because] I didn't speak English ~~and~~ [.] I didn't know how I was going to talk to people. I didn't have any friends. I felt like a chair. I tried to understand the teacher, but I couldn't.

Ingrid said it would be better if I put how I felt last.

Suddenly, a very loud bell rang. The teacher opened the door, and all the kids ~~stood~~ [jumped] up and ~~left the room.~~ [rushed out the door.]

These changes will give my readers a better picture of what happened.

The Good Writer Guide on pages 178–188 for tips on improving your writing.

Keys to the Computer

The computer allows you to **revise** your writing easily.

How to Delete Something

You can **delete**, or take out, whole words or single characters. A **character** is a letter, number, or other typed item.

To delete a character or space between characters:

1. Place your cursor just after the character or space.
2. Press the **delete** key. The cursor will move backward and "erase" whatever was before it.

To delete a whole word:

1. Place the cursor anywhere on the word.
2. Click the mouse twice to highlight the word.
3. Press the **delete** key. This "erases" the whole word.

Before

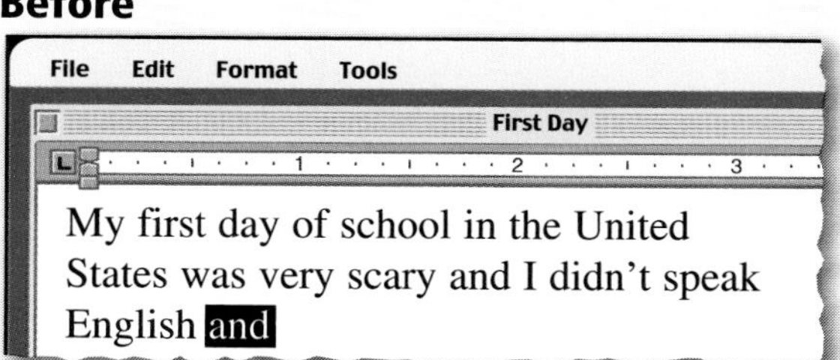

After

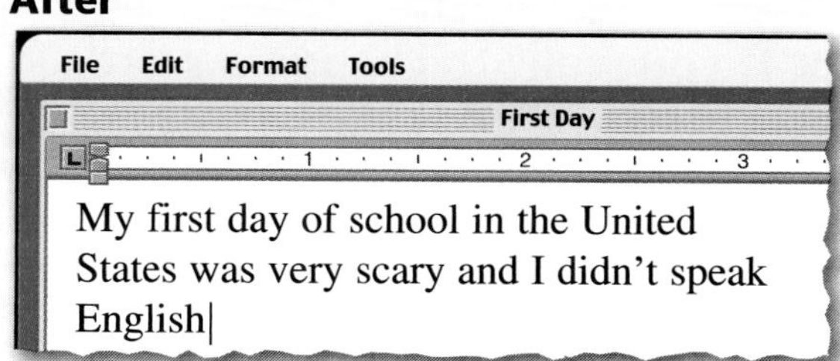

To delete more than one word:

1. **Click and drag** to highlight the words you want to delete. To do this, click on the mouse and hold it down as you slide it over the words.
2. Press the **delete** key. This will "erase" everything you highlighted.

Before

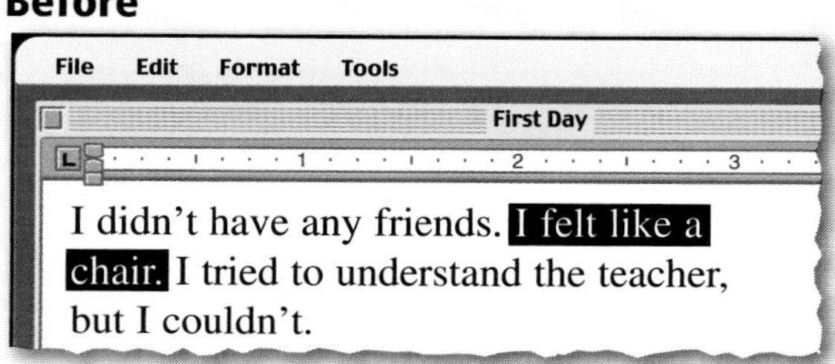

After

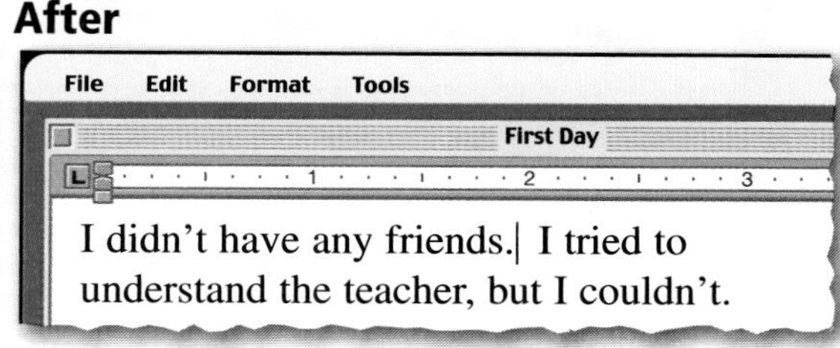

How to Add Something

■ **If you want to add, or insert, characters, words, or spaces:**

1. Put your cursor where you want to insert something.
2. Click the mouse once. The cursor will start to flash.
3. Type what you want to add.

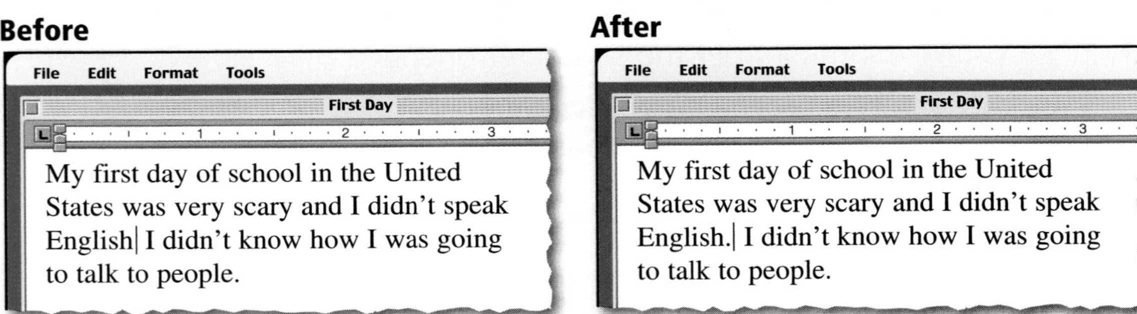

How to Change a Word

■ **If you want to change a word:**

1. Highlight the word that you want to change.
2. Start typing the new word. The new word will erase the old one.

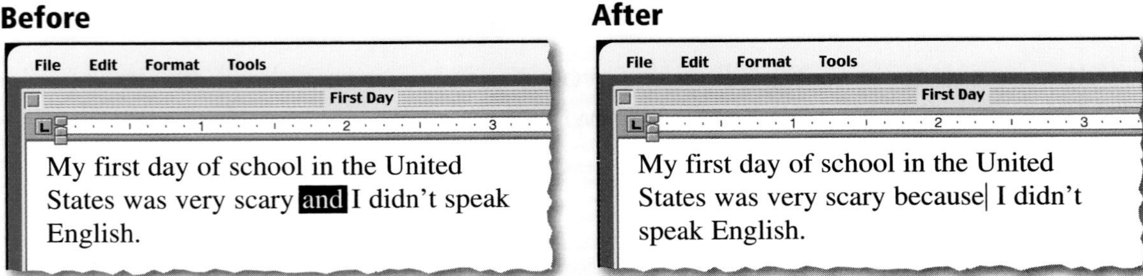

How to Cut and Paste

You can **cut and paste** to move parts of your writing from one place to another.

■ **To move something, first you have to cut it.**

1. Highlight the part you want to move.
2. Go to the **Edit** menu and click **Cut**. This will take out the highlighted part.

Before

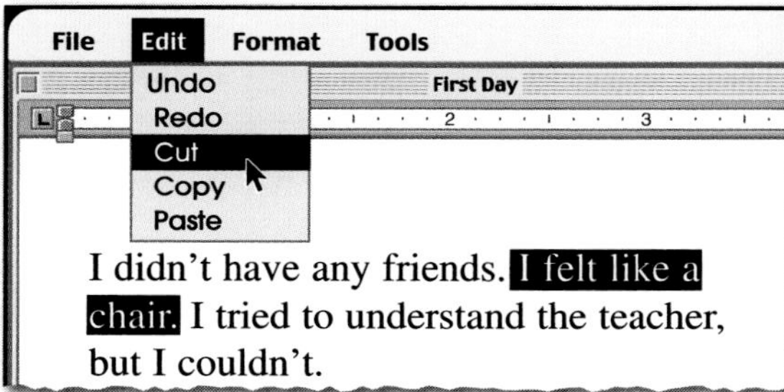

After

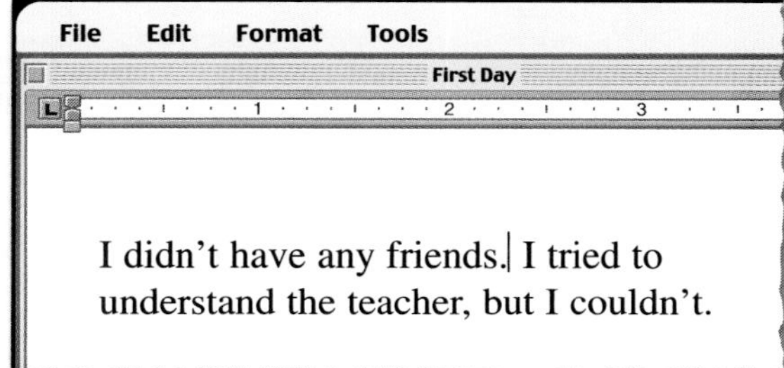

■ **Then you paste, or put back in, the part you cut.**

1. Use the mouse to place your cursor where you want the words to go.
2. Go to the **Edit** menu and click **Paste**. Your words will appear again—in the new place!

Before

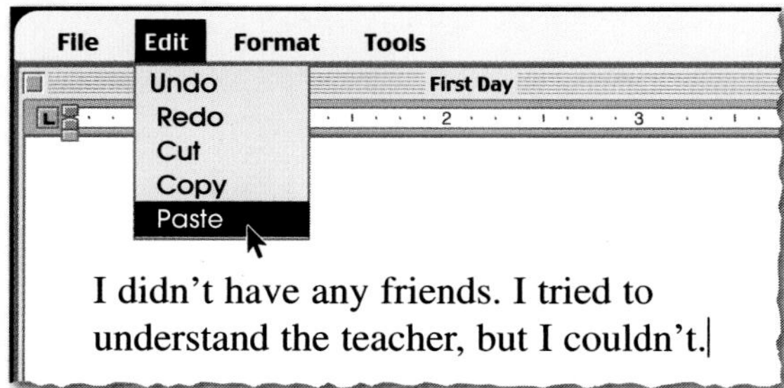

After

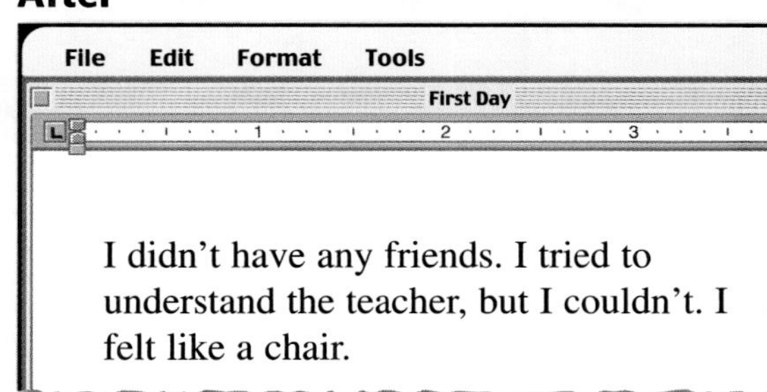

STEP

4 Editing and Proofreading

After revising your draft, you **edit** it. That means you **proofread,** or look for mistakes in capitalization, spelling, and punctuation. Use the **proofreading marks** to show what you need to fix.

Proofreading Marks	Meaning
^	Add.
^,	Add a comma.
⊙	Add a period.
≡	Capitalize.
◯	Check spelling.
/	Make lowercase.
¶	Start a new paragraph.
⌒	Take out.

Why was everyone leaving? In Haiti we stayed in the same Classroom all day. I followed the class and we went into a new room. A stranger gave me a book and some papers. I was really puzzled. Fortunately, the man spoke some Creole and explained that he was my science teacher. ¶ Finally i understood. In america, there are special teachers for science, music and gym. Students also move to new classrooms. At first it was very confusing but now I like having diferent (different) teachers for my subjects

Go To Pages 276–287 for capitalization and punctuation tips.

Keys to the Computer

The computer can help you proofread your writing. Most word processing programs have a tool to **check spelling.**

1. Click on **Tools** in the menu bar.
2. Click **Spelling** in the **Tools** menu. The computer will show you misspelled words in color.

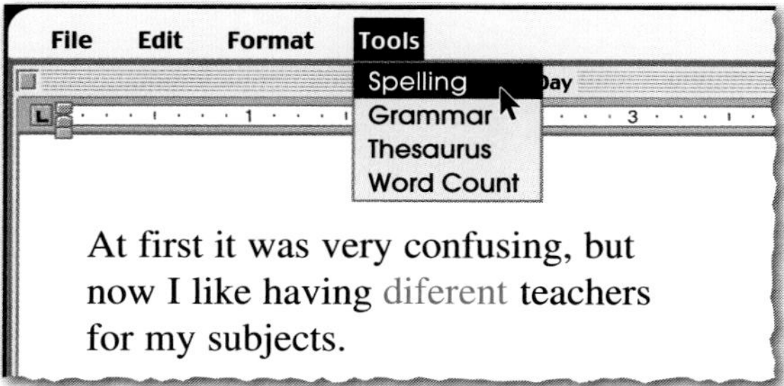

3. Click on the correct spelling from the list of suggestions. If the word you want is not listed, check a dictionary.

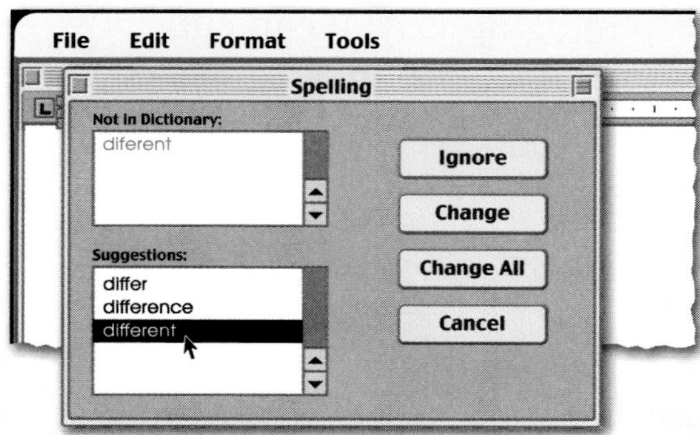

4. Click **Change**. The word will be fixed in your writing.

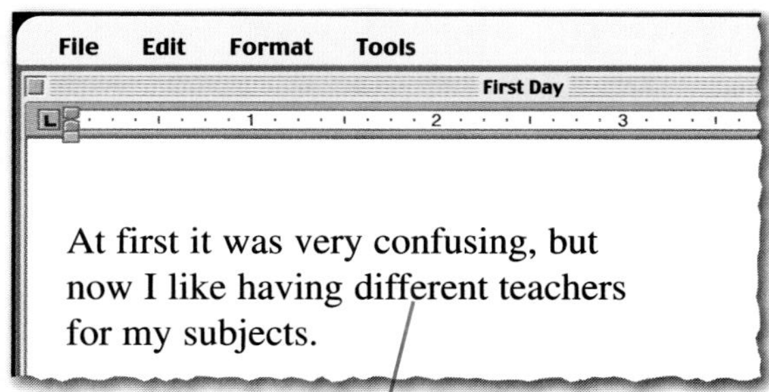

The word **diferent** was changed to **different**.

STEP
5 Publishing

Publishing is the best part of the writing process! Now you can make a final copy of your writing and share it with others.

Add Visuals

Visuals such as drawings, photographs, charts, and diagrams can make your writing more interesting. They also help your audience understand your writing.

- **Draw pictures.**

  You can draw pictures to illustrate what you wrote.

- **Include photographs.**

  If you don't have your own photographs, you can cut pictures out of magazines or print them from the Internet.

- **Use computer clip art.**

  Most word processing programs come with **clip art**. These are symbols, or simple pictures, that you can insert in documents.

- **Show graphs, charts, and diagrams.**

  Sometimes you can make your writing clearer by showing information in a graph, chart, or diagram.

Share Your Writing

Here are some ideas for sharing your finished work.

- Send it to a magazine or newspaper.
- E-mail it to a friend.
- Put it in a notebook with other students' work. Make it a reference book for next year's class.
- Read it out loud to your class.
- Turn it into a book.
- Read it out loud on a stage with music playing in the background.
- Videotape yourself reading it.
- Fax it to your mom at her office.

My First Day in an American School

by Marco Quezada

My first day of school in the United States was very scary because I didn't speak English. I didn't know how I was going to talk to people. I didn't have any friends. I tried to understand the teacher, but I couldn't. I felt like a chair.

Suddenly, a very loud bell rang. The teacher opened the door, and all the kids jumped up and rushed out the door.

Why was everyone leaving? In Haiti, we stayed in the same classroom all day. I followed the class, and we went into a new room. A stranger gave me a book and some papers. I was really puzzled. Fortunately, the man spoke some Creole and explained that he was my science teacher.

Finally, I understood. In America, there are special teachers for science, music, and gym. Students also move to new classrooms. At first, it was very confusing, but now I like having different teachers for my subjects.

Keys to the Computer

Use a computer to add visuals to your writing.

Use a Scanner

A **scanner** is a machine that connects to your computer. It works like a photocopy machine, but it copies pictures into your computer instead of making paper copies. You can scan photos, drawings, and even flat objects such as leaves, coins, or fabric.

To use a scanner:

1. Put the item face down on the scanner window.

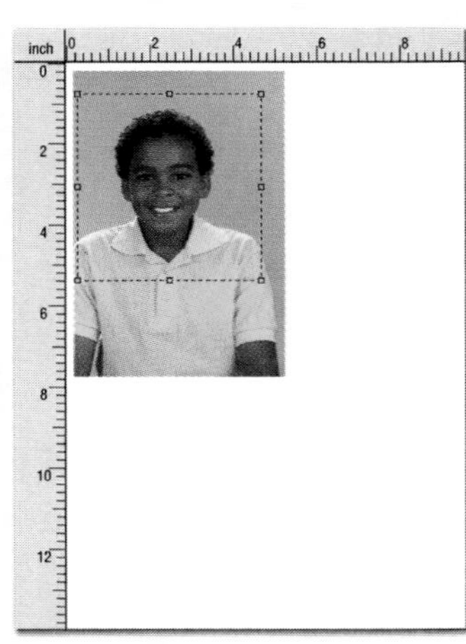

2. Start the scanner program in your computer. (It's separate from the word processing program.) Then go to the **File** menu and choose **Acquire** or **Import**.
3. You will see a **preview** of your picture, or **image**, on the computer screen. Use the mouse to choose the part of the image you want to scan. (The scanner program may ask you to make other choices, too.)
4. Press the **Scan** button on the scanner.
5. After the image is scanned, go to the **File** menu on your computer. Choose **Save As** to save the image as a file.
6. You can now either print out the image and attach the picture to your printed writing, or you can **import**, or place, the image directly into your word processing file on the computer.

Print Your Finished Work

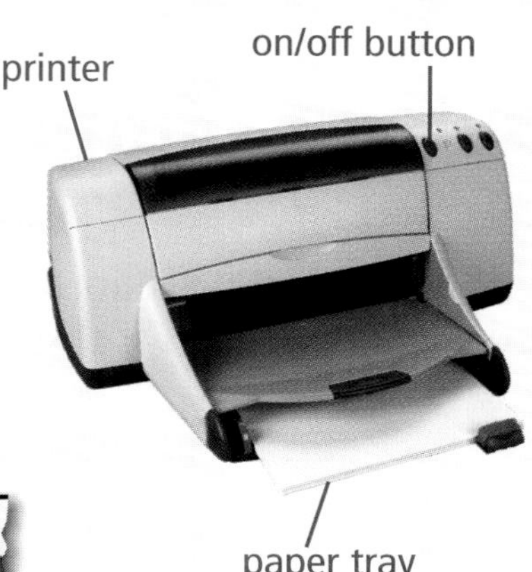

When you're ready to print out the final version of your writing:

1. Turn on the printer. Make sure there is paper in the paper tray.

2. Go to the **File menu** and click **Print**.

3. How many copies do you want? Do you want to print all the pages in your document or just some? Fill in the number and click **Print** to start printing.

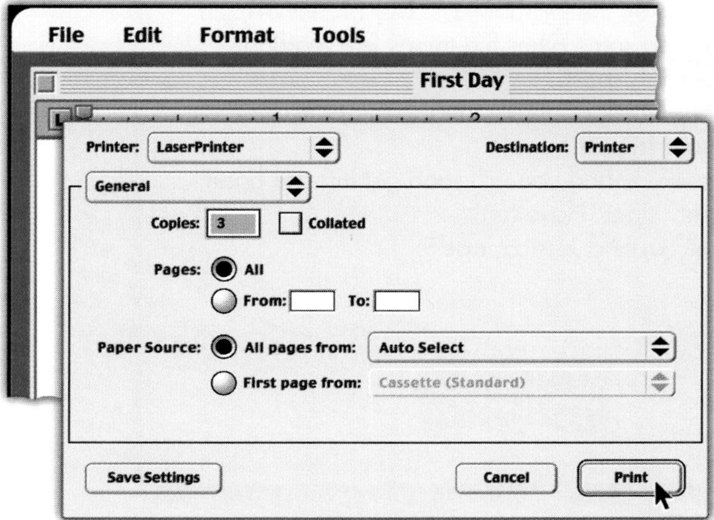

Kinds of Writing

Advice Column

Do you have a problem that you can't figure out? Try writing a letter to an **advice column** in a newspaper, in a magazine, or on the World Wide Web.

An advice column begins with a description of the **problem**.

The **advice** is a way to solve the problem. It's usually helpful to anyone who reads it.

The person asking for advice often uses a **made-up name**.

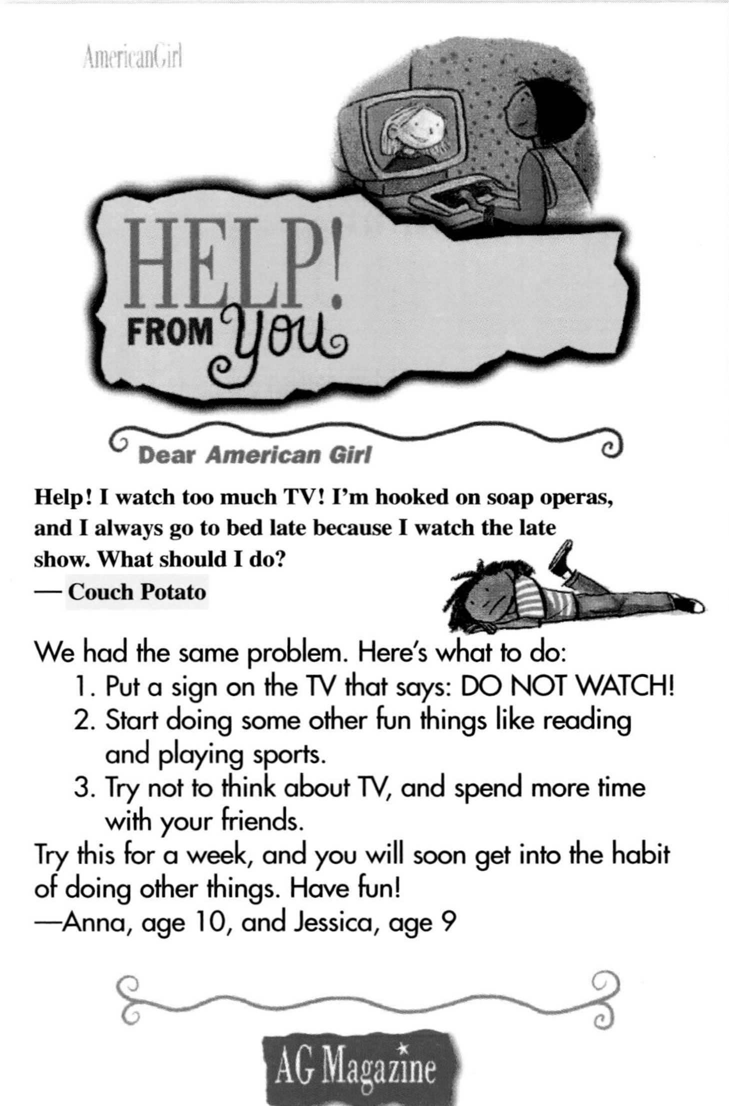

AmericanGirl

HELP! FROM you

Dear American Girl

Help! I watch too much TV! I'm hooked on soap operas, and I always go to bed late because I watch the late show. What should I do?
— Couch Potato

We had the same problem. Here's what to do:

1. Put a sign on the TV that says: DO NOT WATCH!
2. Start doing some other fun things like reading and playing sports.
3. Try not to think about TV, and spend more time with your friends.

Try this for a week, and you will soon get into the habit of doing other things. Have fun!
—Anna, age 10, and Jessica, age 9

AG Magazine

Announcements and Advertisements

An **announcement** is a short message that tells about an event.

Advertisements, or ads, tell about services you might need or special products you can buy.

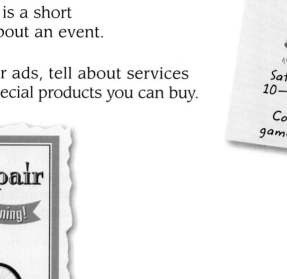

River School's Spring Fair
Saturday, April 15
10–4 at the school
Come for food, games, and prizes!

Bicycle Repair
It's Time for Spring Cleaning!
Complete bike repair and cleaning for road and mountain bikes.
Nathan's Bike Shop
756 Mission Fields Center
Alton, IL 60381
555-0099

A company's **name**, **address**, and **telephone number** is given so you can get in touch with them.

Ads often show pictures of what you can buy.

A description tells you more about the item.

Show Your School Spirit!
OAK GROVE SCHOOL
Your school's name and mascot can be on this 100% cotton shirt. Available in an assortment of colors.
Sizes: ☐ S ☐ M ☐ LG ☐ XL
5D143-714 . . . . $15.00
Mail your order to:
School Colors International
P.O. Box 683
New York, NY 11021
or call : 1-800-555-3671

A **code number** identifies the item. You use that code on the order form.

Classified ads are short notices that are classified, or put into groups. For example, the "New Today" section groups those items that are appearing for the first time. Look at these ads.

New Today

Help Wanted

DOGGY DAY CARE: Wanted dog lover w/ time to care for energetic puppy 2-3 days per week. 555-1759, lv. msg.

For Sale

UNICYCLE: Brand new! We can't ride it! $80 obo. Call 555-2521.

Wanted to Buy

WANTED: Used longboard, 8 ft. or longer. Call Marc 555-8653 pgr.

People pay for classified ads by the line, so they use **abbreviations**, or shortened words, to keep the ad brief.

w/ = with
lv. msg. = leave message
obo. = or best offer
ft. = feet
pgr. = pager

Autobiography

An **autobiography** is the true story of your life, written by you.

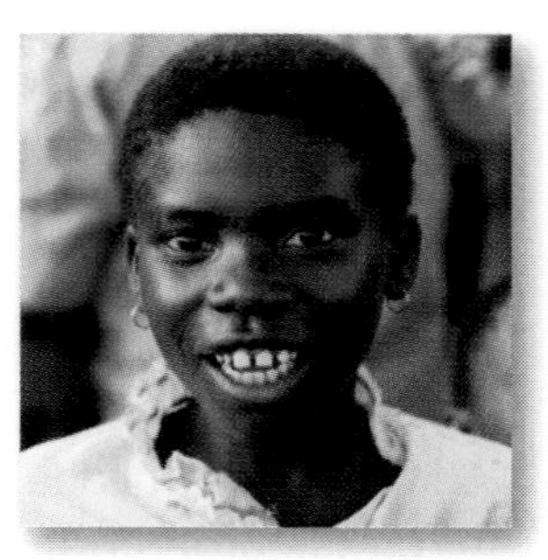

My Haiti

I am from Haiti, a country in the Caribbean Sea. I was born on a hot December day there in 1992.

Every day is warm in Haiti. In fact, until I was ten years old and moved to Boston, I had no idea what snow was like.

Biography

A **biography** is the true story of a person's life. When you write a biography, you tell about the most important events and people in another person's life.

Circus Ponies
by María Izquierdo

A biography has **facts** that tell about the person and what he or she did.

It has **dates** and **order words** that tell when things happened.

María Izquierdo

María Izquierdo was born in 1902 in San Juan de los Lagos, Mexico. Her mother and father died when she was a child, so María lived with her grandmother and aunt. When she was a teenager, she married and moved to Mexico City.

In Mexico City, María attended art classes at the Academia de San Carlos. It was there that a famous Mexican painter, Diego Rivera, saw and liked her paintings. He helped her show them for the first time.

María became very famous for her paintings of the people and landscapes of Mexico and for her pictures of the circus. In 1929, she showed her paintings in New York City. She was the first Mexican woman to have an exhibit that included only her paintings. María painted for the rest of her life until her death in 1955.

Book Review

Sometimes you read a book that you just have to talk about with someone. You can tell about it by writing a **book review**.

In the first paragraph, tell the **title** of the book and the **author**. Then tell what the book is mostly about, or its **main idea**.

Next, tell how you **feel** about the book and why.

Finally, tell the **most important idea you learned** from the book.

The Lost Lake

The Lost Lake by Allen Say is about a boy, Luke, who went to live with his father in New York for the summer. Luke was bored there because his dad was always too busy to spend time with him. One Saturday, Dad took Luke on a hiking trip to a secret "lost lake." The lake wasn't really secret, though, because lots of other people were there. So Luke and Dad looked for another lake. They hiked and talked all the next day. Then they found a place to camp and went to sleep. When they woke up, they saw a lake in front of them! No one else was around.

I like this book because it reminded me of camping trips with my family. I also like that the father and the son talked to each other more when they were out camping.

This book shows how sometimes adults can get so busy that they forget to spend time with their kids. Maybe people should think about going somewhere else to help them remember what is important.

Cartoons and Comic Strips

Cartoons and **comic strips** are drawings that show funny situations. Which of these makes you laugh the most?

"I'm calling it a surprise cake because I lost my bubble gum in the batter."

Descriptions

A **description** uses words to help you picture in your mind what someone or something is like.

Character Sketch

One kind of description is a **character sketch**. It describes a real or an imaginary person.

Name the person in the **topic sentence**.

Give **examples** of what the person does that makes him or her special.

Use **describing words** and other details that tell what the person looks like and how the person acts.

My Friend Germukh

Germukh is my best friend at school. He has dark brown hair and dark eyes. Germukh is shorter than most of the kids in our class, but that doesn't bother him.

Germukh is a great artist. He can draw creepy outer space creatures with antennae and bug eyes. Actually, his creatures are kind of cute!

When there are a lot of people around, Germukh is shy . But he talks a lot when just the two of us work together on a project. Germukh always helps me with my English. Once we had to give an oral report, and Germukh stayed inside during recess to help me practice for it.

Description of a Place

When you describe a place, use lots of details to help your readers imagine that they are there!

Name the subject in the **topic sentence**.

Write the details in **space order**. That means to tell what you see in order from left to right, near to far, or top to bottom.

A Market in Vietnam

The outdoor market in Vietnam is jammed full with food and people. Closest to the street, you'll see a row of square wicker or plastic containers filled with parsley, pineapples, apples, taro, and waterlilies as white as clouds. In the next row up are large, round bowls of fresh beans, bean sprouts, and a special kind of meat piled high like pyramids. Above the bowls, the seller lies in a hammock to free up space for more things to sell. Just above the seller, plastic bags for carrying the food hang down from the wooden beams of the stall.

Use **direction words** and phrases to tell where things are.

Use **sensory words** that tell how things look, sound, feel, smell, or taste.

Use **similes** to help the reader imagine what's being described.

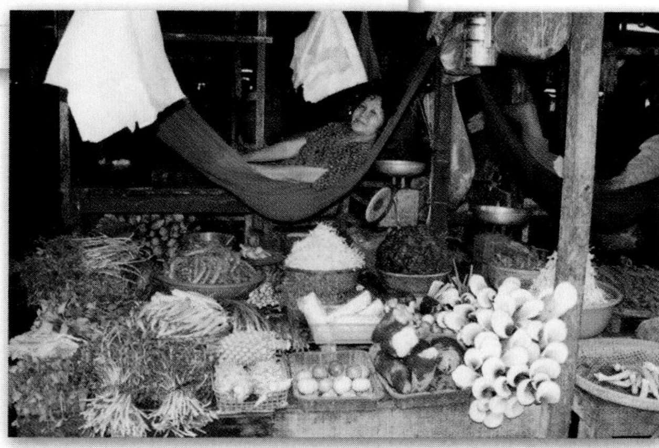

Sensory Words on pages 18 and 19 for more words you can use in a description.

Directions

Directions tell how to play a game, how to get somewhere, or how to make something. When you write directions, the most important thing to do is to put the steps in order.

Game Directions

Tell how many people can play.

Tell how to play the game.

Tell how to win the game.

Rock, Paper, Scissors

Number of Players: 2

How to Play: First make a fist with one hand. Next, shake your fist three times as you say *rock, paper, scissors*. Then do one of these:

- keep a fist for *rock*
- put two fingers out for *scissors*
- put your palm down for *paper*.

Finally, look at your hands to see who wins.

Who Wins: *Rock* beats *scissors*, *scissors* beats *paper*, and *paper* beats *rock*. Play again if both players have the same hand position.

Use **order words** to show the steps.

Directions to a Place

Use **direction words** to tell people which way to go.

To get to the theater, turn left out of the parking lot. Go four blocks, past the school, to Citrus Street. Turn right. The theater is on the left. It's a yellow building with a big, white sign.

Use **describing words** to help someone find the correct place.

Directions for Making Something

In a **recipe**, tell the name of the food.

First, list the ingredients and the amounts of each thing you need.

Write the **steps** in order. Numbers help show the order.

Begin sentences with **verbs** that tell someone exactly what to do.

What's Cooking?

Chocolate Chip Cookies

You will need:

1 cup butter	3 cups flour
1 1/2 cups sugar	1 teaspoon salt
1 tablespoon molasses	1 teaspoon baking soda
1 teaspoon vanilla	2 cups chocolate chips
2 eggs	

1. Preheat the oven to 375°.
2. Mix the butter, sugar, and molasses together in a bowl.
3. Add the vanilla and eggs. Mix well.
4. Add the flour, salt, and baking soda.
5. Fold in the chocolate chips.
6. Drop the batter—a tablespoon for each cookie—on an ungreased cookie sheet.
7. Bake in the oven for 8–10 minutes.

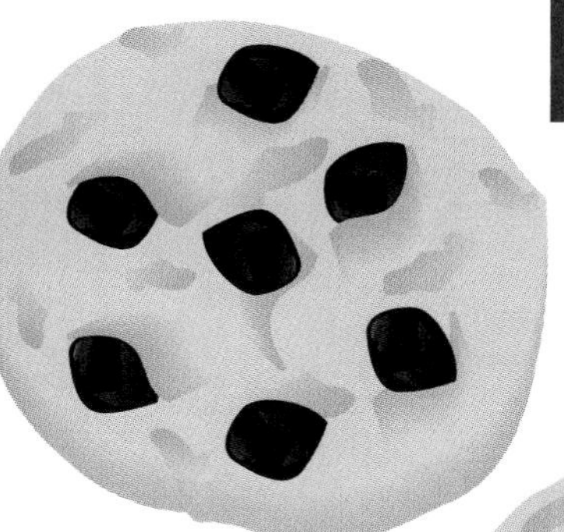
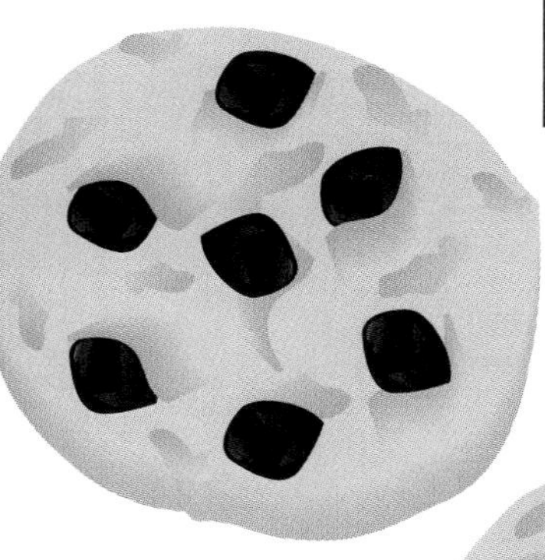

Editorial

An **editorial** is a newspaper or magazine article that is written to persuade people to believe the same way you do. When you write an editorial, tell how you feel about something. That's your **opinion**. Give **facts** to support your opinion.

February 6, 2003

Save the Gentle Manatees

Give your **opinion** about the subject in the first paragraph.

Our manatees need protection from speeding boats. If we don't keep boat speeds slow, more and more of these gentle beasts will die.

Next, give **facts** that explain why you feel the way you do.

A few members of the City Council want to pass a law that will increase boat speeds in some waterways where manatees live. When boats go too fast, the manatees can't get out of the way of the dangerous boat propellers in time.

At the end, tell what people can do to help, and state your opinion again.

We need to tell the City Council that saving the manatees is important to us. Increasing boat speeds is not. You can take action no matter where you live. Call, write, fax, or e-mail City Council members. Ask them to support protection for manatees and their home, and to *keep existing slow speed zones in our waters*! Any type of letter or call helps!

Fable

A **fable** is a story written to teach a lesson. It often ends with a moral that states the lesson.

The **beginning** tells what the story is all about.

The **middle** tells about the events and what the characters do.

The **end** tells what finally happens.

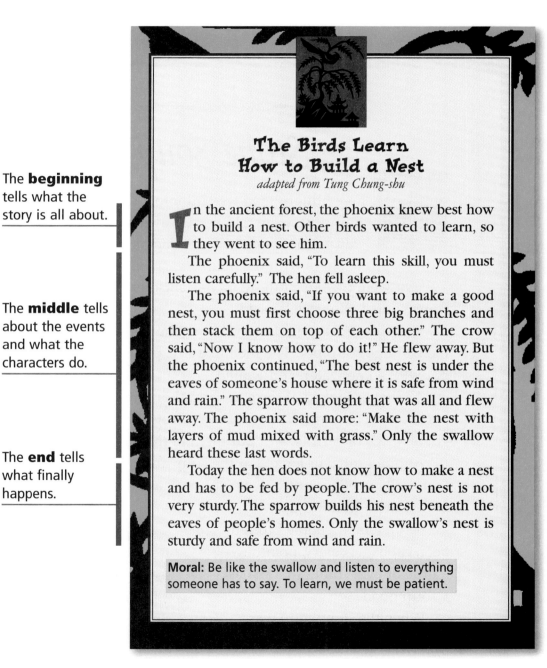

The Birds Learn How to Build a Nest

adapted from Tung Chung-shu

In the ancient forest, the phoenix knew best how to build a nest. Other birds wanted to learn, so they went to see him.

The phoenix said, "To learn this skill, you must listen carefully." The hen fell asleep.

The phoenix said, "If you want to make a good nest, you must first choose three big branches and then stack them on top of each other." The crow said, "Now I know how to do it!" He flew away. But the phoenix continued, "The best nest is under the eaves of someone's house where it is safe from wind and rain." The sparrow thought that was all and flew away. The phoenix said more: "Make the nest with layers of mud mixed with grass." Only the swallow heard these last words.

Today the hen does not know how to make a nest and has to be fed by people. The crow's nest is not very sturdy. The sparrow builds his nest beneath the eaves of people's homes. Only the swallow's nest is sturdy and safe from wind and rain.

Moral: Be like the swallow and listen to everything someone has to say. To learn, we must be patient.

A fable often has **talking animals**.

A fable has a **moral** that tells what you can learn from the story.

Folk Tales and Fairy Tales

Folk Tale

A **folk tale** is a story that people have been telling one another for many years.

The **characters** in a folk tale often have a problem to solve.

The **setting** is often a made-up place, long ago.

The **ending** is usually a happy one.

Stone Soup

Three hungry men walked into a tiny village one day. Everyone told these travelers that there was no food. Really, the villagers were greedy and didn't want to share with the men.

"Oh well, there is nothing more delicious than a bowl of stone soup," one traveler said.

The villagers thought this was odd but agreed to lend the men a huge soup pot. The men lit a fire, put three stones in the pot with some water, and waited.

A villager looked at the soup and thought, "Ridiculous! No soup is complete without some carrots." He went home, got a bunch of carrots, and put them in the pot.

Another villager looked at the soup and thought, "What that really needs is onions!" So she took a few onions and added them to the soup.

Soon, lots of people brought beef, cabbage, celery, potatoes—a little of everything that makes a soup good.

When the stone soup was done and everyone tasted it, they all agreed that they hadn't ever had anything so delicious! And imagine, a soup from stones!

Fairy Tale

A **fairy tale** is a special kind of folk tale. It often has royal characters like princes and princesses, and magical creatures like elves and fairies.

Cinderella

A fairy tale often begins with *Once upon a time*.

nce upon a time, there was a sweet, gentle girl named Cinderella, who wanted to go to the royal ball. Her mean stepmother told her to stay home and scrub the floor while she and her daughters went to the ball. Cinderella wept.

Suddenly, Cinderella's fairy godmother appeared. She waved her magic wand and turned Cinderella's ragged clothes into a sparkling gown and her shoes into glass slippers. She also turned a pumpkin into a coach and mice into horses. Now Cinderella could go to the ball! However, the fairy godmother warned Cinderella that if she wasn't home by midnight, her clothes would change into rags again.

When the prince saw Cinderella, he was overwhelmed by her beauty. All night, he refused to dance with anyone but her. At the stroke of midnight, Cinderella ran away so quickly that she lost a glass slipper, and her clothes turned back into rags. The broken-hearted prince chased her but found only the slipper.

The next day, the prince asked every woman to try on the tiny slipper. No one could squeeze into it except Cinderella. Then the prince knew that he had found the woman of his dreams. Cinderella and the prince were soon married, and they lived happily ever after.

It usually has a happy ending.

Greetings

Cards

Is your cousin having a birthday? Is your aunt in the hospital? Do you want to send Kwanzaa greetings to your friend? All of these are reasons to send a **greeting card**.

Hurry up and feel better.

HAPPY BIRTHDAY

KWANZAA IS A CELEBRATION OF ONE ANOTHER.

Jeffrey Dibrell
1836 Hamlin Road
Washington, D.C. 20017

MAY ALL THE JOY OF KWANZAA BE YOURS THROUGHOUT THE YEAR.

Happy Kwanzaa, Jeffrey!
Love, Chloe

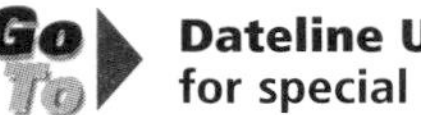

Dateline U.S.A. on pages 340–377 for special days to send greetings.

Postcards

When you go on a trip, you can send greetings to a friend. Just write a postcard!

June 10, 2003

Dear Marc,

Chicago is amazing! O'Hare airport is huge—even bigger than the one in Los Angeles. Can you believe that the Sears Tower is 110 stories tall? I walked along Lake Michigan yesterday and found out why Chicago's nickname is "The Windy City."

I'm having a great time. I can't wait to show you my pictures when I get back.

Your friend,

Felipe

Marc Rountree
347 Driscol Street
Los Angeles, CA 90064

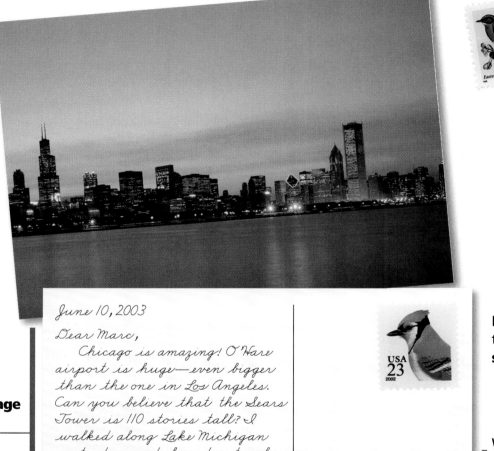

Write your **message** here.

Don't forget to add a **stamp**!

Write your friend's **name and address** here.

Interview

A good way to find out more about someone is to conduct an **interview**. An interview is a meeting where one person asks another person questions to get information.

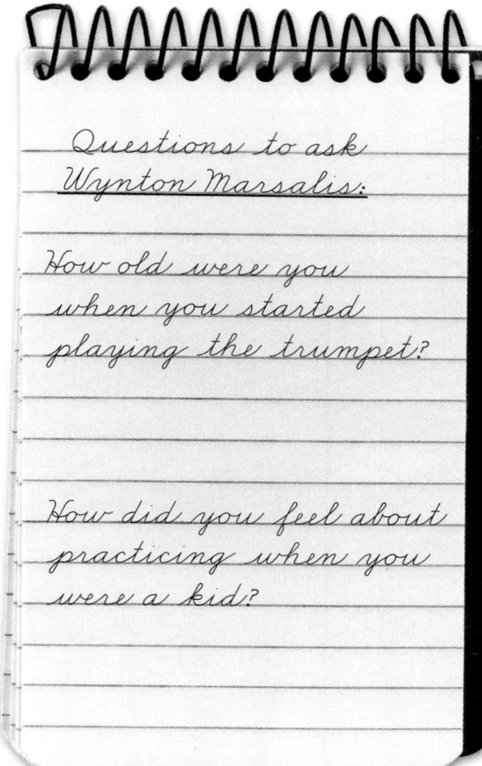
Questions to ask
Wynton Marsalis:
How old were you
when you started
playing the trumpet?
How did you feel about
practicing when you
were a kid?

❶ Prepare for the interview.

- Read any information you can find about the person you want to interview.
- Call or write the person to plan a time when the two of you can meet.
- Make a list of questions that you want to ask.

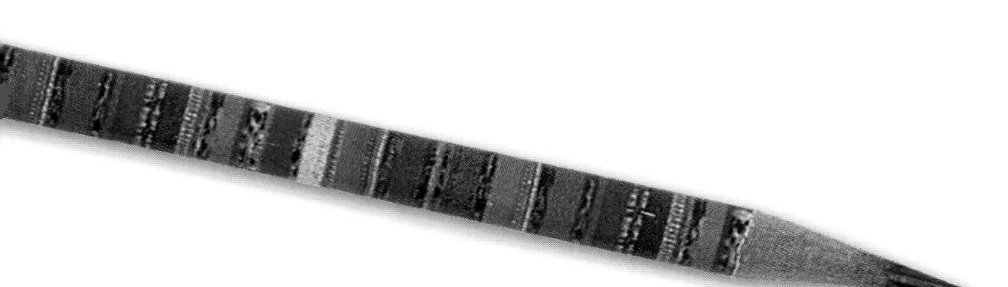

❷ Conduct the interview.

- Be sure you have your questions, a pencil, and some paper to make any notes. Try to have a tape recorder with you. You can play the tape later to help you remember what was said.
- Greet the person you are interviewing.
- Ask the questions you planned and others that come up during the interview.
- Thank the person when you are done.

❸ Share the results of the interview.

- Look over your notes and listen to the tape.
- Choose the information you want to share.
- Decide how you want to share it. You might write an editorial, a description, or an article like this one.

Name the person you interviewed in the title.

List the questions (**Q**) and the answers (**A**).

The answers are exact words spoken by the person you interviewed.

Talking Jazz with Wynton Marsalis

by Judy Burke

Q: How old were you when you started playing the trumpet?

A: I was six. Now, I don't want to give you the impression that I could play. I was just holding the horn, basically. My father was known by all the musicians, and they would say, "Let Ellis's son play."

After they heard me play, they would ask me, "Are you sure you're Ellis's son?"

Q: Did your father give you any advice?

A: He said, "The ability to play has a direct relationship to the amount of hours you practice."

Q: How did you feel about practicing when you were a kid?

A: Oh, I hated it. Just like everybody else. Nobody wants to practice.

Invitation

To invite people to come to a party or other special event, send them an **invitation**!

Tell **what** the event is all about.

Tell **when** and **where** the event will take place.

Come to a Party!
Shhhh!
It's a Surprise Birthday Party!
For: Alma
Date: Saturday, March 19
Time: 3 p.m. (Don't be late, please.)
Place: 263 Newland Street
R.S.V.P. 555-8301 (Ask for Casandra, not Alma.)

R.S.V.P. stands for *répondez, s'il vous plaît* in French. That means "Please answer." Write your telephone number if you want people to call you to let you know they are coming.

Journal Entry

A **journal** is a lot like a diary. Begin each **journal entry** with the date. Then tell about your thoughts and feelings, and describe things that happen to you.

Day Wednesday, May 7, 2003
A couple of days ago
I was thinking, I
really hope to go into
one of the Chinese classes
during my years in
college. I believe that
since that's my original
background and that's
the language of my
ancestors and also my
parents and relatives—
most of my relatives do
not speak English at
all—I think it's really
important to keep the
communication going. Also,
when we travel, I think
it would be hard to
communicate if I didn't
know any Chinese. I am
an American citizen
now, but I still have
that feeling, that
strong feeling, that
I want to know about
my background.

Letters

Friendly Letter

You can write a **friendly letter** to tell a friend what's going on in your life. A friendly letter has five parts.

Heading

29583 Wayfarer Lane
Albany, NY 12258
January 17, 2003

In the **heading**, write your address and today's date.

Greeting

Dear Anders,

Body

You'll never guess what happened today! After months of wishing, my dream finally came true. Grandpa got John and me a new dog! I've been so lonely since Shadow died last year. Anyway, we got a black Labrador and named her Midnight. She is so friendly—she just keeps wagging her tail and following us around. I can't wait for you to see her when you come in March.

How are you doing? Did you learn how to ski yet? Please write soon.

In the **body**, write your news like you're talking to your friend. Ask what your friend is doing.

Closing

Your friend,

Your Signature

Laura

Here are other **closings** you can use in a friendly letter:

Sincerely,
Love,
Yours truly,
Always,

E-Mail

You can use e-mail to send a letter to a friend. E-mail is short for **electronic mail** and is sent by a computer. You can send letters to or receive messages from anyone in the world who has an e-mail address. Here's one kind of computer "mailbox" you might use.

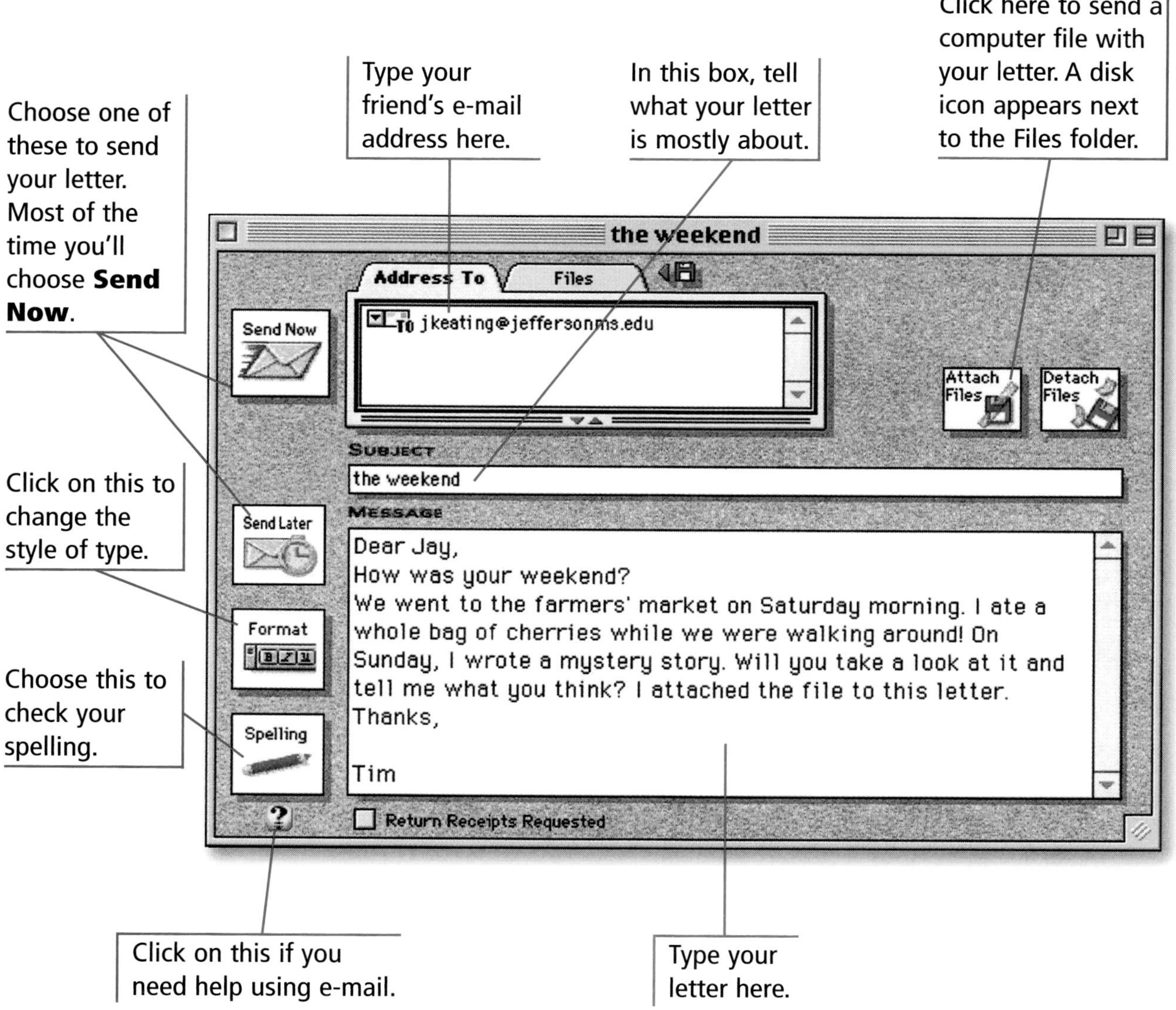

Choose one of these to send your letter. Most of the time you'll choose **Send Now**.
Type your friend's e-mail address here.
In this box, tell what your letter is mostly about.
Click here to send a computer file with your letter. A disk icon appears next to the Files folder.
the weekend
Address To
Files
Send Now
jkeating@jeffersonms.edu
Attach Files
Detach Files
Subject
the weekend
Message
Click on this to change the style of type.
Send Later
Dear Jay,
How was your weekend?
We went to the farmers' market on Saturday morning. I ate a whole bag of cherries while we were walking around! On Sunday, I wrote a mystery story. Will you take a look at it and tell me what you think? I attached the file to this letter.
Thanks,
Tim
Format
Choose this to check your spelling.
Spelling
Return Receipts Requested
Click on this if you need help using e-mail.
Type your letter here.

Business Letter

A **business letter** is written to someone you don't know in a company or an organization. A business letter is more formal than a friendly letter and its parts are a little different.

Letter of Request

Heading

2397 Casanova Street
Neptune Shores, FL 34744
February 6, 2003

Inside Address

Electronic Games, Inc.
57821 Sutter Blvd.
New York, NY 10017

Greeting

Dear Sir or Madam:

Body

Please send me your latest catalogue of electronic games. I am especially interested in your latest version of electronic hockey. Thank you for your prompt attention.

Closing

Respectfully,

Your Signature

Ann Gardner

Your Name

Ann Gardner

In the **body**, tell what you want. Thank the person for paying attention to your request.

Here are more **closings** you can use in a business letter:

Sincerely,

Respectfully yours,

Very truly yours,

With best regards,

Sometimes you'll write a business letter to complain about something.

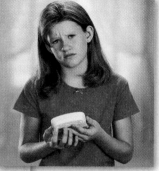

Letter of Complaint

2397 Casanova Street
Neptune Shores, FL 34744
June 30, 2003

Electronic Games, Inc.
57821 Sutter Blvd.
New York, NY 10017

Dear Sir or Madam:

I purchased your electronic game, "Invaders from the Purple Planet," on May 30, 2003, at the Fun and Games Store in Neptune Shores. After playing with it for just three weeks, the button that you press to move the spaceship stopped working. Since your product is guaranteed to work for one year, I am requesting a replacement game. Enclosed is the broken one.

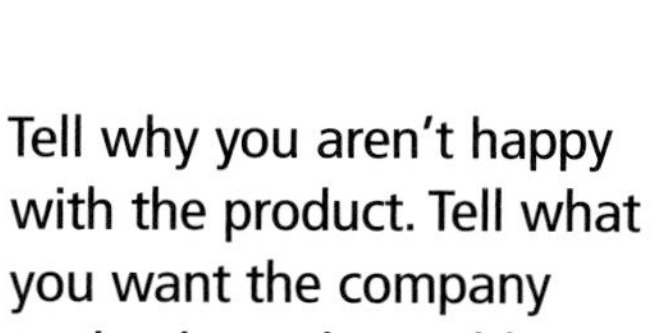

Tell why you aren't happy with the product. Tell what you want the company to do about the problem.

Respectfully,

Ann Gardner

Ann Gardner

Sometimes you'll write a business letter to persuade someone to do something.

Persuasive Letter

349 Olympic Blvd.
Los Angeles, CA 90064
May 10, 2003

Parent and Teacher Association (PTA)
Valley School
562 North Cañon Drive
Los Angeles, CA 90064

Dear PTA Members:

I think that the PTA should vote to keep a gym teacher for our school. I know that it costs more money to have a teacher who teaches only physical education, but I think it's worth it.

Most of the kids in my class love gym, and our teacher, Mrs. Richards, is really great. If Mrs. Richards doesn't teach us physical education, our homeroom teacher will have to, and he already has too much to do. Also, Mrs. Richards helps us learn how to work as a team. Isn't that an important part of our education?

We must have a gym teacher in our school. Please vote "yes" when you meet with the Valley School Board.

Sincerely,

Andy Brown

Andy Brown

Give your **opinion** in the first paragraph.

Next, give **reasons** for your opinion.

Finally, tell what action you want people to take.

Use **opinion words** to tell how you feel. Other ways to begin an opinion are:

I feel that

I believe

My opinion is

Use **persuasive words** to get people to think the way you do.

Envelope

To send a letter, put it in an **envelope**.

Use **abbreviations** for the names of states. See page 279 for a complete list.

Write the **return address** at the top. That's your address.

Write the **mailing address** in the middle. That's the address of the person you are writing to.

Ann Gardner
2397 Casanova Street
Neptune Shores, FL 34744
37 USA
Electronic Games, Inc.
57821 Sutter Blvd.
New York, NY 10017

Include the **ZIP Code**. This number helps the post office deliver your letter quickly.

List

What foods does your family need at the store? What chores do you need to do today? You can write a quick **list** to help you remember things.

eggplant
red peppers
pineapple
lime
coconut milk
curry
red chile peppers
peanuts

Menu

A **menu** lists the food that a restaurant serves and tells the prices. It usually gives a description of the meals.

MAIN DISHES

Shrimp Rice Bowl
Shrimp, red chiles, and garden-fresh vegetables, served over rice . . . **$6.50**

Risotto Italian rice dish with chicken and cheese . . . **$7.95**

Southwestern-Style Burrito
Refried beans, beef, and cheddar cheese wrapped in a flour tortilla . . . **$5.75**

Tafelspitz Beef cooked in its own broth with horseradish . . . **$7.25**

Hawaiian Pizza
Thin slices of ham, pineapple, and extra mozzarella cheese . . . **$6.75**

SALADS

Caesar Salad Romaine lettuce with homemade croutons and our own Caesar dressing . . . **$3.95**

Oriental Chicken Salad
All breast meat, spices, almonds, celery, fried wontons, lettuce, and soy sauce dressing . . . **$5.95**

Garden Salad
Lettuce, tomatoes, cucumbers, mushrooms, carrots, onions, and your choice of dressing . . . **$2.50**

DRINKS

Soft Drinks . . . **$1.50**
Iced Tea . . . **$1.00**
Coffee . . . **$1.00**

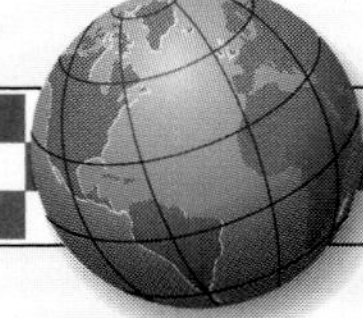

Myth

A **myth** is a very old story. It usually explains something about the world or teaches a lesson. Most myths are about gods or other super-human characters, or about people who try to act like gods.

DAEDALUS AND ICARUS

A long time ago in Greece, there lived an inventor named Daedalus. An angry king had imprisoned Daedalus and his young son, Icarus, on an island.

Daedalus planned to escape by flying away. He used melted wax and bird feathers to make bird wings. Daedalus practiced flying and then taught Icarus how to fly.

Before they took off, Daedalus warned Icarus, "No one has ever done what we are about to do. But do not feel too proud as you soar. If you fly too high, the sun will melt your wings."

Finally, father and son took off. They flew over the island. People thought they were gods. Icarus became so excited and proud that he headed up into the brilliant sun.

"No, Icarus!" his father cried. But Icarus was too far away. The feathers on his wings melted off, and he plunged into the dark ocean. Daedalus couldn't save him. Later, Daedalus buried his son and called the place Icaria in his memory.

Most cultures have myths. Many myths come from Greek culture.

This myth is about humans who give themselves god-like powers.

A myth can tell how a place got its name.

News Story

A **news story** tells about an event that really happened. It includes only **facts**. Most news stories tell about **current events**, or things that happened recently.

The **headline** gives a quick idea of what the story is about.

The **lead paragraph** gives a summary of the story. It tells *who, what, when, where, why,* and sometimes *how* something happened.

The **body** gives more facts about the event.

This tells you where the story continues.

A2

Kids Rescue Puffins–Again

BY EVELYN DAVIS
Banner News Service

VESTMANNAEYJAR, Iceland–Last night many of the children of Vestmannaeyjar were out rescuing birds. Pufflings, or young puffins, have wandered into the towns again this year. The children stayed awake to capture them and take them back to the ocean where they belong.

Pufflings were everywhere, under bushes and cars, in the streets, on the grass. The six-week-old birds aren't old enough to fly well and are a bit disoriented. The birds went looking for open water but ended up in the city, far from the ocean.

In preparation, the children gathered cardboard boxes all last week. Then, this week, they stayed up and walked around the city with their boxes and flashlights to look for stray birds. The children say that they listen for the sound of flapping wings to lead them to the little birds.

In the early hours this morning, the kids took their boxes of birds to the ocean and let the birds go.

*See **Puffins, page A7***

A7

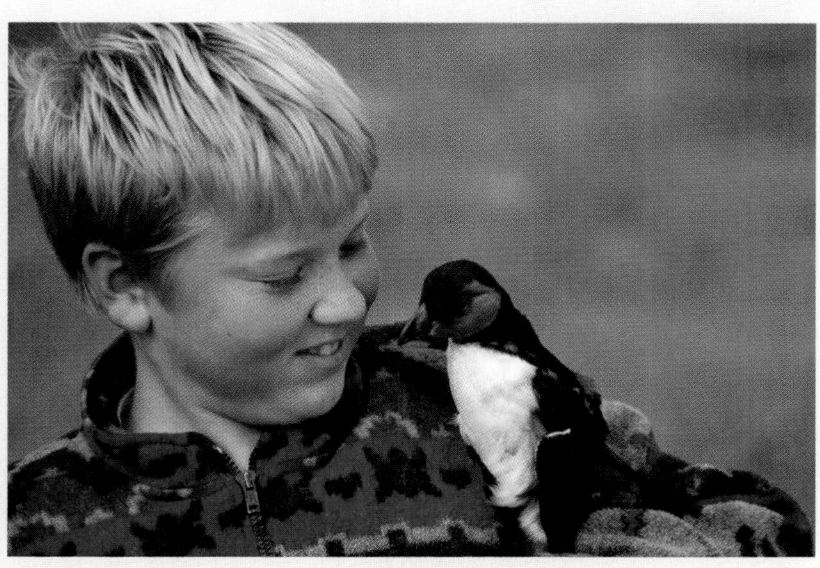

An Icelandic boy greets a puffling.

This tells you where to find the beginning of the story.

Puffins

From **page A2**

"We have to save them," said Arnar Ingi, a young Icelandic boy. "These birds won't live for long if they stay around the city."

It is a local tradition to bring the birds to the sea. The children have been saving young pufflings at the end of the summer every year.

"The kids look forward to it very much. It's quite moving to see children saving the little birds," said Ingrid Karason, a local parent.

After freeing the pufflings over the ocean water, the kids watched them fly away. "Goodbye, goodbye," the kids called out, wishing the little birds a safe journey.

News stories often include **quotations**, or the actual words a person said.

Notes

A **note** is a short written message.

Telephone Message

When someone calls your mom and she isn't home, what can you do? Write a note, of course. This kind of note is called a **telephone message**.

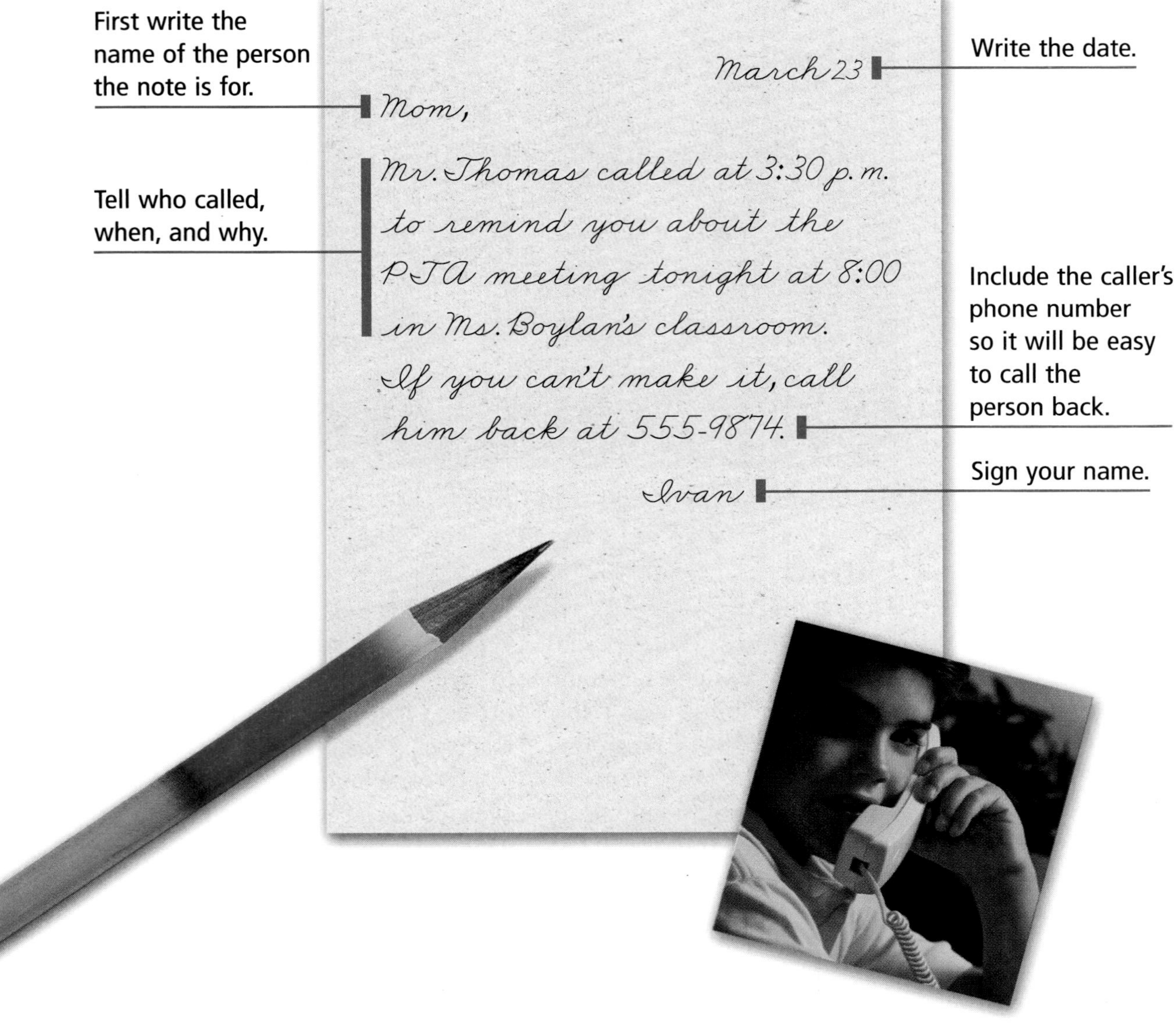

First write the name of the person the note is for.
Write the date.
March 23
Mom,
Mr. Thomas called at 3:30 p.m. to remind you about the PTA meeting tonight at 8:00 in Ms. Boylan's classroom. If you can't make it, call him back at 555-9874.
Ivan
Tell who called, when, and why.
Include the caller's phone number so it will be easy to call the person back.
Sign your name.

Thank-you Note

A **thank-you note** thanks someone for doing something or for giving you a gift. It's a lot like a friendly letter.

Write the **date**.

Write a **greeting**.

October 31, 2003

Dear Grandma and Grandpa,

Thank you so much for the game. It is so fun that my friend Sonia and I play every single afternoon after school. Sometimes I win and sometimes she wins. I am so glad that you showed me how to play when I was at your house last summer. I hope that we can play again together soon—this time I might beat Grandpa!

Love,
Liz

In the **body**, say "thank you" and name the gift. Tell why you like it or how you are using it.

Write a **closing** and sign your name.

Here are some other ways to say *thank you*:

Many thanks...
I really appreciate...
Thanks a million...
You are so thoughtful...
I'm so grateful...

Observation Log

An **observation log** is a written record of things you see, or **observe**. Date your entries to help you remember and study what you observed.

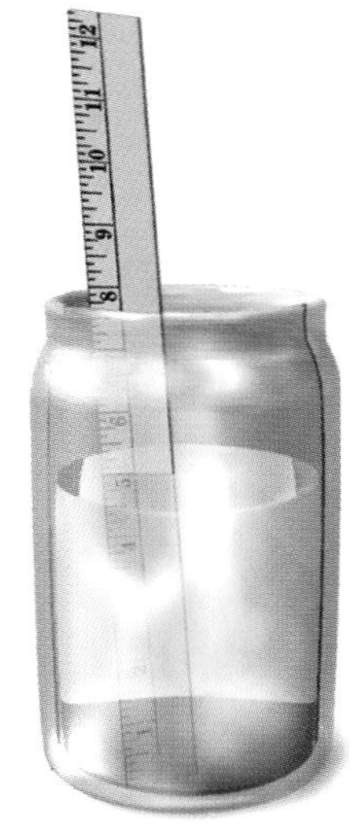

Heat and Water

Start: The water level in the jar is 6 inches.

	Temperature	Water Level at End of Day
Monday	90°	5 inches
Tuesday	78°	4 1/2 inches
Wednesday	79°	4 inches
Thursday	92°	3 inches
Friday	91°	2 inches
Saturday	78°	1 1/2 inches
Sunday	77°	1 inch

Conclusion: Water evaporates faster in hot weather.

This log records daily temperatures and the amount of water left at the end of each day.

This log records weekly observations of a plant's growth.

Observations: Growing a Plant
Week 1: Brown dirt, no plant
Week 2: See a tiny, green shoot
Week 3: Shoot is now about 1/2 inch tall
Leaf starting to grow
Week 4: Plant taller
See two leaves
Week 5: Plant bigger
More leaves

Paragraphs

A **paragraph** is a group of sentences that all tell about the same idea. One sentence gives the main idea of the paragraph. The other sentences give details that support the main idea.

Sometimes the paragraph begins with the main idea.

The **topic sentence** tells the main idea of the paragraph.

The **details** in these sentences tell more about the main idea.

There are so many treasures to see at the beach! Tiny shells, shaped like fans, are everywhere. Colorful rocks sparkle on the soft, warm sand. A little, pink crab shell sits in the middle of a log that has washed up on the sandy shore.

Indent the first sentence of a paragraph. *Indent* means to leave a space before you start to write.

Sometimes the main idea comes at the end of a paragraph.

These sentences give the **details**.

Tiny shells, shaped like fans, are everywhere. Colorful rocks sparkle on the soft, warm sand. A little, pink crab shell sits in the middle of a log that has washed up on the sandy shore. There are so many treasures to see at the beach!

The **topic sentence** that tells the main idea is last.

Main Idea Diagram on page 74. It shows how to make a picture of your main idea and details before you write a paragraph.

Paragraph with Examples

In some paragraphs, the detail sentences give **examples** that go with the main idea.

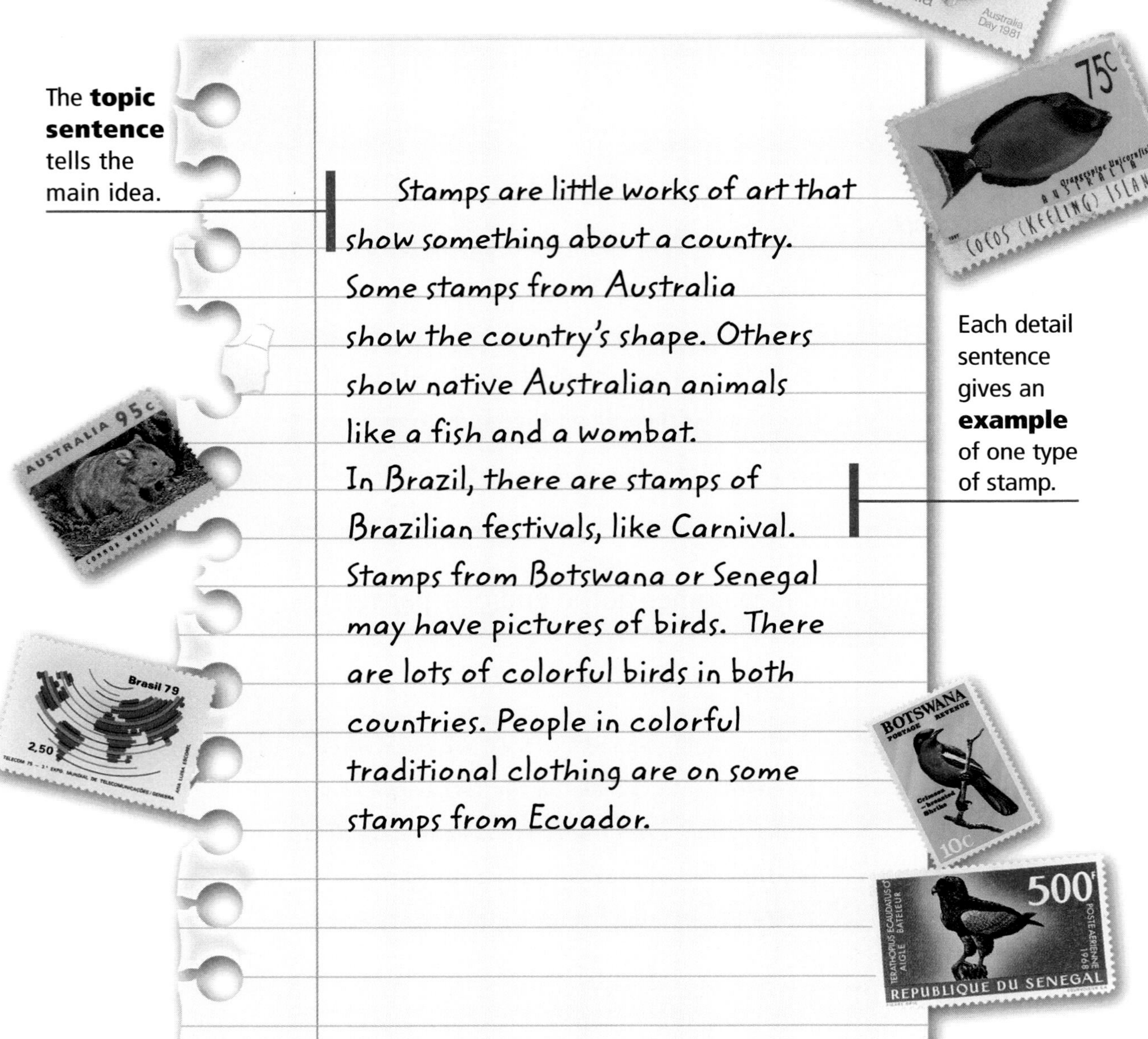

Stamps are little works of art that show something about a country. Some stamps from Australia show the country's shape. Others show native Australian animals like a fish and a wombat. In Brazil, there are stamps of Brazilian festivals, like Carnival. Stamps from Botswana or Senegal may have pictures of birds. There are lots of colorful birds in both countries. People in colorful traditional clothing are on some stamps from Ecuador.

Cause-and-Effect Paragraph

In a cause-and-effect paragraph, you tell what happens and why. An **effect** is what happens. The **cause** is why it happened.

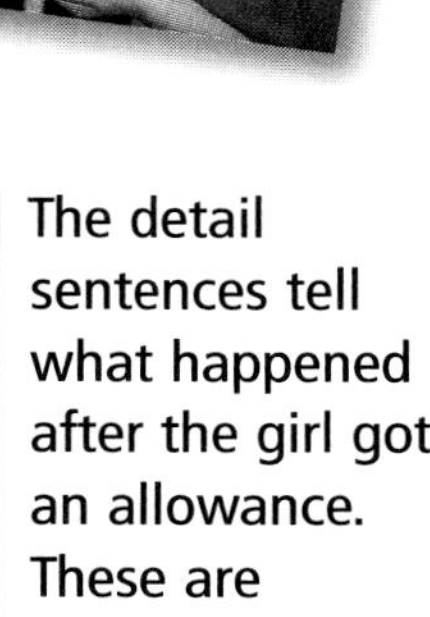

The topic sentence tells the **cause**.

Last week, my father started giving me a weekly allowance. Now, when I go to the store or the movies with my friends, I have my own money. Also, I can save some of my allowance every week to buy something nice for my sister's birthday. My allowance isn't a lot of money, but it is special to me.

The detail sentences tell what happened after the girl got an allowance. These are the **effects**.

Paragraph That Compares

Some paragraphs tell how two people, places, things, or ideas are alike. This paragraph **compares** alligators and crocodiles.

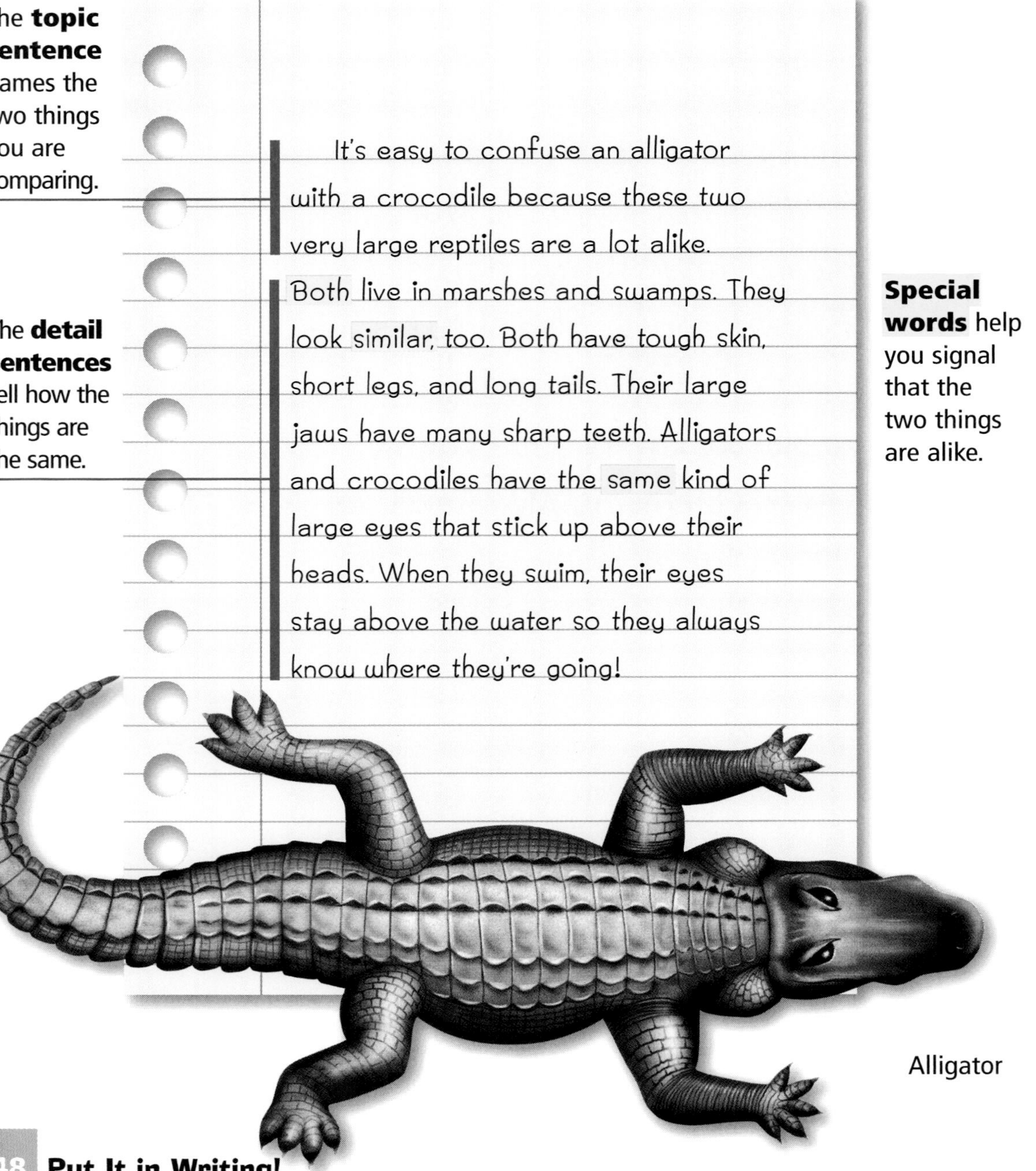

The **topic sentence** names the two things you are comparing.
It's easy to confuse an alligator with a crocodile because these two very large reptiles are a lot alike.
The **detail sentences** tell how the things are the same.
Both live in marshes and swamps. They look similar, too. Both have tough skin, short legs, and long tails. Their large jaws have many sharp teeth. Alligators and crocodiles have the same kind of large eyes that stick up above their heads. When they swim, their eyes stay above the water so they always know where they're going!
Special words help you signal that the two things are alike.

Alligator

Paragraph That Contrasts

Some paragraphs tell how two people, places, things, or ideas are different. This paragraph **contrasts** alligators and crocodiles.

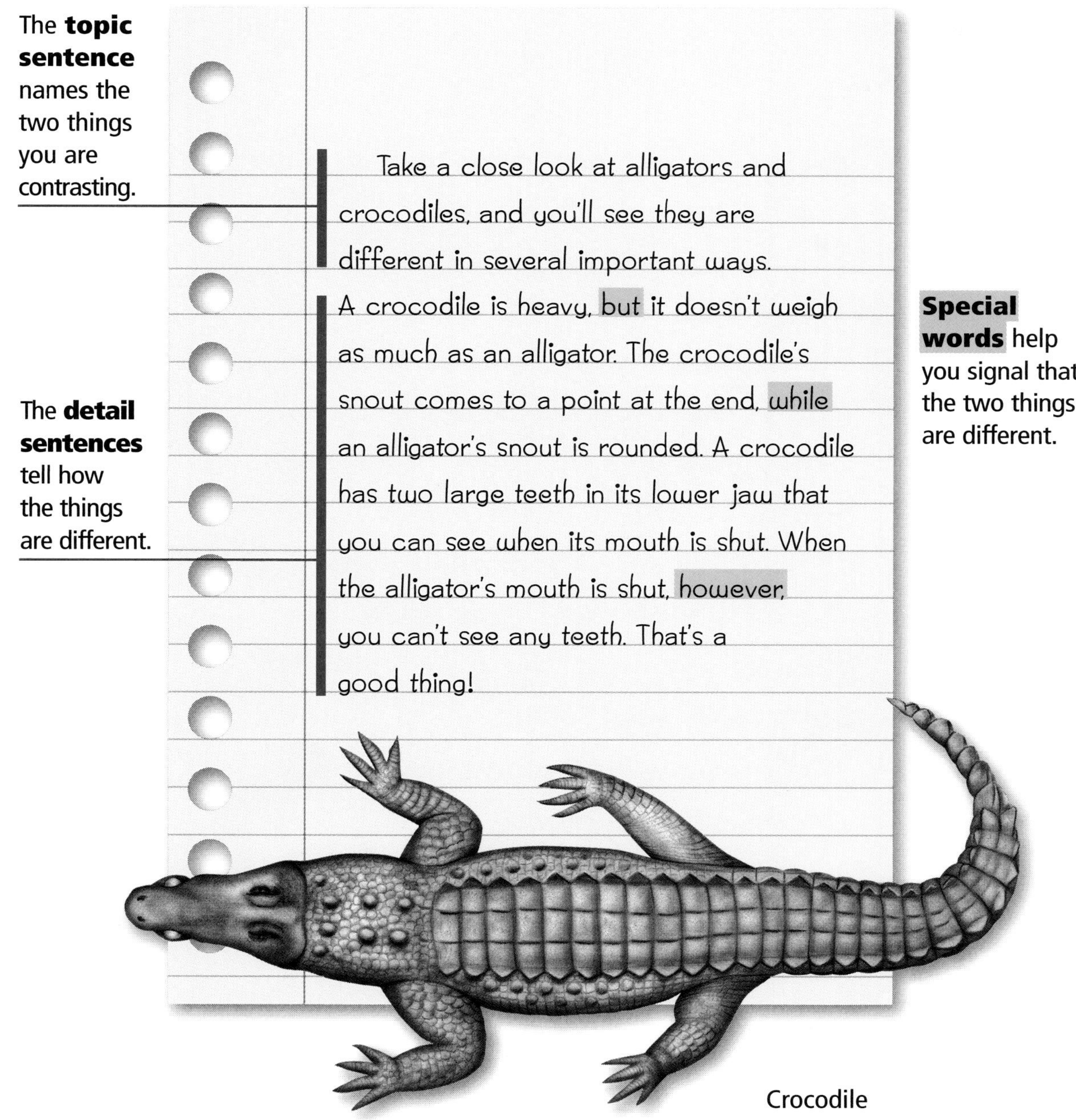

The **topic sentence** names the two things you are contrasting.
Take a close look at alligators and crocodiles, and you'll see they are different in several important ways.
The **detail sentences** tell how the things are different.
A crocodile is heavy, but it doesn't weigh as much as an alligator. The crocodile's snout comes to a point at the end, while an alligator's snout is rounded. A crocodile has two large teeth in its lower jaw that you can see when its mouth is shut. When the alligator's mouth is shut, however, you can't see any teeth. That's a good thing!
Special words help you signal that the two things are different.

Crocodile

Persuasive Paragraph

When you write a **persuasive paragraph**, you tell your opinion about something. You try to persuade your readers. That means you try to get them to agree with you.

Give your opinion in the **topic sentence**.

When you change the motor oil in your car, you should recycle the used oil. If you pour the used oil onto the ground, it harms the soil where plants are trying to grow. If you dump the used oil down a storm drain, it will end up in the ocean where it could kill a lot of fish. If you recycle used oil, however, it can be cleaned and reused. Please, you must help our planet! Just take your used oil to a gas station or other place where it can be recycled.

Give the reasons for your opinion in the **detail sentences**.

Use **facts** to support your argument.

Use **persuasive words** to get your readers to take action.

Personal Narrative

When you write a **personal narrative**, you tell a story about something that happened to you. Because the story is about you, you'll write it in the **first person**. That means you'll use the words *I*, *me*, and *my* a lot.

The **beginning** tells what the event is all about.

The **middle** tells more about the event.

The **end** tells what finally happened.

A Good Luck Valentine

I'll never forget my first Valentine's Day. When I got to school, I was surprised to find some bright red envelopes on my desk.

At first, I thought they were gifts for Chinese New Year. Each new year my family gives me money in red envelopes to wish me good luck. But when I opened the little envelopes, I only found some paper hearts.

Then my teacher explained what happens on Valentine's Day. The notes in the envelopes were valentines. Now when I look at my valentines, I feel just as wonderful as when I get gifts for the new year!

A personal narrative has **order words** that tell when something happened.

It has **describing words** that tell what things were like and how you felt.

Dateline U.S.A. on pages 340–377 for more information about Valentine's Day and other special days.

Play

A **play** is a story that is acted out on a stage. Real people, or **actors**, pretend to be characters in the story.

The actors perform the play *Annie* **on stage**.

The **audience** watches the play in a **theater**.

The author of a play is called a **playwright**. The playwright writes the script.

An actor's part in a play is called a **role**. The girl is performing the role of Annie.

This **scene**, or part of the play, takes place in the city. The **scenery** shows what this place looks like. The scenery can change between scenes.

The actors wear different **costumes** to look like their characters. **Props**, or objects on stage, help the action seem more real.

Play, continued

You can turn any story into a play. Follow these steps.

1 Start with a story. Make one up or choose one from a book.

The Legend of the Chinese Zodiac

In ancient times, the Jade Emperor wanted to name each year in the twelve-year cycle after an animal. He couldn't decide which animals to honor, however. He invited all the animals on earth to participate in a race. The first twelve to finish the race would each have a year named for them. The rat won the race; the ox was second. The tiger, rabbit, dragon, snake, horse, sheep, monkey, rooster, dog, and boar were the next ten animals to cross the finish line. The Jade Emperor named a year for the animals in the order they finished the race, starting with the rat and ending with the boar.

❷ Turn the story into a script.

The **script** names the characters and the setting. It describes what the characters say and do.

Write a **title** and **act number**. An **act** in a play is just like a chapter in a book.

List all the **characters**.

Tell about the **setting**.

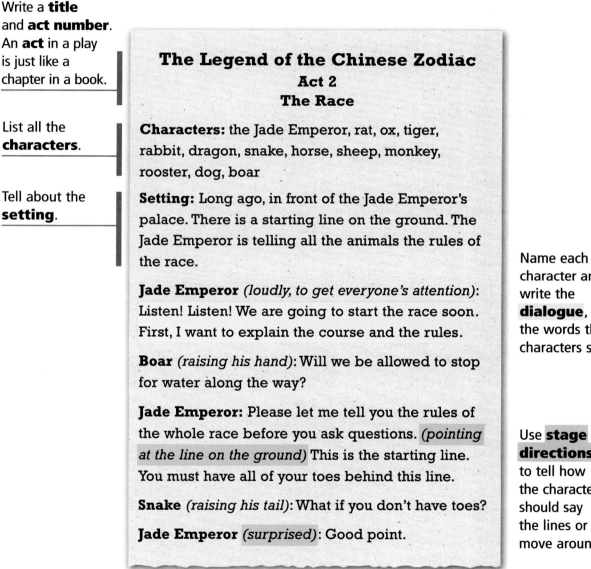

The Legend of the Chinese Zodiac
Act 2
The Race

Characters: the Jade Emperor, rat, ox, tiger, rabbit, dragon, snake, horse, sheep, monkey, rooster, dog, boar

Setting: Long ago, in front of the Jade Emperor's palace. There is a starting line on the ground. The Jade Emperor is telling all the animals the rules of the race.

Jade Emperor *(loudly, to get everyone's attention)*: Listen! Listen! We are going to start the race soon. First, I want to explain the course and the rules.

Boar *(raising his hand)*: Will we be allowed to stop for water along the way?

Jade Emperor: Please let me tell you the rules of the whole race before you ask questions. *(pointing at the line on the ground)* This is the starting line. You must have all of your toes behind this line.

Snake *(raising his tail)*: What if you don't have toes?

Jade Emperor *(surprised)*: Good point.

Name each character and write the **dialogue**, or the words the characters say.

Use **stage directions** to tell how the characters should say the lines or move around.

❸ Perform the play.

Choose people to play the characters. Have them use the script to practice. Then put on the play.

Poem

A **poem** looks and sounds different from other kinds of writing. Poems use rhyme, rhythm, and colorful language to give the reader a special feeling.

Cinquain

There are five lines in a **cinquain**. One kind of cinquain has a certain number of syllables in each line.

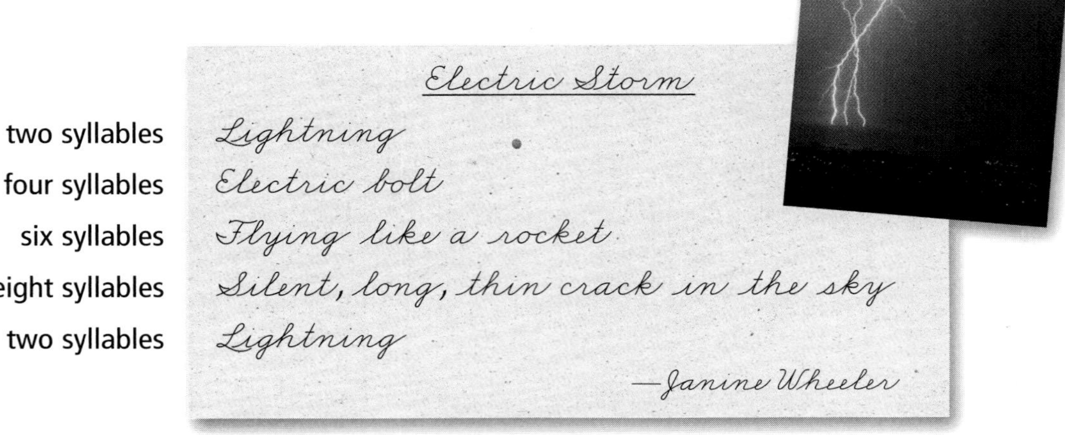

Electric Storm
two syllables
Lightning
four syllables
Electric bolt
six syllables
Flying like a rocket
eight syllables
Silent, long, thin crack in the sky
two syllables
Lightning
—Janine Wheeler

Diamante

A **diamante** is seven lines long. When you write it, it looks like a diamond.

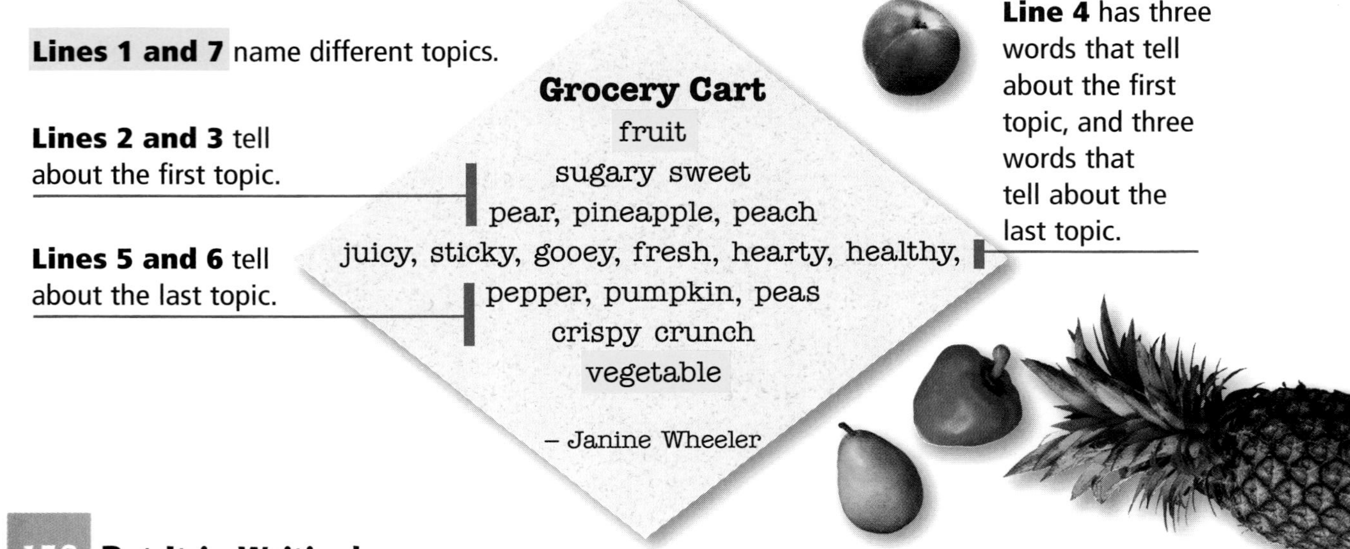

Lines 1 and 7 name different topics.
Lines 2 and 3 tell about the first topic.
Lines 5 and 6 tell about the last topic.
Line 4 has three words that tell about the first topic, and three words that tell about the last topic.
Grocery Cart
fruit
sugary sweet
pear, pineapple, peach
juicy, sticky, gooey, fresh, hearty, healthy,
pepper, pumpkin, peas
crispy crunch
vegetable
– Janine Wheeler

Concrete Poem

A **concrete poem** is written so the words make a picture of what they are describing.

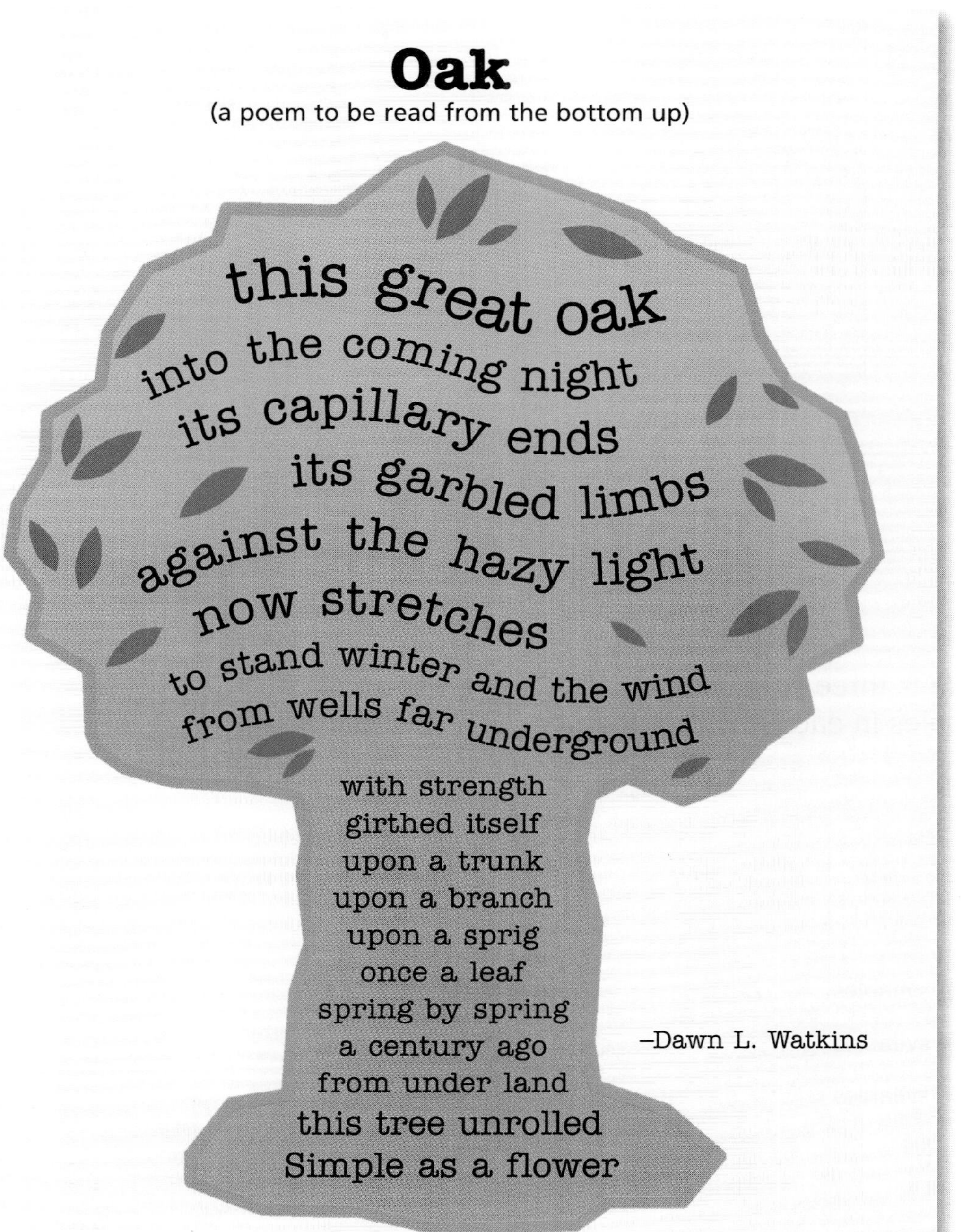
Oak
(a poem to be read from the bottom up)
this great oak
into the coming night
its capillary ends
its garbled limbs
against the hazy light
now stretches
to stand winter and the wind
from wells far underground
with strength
girthed itself
upon a trunk
upon a branch
upon a sprig
once a leaf
spring by spring
a century ago
from under land
this tree unrolled
Simple as a flower
–Dawn L. Watkins

Poem in Free Verse

Free verse is a kind of poetry that doesn't have a regular rhythm. Sometimes a poem written in free verse can have rhyming words, but it doesn't have to.

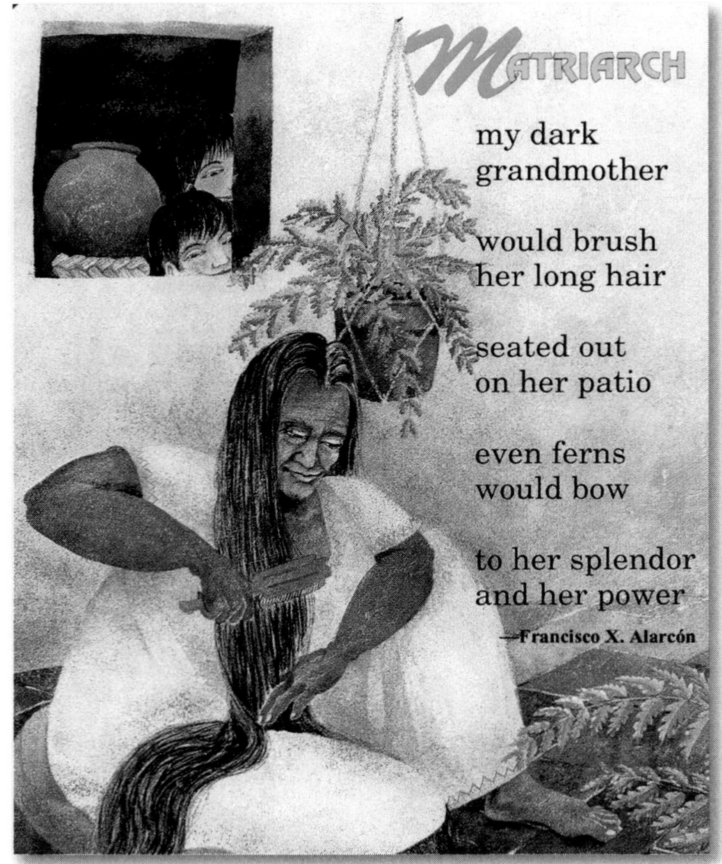

would brush
her long hair
seated out
on her patio
even ferns
would bow
to her splendor
and her power
—Francisco X. Alarcón

Haiku

A **haiku** is three lines long and has a specific number of syllables in each line. A haiku is often about nature.

five syllables
seven syllables
five syllables

Dragon Song
Upon the blue sky
the dragon kite writes a song.
Ah, my heart sings it!
— Shirleyann Costigan

Rhyming Poem

In a **rhyming poem**, some of the words at the end of the lines rhyme. That means the words have the same ending sounds. The rhyming words help give the poem a special rhythm, or beat.

Today is Very Boring

Today is very boring,
it's a very boring day,
there is nothing much to look at,
there is nothing much to say,
there's a peacock on my sneakers,
there's a penguin on my head,
there's a dormouse on my doorstep,
I am going back to bed.

Today is very boring,
it is boring through and through,
there is absolutely nothing
that I think I want to do,
I see giants riding rhinos,
and an ogre with a sword,
there's a dragon blowing smoke rings,
I am positively bored.

Today is very boring,
I can hardly help but yawn,
there's a flying saucer landing
in the middle of my lawn,
a volcano just erupted
less than half a mile away,
and I think I felt an earthquake,
it's a very boring day.

–Jack Prelutsky

Limerick

A **limerick** is a funny poem with five lines. It has a special pattern. Lines 1, 2, and 5 rhyme. Lines 3 and 4 also rhyme. Lines 1 and 5 sometimes end with the same word.

Line 1 often introduces a person or place.
Lines 3 and 4 are shorter than the others. This gives the poem its rhythm.
There was an Old Man with a beard,
Who said, "It is just as I feared!
Two Owls and a Hen,
Four Larks and a Wren,
Have all built their nests in
my beard!"
—Edward Lear

Records and Forms

Record Sheet

You can use a **record sheet** to keep track of information. Usually there are places to write your name, age, school, and other information.

Keep the record over time. This sheet is for one month.

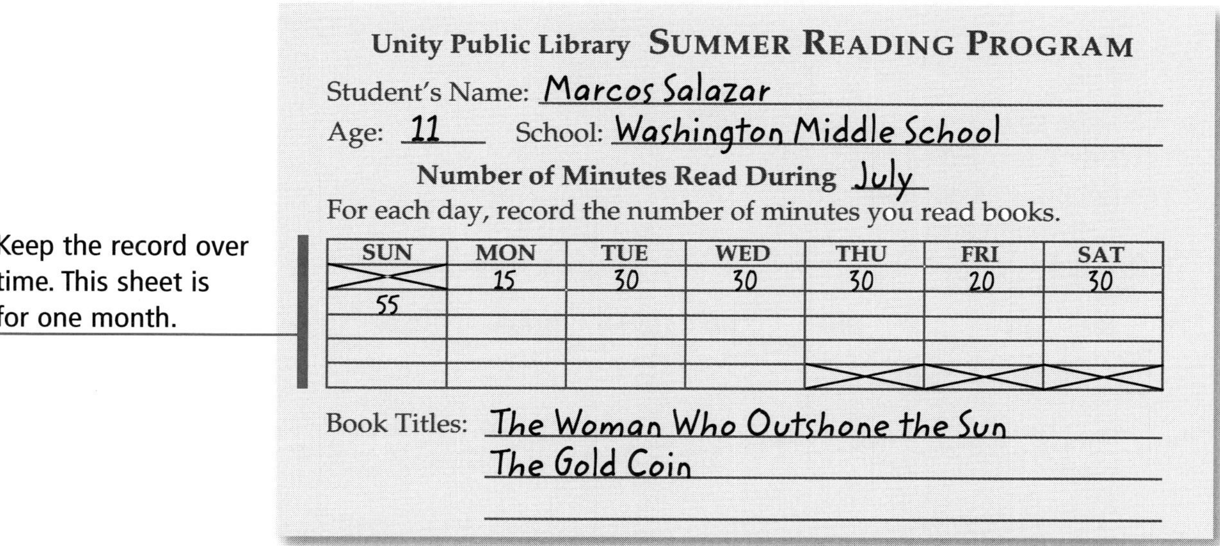

Unity Public Library SUMMER READING PROGRAM

Student's Name: Marcos Salazar

Age: 11 School: Washington Middle School

Number of Minutes Read During July

For each day, record the number of minutes you read books.

SUN	MON	TUE	WED	THU	FRI	SAT
X	15	30	30	30	20	30
55						
				X	X	X

Book Titles: The Woman Who Outshone the Sun

The Gold Coin

Order Form

Use an **order form** to buy something from a catalog or magazine. Include all the information about the item and where to send it.

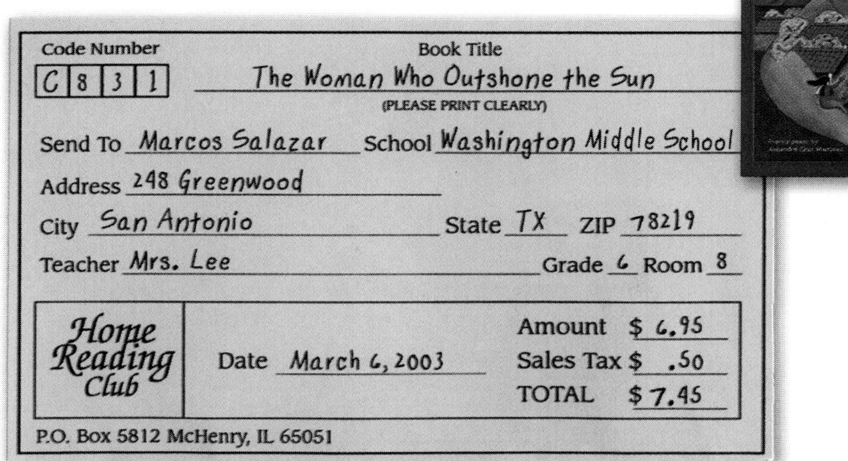

Code Number: C 8 3 1

Book Title: The Woman Who Outshone the Sun

(PLEASE PRINT CLEARLY)

Send To Marcos Salazar School Washington Middle School

Address 248 Greenwood

City San Antonio State TX ZIP 78219

Teacher Mrs. Lee Grade 6 Room 8

Home Reading Club

Date March 6, 2003

Amount $ 6.95

Sales Tax $ .50

TOTAL $ 7.45

P.O. Box 5812 McHenry, IL 65051

Report

A **report** presents facts about a topic. You can gather facts by reading books, interviewing people, searching for information on the Internet, and doing other kinds of research. Then you can organize the information you find and write the report.

The **title** and **introduction** tell what your report is all about. They get your reader interested.

Each **topic sentence** tells one main idea about your topic.

A **picture** and **caption** help the reader understand.

Types of Fossils

Have you ever wondered about the creatures that roamed the earth thousands of years ago? Take a look at fossils! They can tell us a lot about what those creatures were like.

Long ago, dead plants and animals were buried under the earth or the ocean. For many years, materials like dirt, sand, and oil covered their remains. As the materials hardened, they trapped the remains inside to make fossils. There are many kinds of fossils.

The most common fossils are mold and cast fossils. In a mold fossil, rock hardened around the remains. Parts of the plant or animal then dissolved or disappeared, leaving just an outline shape in the rock.

A fish left behind this **mold fossil**.

In a cast fossil, minerals filled up an empty space left by an animal's body. It looks like a whole animal buried in the rock.

A trace fossil is another type of fossil. It shows the activities of an animal. An example is a dinosaur footprint in mud that later hardened into rock. Other trace fossils show animal trails or burrows.

True form fossils are the actual animals or parts of animals, such as teeth, bones, and shells. An ant caught in tree sap which hardened into amber is a true form fossil. A woolly mammoth frozen in a block of ice and a saber-toothed tiger stuck in a sticky tar pit are also true form fossils.

Fossils come in many forms. They may be in rock, tar, ice, or amber. They are all evidence of animals from long ago.

The **body** of the report has all the facts you found.

The last paragraph is the **conclusion**. It sums up your report.

Go To **The Research Process** on pages 290–305 to find out how to do research.

Story

Writers use their imaginations and make up different kinds of **stories** to entertain their readers. They decide where a story will happen, who will be in it, and what will happen.

Parts of a Story

Every story happens in a place at some time. That place and time are called the **setting**.

Saturday morning in our apartment

The people or animals in a story are called the **characters**. In most stories, the characters speak. Their words are called the **dialogue**.

Come by this afternoon to see if you have won.

woman from the bike store

Anything is possible, but don't count on winning the bike, Alex.

Alex and his mom

The things that happen in a story are the events. The order, or **sequence of events**, is called the **plot**.

1. Mom filled out a form for the bike drawing.

2. We went to the bike store.

MOUNTAIN
BIKE
WINNER:
Alex Sanchez

3. I saw a huge sign that said that I won!

Realistic Fiction

Some stories have characters that seem like people you know. They happen in a place that seems real. These stories are called **realistic fiction** because they tell about something that could happen in real life.

The **characters** are like people you know.

The events in the **plot** could really happen.

Another Saturday Morning

Mom and I were eating breakfast Saturday morning when a woman knocked on the door to our apartment.

"Hello," she said. "I'm from Bikes and Stuff. We're having a drawing for a mountain bike. Would you be interested in signing up?" Mom agreed and filled out a form for me.

"Come by this afternoon to see if you have won," the woman said.

"Anything is possible, but don't count on winning the bike, Alex," Mom said when the woman left.

So I forgot all about the bike and started reading my new book. Before I knew it, Mom came in the room and said it was time to go to the bike store.

When I walked in, the first thing I saw was a huge sign that said: *Mountain bike winner: Alex Sanchez!* I couldn't believe it!

They put my name and photograph in the newspaper in an ad for Bikes and Stuff. That was the day I learned anything is possible on a Saturday morning.

The **setting** is in a time and a place you know.

The **dialogue** sounds real.

Historical Fiction

Historical fiction is a story that takes place in the past during a certain time in history. Some of the characters may be real people, and some of the events really happened. Even so, the story is fiction because the writer made it up.

January 13, 1778

Today when we returned the laundry to the army headquarters, I was astounded to see only General Washington in the parlour, no other officers. I know not where Billy Lee was. The General was sharpening his quill with his penknife. He looked up at us and smiled.

"Thank you, Abigail. Thank you, Elisabeth," he said.

I curtsied, unable to speak. How did he know our names?

He looked at us with kind eyes—they're gray-blue—then he returned to his pen and paper. Mrs. Hewes says Mr. Washington writes at least fifteen letters a day, mostly to Congress. He is pleading for food, clothing, and other supplies for the soldiers, she told us.

The characters act and talk like the people in that time did.

It can have **real people** and **made-up characters** who lived during that time.

Fantasy

A **fantasy** is a story that tells about events that couldn't possibly happen in real life. Here is part of a fantasy about some children playing a very unusual board game.

from *Jumanji* by Chris Van Allsburg

The **characters** can be like real people.

Some of the **events** could never happen in real life.

At home, the children spread the game out on a card table. It looked very much like the games they already had.

"Here," said Judy, handing her brother the dice, "you go first."

Peter casually dropped the dice from his hand.

"Seven," said Judy.

Peter moved his piece to the seventh square.

"'Lion attacks, move back two spaces,'" read Judy.

"Gosh, how exciting," said Peter, in a very unexcited voice. As he reached for his piece he looked up at his sister. She had a look of absolute horror on her face.

"Peter," she whispered, "turn around very, very slowly."

The boy turned in his chair. He couldn't believe his eyes. Lying on the piano was a lion, staring at Peter and licking his lips. The lion roared so loud it knocked Peter right off his chair. The big cat jumped to the floor. Peter was up on his feet, running through the house with the lion a whisker's length behind. He ran upstairs and dove under a bed. The lion tried to squeeze under, but got his head stuck. Peter scrambled out, ran from the bedroom, and slammed the door behind him. He stood in the hall with Judy, gasping for breath.

"I don't think," said Peter in between gasps of air, "that I want... to play... this game... anymore."

"But we have to," said Judy as she helped Peter back downstairs. "I'm sure that's what the instructions mean. That lion won't go away until one of us wins the game."

Summary

In a **summary**, you write the most important ideas in something you have read or seen. Read this magazine article. Then follow the steps to see how to write a summary of it.

The first supersonic car, Thrust SSC, set a record at 763 miles per hour in Nevada's Black Rock Desert last week.

The World's Fastest Car

Thrust SSC zips through the sound barrier

WHOOSH! KABOOM! For Andy Green, a Royal Air Force pilot, that was the sound of success. Last Wednesday, Green rocketed into the history books by becoming the first person to drive a car faster than the speed of sound. His average speed: **763 miles per hour**!

Green was not driving an ordinary car. He was driving the Thrust SSC (for **S**uper **S**onic **C**ar), which has twin jet engines like those used on Phantom fighter planes. The car packs as much power as 1,000 Ford Escorts. It needs parachutes to help it stop.

Green had been building up speed for more than a month out in Nevada's Black Rock Desert. He had competition from American driver Craig Breedlove. But Breedlove's car couldn't keep up. On September 25, Green blasted away the old land-speed record of 633 miles per hour. His new record: 714 miles per hour.

Richard Noble, Green's fellow Englishman who set the old record in 1983, didn't mind seeing it bite the dust. Noble owns the Thrust SSC, so he was rooting for Green.

The ultimate dream for Noble and Green was to see their car travel faster than sound. The speed of sound varies, depending on weather conditions and altitude. In the Black Rock Desert, it is around 750 m.p.h.

Noble and Green finally saw their dream come true on October 15. When a plane or car reaches the speed of sound, people for miles around hear an explosive noise called a sonic boom. Each time the car broke through the sound barrier, a sonic boom thundered across the Black Rock Desert, announcing Green's amazing feat.

"We have achieved what we set out to do," he said. "We are finished." ■

REUTERS

1 Make a list of the most important ideas in the article.

Look for the important ideas in the title or at the beginning of the paragraphs. In some articles, you can find important details in **bold** letters or *italics*.

2 Read through your list and cross out details that are not important.

A detail is important if it answers one of these questions: Who? What? When? Where? Why? How?

3 Use your own words to turn your notes into sentences.

world's fastest car
~~Whoosh! Kaboom!~~
Andy Green
first person to drive a car faster than the speed of sound
763 miles per hour
Thrust SSC (Super Sonic Car)
~~1000 Ford Escorts~~
Nevada's Black Rock Desert
October 15— had been trying for more than a month
~~speed of sound in desert: about 750 m.p.h.~~

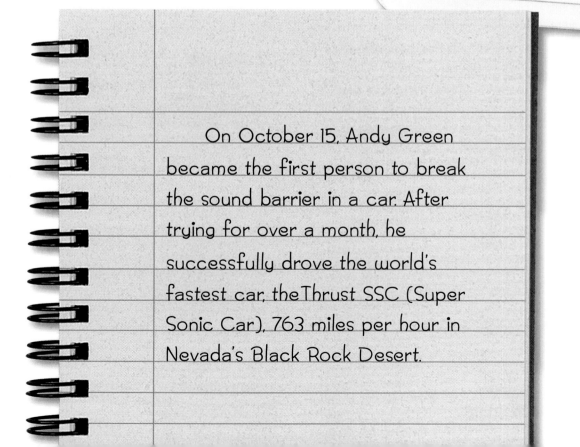

On October 15, Andy Green became the first person to break the sound barrier in a car. After trying for over a month, he successfully drove the world's fastest car, theThrust SSC (Super Sonic Car), 763 miles per hour in Nevada's Black Rock Desert.

Tall Tale

A **tall tale** is a story told just for fun. It has lots of exaggerated details. When details are exaggerated, they make the story impossible to believe.

from *Paul Bunyan* by Steven Kellogg

Paul's next job was to clear the heavily forested Midwest. He hired armies of extra woodsmen and built enormous new bunkhouses. The men sailed up to bed in balloons and parachuted down to breakfast in the morning.

Unfortunately the cooks couldn't flip flapjacks fast enough to satisfy all the newcomers.

To solve the muddle, Paul built a colossal flapjack griddle.

The surface was greased by kitchen helpers with slabs of bacon laced to their feet.

Every time the hot griddle was flooded with batter, it blasted a delicious flapjack high about the clouds. Usually the flapjacks landed neatly beside the griddle, but sometimes they were a bit off target.

Paul took a few days off to dig the St. Lawrence River and the Great Lakes so that barges of Vermont maple syrup could be brought to camp.

Fueled by the powerful mixture of flapjacks and syrup, the men leveled the Great Plains and shaved the slopes of the Rocky Mountains.

The **main character** has special powers or great strength and solves a problem in an unusual or exaggerated way.

Tongue Twister

A tongue twister is a phrase that is so difficult to say your tongue gets all twisted! Tongue twisters usually don't make much sense—they're just for fun.

Don't light a night-light on a light night like tonight.

Surely Shawn should show Sherry Shawna's shoes.

Chuck chews cherries by the cheekful.

What noise annoys an oyster most? A noisy noise annoys an oyster most.

The Good Writer Guide

A skater can't skate without skates, and a writer can't write without ideas. Just like skaters, writers get better and better with practice.

How to Collect Ideas

First, set up a file to store your ideas.

- You might want to keep a **notebook** or a **journal** close by so you can write down ideas as you think of them.
- Maybe you want to save ticket stubs, special photos, cards from your friends, or other things that remind you of people and events. You'll need a box or folder that is big enough for all these things plus your lists and notes, too.
- A great place to keep a list of ideas is in a file on the computer. Your file can get as big as your ideas!

Then gather the ideas that interest you. Here are some tips.

1 Look and listen.

Keep your eyes and ears open. You'll be surprised at how many ideas you get!

- What are your friends talking about?
- Did you see something funny or amazing on TV?
- Did you find something interesting on the Internet? Do you want to know more about the topic?
- Is the weather really hot or really cold?
- Is it quiet outside or is it noisy? What do you see? What do you hear?

2 Read a lot!

When you read something you like, take notes about:

- your favorite characters
- interesting or unusual facts
- words and phrases that sound good
- topics that interest you.

roller hockey—
"Dribble, pass, shoot, and score."

3 Make charts and lists.

List these headings in your file. Add examples to them throughout the year.

- Things I Wonder About
- What I'll Never Forget
- Things I Like to Do
- Funny Things That Have Happened to Me
- Places I'd Like to Go
- My Favorites
- When I Felt Proud
- The Most Beautiful Things I've Seen

Things I Wonder About

How our team will do in the roller hockey league

If I'll get to play goalie this year

How many teams will be in the league

4 Draw pictures.

Draw pictures to show what you are thinking, or try drawing a time line of your life. Look at it when you need a writing idea.

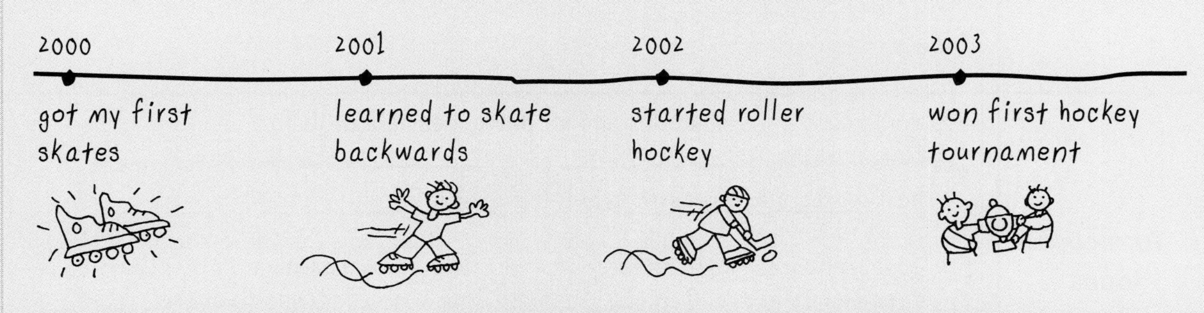

How to Write for a Specific Purpose

Why are you writing? That's your **purpose**. Good writers identify their purpose and then choose a **writing form** to fit that purpose.

Purpose	Writing Forms	
To inform or to explain	You might give directions to explain how to do something. To stop on your skates, have your brake foot in front. Then, bend your knees. Finally, put your brake down. If this doesn't work, hop onto some grass!	You could write a paragraph that gives important facts about a topic. Safety equipment protects you when you skate. A hard helmet protects the head in case of a fall. Plastic knee and elbow pads keep knees and elbows from getting scraped.
To describe	You could write a description that has lots of descriptive details to help your reader "see" what you are describing. My new in-line skates are fantastic! They are a shiny blue with bright red trim.	For a poem, use many colorful verbs to describe how something moves. Clicking and Clacking Clicking and clacking over the concrete cracks, skates swish and slip by.
To record ideas	You could copy parts of stories and jot down ideas about them. From Brothers by Vincent Ayala: "I wasn't sure I wanted to learn how to skate. Teo had taught me to swim. But that was different. Water was soft. The sidewalk was hard! . . ."	What I Think: 1. This story makes me think about the time I learned to skate. 2. I could write about skating, or maybe a story about a boy who teaches his sister to ride a bike.

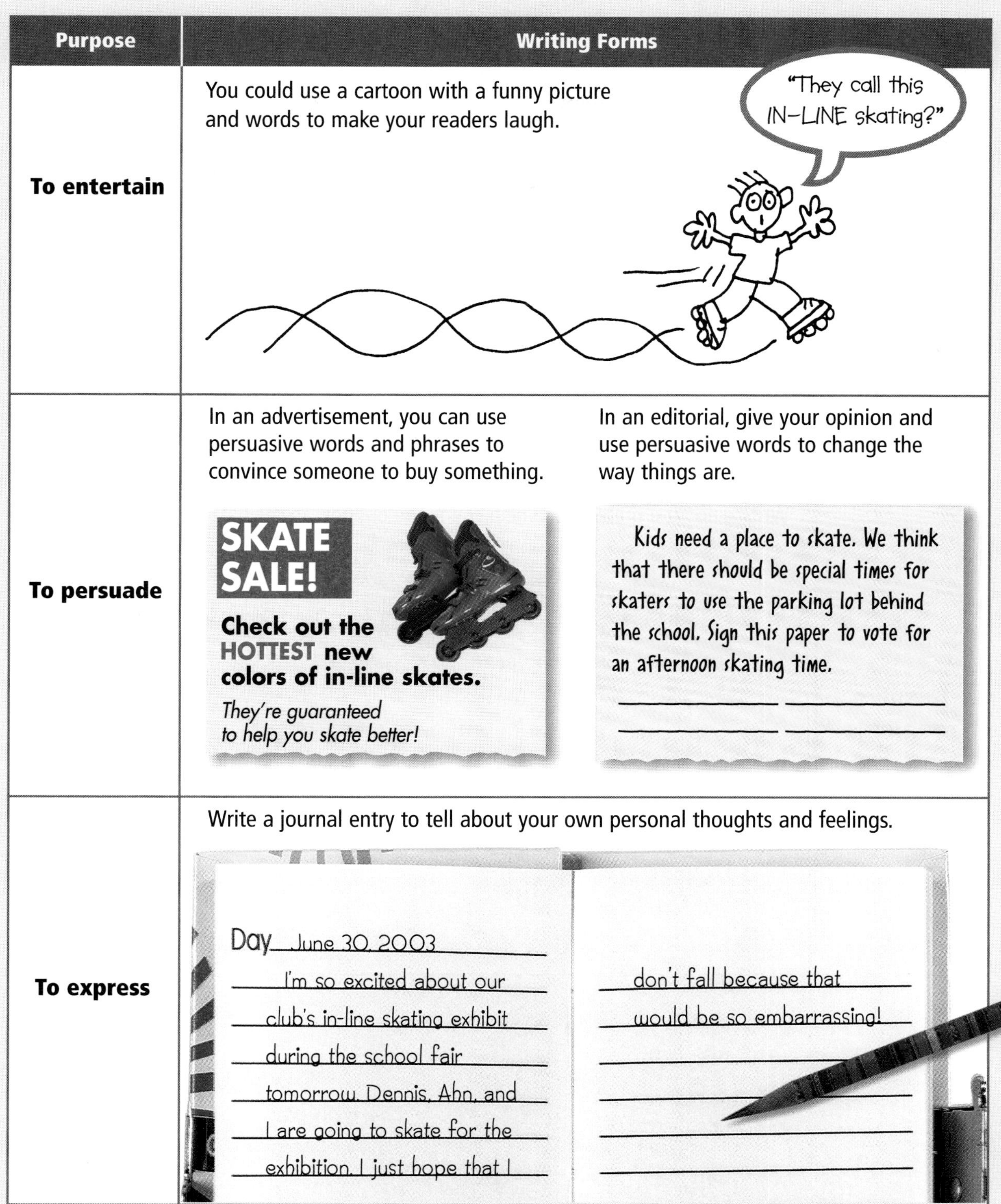

Purpose	Writing Forms
To entertain	You could use a cartoon with a funny picture and words to make your readers laugh.
To persuade	In an advertisement, you can use persuasive words and phrases to convince someone to buy something. In an editorial, give your opinion and use persuasive words to change the way things are.
To express	Write a journal entry to tell about your own personal thoughts and feelings.

<table>
<tr><th>Purpose</th><th>Writing Forms</th></tr>
<tr><td>To learn and discover</td><td>It helps to write things down when you are learning about a topic. You can see what you know—and what you don't know!

In-line skating is good exercise. Now I want to know why, and if it's good for everyone.

Sometimes when you write about a topic, you discover new ideas!

Skating is probably good exercise because you move so much of your body. It's a lot like running! I will find out if that's true.</td></tr>
<tr><td>To solve problems</td><td>Writing about a problem can help you figure out how to solve it.

Problem:
I have a guitar lesson Saturday, but everyone is going skating at the park that day.

Options:
1. try to get everyone to meet after guitar lessons
2. skip my guitar lesson
3. ask my teacher to change my guitar lesson
4. skip skating</td></tr>
</table>

How to Write for a Specific Audience

Who will read what you write? Your **audience** will. Sometimes you are not writing for anybody special. Sometimes you know exactly who will read your writing, such as your teacher, classmates, or the judges of a contest. Knowing your audience will help you decide what words to use and what details to include.

Audience	Writing Forms
Adults and people you don't know	Use formal language and details to help them understand what they might not know. My skating lesson was great. I learned how to cross my right foot over my left foot while making a turn. That's called a crossover.
Your friends	Use informal language because they'll probably understand exactly what you mean. My blading lesson was awesome! Now I can do crossovers like a pro.
Someone younger than you	Use simple language so they'll understand. My skating lesson was fun. Now I can make turns on my skates without stopping.

How to Make Your Writing Better

Good writers work on their writing until it's the best it can be. Here are eight important ways to make your writing spectacular!

1 Choose the right words.

Help your reader see what you are writing about by using just the right words.

Marcy got her things.

Use **specific nouns** to tell exactly what you mean.

Marcy got her skates and helmet.

Use **colorful verbs** to give the best picture of the action.

Marcy grabbed her skates and helmet.

Add **describing words** to tell what things are like.

Marcy grabbed her new skates and the blue helmet with the silver spots.

You can also describe something by making a **comparison**. That's when you use special words and language to tell how something is similar to or different from something else.

Use words that mean **more** or **the most** to tell exactly how much.

Use a **simile** to compare what you are describing to something the reader already knows. A simile contains the word **like** or **as**.

Use **vivid sensory words** about opposite things to help your reader see, hear, smell, taste, or feel what you describe.

Marcy was skating faster than the wind! Her purple and red skates were the brightest in the park. She slowed down smoothly, like a train entering the station. When she stopped, the soft, cool breeze she had felt on her face was replaced by the burning hot sun on her arms and back.

2 Use a thesaurus.

A **thesaurus** is a book that lists synonyms and antonyms for words.

- A **synonym** is a word with almost the same meaning as another word.

  Example: Little means the same as **tiny.**

- An **antonym** means the opposite of another word.

  Example: Little means the opposite of **big.**

You can use a thesaurus to replace words that are boring, words that you use too much, or words that don't say exactly what you mean.

For example, here's how to replace the word **bad**:

1. The words in a thesaurus are listed in alphabetical order. Use the **guide words** at the top of each page to find the page where **bad** appears. Look down the list of **entry words** until you see **bad**.
2. Read the definition and example sentence for **bad**. Then read the definition and example sentences for its synonyms.

bad *adj.* of poor quality, not good: That's a really *bad* movie.
Synonyms
terrible, awful very bad: Those stale cookies taste *awful*!
unsatisfactory not good enough: I got an *unsatisfactory* grade on my book report.
Antonyms *good, great*

3. Choose the synonym that best describes what you want to say.

We had ~~a bad~~ an awful time because of the rain.

Guide words show the first and last **entry word** on each page.

This **guide word** matches the first word on the page.

This **guide word** matches the last word on the page.

baby **beautiful**

baby *n.* a very young child or animal: The *baby* is only ten months old.
Synonyms
infant a child too young to walk or talk: You need to carry an *infant*.
newborn a baby that has just been born: The *newborn* and her mother go home from the hospital today.
Antonyms *adult, grown-up*

baby *v.* to treat like a baby, with care: My dad likes to *baby* me when I'm sick.
Synonym
coddle to treat too much like a baby: The teacher tries to help students but not *coddle* them too much.

bad *adj.* of poor quality, not good: That's a really *bad* movie.
Synonyms
terrible, awful very bad: Those stale cookies taste *awful*!
unsatisfactory not good enough: I got an *unsatisfactory* grade on my book report.
Antonyms *good, great*

beat *n.* a repeated sound, usually with a regular occurrence: Tap your foot to the *beat*.
Synonyms
pounding I could feel the *pounding* of my own heart.
rhythm The *rhythm* of the rain put me to sleep last night.

beat *v.*
1) to hit repeatedly: He *beat* the drum to begin the ceremony.
Synonyms
pound Use a hammer to *pound* the nail.
strike *Strike* the piano keys.
2) to win out over: She can *beat* me at checkers every time.
Synonym
defeat A community police station can help *defeat* crime in the neighborhood.
Antonym *lose*

beautiful adj. very pretty: There is a *beautiful* painting on the wall.
Synonyms
pretty, pleasing, lovely very nice: The band played *lovely* music.
Antonym *ugly*

21

Some words have more than one entry. They show different **parts of speech** or different meanings for the same part of speech.

3 Improve your sentences.

Use Complete Sentences

A complete sentence tells a complete thought. It has a **subject** and a **predicate**. A complete sentence starts with a capital letter and has an end mark.

Example: My friend Andrea got new skates.

Not OK	OK
Andrea's new skates.	Andrea's new skates were very shiny.
sat down to put them on	She sat down to put them on.

Combine Short Sentences

Too many short sentences in a row sound choppy. Whenever you have a lot of short sentences, try combining some of them.

Just OK	Better
Kwai loves to skate. His friends love to skate. They skate at the park.	Kwai and his friends love to skate at the park.
They skate around. They do tricks. Kwai skates backward. His friend does a spin.	They skate around and do tricks. Kwai skates backward, and his friend does a spin.
Then they rest. They are very tired!	Then they rest because they are very tired!

Vary Your Sentences

Mix short and long sentences together. This makes your writing sound more interesting.

Just OK

Rita felt ready. She took off. Right away she was skating fast! Then Rita decided to stop. She found out she couldn't. She didn't know how!

Better

Rita felt ready. She took off, and right away she was skating fast! Then Rita decided to stop. That's when she found out she couldn't, because she didn't know how!

Break Up Run-on Sentences

Sometimes a long sentence uses the word **and** too many times. Break a sentence like this into two sentences.

Not OK

Victor loves to play roller hockey, and he practices every Tuesday after school, and he has a game every Saturday.

OK

Victor loves to play roller hockey. He practices every Tuesday after school, and he has a game every Saturday.

Start Sentences in Different Ways

If all your sentences start in the same way, your readers might get bored. Try changing the way some of your sentences begin.

Just OK

Matt went skating for the first time yesterday. Matt fell forward on his knees as he was trying to stand up on his skates. Matt tried to stand up again and fell backward. Matt tried a third time. Matt finally rolled forward!

Better

Yesterday, Matt went skating for the first time. As he tried to stand on his skates, Matt fell forward on his knees. When he tried to stand up again, he fell backward. He tried a third time. Finally, Matt rolled forward!

4 Group your sentences into good paragraphs.

Your writing will be easier to read if you group your sentences into paragraphs that make sense. Each paragraph should have a main idea and sentences that give details about it.

Not OK

Sam could hardly wait for the race to start. It was his first one since he had broken his leg in the car accident. His leg was still a little weak, but he had worked hard to get back in shape. The announcer called the skaters to the starting line. Sam just wanted to prove that he could still race. There was another reason this race was special. Sam's older brother Josh was coming to watch. Sam's heart pounded as he thought about it. Would he be able to make Josh proud? Sam skated up to the line and took his place. "Good luck," shouted Josh. "Just do your best!"

Much Better

Give your **main idea** in the first paragraph. Write a **topic sentence**.

Write **detail sentences** to tell more about the topic.

Sam could hardly wait for the race to start. It was his first one since he had broken his leg in the car accident. His leg was still a little weak, but he had worked hard to get back in shape. He just wanted to prove that he could still race.

Start a new paragraph when you introduce a **new topic**.

There was another reason this race was special. Sam's older brother Josh was coming to watch. Sam's heart pounded as he thought about it. Would he be able to make Josh proud?

Start paragraphs with **transition words** to make the writing sound smooth.

Finally the announcer called the skaters to the starting line. Sam skated up to the line and took his place.

Start a new paragraph when someone speaks.

"Good luck," shouted Josh. "Just do your best!"

❺ Start and end in an interesting way.

Start Off with a Great Sentence

A good beginning sentence gets your readers' attention. They'll want to start reading right away!

Just OK

Once there was a boy named Sam who liked to skate.

Much Better

Sam could hardly wait for the race to start.

End with a Great Conclusion

A good **conclusion**, or ending, leaves your reader feeling satisfied. In a story, sum up the characters' feelings about what happened—or write a surprise ending! In reports and other nonfiction writing, summarize your writing and a give a little extra information to help your reader really get the picture.

Just OK

After the race, Sam went home. He felt happy.

Much Better

After the race, Sam went home feeling happy and tired. He didn't care that he had only come in second place. No one had expected him to finish at all!

Just OK

Ms. Rodríguez shared her in-line skating experiences for four hours. We thanked her for her time.

Much Better

For four hours, Ms. Rodríguez shared her in-line skating experiences, including that she owns fifteen pairs of skates! This is a person who really loves what she does.

6 Add details.

Details make writing interesting to read.

Just OK

This article is about Josie Rodríguez. She has been skating for a long time. She really likes it. I talked to her for a long time.

Much Better

Add **specific details** that tell who, what, how, and when.

"On your left," yelled Josie Rodríguez as she zipped by another skater on the bike path. Josie arrived in front of her apartment just in time for our interview last week.

Use **prepositional phrases** to describe things such as where the action takes place.

It was a thrill to meet Josie Rodríguez. She is a professional in-line skater who always has her skates on. ~~She has brown hair.~~

Leave out **unimportant details**. They get in the way and make your writing unclear or boring.

Include **dialogue**.

"I feel strange without them," she said. "I've been skating since I was two. I had to do something to keep up with my four older brothers."

Add **examples.**

For four hours Ms. Rodríguez shared her in-line skating experiences, including that she owns fifteen pairs of skates! This is a person who really loves what she does!

Include **your own thoughts**.

7 Show, don't tell.

Don't just *tell* about a person or an event. To give your readers the best picture, *show* exactly what you mean!

- Use actions to show how a person feels or thinks.
- Use **dialogue**, or a person's words, to show what the person is like.

This Tells

> Kristen likes in-line skating because it's great exercise. She skates for a long time after school every day.

This Shows

Kristen's **words** show that she thinks skating is good exercise.

> "If I didn't do in-line skating, I would probably be a couch potato," says Kristen, a very athletic fifth grader. As soon as Kristen gets home, she puts her books down, grabs her skates, and doesn't come back in the door until dinner.

Kristen's **actions** show how much she likes to skate.

8 Develop your voice and style.

Just like you have a certain style when you talk, you can develop your own special style, or **voice**, when you write. That's the difference between good writing and *great* writing. Here are some ways to develop your writing voice:

- Let your personality come out! Are you funny or serious? Are you quiet or bold? Choose words that make your writing sound like *you*.
- Write about things that you care about or know a lot about.
- Don't be afraid to show your personal thoughts and feelings in your writing.
- Write as if you are talking directly to your reader.

Just OK

Some people think that kids today only like to play video games and watch TV. That is not true about the sixth graders at Hope Middle School. Fifteen of them play a team sport, seven are in Outdoor Scouts, and five go in-line skating together every day.

Much Better

It makes me angry that some people think kids today don't do anything except play video games and watch TV. That sure isn't true about the awesome sixth graders at Hope Middle School. How do I know? I'm one of them! Out of the twenty-six students in my class, fifteen play a team sport, seven are in Outdoor Scouts, and five go in-line skating together every day. Now, does that sound like kids who only care about staring at a video screen?

When you say what you think and feel, you sound like you!

Use **your own words** to let your personality shine through.

Ask questions to make your readers feel like you're talking right to them.

How to Evaluate Your Writing

Save everything you write! A collection of your writing is called a **portfolio**. It can be in a notebook, big envelopes, or file folders. The writing in your portfolio will help you see how you are doing as a writer.

Organize Your Portfolio

Organize your writing so you can find what you are looking for. You might want to:

- put all the writing you've done in order by date
- make special sections for pieces you've written for the same purpose or the same audience
- organize by kinds of writing. In other words, put all stories together, all reports together, and all poems together.

Look Over Your Writing

Look at your writing every now and then to see how you are doing. Ask yourself:

- [ ] What is my favorite piece of writing?
- [ ] How is the first thing I wrote different from the last?
- [ ] What do I need to work on?
- [ ] What other kinds of writing can I try?

Set Goals for Your Writing

Make a list of ways to improve your writing. Include:

- the kind of writing you need the most practice in
- a new purpose for writing and an audience you would like to address
- two or more ways you can improve your sentences
- one new kind of writing you will try.

Chapter 4

Present It!

Kim has some interesting information to share about birds. She'll use more than just words to get her audience's attention. She'll use pictures, props, and sounds, too. In this chapter, find out how you can present information and communicate ideas. Learn how to give a talk, create visuals, and make your spelling and handwriting the best it can be. That way, people will get the message!

Give a Presentation

To share your ideas with others, you can give a **presentation**. A presentation is more than just writing down your ideas. You write to plan what you will say, but then you share it with your audience by giving a **talk**.

A presentation can include **visuals**, such as pictures, diagrams, and props.

You can also combine visuals with technology to create a **multimedia presentation**. You can show **video clips**, or short parts of TV shows or movies. You can use slides or a computer, too.

You can even give a **hands-on demonstration** to show others how to do something, such as cook a special dish or make a decoration.

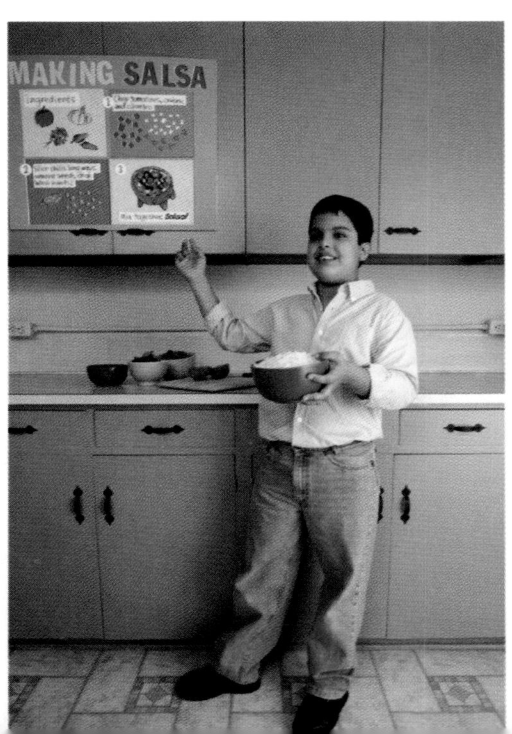

The kind of presentation you give will depend on your **topic**, **purpose**, and **audience**. Follow the steps on pages 193–206 to plan, prepare, and give a great presentation!

STEP
1 Choose Your Purpose

Your **purpose**, or reason for your presentation, depends on the topic you choose. Knowing your purpose can help you figure out how to present your topic. For example:

■ Do you want to entertain your audience?

Tell a story. Use different **voices** for different characters. Wear a **costume** that matches the setting. Play recorded **sound effects**, or use objects to make sound effects as you tell the story.

■ Do you want to share your thoughts and feelings?

Recite a poem. Use your **voice** to show how you feel as you say the lines. Create an audiotape of **sounds** to capture the setting of the poem. Use flowers, foods, perfume, or other **smells** mentioned in the poem.

Give a book review. Show the book **cover** and some of the **art** or **photos** inside it. Read an **excerpt**, or small part from the book, and explain what you think it means or how it makes you feel. Tell others why they should read it.

Do you want to persuade your audience?

Give a speech. Show **charts** or **graphs** to give facts that support your ideas. Display **pictures** that show your point.

Do you want to inform, or teach, your audience?

Present a report or **news story**. Play a **video** of an event that took place. Display **pictures** of your subject. Show **charts** and **graphs** to supply facts.

Demonstrate how to do or make something. Show a chart with a drawing of **each step**. Perform the **actions** as you talk about them. You can even have your audience do or make the same thing as you explain!

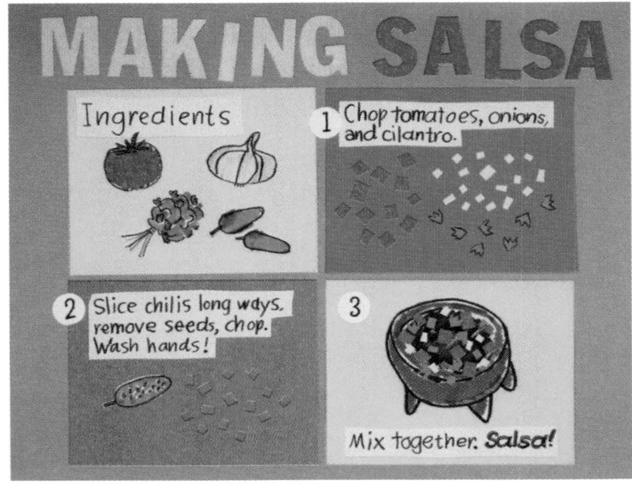

MAKING SALSA
Ingredients
1 Chop tomatoes, onions, and cilantro.
2 Slice chilis long ways, remove seeds, chop. Wash hands!
3
Mix together. Salsa!

STEP

2 Think About Your Audience

■ Think about who will listen to your talk.

Knowing who your **audience** is will help you plan the best way to present the information.

Your Audience	How to Plan
Friends or classmates	You probably know these people well, so you know what interests them and how to get their attention. Plan your presentation as if you're giving it to yourself!
Younger children	It's hard to keep young children's attention for a long time. Plan to keep your talk short and to use a lot of visuals. Use simple language and easy explanations that children can understand.
Teachers and other adults	Your presentation should be more formal. Give more detailed or complicated information about your topic.
People who share your interests • **Club members** • **Teammates** • **After-school groups**	When you speak to people who already know a lot about your topic, don't include as much background information. For example, if you are telling your scout club about a camping trip, you probably don't have to explain what you took with you. Talk about the place and what you liked about it.

■ Think about how many people there will be.

- For a **large audience**, you will need a large space. Your pictures, charts, and other props will have to be big enough for the people in the back to see.
- For a **small audience**, everyone can gather near you. Think of ways to **involve** the audience, or have them participate in your presentation.

STEP
3 Plan Your Presentation

The more you plan, the better your presentation will go.

■ **Make a chart to focus your thoughts and ideas.**

Topic:	How to make a milk-carton birdfeeder
Purposes:	1. To explain how to make a birdfeeder 2. To inform people about birds
Audience:	Members of the Backyard Explorers Club (mostly 4th and 5th graders)
Place:	Meeting room at the Afterschool Center
Amount of time:	10 minutes + 5 minutes for questions = 15 minutes

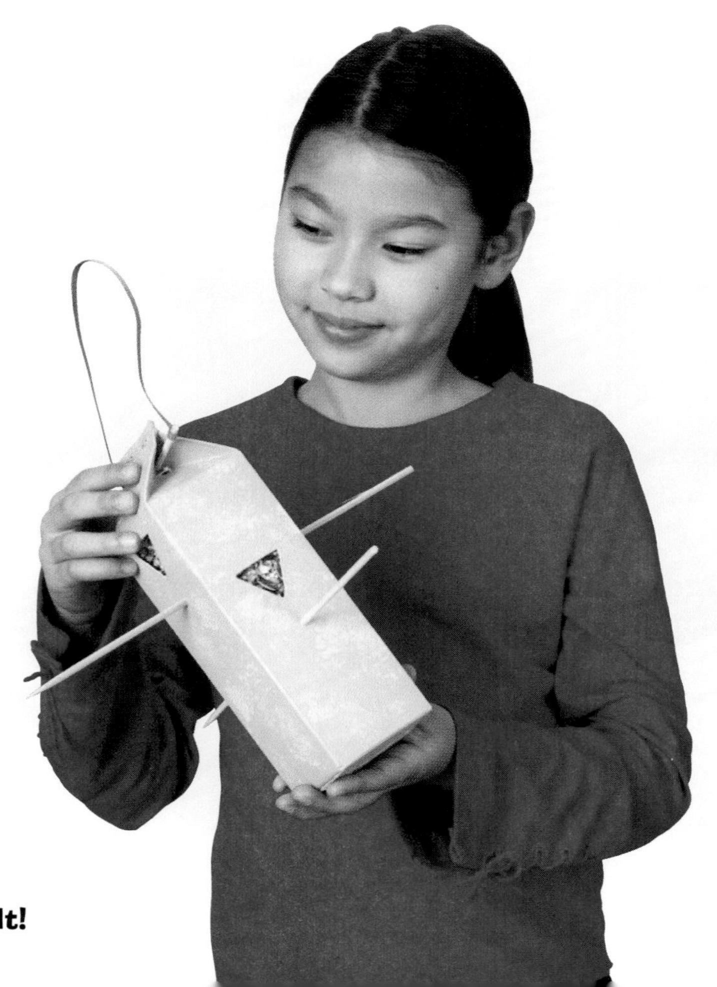

Write an outline to plan what you will say and do.

Think of a **title** that will get your audience's attention and will give an idea of what your talk will be about.

In the **introduction**, plan to introduce yourself and say what you will talk about.

Write a Roman numeral for each **main idea** of your talk. List **details** after capital letters. List **related details** after numbers.

Write notes to remind yourself about **props and other visuals** you'll need and when to show them.

In your **conclusion**, sum up what you talked about. Ask if there are any questions.

A Bird-Brain Idea!

I. Introduction
  A. My name is . . .
  B. Here to show easy way to make bird feeder (SHOW FINISHED BIRDFEEDER), get birds to come to yard.

II. How to make a bird feeder
  A. Things you'll need to make bird feeder (HOLD UP MATERIALS)
  B. Steps (POINT TO DIAGRAM FOR EACH STEP)
    1. Fill bottom of carton with gravel or sand.
    2. Poke sticks through carton to make perches.
    3. Cut windows for feeding.
    4. Fill with seeds and close.
    5. Decorate and hang.

III. Birds to look for (SHOW CHART)
  A. Year-round birds
  B. Migrating birds (SHOW MAP)

IV. Conclusion
  A. Hope you enjoyed; hope birds come to your feeder!
  B. Answer questions.

Copy your outline onto notecards.

Notecards are easier to read from than a sheet of paper. You can look quickly at them. Put one idea or detail on each card. Use only a few key words.

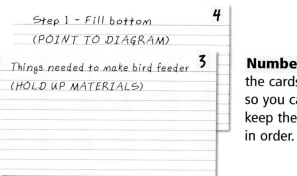

4
Step 1 - Fill bottom
(POINT TO DIAGRAM)

3
Things needed to make bird feeder
(HOLD UP MATERIALS)

Number the cards so you can keep them in order.

How to Use Visuals

A **visual** is something you show. It can be a picture or a real object. Using visuals will make your presentation more interesting and will help your audience understand the information better.

Props

Props are objects that you use to demonstrate an action or to show what something looks like.

Pictures

When you can't show the "real thing," show pictures instead. You can make your own **drawings** and **photographs**, cut them out of magazines, or print them from the Internet. You can even use **clip art** from the computer.

Charts

You can use a chart to show **data**, or information you have gathered. The chart should be easy to read from a distance.

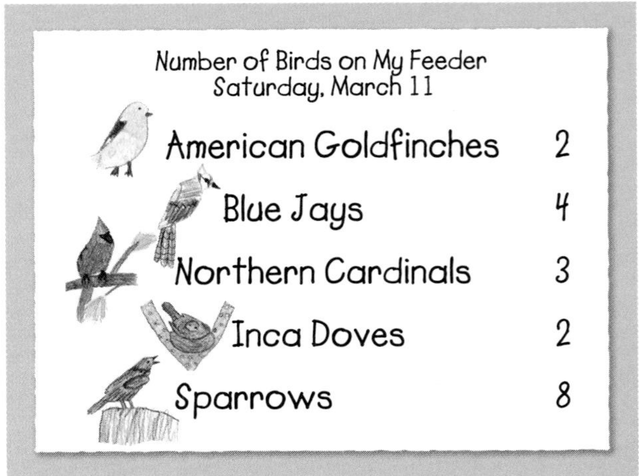

Diagrams

A **diagram** uses words and pictures to show how something works or what its parts are. Write **labels** to identify the parts or steps that the diagram shows.

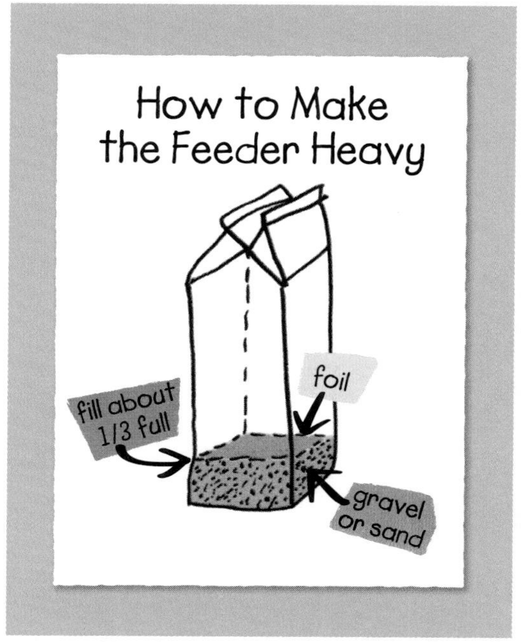

Maps

If you talk about places, use a **map** to help your audience see where the places are. You can use a published map or draw your own.

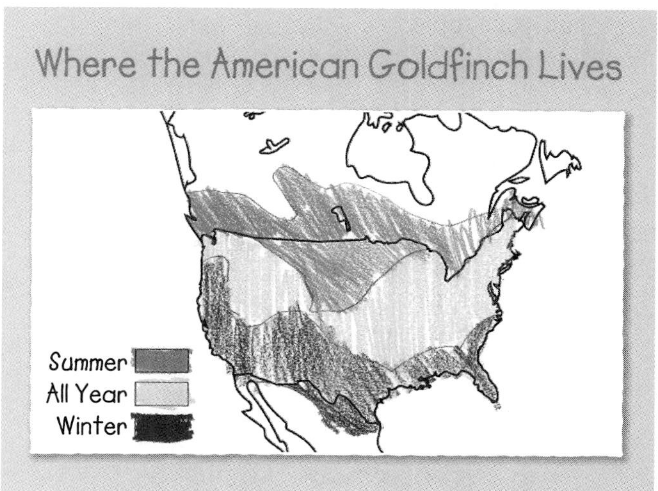

Videos

You can use a **video clip**, or short videotape, to show your audience things or people in action. Here are some ways to find or make videos for your presentation.

You can rent **videos** from a video store. Many libraries lend videos for free, too. Ask the store clerk or librarian to help you find a video on your topic.

You can use a **videocassette recorder**, or VCR, to tape-record programs from television.

You can **download** video clips from the Internet. You will need special equipment and software to play the video for your audience. Ask for help at school or the library.

If your family or your school has a video camera, you can make your own video! Practice with the camera before you shoot the final clip.

Tips for Using Videos 

- If you record something from TV or shoot your own video, use a blank tape. The picture and sound will be clearer than if you record over an old tape.
- Keep your video clip short. Two to three minutes is about the right amount of time.
- Make sure there will be a VCR and a TV monitor at your presentation to show your video. Have someone show you how to work the equipment ahead of time.
- Practice using the video equipment. Find the right volume. It should be loud enough for everyone to hear, but not too loud.
- Figure out where to stand so you don't block the video.
- Make sure your video is **cued**, or set to go before your presentation. Don't make your audience wait while you rewind!
- Practice turning off the tape at the right time. Plan to sum up what you just showed before you begin the next part of your presentation.

Multimedia Presentation

In a **multimedia presentation**, you use technology to put pictures and sounds together.

You can use slides, transparencies, or a computer to **project**, or show, images on a large screen.

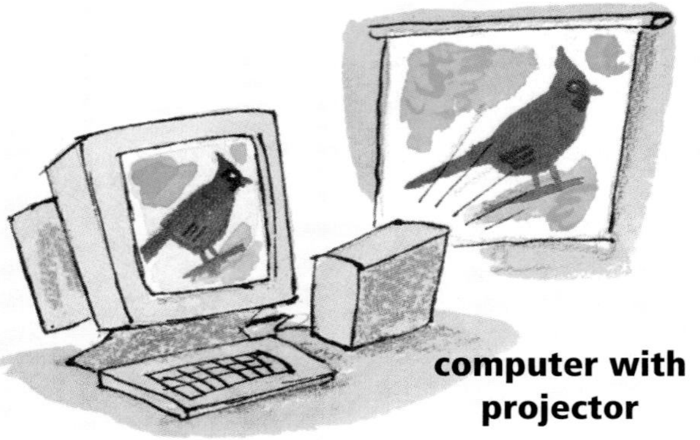

To add sound, you can:

- record **yourself** or **another person** talking
- record **sound effects**
- play **music** from a CD or cassette
- download **sound files** from the Internet.

Put It All Together

In what order will you put your pictures and sounds? What will you say in between to connect them? Make a **flow chart** like this one to plan your multimedia presentation. You can use the chart as your notes when you give your presentation, too.

Use **numbers** to show the order of the pictures or sounds.

Use different colors to help you see things at a glance.

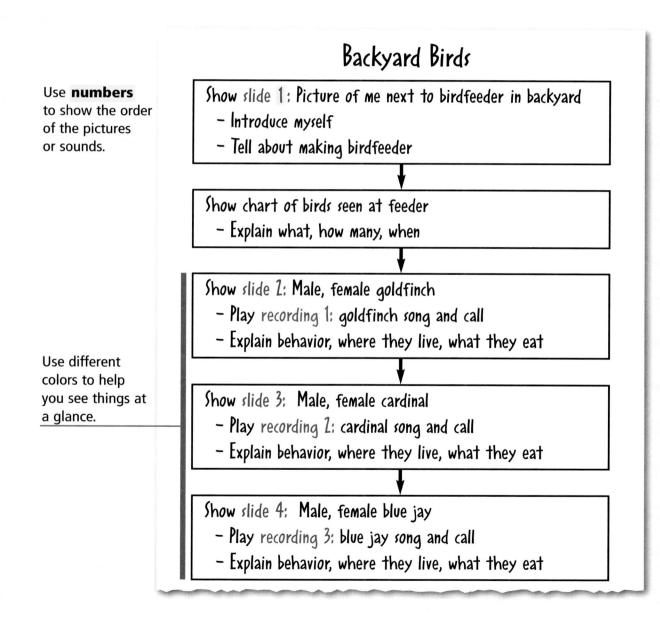

Backyard Birds

Show slide 1: Picture of me next to birdfeeder in backyard
- Introduce myself
- Tell about making birdfeeder

↓

Show chart of birds seen at feeder
- Explain what, how many, when

↓

Show slide 2: Male, female goldfinch
- Play recording 1: goldfinch song and call
- Explain behavior, where they live, what they eat

↓

Show slide 3: Male, female cardinal
- Play recording 2: cardinal song and call
- Explain behavior, where they live, what they eat

↓

Show slide 4: Male, female blue jay
- Play recording 3: blue jay song and call
- Explain behavior, where they live, what they eat

STEP

4 Practice Your Presentation

The more you practice, the more prepared you'll be. You won't feel as nervous, either.

■ Practice by yourself.

- Practice in front of a mirror so you can see how you look. Are you standing straight? Are you smiling? Do you need to look up from your notes more as you talk?
- Practice talking slowly and clearly. Use a watch to time yourself. Is your talk too short or too long?
- Practice using your props and visuals. Get comfortable with any **audio-visual (AV) equipment** such as a tape recorder or slide projector.
- Try to practice in the place where you will give your presentation. That way, you can see how loudly you will need to speak, where you will stand, and how you will display posters, props, and other visuals.

■ Practice in front of an audience.

Ask a friend, family member, or teacher to be your "audience." After you give your presentation, ask for feedback:

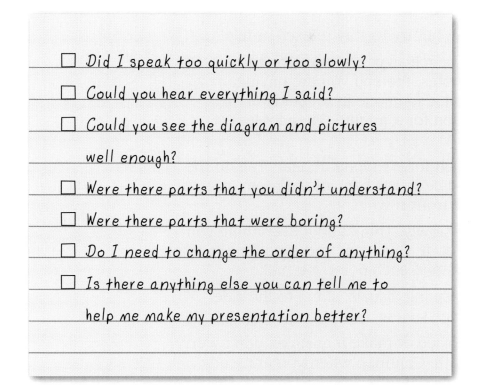

- ☐ *Did I speak too quickly or too slowly?*
- ☐ *Could you hear everything I said?*
- ☐ *Could you see the diagram and pictures well enough?*
- ☐ *Were there parts that you didn't understand?*
- ☐ *Were there parts that were boring?*
- ☐ *Do I need to change the order of anything?*
- ☐ *Is there anything else you can tell me to help me make my presentation better?*

STEP
5 Give Your Presentation

It's finally time for your talk! Set up your visuals and equipment. Check to make sure your notes are in order. Then greet your audience and begin! Remember:

- Stand up straight, but try to stay relaxed. Smile!
- Look at your audience as you speak. Don't just read from your notes. Pretend you are having a conversation with someone in the audience. Look at one person for a minute. Then look at another person.
- Talk loudly enough for everyone to hear. Talk to the people in the middle or the back of the room, not just the people in the front row.
- Don't rush! Talk slowly. Think about everything you say, before you say it. Give your audience time to think about and understand each point you make.
- When you are showing visuals, stand to the side. Don't block anyone's view.
- If you lose your place or make a mistake, don't worry. Take a deep breath. Continue when you are ready.

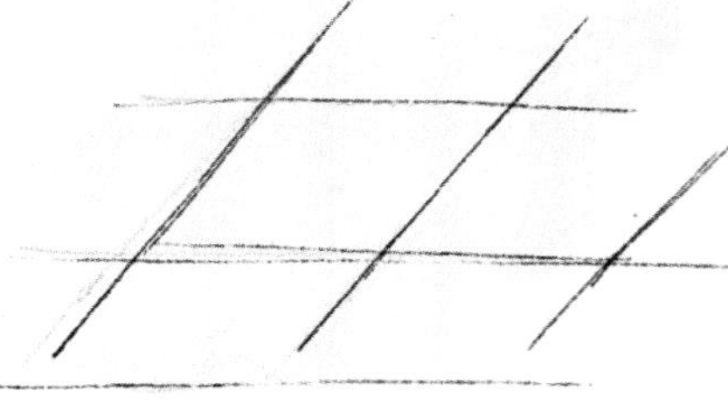

When You're in the Audience

When you are **listening** to a presentation, you have a job to do, too! Here's how to be a good audience member:

- Arrive on time. If you come in late, sit down quickly. Don't walk in front of the speaker.
- Don't move around in your chair. Sit quietly. Look at the speaker or what the speaker is showing.
- Raise your hand if you can't hear. Politely ask the speaker to talk louder.
- Listen carefully to what the speaker is saying. Decide why you're listening. Are you going to be entertained? Will you learn something? Is the speaker trying to get you to do or believe something?

Speaker's Purpose	How to Listen
To inform	Take **notes** to help you understand and remember. Write down **questions** to ask at the end of the presentation.
To entertain	Pay attention to the speaker's face and voice. How do the words, sounds, or pictures make you feel?
To persuade	Identify the speaker's **point of view**. Listen for **facts** and **opinions**. Think about whether you agree or disagree with the speaker.

STEP

6 Conclude Your Presentation

How do you **conclude**, or finish, your presentation? First, thank your audience for listening. Then ask if there are any questions. Remember:

- Ask people to raise their hands. Call on people by name if you know them.
- Listen carefully. Let the person finish the question before you start talking, even if you are sure you already know the answer.
- Ask the person to repeat the question if you didn't hear or understand it completely.
- Be polite. Don't make the person feel silly for asking. Say, "That's a good question!" or "I'm glad you asked!"
- Before you answer the question, repeat it so everyone in the audience can hear. Then answer as if you are talking to the whole audience, not just to the person who asked.
- Don't be embarrassed if you don't know the answer. Say, "I don't know, but I can find out." You can also ask if anyone in the audience knows.

When You're in the Audience

There's one important thing to do before the presentation ends—**clap**! Clapping is a great way to thank the speaker and to say, "Good job!"

Now is also the time to **ask questions** if you have them. Don't be shy! When you ask a question, you let the speaker know that you are interested in the topic and that you want to learn more.

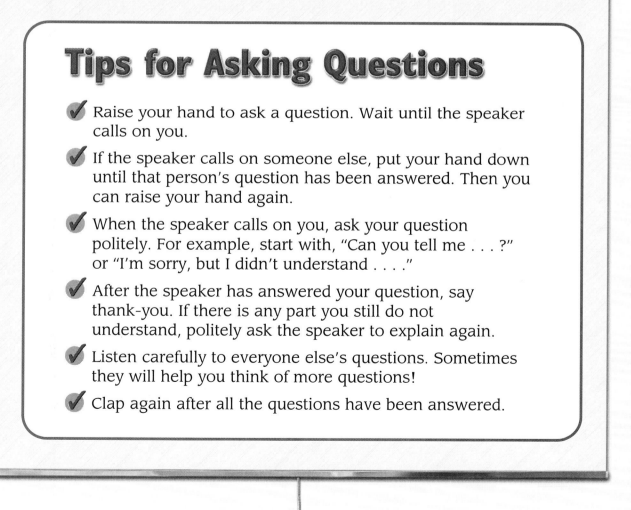

Tips for Asking Questions

- ✓ Raise your hand to ask a question. Wait until the speaker calls on you.
- ✓ If the speaker calls on someone else, put your hand down until that person's question has been answered. Then you can raise your hand again.
- ✓ When the speaker calls on you, ask your question politely. For example, start with, "Can you tell me . . . ?" or "I'm sorry, but I didn't understand . . . ."
- ✓ After the speaker has answered your question, say thank-you. If there is any part you still do not understand, politely ask the speaker to explain again.
- ✓ Listen carefully to everyone else's questions. Sometimes they will help you think of more questions!
- ✓ Clap again after all the questions have been answered.

Handwriting and Spelling Guide

It's important to use your best **penmanship**, or handwriting, and to spell words correctly. That way your audience will be able to read what you write!

Handwriting Hints

You can **print** your words or write in **cursive**. Printing is sometimes called **manuscript**.

Manuscript

Manuscript is less formal than cursive and is usually easier to read at a glance. That makes manuscript good to use for filling out forms and for writing things like posters, ads, and short notes. When you write in manuscript, hold the pencil and paper this way:

Left-handed

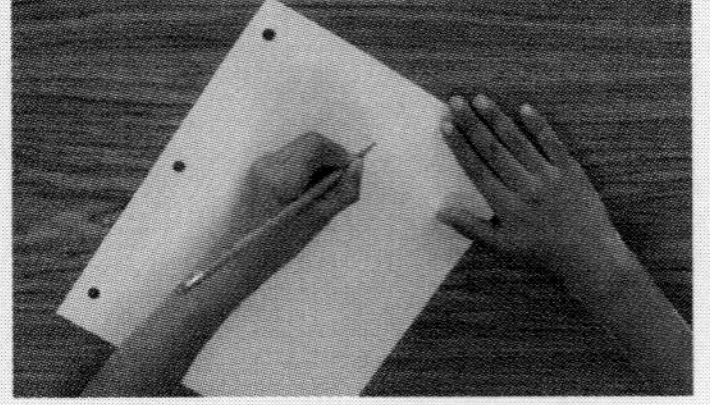

Right-handed

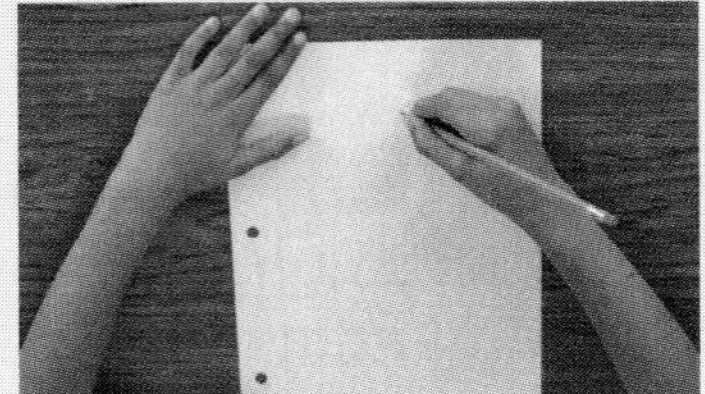

Cursive

Cursive is good to use for longer pieces, such as letters or stories, because you can write faster. You don't have to lift your pencil between letters. Also, cursive writing gives your finished pieces a polished look. When you write in cursive, hold the pencil and paper this way:

Left-handed

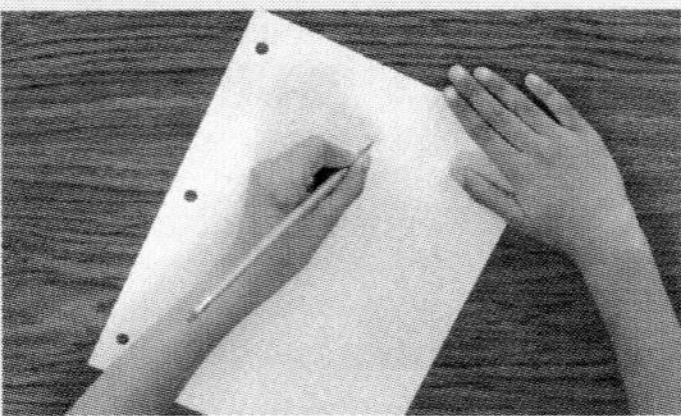

Right-handed

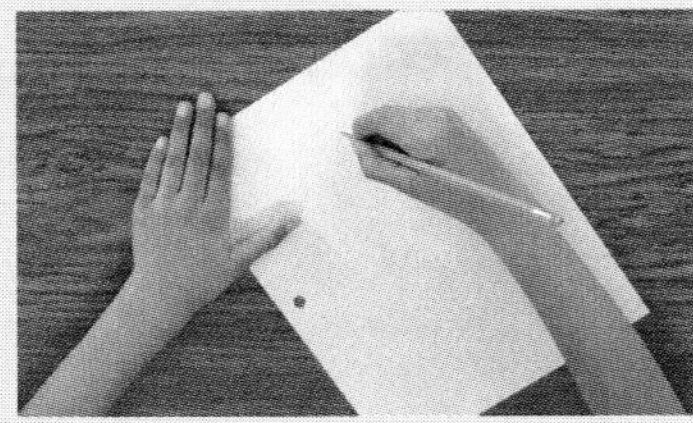

Manuscript Alphabet

Capital Letters

Lowercase Letters, Numbers, and Punctuation

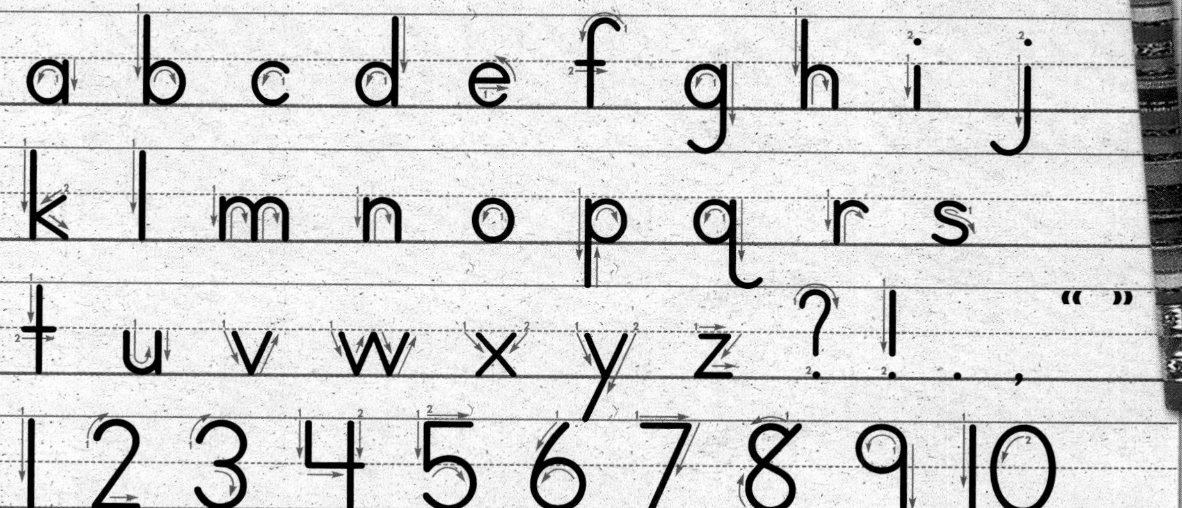

Writing Manuscript Letters

- Make letters sit on the **baseline**, or bottom line. Make letters the same size.

Not OK

a b c d e f

OK

a b c d e f

- Letters that go past the **midline**, or middle line, should all be the same height.

Not OK

walked

OK

walked

- Make your capital letters touch the **headline**, or top line. Make half-size letters touch the midline.

Not OK

United States

OK

United States

- Letters should be **vertical**, or standing up straight.

Not OK

a b c d e f

OK

a b c d e f

Writing Words and Sentences

■ **Put the same amount of space between each word.**

Not OK

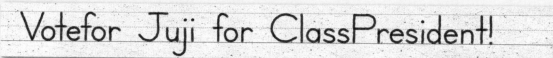

Votefor Juji for ClassPresident!

OK

Vote for Juji for Class President!

■ **Put the right amount of space between each letter.**

Not OK

She wi l l work hard for our school.

OK

She will work hard for our school.

■ **Write smoothly. Do not press too hard or too light.
Make your lines the same thickness.**

Not OK

Who will you vote for?

OK

Who will you vote for?

Writing a Paragraph in Manuscript

Indent, or leave a space at the beginning of each paragraph. Leave blank spaces, or **margins**, around the top, bottom, left, and right sides of your writing.

Indent the first sentence of a paragraph.

After the first line, continue your writing at the left **margin**.

Sally Ride is a scientist and an astronaut. She was born on May 26, 1951, and lives in California. She was the first American woman in outer space. She was a mission specialist in space. Later she wrote three books about space. Now she is a physics teacher at a university in San Diego.

Cursive Alphabet

Capital Letters

A B C D E F
G H I J K L
M N O P Q R
S T U V W X
Y Z

Lowercase Letters

a b c d e f g
h i j k l m
n o p q r s t
u v w x y z

Writing Cursive Letters

Be careful not to make these common mistakes when you write in **cursive**.

Mistake	Not OK	OK	In a Word
The **a** looks like a **u**.	a	a	again
The **d** looks like a **c** and an **l**.	d	d	dad
The **e** is too narrow.	e	e	eagle
The **h** looks like an **l** and an **i**.	h	h	high
The **i** has no dot.	i	i	inside
The **n** looks like a **w**.	n	n	none
The **o** looks like an **a**.	a	o	onion
The **r** looks like an **i** with no dot.	r	r	roar
The **t** is not crossed.	t	t	title
The **t** is crossed too high.	t	t	that

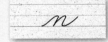

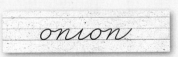

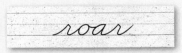

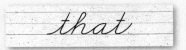

Writing Words and Sentences

■ **Slant your letters all the same way.**

Not OK

My Chinese-language class today was interesting.

OK

My Chinese-language class today was interesting.

■ **Put the right amount of space between words.**

Not OK

I learned how togreet adults.

OK

I learned how to greet adults.

■ **Write smoothly. Do not press too hard or too lightly.**

Not OK

I practiced on my teacher. He was impressed.

OK

I practiced on my teacher. He was impressed.

Writing a Paragraph in Cursive

Indent, or leave a space, at the beginning of each paragraph. Leave blank spaces, or **margins**, around the top, bottom, left, and right sides of your writing.

Indent the first sentence of each paragraph.

After the first line, continue your writing at the left margin.

Leave a margin at the bottom of the page.

Day *Wednesday, May 7, 2003*

A couple of days ago I was thinking, I really hope to go into one of the Chinese classes during my years in college. I want to learn Chinese since that's my original background and the language of my ancestors and also of my parents and relatives. (Most of my relatives do not speak English at all.) I think that it's really

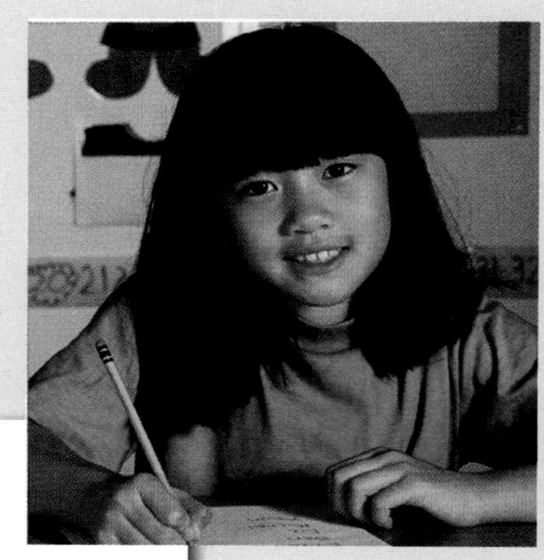

Stop before the right margin.

important that I keep the communication going.

Also, when we travel, I think it would be hard to communicate if I didn't know any Chinese.

I am an American citizen now, but I still have that feeling, that strong feeling, that I want to know about my background.

Spelling Tips

Here are some tips to help you spell words correctly.

1.

Look at the new word.

2.

Look again as you **say** the word out loud.

3.

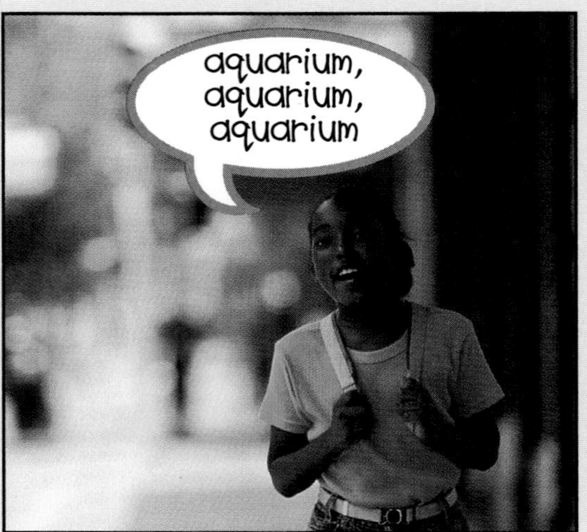

Listen to the word as you say it again.

4.

Make a picture of the word in your head.

5.

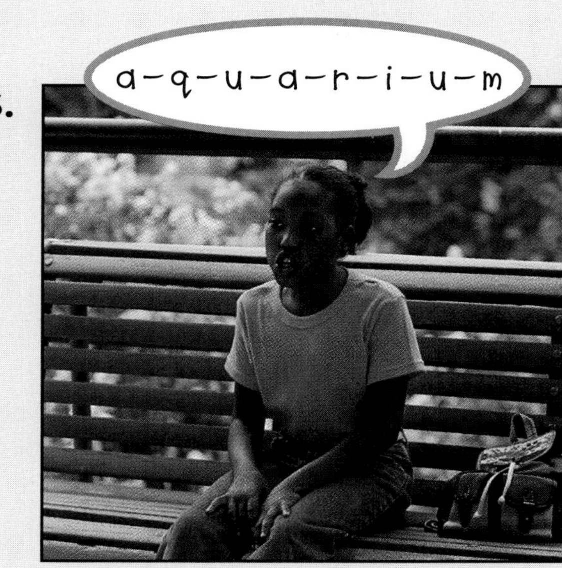

Spell the word out loud several times.

6.

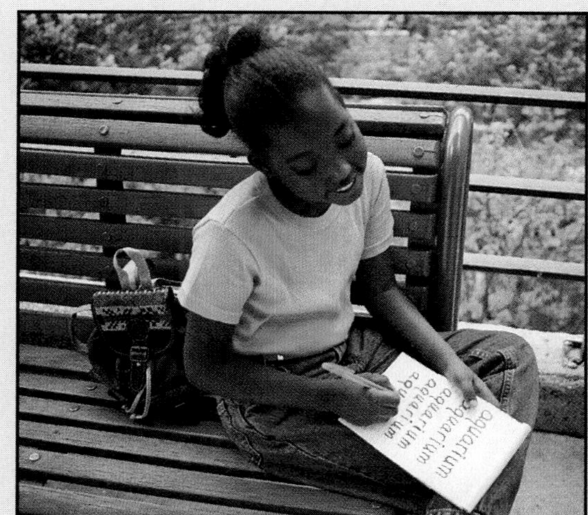

Write the word for practice. Write it five or ten times.

7.

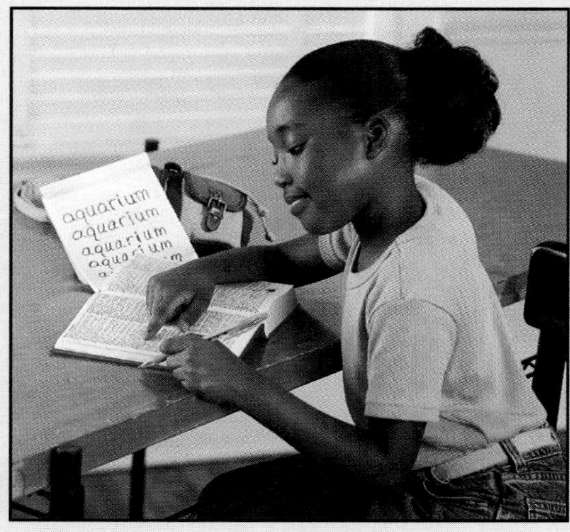

Check the word. You can use a dictionary, a computer spell-check, or a word list. See pages 322-323 to learn how to look up a word in a dictionary.

8.

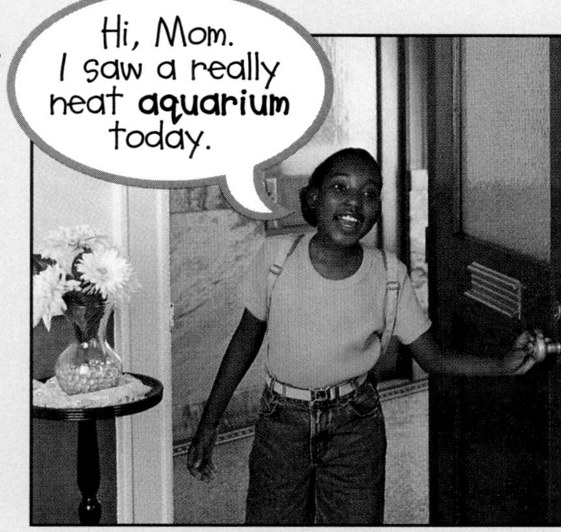

Make a sentence with the word to be sure that you understand what the word means.

Spell Words with *-ed*, *-ing*, *-er*, *-est*

■ Add the ending directly to:

- words that end with one vowel and two consonants

Examples: crack + ed = crack**ed** turn + ed = turn**ed**

crack+ ing = crack**ing** turn + ing = turn**ing**

invent + ed = invent**ed** smell + ed = smell**ed**

invent + ing = invent**ing** smell + ing = smell**ing**

- words that end with two vowels and one consonant

Examples: clean + ed = clean**ed** scoop + ed = scoop**ed**

clean + ing = clean**ing** scoop + ing = scoop**ing**

peel + ed = peel**ed** explain + ed = explain**ed**

peel + ing = peel**ing** explain + ing = explain**ing**

■ When a word ends in silent e, drop the e. Then add the ending.

Examples: bak~~e~~ + ed = bak**ed** wis~~e~~ + er = wis**er**

bak~~e~~ + ing = bak**ing** wis~~e~~ + est = wis**est**

smil~~e~~ + ed = smil**ed** larg~~e~~ + er = larg**er**

smil~~e~~ + ing = smil**ing** larg~~e~~ + est = larg**est**

late

later

- **When a word ends in one vowel and one consonant, double the consonant. Then add the ending.**

Examples: scrub + b + ed = scrubb**ed** thin + n + er = thinn**er**

scrub + b + ing = scrubb**ing** thin + n + est = thinn**est**

jog + g + ed = jogg**ed** wet + t + er = wett**er**

jog + g + ing = jogg**ing** wet + t + est = wett**est**

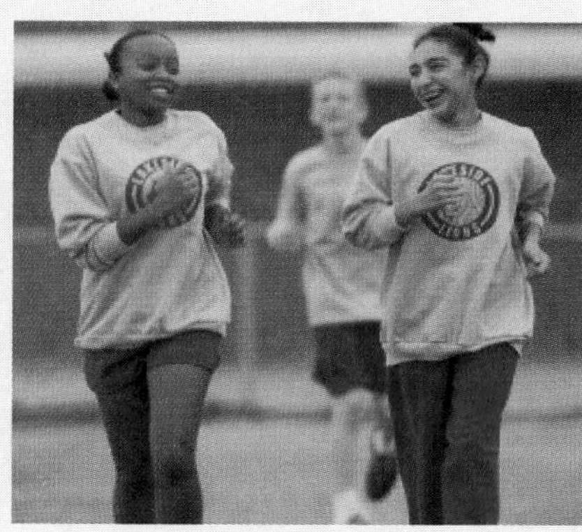

- **When a word ends in a consonant plus y, change y to i. Then add -ed, -er, or -est.**

Examples: study + ed = studi**ed** marry + ed = marri**ed**

busy + er = busi**er** happy + er = happi**er**

busy + est = busi**est** happy + est = happi**est**

- **Keep the y when a word ends in a vowel plus y or when you add -ing.**

Examples: enjoy + ed = enjoy**ed**

play + er = play**er**

stay + ing = stay**ing**

fry + ing = fry**ing**

study + ing = study**ing**

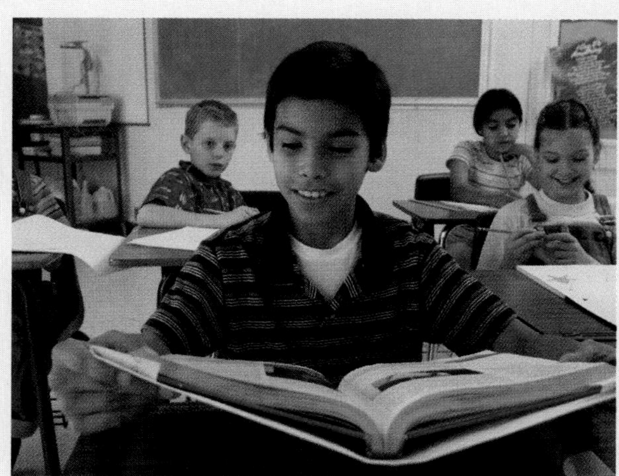

Spell Words with Prefixes and Suffixes

Prefixes

A **prefix** is a word part that comes at the beginning of a word. The spelling of the word does not change when you add a prefix.

Examples: dis + agree = **dis**agree
un + necessary = **un**necessary
re + write = **re**write

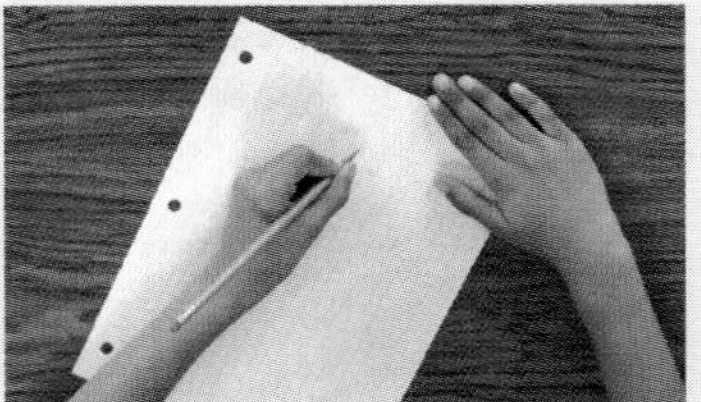

Suffixes

A **suffix** is a word part that comes at the end of a word.

- **The spelling of some words does not change when you add a suffix.**

Examples: develop + ment = develop**ment**
thought + ful = thought**ful**

- **For most words that end in silent e, drop the e if you are adding a suffix that starts with a vowel.**

Examples: us~~e~~ + able = us**able**
nerv~~e~~ + ous = nerv**ous**

- **Keep the silent e at the end of a word if the suffix begins with a consonant.**

Examples: amuse + ment = amuse**ment**
care + ful = care**ful**

- **For most words that end in a consonant and y, change the y to i. Then add the suffix.**

Examples: happy + ness = happi**ness**
beauty + ful = beauti**ful**

- **When a word ends in a vowel and y, keep the y.**

Examples: joy + ous = joy**ous**
play + ful = play**ful**

- **When a word ends in le, drop the final le before adding the suffix ly.**

Examples: possible + ly = possib**ly**
comfortable + ly = comfortab**ly**

- **When a word ends in l, leave the l before adding ly.**

Examples: real + ly = real**ly**
wool + ly = wool**ly**

Spell Plurals

■ **Add -s to most words.**

Examples:

lamp + s = lamp**s**

stone + s = stone**s**

■ **Add -es to words that end in s, ch, sh, x, or z.**

Examples:

dress + es = dress**es**

peach + es = peach**es**

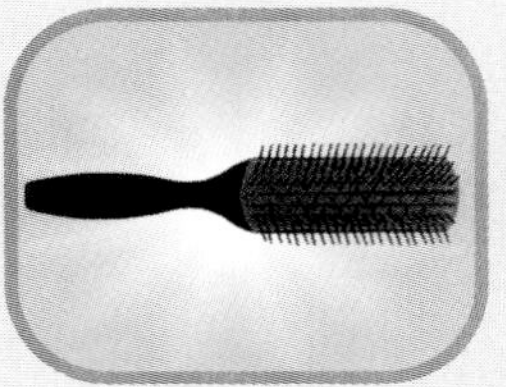
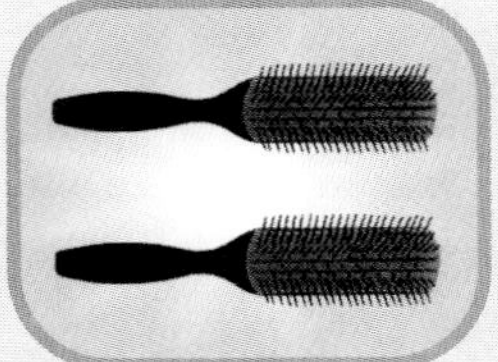

brush + es = brush**es**

fox + es = fox**es**

■ **Change y to i . Then add -es.**

Examples:

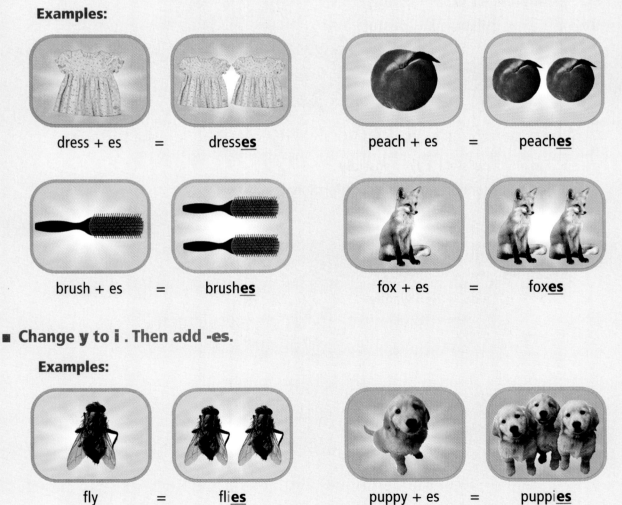

fly = fli**es**

puppy + es = puppi**es**

Spell Long Words

- **Say the word and count the syllables, or word parts. Then spell each syllable and read the word.**

  Example: mag + net = magnet

The word **magnet** has two syllables. I'll write the first syllable: **mag**. Then I'll write the second syllable: **net**.

- **Some long words are called compound words. They're made up of two smaller words. Write each word.**

  Example: side + walk = sidewalk

- **Some long words start with a syllable that sounds like the a in about.**

  Examples: above across alone along around

- **Many words end in a consonant + le.**

  Examples: table title little article handle

Words That Sound Alike

Some words that sound alike are hard to spell, but you can look here or in a dictionary to check your spelling.

knew

new

She **knew** every answer on the test.

She used a **new** pencil.

close

clothes

The store will **close** soon.

I see new **clothes** on sale!

its

it's

The dog is wagging **its** tail.

It's time to feed the dog.

Spelling Tip

It's is short for "it is." Say the sentence to see if "it is" makes sense. If not, don't use **it's**!

heard

herd

I **heard** a loud noise.

It was a **herd** of cows.

dear

deer

My **dear** friend lives in the country.

There are many **deer** where she lives.

read
red

Yesterday I **read** a beautiful poem.

It was about the color **red**.

peace
piece

I wished for world **peace**.

I wrote my wish on a **piece** of paper.

two
to
too

Two friends went **to** the beach.

I wanted **to** go, **too**.

they're
there
their

They're playing soccer in the park.

There is a bee on **their** dad!

weather
whether

The **weather** might be rainy today.

I can't decide **whether** or not to stay home.

wear
where

Wear this to the picnic.

Where is my blue jacket?

you're
your

Your report is great!

You're a real expert!

Spelling Tip

Does "you are" makes sense in the sentence? If so, use **you're**!

Grammar Made Graphic

Pedro loves to fly kites. To tell about his kite, he is putting words together to make a sentence. Pedro makes sure to use the correct pronoun, verb, and adverbs so everyone can understand exactly what the kite does.

This chapter will help you make your writing clear, too. Here you'll find all the rules you need to know to write in English.

Sentences

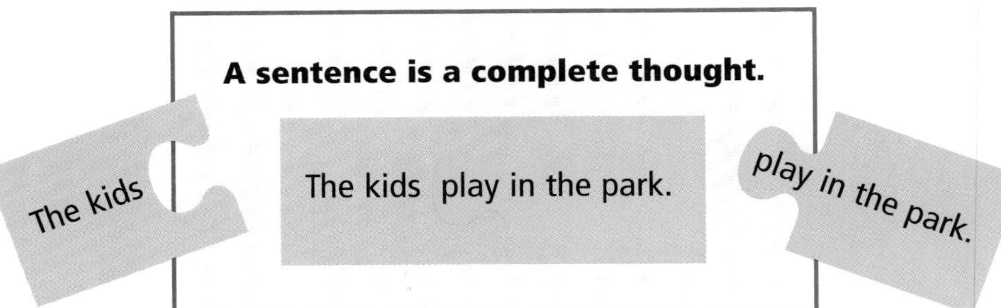

A sentence is a complete thought.
The kids
The kids play in the park.
play in the park.

Kinds of Sentences

■ **There are four kinds of sentences.**

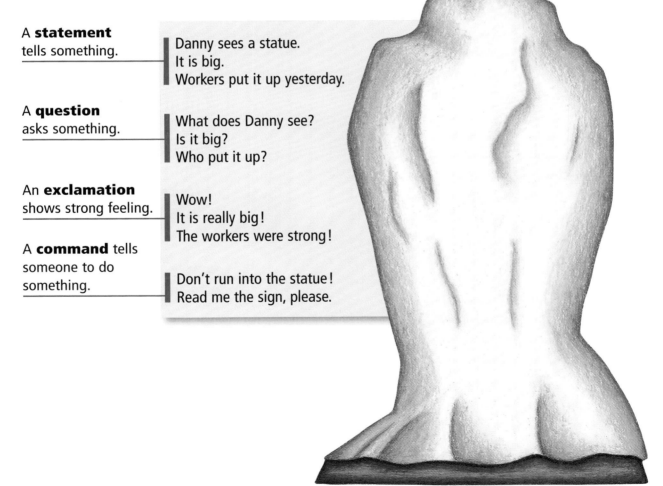

A **statement** tells something.	Danny sees a statue. It is big. Workers put it up yesterday.
A **question** asks something.	What does Danny see? Is it big? Who put it up?
An **exclamation** shows strong feeling.	Wow! It is really big! The workers were strong!
A **command** tells someone to do something.	Don't run into the statue! Read me the sign, please.

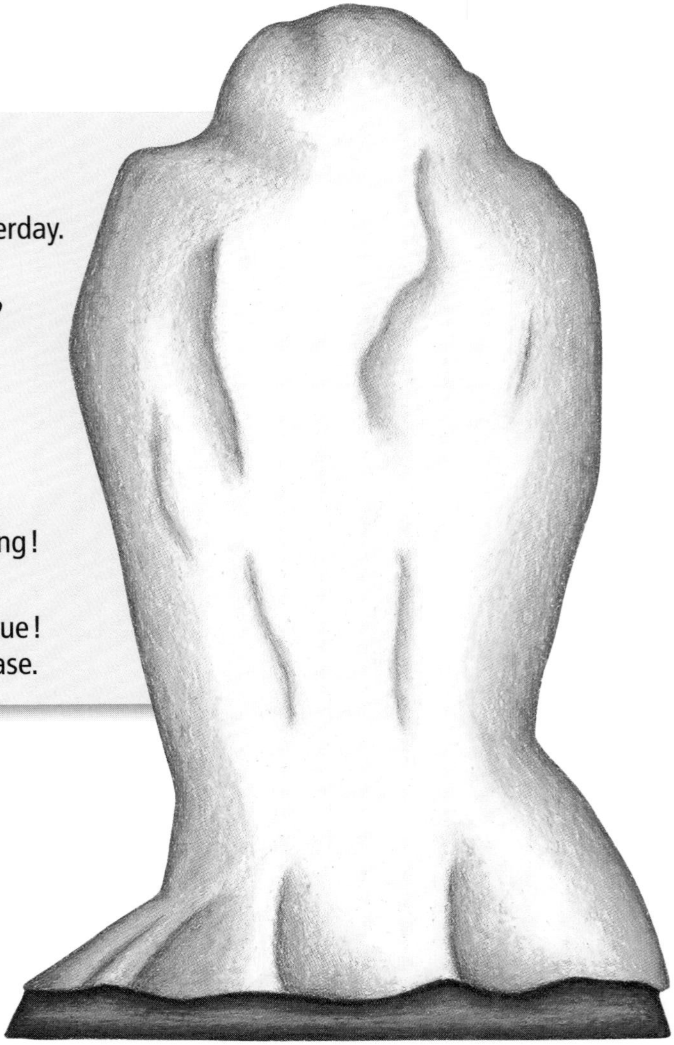

■ Ask a question to get information.

Some questions ask for a "yes" or "no" answer.

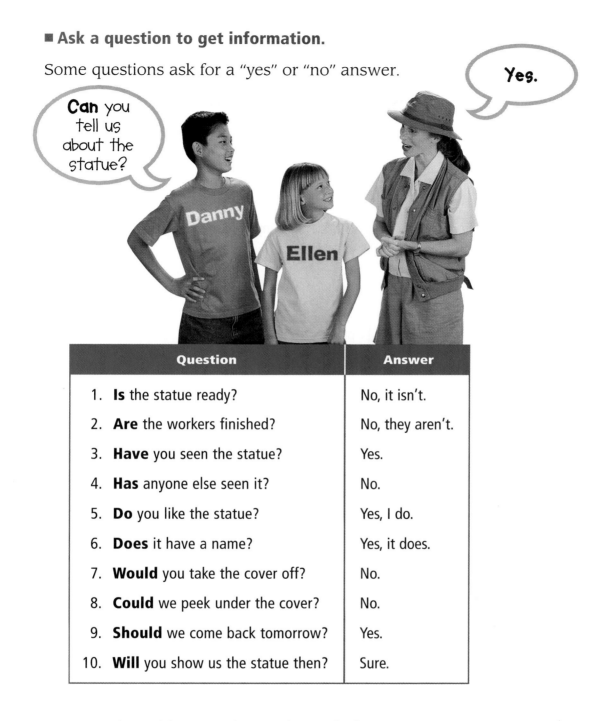

Can you tell us about the statue?

Question	Answer
1. **Is** the statue ready?	No, it isn't.
2. **Are** the workers finished?	No, they aren't.
3. **Have** you seen the statue?	Yes.
4. **Has** anyone else seen it?	No.
5. **Do** you like the statue?	Yes, I do.
6. **Does** it have a name?	Yes, it does.
7. **Would** you take the cover off?	No.
8. **Could** we peek under the cover?	No.
9. **Should** we come back tomorrow?	Yes.
10. **Will** you show us the statue then?	Sure.

You can also add a question to the end of a statement.

Examples: You are busy.
You are busy, aren't you? Yes, I am.

You're not busy.
You're not busy, are you? No, I'm not.

Kinds of Sentences, continued

When you want more information than just "yes" or "no," start your question with one of these words.

Question	Answer
1. **When** did you uncover the statue?	I uncovered it this morning.
2. **How much** does the statue weigh?	I don't know. It's very heavy.
3. **Who** is it?	That's Paul Bunyan.
4. **What** did he do?	He was a lumberjack.
5. **Where** did he live?	He lived in Minnesota.
6. **How** big was he?	He was big enough to pick up railroad tracks.
7. **Why** is he famous?	Some stories say he made all the lakes in Minnesota.
8. **How many** lakes did he make?	He made more than 10,000!
9. **Which** story about Paul Bunyan is your favorite?	I like the stories about Paul and Babe, his blue ox.
10. **How** can we find out more about Paul Bunyan?	Use the computer at the library.

Go To Practices A and B on page 381.

■ Some sentences mean "no."

A negative sentence uses a negative word to say "no."

Examples: no, not, nothing, none, nobody, no one, never, nowhere

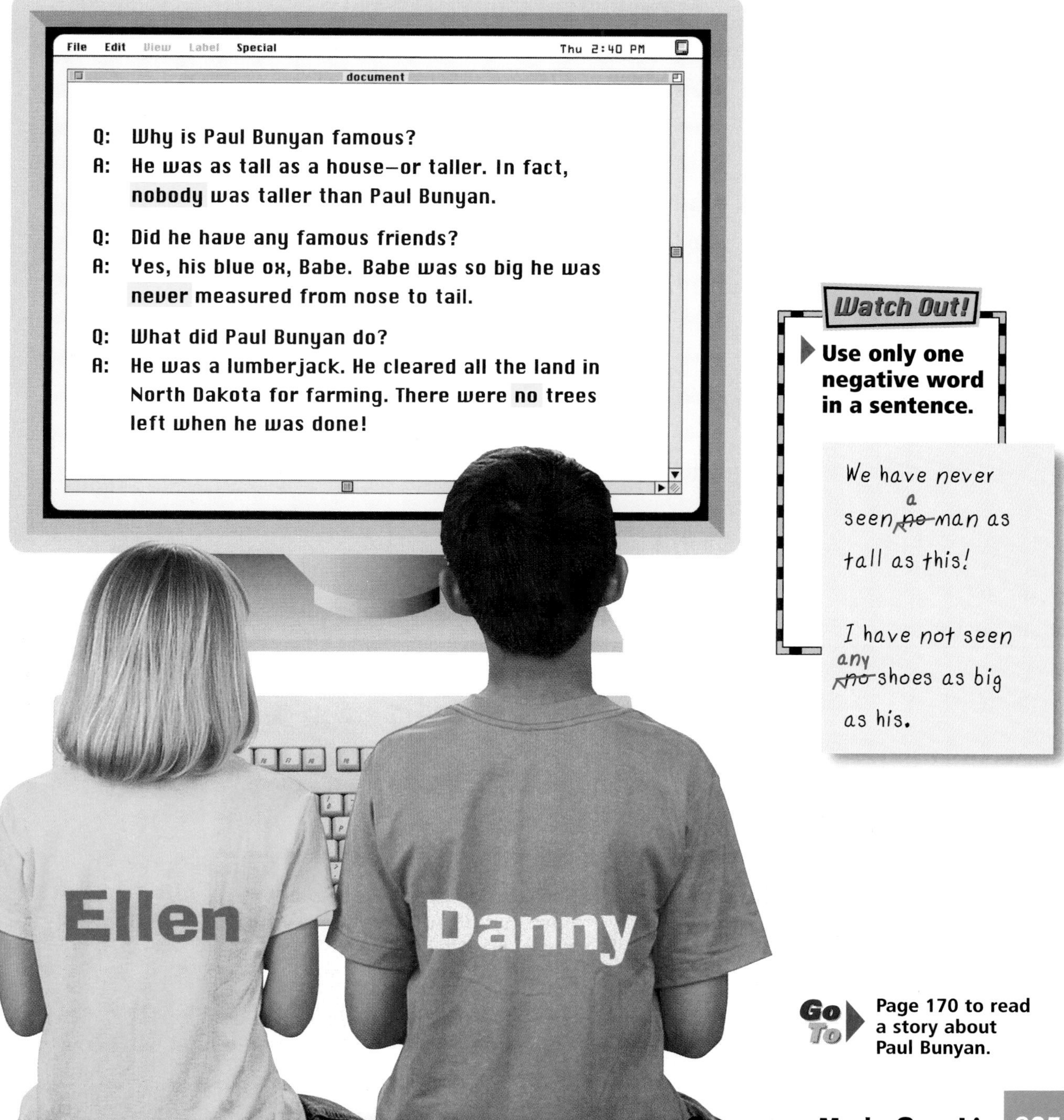

File Edit View Label Special Thu 2:40 PM
document
Q: Why is Paul Bunyan famous?
A: He was as tall as a house—or taller. In fact, nobody was taller than Paul Bunyan.
Q: Did he have any famous friends?
A: Yes, his blue ox, Babe. Babe was so big he was never measured from nose to tail.
Q: What did Paul Bunyan do?
A: He was a lumberjack. He cleared all the land in North Dakota for farming. There were no trees left when he was done!
Ellen
Danny

Watch Out!

Use only one negative word in a sentence.

We have never seen ~~no~~ a man as tall as this!

I have not seen ~~no~~ any shoes as big as his.

Go To Page 170 to read a story about Paul Bunyan.

Subject and Predicate

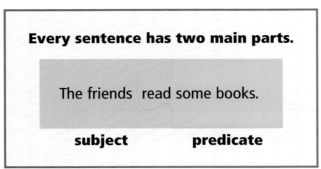

Every sentence has two main parts.

The friends read some books.

subject **predicate**

■ **The subject tells whom or what the sentence is about.**

The subject usually comes at the beginning of the sentence. It can have more than one word.

The **simple subject** is the most important word in the subject.

The **complete subject** includes all the words that tell about the subject.

A **compound subject** has two or more simple subjects. They are often joined by **and** or **or**.

Danny finds a book with tall tales.

It has stories about Paul Bunyan.

One funny **story** is about Babe, his ox.

This big, blue **ox** drank a lake every morning!

Danny and **Ellen** enjoy the tale.

They smile and laugh.

Watch Out!

- **Sometimes a subject comes at or near the end of a sentence.**

  Here is my **book**.
  There are many **books** to read.

- **Sometimes the subject is not named, but you can guess who the subject is!**

  Don't talk in the library!
  Please return your books here.

■ The predicate tells what the subject is, does, or has.

The predicate usually comes at the end of a sentence.

The **simple predicate** is the most important word in the predicate. It is the **verb**.

Danny **finds** a book with tall tales.

It **has** stories about Paul Bunyan.

One funny story **is** about Babe, his ox.

This big, blue ox **drank** a lake every morning!

Danny and Ellen **enjoy** the tale.

They **smile** and **laugh**.

The **complete predicate** includes all the words in the predicate part of the sentence.

A **compound predicate** has two or more verbs that tell about the same subject.

Go To ▶ **Practices C–F on page 382.**

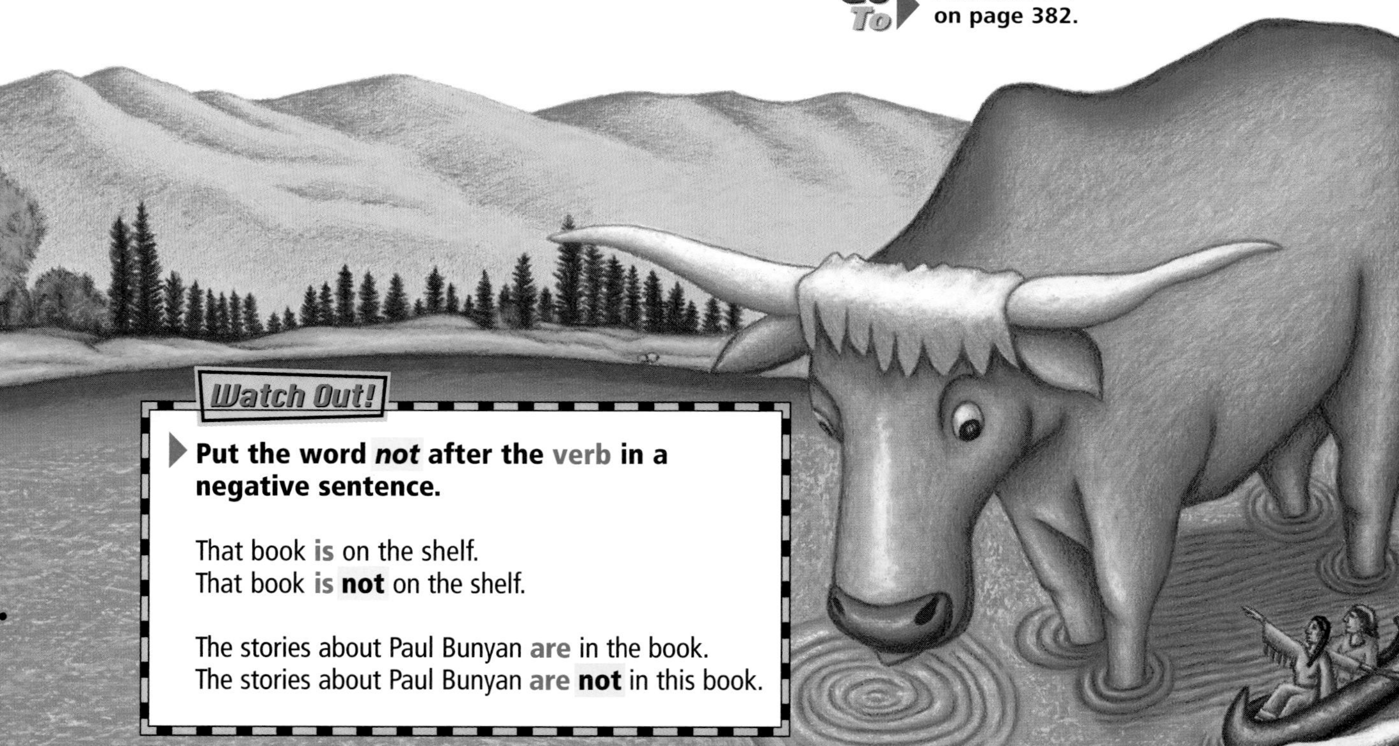

Watch Out!

▶ **Put the word *not* after the verb in a negative sentence.**

That book **is** on the shelf.
That book **is** **not** on the shelf.

The stories about Paul Bunyan **are** in the book.
The stories about Paul Bunyan **are** **not** in this book.

Compound Sentences

You can put two sentences together to make a compound sentence. Just use a comma in front of:

and **but** **or**

When you put together two ideas that are alike, use **and**.

Example:
Paul cut down many trees.
Babe carried the logs to the river.

Paul cut down many trees, **and** Babe carried the logs to the river.

When you want to show a difference between two ideas, use **but**.

Example:
The farmers could not clear their land.
Paul did it overnight.

The farmers could not clear their land, **but** Paul did it overnight.

When you want to show a choice between two ideas, use **or**.

Example:
You can find books about Paul Bunyan in the library.
You can download stories from the Internet.

You can find books about Paul Bunyan in the library, **or** you can download stories from the Internet.

Watch Out!

▶ **If a sentence uses *and* too many times, make two sentences.**

We saw the new statue of Paul Bunyan, and we asked a lot of questions ~~and~~ then we went to the library to find some books.

Go To Practice G on page 383.

Nouns

A noun is the name of a person, place, or thing.

Examples: Say hello to **Luisa**.
She lives in **Galveston**.
She rides a purple **bicycle**.

Common and Proper Nouns

- **A common noun names any person, place, or thing.**
- **A proper noun names one particular person, place, or thing.**

All the important words in a proper noun start with a capital letter.

COMMON NOUNS	PROPER NOUNS
Any Person The **girl** rides her bike. A **runner** jogs by her.	**One Particular Person** **Luisa** rides her bike. **Max Medina** jogs by her.
Any Place Our **state** has many cities. This **city** is pretty. We ride by the **bay**.	**One Particular Place** **Texas** has many cities. **Galveston** is pretty. We ride by **Galveston Bay**.
Any Thing The **building** is historic. That **street** is famous. Luisa sees the **boat**.	**One Particular Thing** **Ashton Villa** is historic. **Hope Boulevard** is famous. Luisa sees **Tall Ship *Elissa***.

Go To Practice A on page 383.

Singular and Plural Nouns

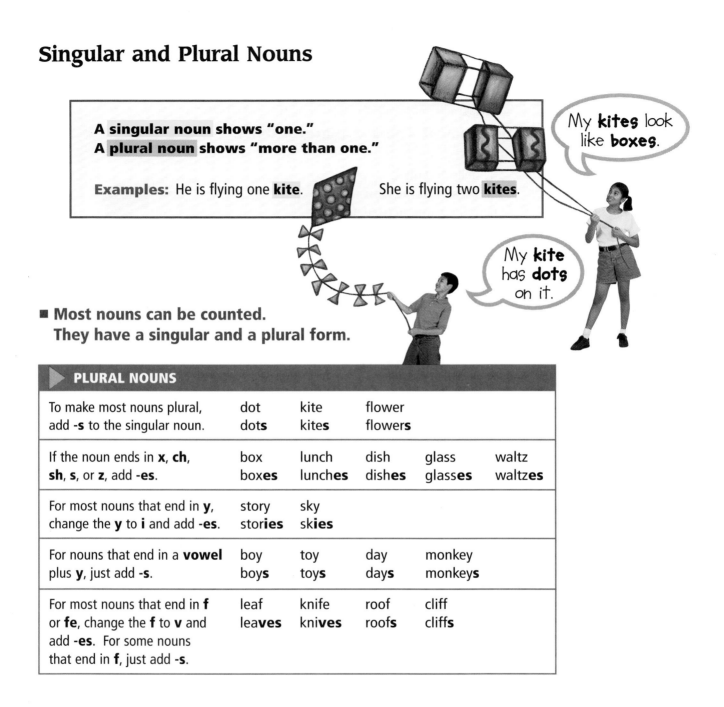

A singular noun shows "one."
A plural noun shows "more than one."

Examples: He is flying one **kite**. She is flying two **kites**.

My **kites** look like **boxes**.

My **kite** has **dots** on it.

■ **Most nouns can be counted.**
They have a singular and a plural form.

PLURAL NOUNS					
To make most nouns plural, add **-s** to the singular noun.	dot dot**s**	kite kite**s**	flower flower**s**		
If the noun ends in **x**, **ch**, **sh**, **s**, or **z**, add **-es**.	box box**es**	lunch lunch**es**	dish dish**es**	glass glass**es**	waltz waltz**es**
For most nouns that end in **y**, change the **y** to **i** and add **-es**.	story stor**ies**	sky sk**ies**			
For nouns that end in a **vowel** plus **y**, just add **-s**.	boy boy**s**	toy toy**s**	day day**s**	monkey monkey**s**	
For most nouns that end in **f** or **fe**, change the **f** to **v** and add **-es**. For some nouns that end in **f**, just add **-s**.	leaf lea**ves**	knife kni**ves**	roof roof**s**	cliff cliff**s**	

A few nouns change in different ways to show "more than one."

One	**man**	**woman**	**foot**	**tooth**	**mouse**	**goose**	**child**	**person**
More than One	**men**	**women**	**feet**	**teeth**	**mice**	**geese**	**children**	**people**

Go To Practice B on page 384.

- **Some nouns cannot be counted. They have only one form for "one" and "more than one."**

NOUNS THAT CANNOT BE COUNTED		
Weather Words Many nouns that refer to weather cannot be counted. **Example:** **Thunder** and **lightning** scare my dog.	hail ice lightning rain	snow heat thunder fog
Food Many food items cannot be counted unless you use a measurement word like **cup**, **slice**, or **head**. Make the measurement word plural to show "more than one." **Examples:** I love **lettuce**! Mom bought **two heads of lettuce**.	bread cereal cheese corn flour lettuce	meat milk rice soup sugar tea
Ideas and Feelings **Examples:** I need some **help**. What **information** do you need?	democracy fun health help happiness	homework information luck trouble work
Category Nouns These nouns name a group, or category. Some of the items within the category can be counted. **Example:** I have some **money** in my pocket. There are **four dollars** and **two dimes**.	equipment energy fruit furniture	machinery mail money time
Materials **Example:** Is the table made of **wood** or **metal**?	metal paper	water wood
Activities and Sports **Examples:** My mom and dad love to play **golf**. **Camping** is my favorite thing to do.	baseball camping dancing football	golf singing soccer swimming

Watch Out!

Some nouns have more than one meaning. Add -s for the plural only if the noun means something you can count.

football

1. **a ball** *We need two **footballs** for the game.*
2. **a sport** *I like to watch **football**.*

Go To Practice C on page 384.

Words That Signal Nouns

Some words help identify a noun:

a an some the this that these those

Examples: I'd like to buy **a** shirt.
How about **this** nice shirt?
Do you like **the** collar?

■ Use *a, an,* or *some* to talk about something in general.

One	More than One
a hat **an umbrella**	**some hats** **some umbrellas**

Examples: I'll buy **a hat** for me and **an umbrella** for you.

Some hats are too fancy.

Some umbrellas are too expensive.

Use **an** before a noun that begins with a vowel like:

a in **a**nt, **a**pron, **a**mount
e in **e**lbow, **e**el, **e**lection
i in **i**nch, **i**dea
o in **o**tter, **o**cean, **o**wl
u in **u**mbrella

Don't forget to use **an** before a word with a silent **h**: **an h**our

■ Use *the* to talk about something specific.

One	More than One
the pink hat **the small umbrella**	**the blue hats** **the large umbrellas**

Examples: I'll buy **the pink hat** for me and **the small umbrella** for you.

The blue hat is too fancy.

The large umbrellas are too expensive.

Here are some tips to help you use **a** and **the** correctly.

Never use **the** before the name of a:

Galveston is a city in **Texas**. — • city or state

Many people there speak **English** and **Spanish**. — • language

We visited the city in **September** on **Labor Day**. — • day, month, or holiday

If you talk about the same thing a second time, use **the**. — I found a great beach by the seawall. **The** beach was nice and big.

Several of us played **volleyball**. — • sport or activity

Then we went to lunch at **Joe's Cafe**. — • business

When you compare three or more things, use **the**. — Joe serves **the** best hamburgers in the city.

- **Use *this, that, these,* and *those* to talk about something specific.**

	One	More than One
Close By	**this** T-shirt	**these** T-shirts
Far Away	**that** umbrella	**those** umbrellas

Do you like **these** pink T-shirts or **this** red one?
That purple umbrella is bigger than **those** green ones.

Go To Practices D and E on page 385.

Possessive Nouns

A possessive noun is the name of an owner.
The name always has an apostrophe: '

Examples: **Luisa's** T-shirt is from the Springfest.
The **boys'** T-shirts are from the Flight Museum.

The placement of the apostrophe depends on whether there is one owner or more than one owner. Look at these examples.

One Owner	More than One Owner
Martin's cap	the **boys'** caps
Mom's umbrella	my **parents'** umbrella
the **umbrella's** handle	the **umbrellas'** stripes
the **student's** T-shirt	the **students'** T-shirts

I just love **Galveston's** shops! This cap will look perfect with my **brother's** T-shirt.
But the **cap's** bill is torn. Maybe you would like this one.
Galveston

Go To Practice F on page 386.

Using Nouns in Writing

Use specific nouns to help your reader see what you are writing about.

Example: Two **birds** flew around the restaurant.
Two **parrots** flew around the restaurant.

The writer replaced **restaurant** with **Parrot Cafe** to let readers know exactly which restaurant it is.

Time for Lunch

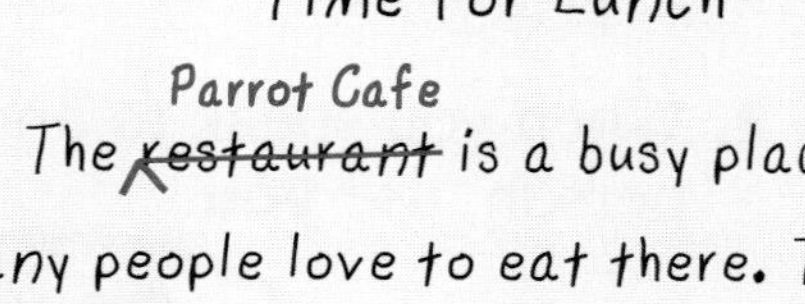

The ~~restaurant~~ Parrot Cafe is a busy place. Many people love to eat there. They serve tasty tacos all through the day. The chef's best dish is black beans and rice.

He also serves great pizza. Have you ever tried a tuna pizza? How about a pizza with apples and walnuts? Now there's a taste not to miss!

Don't forget to save room for ~~dessert~~ chocolate fudge cake. It's thick and rich. You shouldn't skip this two-napkin treat.

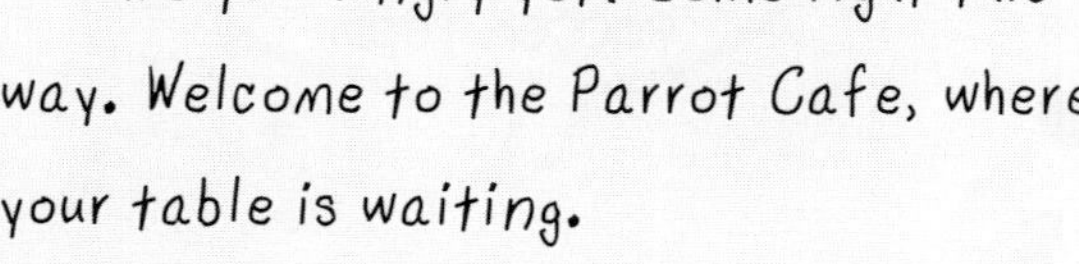

Are you hungry yet? Come right this way. Welcome to the Parrot Cafe, where your table is waiting.

Replacing **dessert** with **chocolate fudge cake** gives a much clearer picture of the treat. You can almost taste it!

Practices G and H on page 386.

Pronouns

A pronoun takes the place of a noun.

Example: **Lisa** wears a cap.

⬇

She wears a cap.

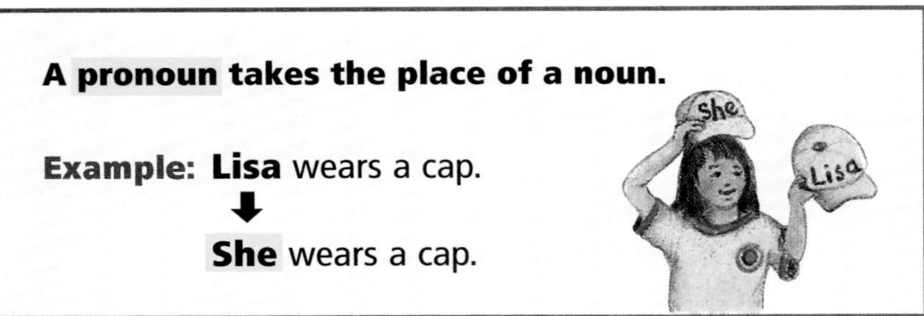

Using Different Kinds of Pronouns

■ **When you use a pronoun, be sure you are talking about the right person.**

1. For yourself, use **I**.

Hi! **I** am Mr. Brown.

2. When you speak to another person, use **you**.

Are **you** the coach?

3. For a boy or a man, use **he**.

Yes! **He** is the coach.
Lisa

4. For a girl or a woman, use **she**.

That's Lisa. **She** is on the soccer team.

5. For a thing, use **it**.

Oh, the ball. Where is **it**?

- **Be sure you are talking about the right number of people or things.**

One	More than One
I **you** **he, she, it**	**we** **you** **they**

1. When you speak to two or more people, use **you**.

2. For yourself and another person, use **we**.

3. For other people, use **they**.

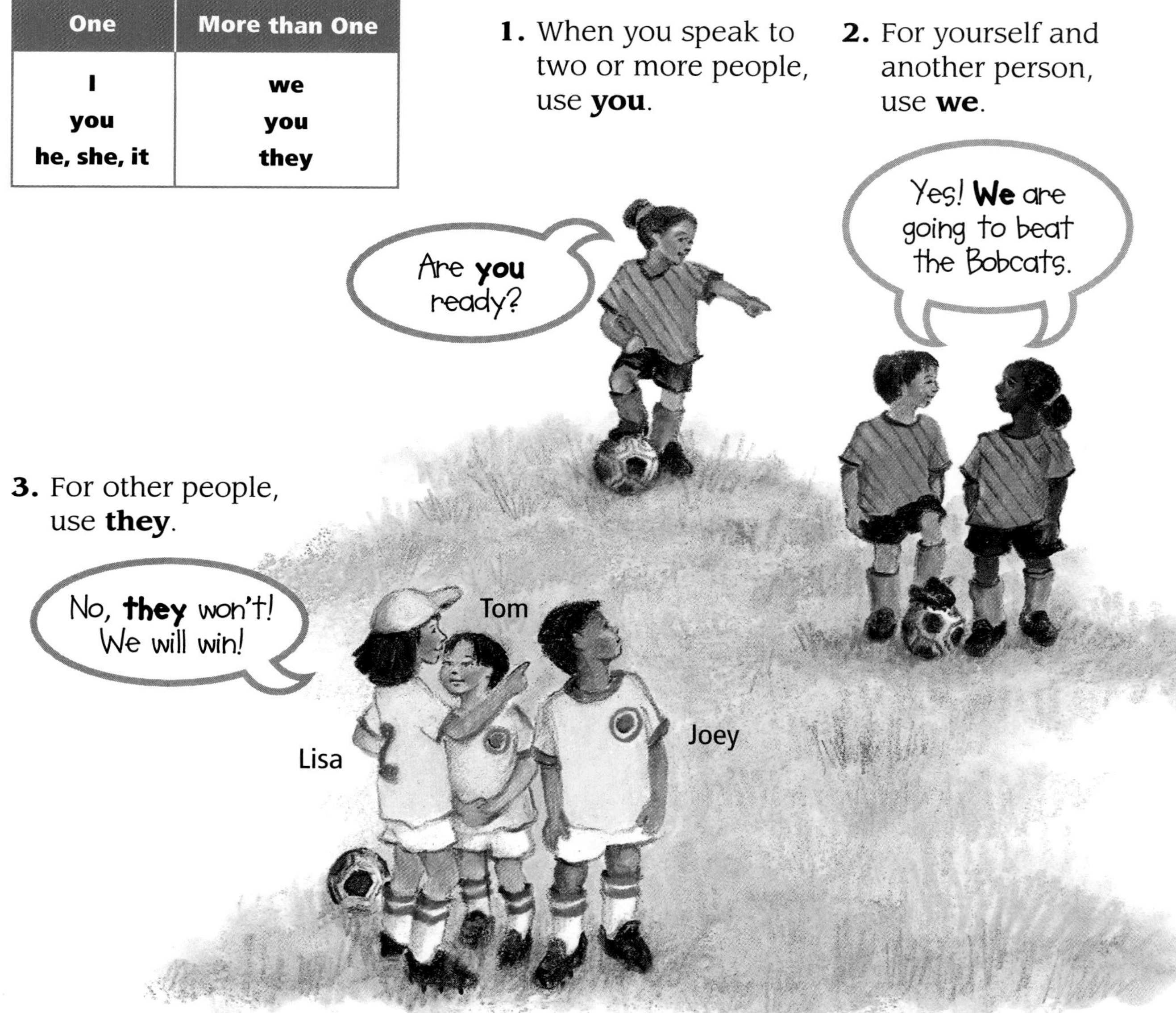

- **If you talk about a person twice in a sentence, use these pairs of pronouns.**

One		More than One	
I	**myself**	**we**	**ourselves**
you	**yourself**	**you**	**yourselves**
he	**himself**	**they**	**themselves**
she	**herself**		
it	**itself**		

Examples:

I hurt **myself**.
She found the ball **herself**.

Using Different Kinds of Pronouns, continued

■ Be sure you use the right pronoun in the right place.

Use these pronouns to tell who or what is doing something. They take the place of the subject in the sentence.

One	More than One
I **you** **he, she, it**	**we** **you** **they**

Examples:

Juan and Lisa are kicking the ball back and forth.

They are kicking the ball back and forth.

Juan kicks the ball up in the air.

⬇

He kicks the ball up in the air.

Use these pronouns after a verb or a preposition.

One	More than One
me **you** **him, her, it**	**us** **you** **them**

Examples:

The ball flies past **Jasmine and Tom**.

⬇

The ball flies past **them**.

The goalie reaches for **the ball**.

The goalie reaches for **it**.

Go To ▶ Practice A on page 387.

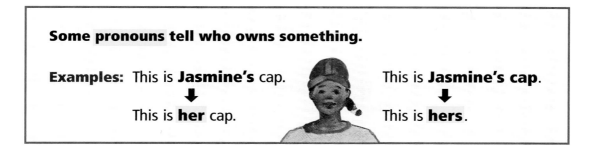

Some pronouns tell who owns something.

Examples: This is **Jasmine's** cap. → This is **her** cap.

This is **Jasmine's cap**. → This is **hers**.

These pronouns take the place of a person's name.

One	More than One
my	**our**
your	**your**
his, her, its	**their**

1.
Is this **Jasmine's** cap?
2.
No. I think **her** cap is red.
Lisa
Joey

These pronouns take the place of a person's name and what the person owns.

One	More than One
mine	**ours**
yours	**yours**
his, hers	**theirs**

Hmm. Is this **my cap**?

Yes. It's **mine**.

Watch Out!

its = pronoun
it's = it is

Nuff

The dog is wearing **its** cap, too. I like the cap. **It's** cute!

Go To Practice B on page 388.

When you don't name a specific person or thing, use one of these special pronouns.

anyone	someone	everyone
anybody	somebody	everybody
anything	something	everything

Example: Who left a cap on the table?
I don't know, but **someone** did.

CONGRATULATIONS!
1. Is **anybody** missing?
2. No, **everybody** is here.
3. Well, congratulations, **everyone**.
LISA
4. **Everything** looks good. Let's eat!
5. **Someone** made cookies. Yum.
6. Did **anyone** bring milk?
7. Can **somebody** hand me a napkin?
8. Hmm. There's **something** under the napkin.
3

Go To Practice C on page 388.

Using Pronouns in Writing

In a paragraph, each pronoun must agree with its noun.

Example:

Mr. Brown wears **his** cap at every game. The players say the **cap** is lucky. One day, **it** was missing. Mr. Brown looked everywhere, and finally the **players** found it in his back pocket. He thanked **them** again and again.

By replacing **the Bobcats** ⬇ with **they**, the writer makes this paragraph sound better.

Kicking Around!

Soccer Team Wins Again!

by Andy Thomas

Let's hear it for our team! Yesterday the Bobcats won their match. ~~The Bobcats~~ They played hard against the Eagles and won by one goal. Lisa Anderson kicked the winning goal. Juan Chávez, her teammate, assisted on the goal.

The team's record is now five wins and one loss—their best record in four years. Juan Silva and Jasmine Cummins also scored one goal each, and Joey Lee, the goalie, had six saves. Congratulations to them, too!

After the game, everyone celebrated at the coach's house. He and his wife thanked all the people who helped organize the celebration.

The players will go to Valley School next Wednesday. We hope they can win again!

The pronoun **them** agrees with ⬇ **Juan Silva, Jasmine Cummins,** and **Joey Lee**.

Go To Practices D and E on page 389.

Adjectives

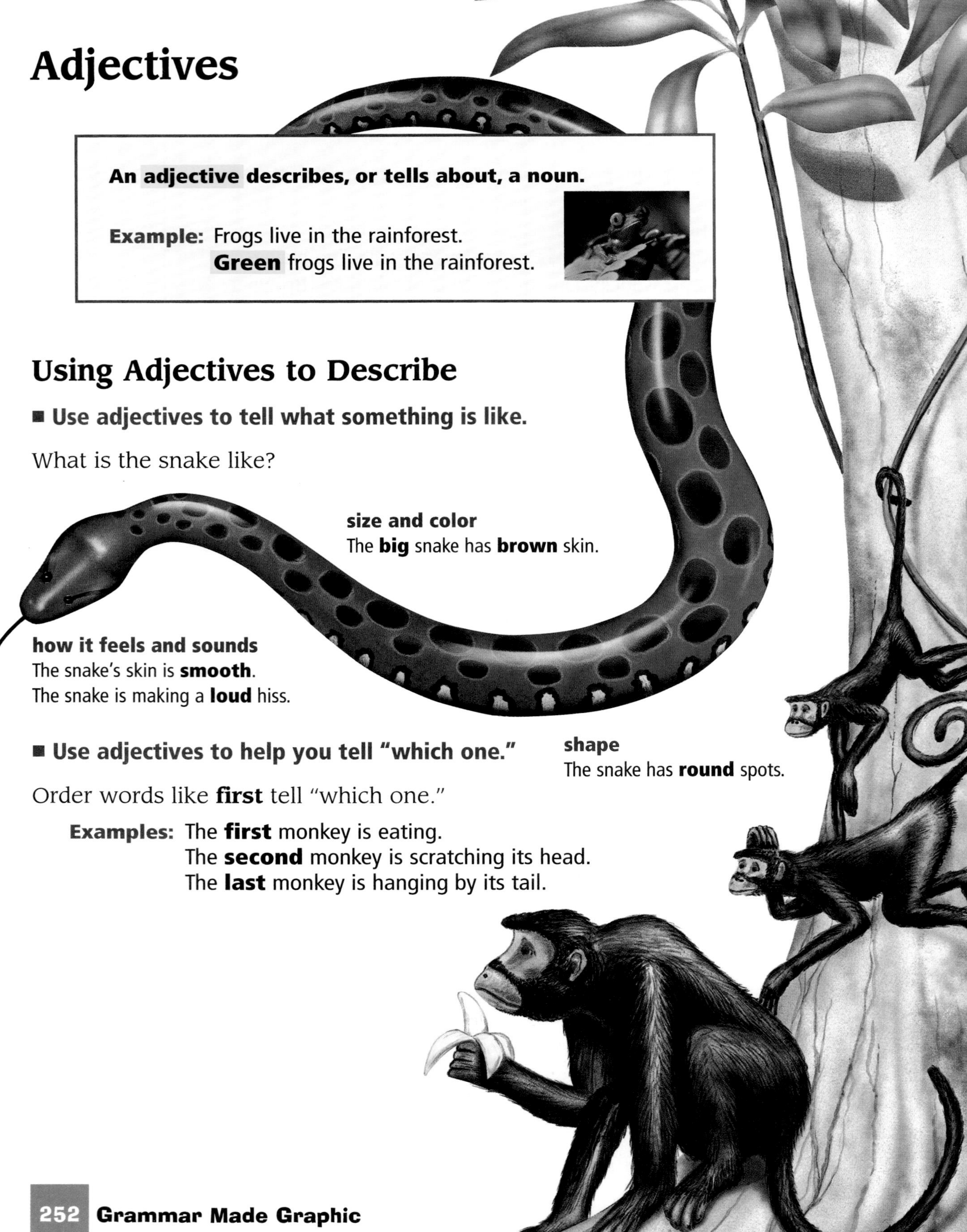

An adjective describes, or tells about, a noun.

Example: Frogs live in the rainforest.
Green frogs live in the rainforest.

Using Adjectives to Describe

■ Use adjectives to tell what something is like.

What is the snake like?

size and color
The **big** snake has **brown** skin.

how it feels and sounds
The snake's skin is **smooth**.
The snake is making a **loud** hiss.

shape
The snake has **round** spots.

■ Use adjectives to help you tell "which one."

Order words like **first** tell "which one."

Examples: The **first** monkey is eating.
The **second** monkey is scratching its head.
The **last** monkey is hanging by its tail.

■ **Use adjectives to help you tell "how many" or "how much."**

Sometimes you know exactly how many things you see. Use number words to describe them.

Examples: A sloth has **four** feet.
Some sloths have **three** toes on each foot.
A **dozen** sloths can have **144** toes in **one** tree!

If you don't know the exact number, use the words in this chart.

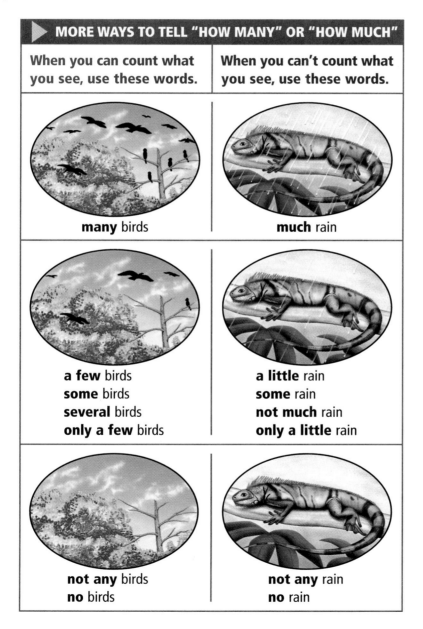

MORE WAYS TO TELL "HOW MANY" OR "HOW MUCH"

When you can count what you see, use these words.	When you can't count what you see, use these words.
 **many** birds	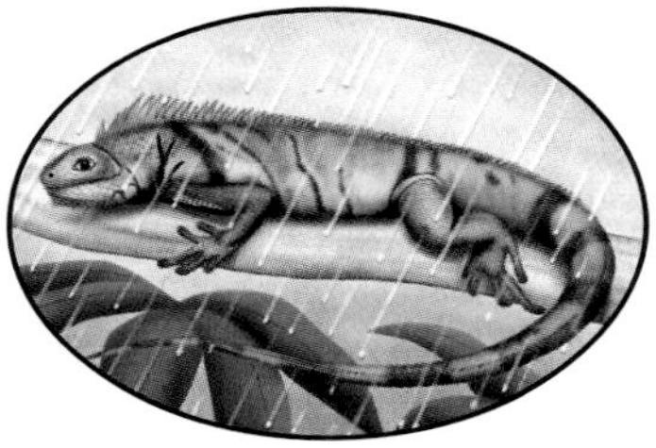 **much** rain
 **a few** birds **some** birds **several** birds **only a few** birds	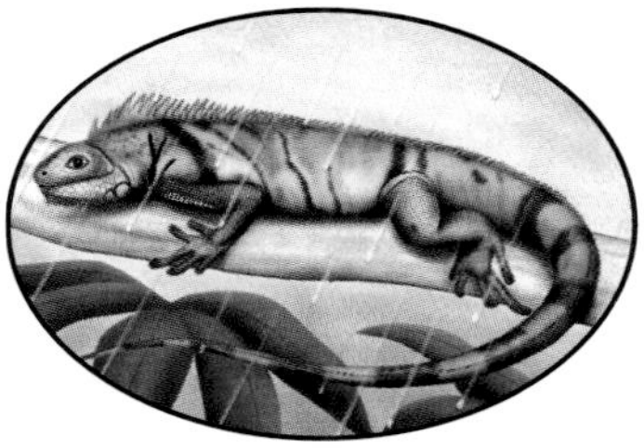 **a little** rain **some** rain **not much** rain **only a little** rain
 **not any** birds **no** birds	 **not any** rain **no** rain

Go To Practices A and B on pages 389–390.

Using Adjectives to Compare

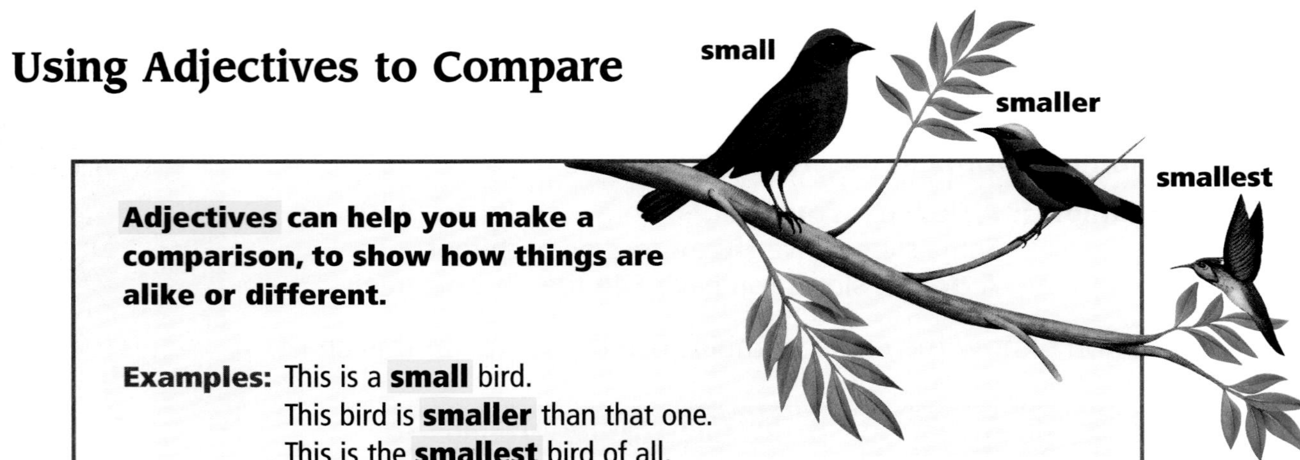

Adjectives can help you make a comparison, to show how things are alike or different.

Examples: This is a **small** bird.
This bird is **smaller** than that one.
This is the **smallest** bird of all.

■ When you compare two things, add *-er* to the adjective.

You'll probably use the word **than** in your sentence, too.

Example: The parrot's beak is **long**.
The motmot's beak is **longer than** the parrot's beak.

parrot

■ When you compare three or more things, add *-est* to the adjective.

Remember to use **the** before the adjective.

Example: The toucan's beak is **the longest** of them all.

toucan

motmot

You may have to change the spelling of the adjective before you add **-er** or **-est**.

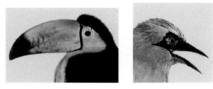

SPELLING RULES		
For adjectives that end in a silent **e**, drop the **e** and add **-er** or **-est**.	larg~~e~~ larg**er** larg**est**	nic~~e~~ nic**er** nic**est**
For adjectives that end in **y**, change the **y** to **i** and add **-er** or **-est**.	pretty prett**ier** prett**iest**	sleepy sleep**ier** sleep**iest**
Does the adjective end in one vowel and one consonant? If so, double the final consonant and add **-er** or **-est**.	big big**ger** big**gest**	sad sad**der** sad**dest**

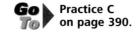

Go To Practice C on page 390.

■ If the adjective is a long word, do not add *-er* or *-est* to make a comparison.

Adjectives with three or more syllables would be too hard to say if you added **-er** or **-est**. To make a comparison with these adjectives, use **more**, **most**, **less**, or **least** instead.

hummingbird

motmot

macaw

Examples:
The hummingbird is **colorful**.
The motmot is **more colorful** than the hummingbird.
The macaw is **the most colorful** bird of all.

Examples:
The first monkey was **frightened**.
The second monkey was **less frightened**.
The third monkey was the **least frightened** of all.

When you make a comparison, use either **-er** or **more**, but not both.

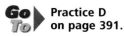

The hummingbird is ~~more~~ smaller than the monkey.

The macaw is ~~more~~ prettier than the motmot.

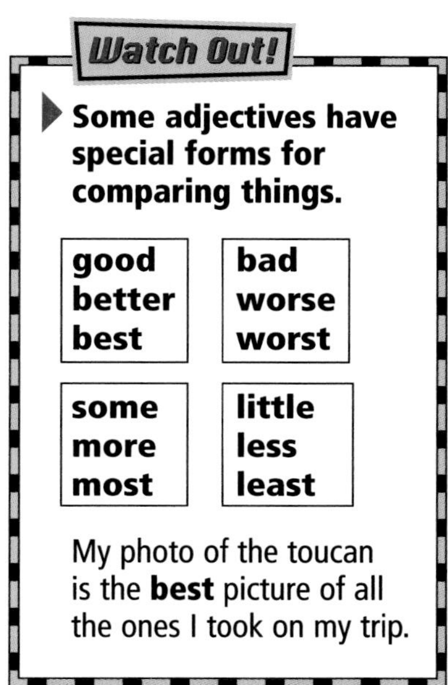
Watch Out!

Some adjectives have special forms for comparing things.

good **better** **best**	**bad** **worse** **worst**
some **more** **most**	**little** **less** **least**

My photo of the toucan is the **best** picture of all the ones I took on my trip.

Go To Practice D on page 391.

Adding Adjectives to Sentences

Adjectives can appear anywhere in a sentence.

Examples: Look at that **big** jaguar.
Its eyes are **big**, too.
The **big** jaguar just looks back at me.

Usually, an adjective comes before the noun it tells about.

Examples: An **old** jaguar hides in the **green** leaves.

Its **spotted** coat makes the **big** jaguar hard to see.

Two or more adjectives can also come before a noun.
A comma usually comes between them.

Example: The **wise, old** jaguar knows where to hide.

An adjective can come after words like **is**, **are**, **look**, **feel**, **smell**, and **taste**. The adjective describes the noun in the subject.

Examples: A rainforest is **beautiful**.

The air smells **clean**.

Each day in the rainforest feels **fresh**.

Using Adjectives in Writing

katydid

Use adjectives to help your reader "see" what you are writing about.

Example: The katydid chewed on the leaf.
The **shiny** katydid chewed on the **green** leaf.

Animal Disguises

These two **adjectives** help you picture the insect.

Some animals in the rainforest are hard to find. That's because their special colors help them hide. For example, a stick insect can look like a skinny, brown twig.

Some katydids have bodies that look like green and brown leaves. One kind of katydid has wings with spots that look like big eyes. These two spots help the katydid fool the animals that try to eat it.

Now you know how many spots are on the katydid's wings.

The black spots on jaguars make it easy for them to hide in the leaves. Then they can watch for animals on the ground without being seen.

This **adjective** helps you know *which* disguises.

These disguises protect animals from other animals, but sometimes they can help an animal sneak up on its own food. This is how rainforest creatures survive.

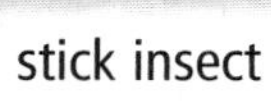

stick insect

katydid

Go To Practices E and F on page 391.

Verbs

Some verbs show action:

Example: The clouds **float** across the sky.

Some verbs link words in a sentence.

Example: The sky **is** blue.

Action and Linking Verbs

■ An action verb tells what the subject does.

Most verbs are action verbs.

The wind **blows** the clouds.
The clouds **cover** the sun.
Then the clouds **move** again.

Some **action verbs** show action that you cannot see.

We **learn** about clouds in school.
The class **enjoys** the lesson.

■ A linking verb connects, or links, the subject of a sentence to a word in the predicate.

The word in the predicate can describe the subject.

Examples: Some clouds **look** fluffy on the top.

They **are** flat on the bottom.

Or, the word in the predicate can name the subject in another way.

Example: Those white streaks **are** clouds, too.

LINKING VERBS

Forms of the Verb *be*

am	was
are	were
is	

Other Linking Verbs

appear	seem
feel	taste
look	

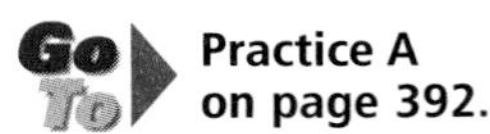

Practice A on page 392.

Helping Verbs

■ **Some verbs are made up of more than one word.**

In these verbs, the last word is called the **main verb**. The verbs that come before are called **helping verbs**.

The **helping verb** agrees with the subject. The **main verb** shows the action.

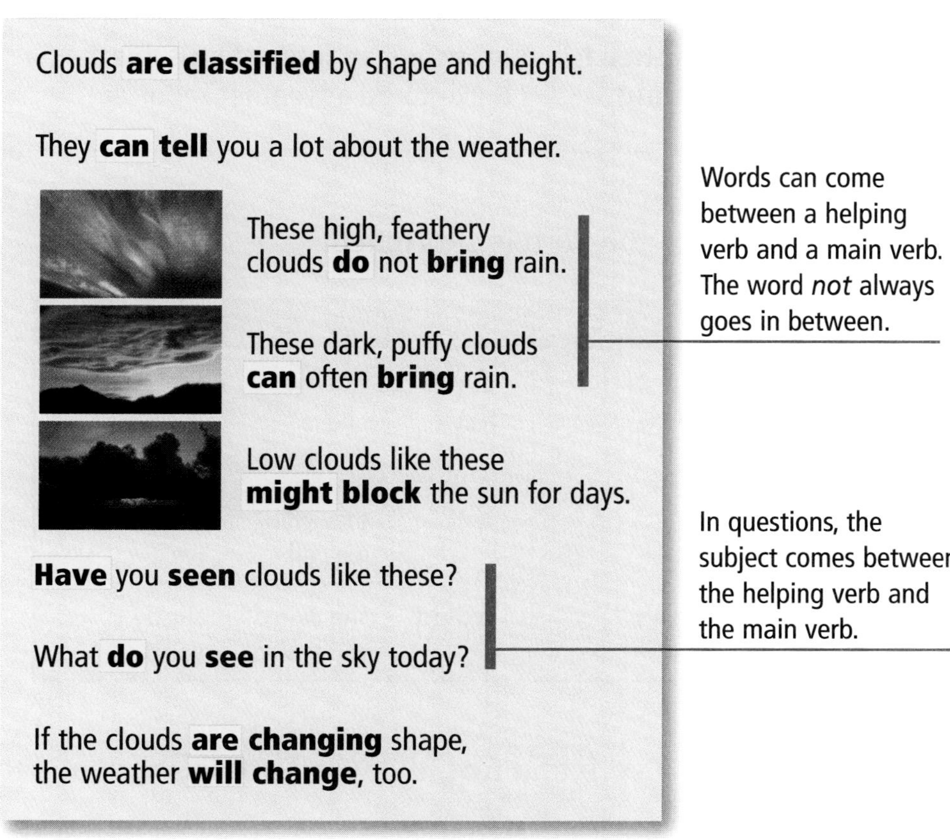

Clouds **are classified** by shape and height.
They **can tell** you a lot about the weather.
These high, feathery clouds **do** not **bring** rain.
These dark, puffy clouds **can** often **bring** rain.
Low clouds like these **might block** the sun for days.
Have you **seen** clouds like these?
What **do** you **see** in the sky today?
If the clouds **are changing** shape, the weather **will change**, too.

Words can come between a helping verb and a main verb. The word *not* always goes in between.

In questions, the subject comes between the helping verb and the main verb.

Here are some useful helping verbs.

HELPING VERBS

Forms of the Verb *be*	Forms of the Verb *do*	Forms of the Verb *have*	Other Helping Verbs	
am	do	have	can	might
are	does	has	could	should
is	did	had	may	will
was			must	would
were				

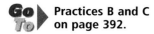

Go To Practices B and C on page 392.

Contractions with Verbs

You can put two words together to make a contraction.
An apostrophe shows where one or more letters have been left out.

Examples: **Weather ~~i~~s** **Weather's** an interesting subject.
I ~~would~~ **I'd** like to be a weather reporter.

In many contractions, the verb is shortened.

CONTRACTIONS WITH VERBS

Verb	Phrase	Contraction	Verb	Phrase	Contraction
am	I ~~a~~m	I'm	**have**	I ~~ha~~ve	I've
				they ~~ha~~ve	they've
are	they ~~a~~re	they're			
			will	they ~~wi~~ll	they'll
is	he ~~i~~s	he's		we ~~wi~~ll	we'll
	it ~~i~~s	it's			
	where ~~i~~s	where's	**would**	she ~~woul~~d	she'd
	what ~~i~~s	what's		you ~~woul~~d	you'd

In contractions with a verb and **not**, the word **not** is shortened to **n't**.

CONTRACTIONS WITH *not*

Verb	Phrase	Contraction	Verb	Phrase	Contraction
do	I do n~~o~~t	I don't	**have**	I have n~~o~~t	I haven't
does	he does n~~o~~t	he doesn't	**could**	you could n~~o~~t	you couldn't
did	we did n~~o~~t	we didn't	**would**	she would n~~o~~t	she wouldn't
are	you are n~~o~~t	you aren't	**should**	we should n~~o~~t	we shouldn't
is	he is n~~o~~t	he isn't			
was	she was n~~o~~t	she wasn't	**Exception**		
were	they were n~~o~~t	they weren't	**can**	you can~~no~~t	you can't

Practice D on page 393.

Present-Tense Verbs

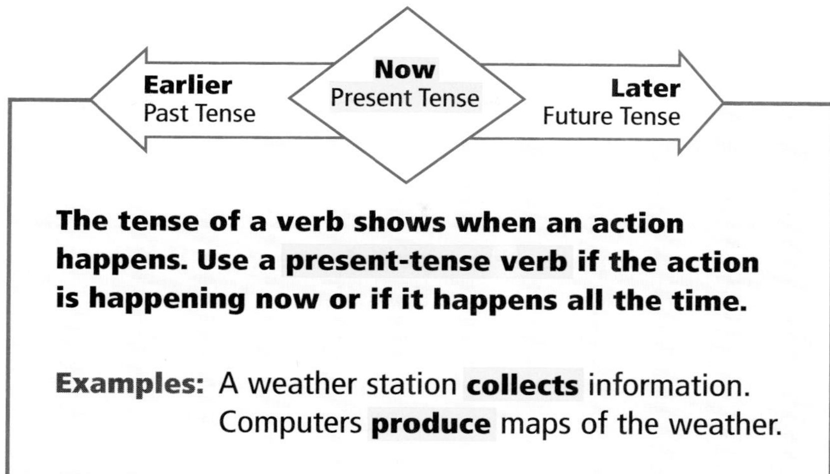

The tense of a verb shows when an action happens. Use a present-tense verb if the action is happening now or if it happens all the time.

Examples: A weather station **collects** information.
Computers **produce** maps of the weather.

■ Some present-tense verbs end in *-s*, and some do not.

One	More than One
I like rain.	**We like rain.**
You like rain.	**You like rain.**
He, she, or it likes rain.	**They like rain.**

The use of **-s** depends on who the subject is.

Subjects	Present-Tense Verbs Ending in *-s*
She	The TV reporter **gives** the weather forecast for the day. She **gives** the weather forecast for the day. Sarita Pérez **gives** the weather forecast for the day.
He	The scientist **gathers** data on big storms. He **gathers** data on big storms. Mr. Taylor **gathers** data on big storms.
It	A newspaper **prints** weather stories. It **prints** weather stories.

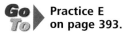

Go To Practice E on page 393.

Past-Tense Verbs

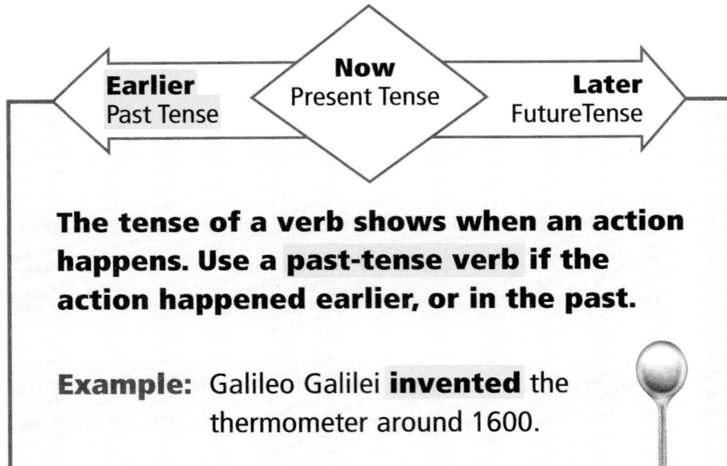

The tense of a verb shows when an action happens. Use a past-tense verb if the action happened earlier, or in the past.

Example: Galileo Galilei **invented** the thermometer around 1600.

■ Many past-tense verbs end in *-ed*.

These verbs are called **regular verbs**.

Example: **measure** Galileo's thermometer **measured** the air's temperature.

Galileo's thermometer

Follow these rules to add **-ed** to a verb.

SPELLING RULES		
For most verbs, add **-ed**.	**launch**	Scientists **launched** the first weather satellite in 1960.
For verbs that end in silent **e**, drop the **e** and add **-ed**.	**circle**	It **circled** Earth every two hours.
Does the verb end in one vowel and one consonant? If so, double the final consonant and add **-ed**.	**snap**	It **snapped** pictures of the clouds around Earth.
For verbs that end in a consonant and **y**, change the **y** to **i** and add **-ed**.	**study**	Scientists **studied** the pictures to predict a heat wave.
For verbs that end in a vowel and **y**, just add **-ed**.	**stay**	The weather **stayed** hot for a few days, but then it changed!

Go To Practice F on page 394.

- **Irregular verbs do not add *-ed* to show past tense.**

IRREGULAR VERBS		
Verb	Now–In the Present	Earlier–In the Past
be	Our family **is** in Arizona.	Our family **was** in Arizona.
	We **are** excited.	We **were** excited.
begin	Our desert vacation **begins**.	Our desert vacation **began**.
break	The temperature **breaks** 100°.	The temperature **broke** 100°.
bring	My mom **brings** sunscreen.	My mom **brought** sunscreen.
buy	We **buy** special hats.	We **bought** special hats.
do	We **do** the same things every day.	We **did** the same things every day.
drink	We **drink** a lot of water.	We **drank** a lot of water.
eat	We **eat** very little.	We **ate** very little.
find	My sister and I **find** interesting rocks.	My sister and I **found** interesting rocks.
go	I **go** back to camp at noon.	I **went** back to camp at noon.
get	It **gets** even hotter at that time!	It **got** even hotter at that time!
give	The afternoon **gives** us time to rest.	The afternoon **gave** us time to rest.
hear	We **hear** a sound nearby.	We **heard** a sound nearby.
hide	Something **hides** by our tent.	Something **hid** by our tent.
hold	I **hold** my breath.	I **held** my breath.
keep	I **keep** listening.	I **kept** listening.
know	My dad **knows** it is a lizard.	My dad **knew** it was a lizard.
make	We **make** a drawing of the lizard.	We **made** a drawing of the lizard.
ride	In the evening, we **ride** horses.	In the evening, we **rode** horses.
run	Something **runs** by us.	Something **ran** by us.
say	"Look at that," I **say**.	"Look at that," I **said**.
see	We **see** a big roadrunner.	We **saw** a big roadrunner.
sing	At night, we **sing** together.	At night, we **sang** together.
take	I **take** photos of our family.	I **took** photos of our family.
think	Everyone **thinks** the trip was great.	Everyone **thought** the trip was great.
write	We **write** about our hot vacation in school, and I add my photos.	We **wrote** about our hot vacation in school, and I added my photos.

Go To Practices G and H on page 395.

Future-Tense Verbs

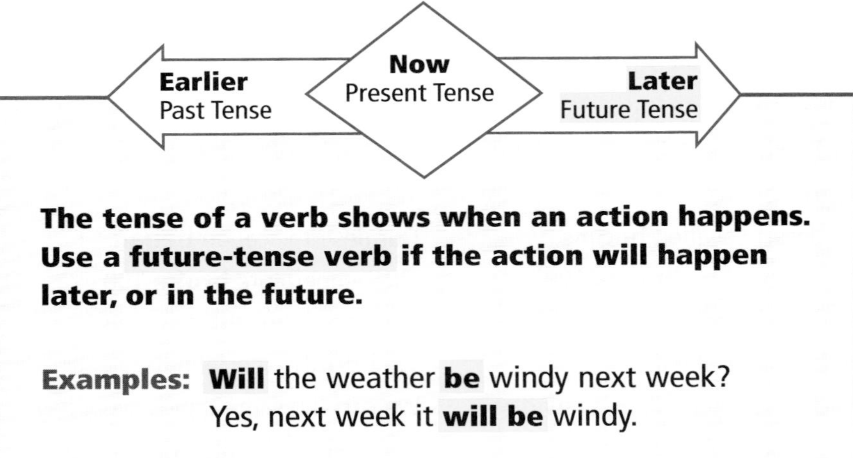

The tense of a verb shows when an action happens. Use a future-tense verb if the action will happen later, or in the future.

Examples: **Will** the weather **be** windy next week?
Yes, next week it **will be** windy.

■ **There are two ways to show the future tense.**

1. Use the helping verb **will** along with a main verb.

Tomorrow I **will build** a weather vane.

2. Use the phrase **going to**.

The word **won't** also shows future tense. **Won't** is a contraction, or shortened form, of the words **will** and **not**.

We will check the wind direction every day.
I bet we **won't** get the same results.

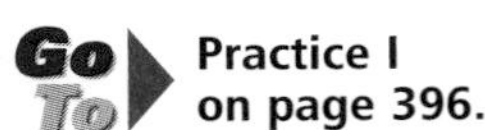

Go To

Practice I on page 396.

Principal Parts of a Verb

■ **A verb has four principal, or main, parts.**

PRINCIPAL PARTS

Present	Past	Present Participle	Past Participle
bake	baked	baking	baked
stop	stopped	stopping	stopped
look	looked	looking	looked
bring	brought	bringing	brought
begin	began	beginning	begun
do	did	doing	done
eat	ate	eating	eaten
feel	felt	feeling	felt
get	got	getting	got, gotten
go	went	going	gone
hear	heard	hearing	heard
make	made	making	made
ride	rode	riding	ridden
run	ran	running	run
see	saw	seeing	seen
take	took	taking	taken

Add *-ed* to regular verbs to form the past and the past participle.

Irregular verbs have special forms.

■ **The *-ing* form of the verb is the present participle. Use it to tell about something that is in the process of happening. The *helping verb* shows when.**

Examples:

Now The clouds **are getting** darker.

The rain **is starting**.

In the Past The clouds **were getting** darker.

The rain **was starting**.

Present-Perfect Tense

Some actions started in the past but are still going on.

Example: The sun **has shined** all month.

Some actions happened in the past, but you're not sure when.

Examples: All my flowers **have bloomed**.

The grass **has grown** so tall.

Use verbs in the present-perfect tense to tell about these actions.

■ **To form the present-perfect tense, use *has* or *have* with the past participle of the main verb.**

Follow these rules:

- Add **-ed** to regular verbs to form the past participle.

  Example: **start** Spring **has started**.

- Some verbs are irregular. You have to learn the past participles of these verbs.

  Examples:
  go The clouds **have gone** away.
  find The squirrels **have found** some nuts.
  be The weather **has been** beautiful.

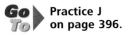

Go To Practice J on page 396.

Past-Perfect Tense

Sometimes you want to tell about an action that was completed before another action in the past. Use a verb in the past-perfect tense .

Example: We **had planted** our garden before spring began.

March
21
March 1:
garden planted
March 21:
spring began

■ **To form the past-perfect tense, use *had* with the past participle of the main verb.**

Follow these rules:

- Add **-ed** to regular verbs to form the past participle.

Examples: **talk** We **had talked** about our garden before we planted it.

melt The ground was wet because the snow **had melted**.

- Some verbs are irregular. You have to learn the past participles of these verbs.

Examples: **break** We bought a new rake because we **had broken** our old one.

grow Many flowers **had grown** before I picked some of them.

Go To Practice K on page 397.

Using Verbs in Writing

Use colorful verbs to help your reader see what you are talking about.

Example: An icicle **fell** to the ground.
An icicle **crashed** to the ground.

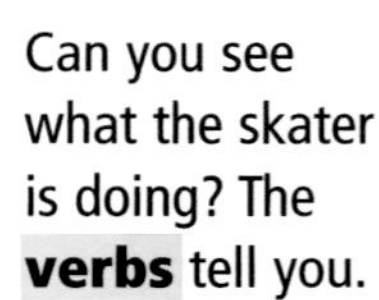

Can you see what the skater is doing? The **verbs** tell you.

ICY

I slip and I slide
On the slippery ice;
I skid and I glide—
Oh, isn't it nice
To lie on your tummy
And slither and skim
On the slick crust of snow
Where you skid as you swim?

—*Rhoda W. Bacmeister*

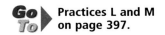

Go To Practices L and M on page 397.

Adverbs

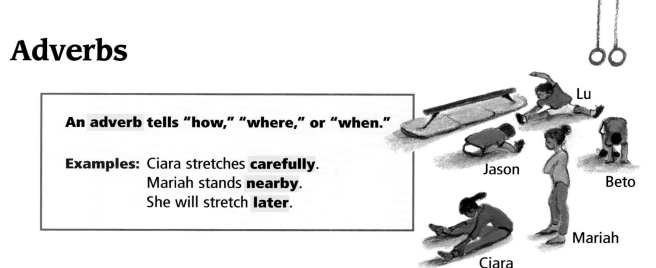

An adverb tells "how," "where," or "when."

Examples: Ciara stretches **carefully**.
Mariah stands **nearby**.
She will stretch **later**.

Using Adverbs

■ **Adverbs usually tell more about a verb.**

An **adverb** can come before or after a **verb**.

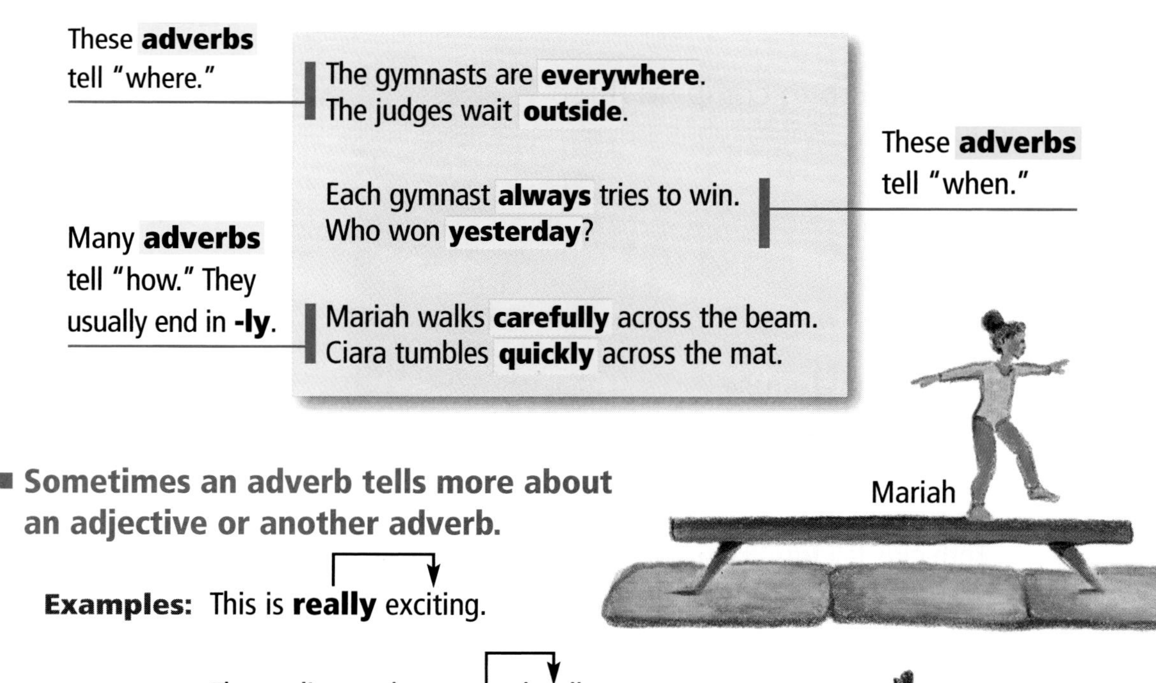

These **adverbs** tell "where."

The gymnasts are **everywhere**.
The judges wait **outside**.

These **adverbs** tell "when."

Each gymnast **always** tries to win.
Who won **yesterday**?

Many **adverbs** tell "how." They usually end in **-ly**.

Mariah walks **carefully** across the beam.
Ciara tumbles **quickly** across the mat.

■ **Sometimes an adverb tells more about an adjective or another adverb.**

Examples: This is **really** exciting.

The audience claps **very** loudly.

Using Adverbs to Compare

■ **You can use an adverb to compare actions.**

Lu jumps **high**.
Jason jumps **higher** than Lu.
Beto jumps the **highest** of all.

1. Add **-er** to an adverb to compare two actions. You'll probably use the word **than** in your sentence, too.
2. Add **-est** to an adverb to compare three or more actions.

3. If the adverb ends in **-ly**, use **more**, **most**, **less**, or **least** to compare the actions.

Examples: Ciara walks **more quickly** than Mariah.
Both girls fall **less frequently** than other gymnasts.

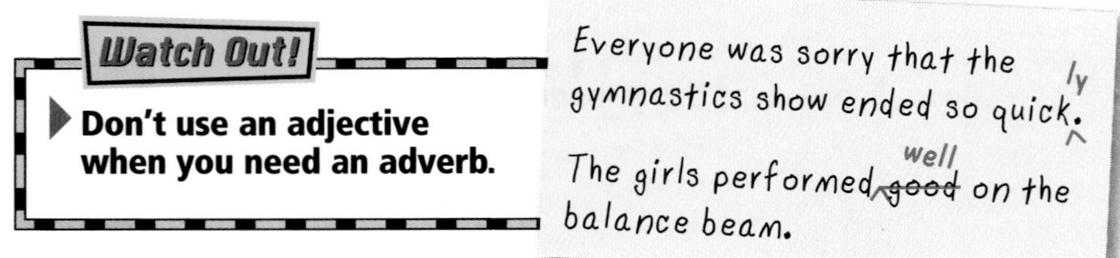

Watch Out!
Don't use an adjective when you need an adverb.
Everyone was sorry that the gymnastics show ended so quick. ly
The girls performed good well on the balance beam.

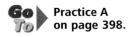

Go To Practice A on page 398.

Using Adverbs in Writing

Use adverbs to tell where, when, and how things happen. These important details will make your writing clear.

Example: Mariah walked **gracefully** across the balance beam.

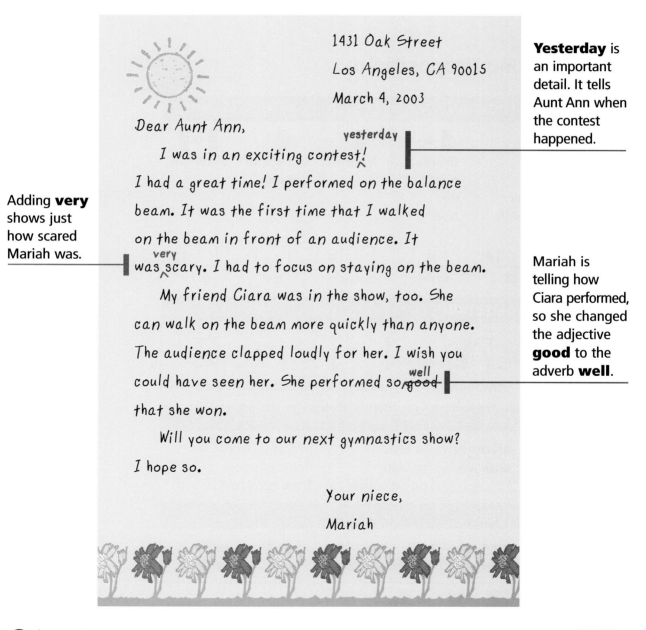

1431 Oak Street
Los Angeles, CA 90015
March 4, 2003

Dear Aunt Ann,

I was in an exciting contest ^yesterday! I had a great time! I performed on the balance beam. It was the first time that I walked on the beam in front of an audience. It was ^very scary. I had to focus on staying on the beam.

My friend Ciara was in the show, too. She can walk on the beam more quickly than anyone. The audience clapped loudly for her. I wish you could have seen her. She performed so ~~good~~ well that she won.

Will you come to our next gymnastics show? I hope so.

Your niece,
Mariah

Yesterday is an important detail. It tells Aunt Ann when the contest happened.

Adding **very** shows just how scared Mariah was.

Mariah is telling how Ciara performed, so she changed the adjective **good** to the adverb **well**.

Go To Practice B on page 398.

Prepositions

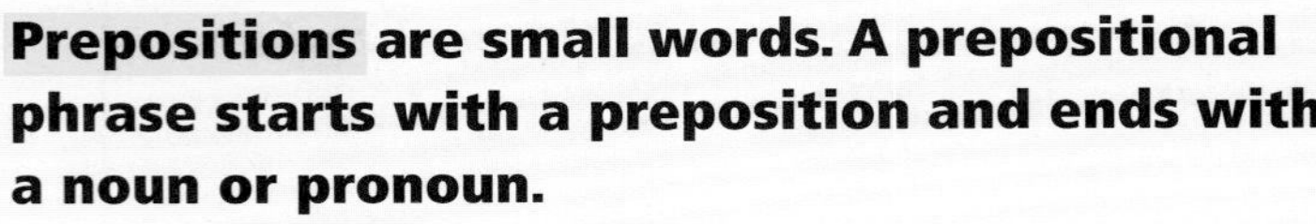
Prepositions are small words. A prepositional phrase starts with a preposition and ends with a noun or pronoun.

Example: Can you make a fish kite **with** green paper?

Ways to Use Prepositions

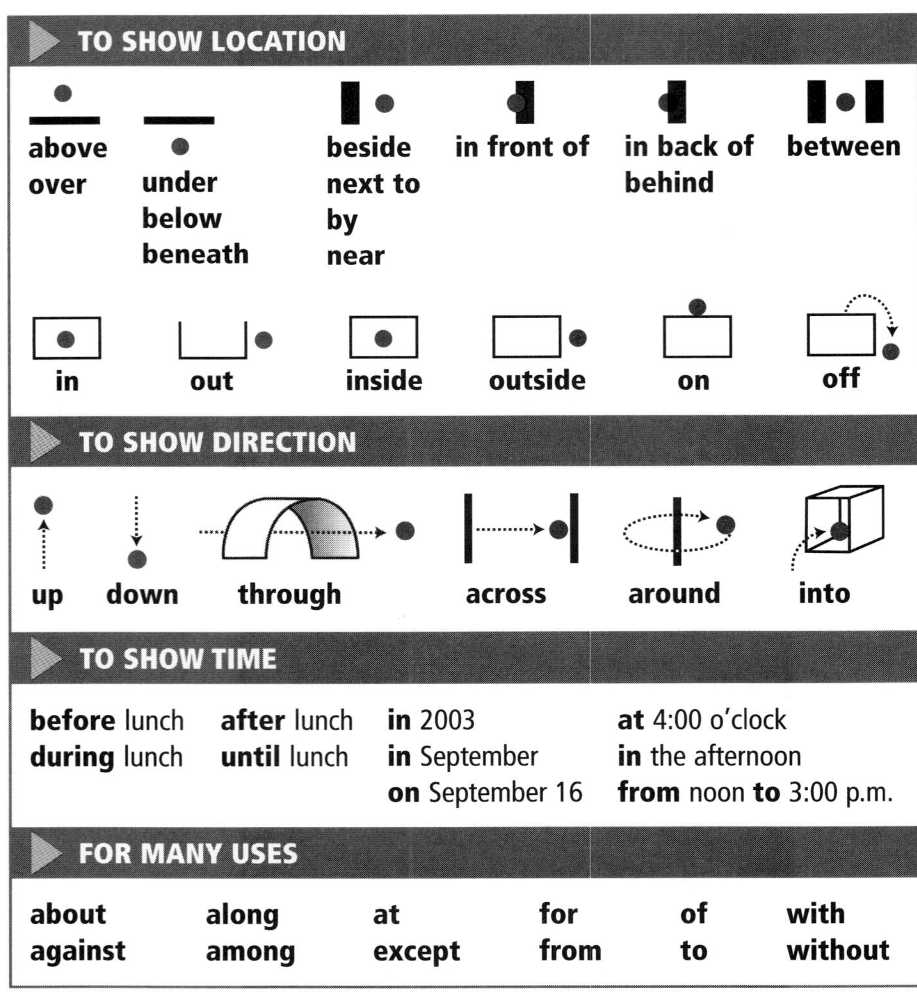

TO SHOW LOCATION

above over	under below beneath	beside next to by near	in front of	in back of behind	between
in	out	inside	outside	on	off

TO SHOW DIRECTION

up	down	through	across	around	into

TO SHOW TIME

before lunch	**after** lunch	**in** 2003	**at** 4:00 o'clock
during lunch	**until** lunch	**in** September	**in** the afternoon
		on September 16	**from** noon **to** 3:00 p.m.

FOR MANY USES

about	along	at	for	of	with
against	among	except	from	to	without

Go To Practices C, D, and E on pages 398–399.

Using Prepositions in Writing

Prepositional phrases add details to your writing.

Example: I will decorate my kite.
I will decorate my kite **with red dots**.

The information in these **prepositional phrases** helps the reader put the kite together correctly.

How to Make a Fish Kite

1. Fold a piece of tissue like this. Do not press the fold. Then, cut the paper in this shape. Unfold the paper.

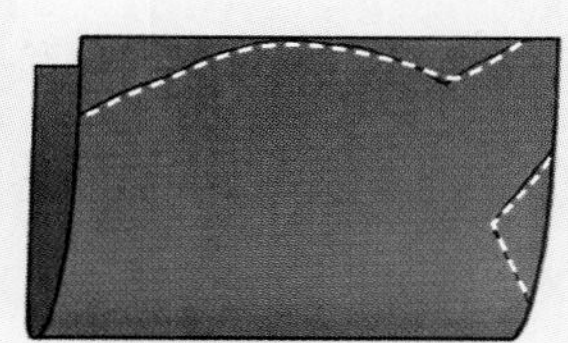

2. Add some glue in a line near the edge of the paper. Put a pipe cleaner by the glue and fold the paper over. Press it down.

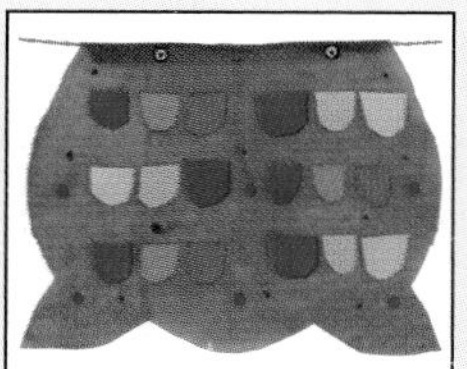

3. Turn the paper over and decorate the fish.

4. Bend the pipe cleaner into a circle and twist the ends together.

5. Glue the bottom edges of the fish together, but be sure to leave the tail end open.

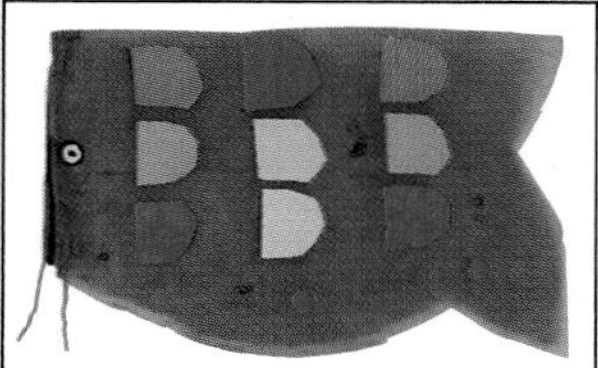

6. Tie a short string to the mouth like this.

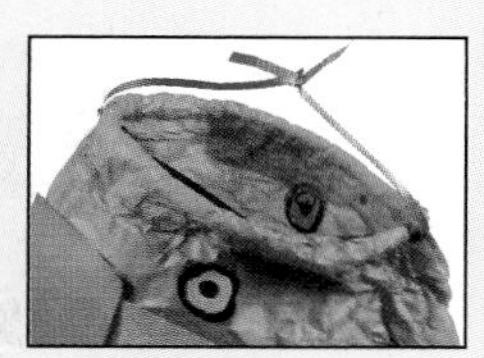

7. Tie the short string to a long string. Tie the long string to a long pole. Then take your fish outside and fly it!

Go To Practices F and G on page 399.

Interjections

Use an interjection to show feelings, like surprise.

Example: **Wow!** That was a great catch.

An interjection can be a word or a phrase.

Examples:	**Help!**	**Hooray!**	**Oh, boy!**	**Wow!**
	Hey!	**Oh!**	**Oops!**	**Yikes!**

A comma follows the interjection if it is part of a sentence. An exclamation point follows an interjection that stands alone.

Examples: **Hooray,** his catch saved a home run!
Oh, boy! Now our team can win.

Conjunctions

To connect words and sentences, use these conjunctions:

and **but** **or**

Example: The Tigers **and** the Eagles are playing today.

HOW TO USE CONJUNCTIONS	
When you want to put together two ideas that are alike, use **and**.	Keith Morrow can hit **and** run well. He hit the ball, **and** then he scored a run.
When you want to show a difference between two ideas, use **but**.	Mom likes the Tigers, **but** I like the Eagles.
When you want to show a choice between two ideas, use **or**.	Either the Tigers **or** the Eagles will be in first place after this game. Mom will be happy, **or** I will be!

Using Conjunctions in Writing

Use conjunctions to avoid short, choppy sentences.

Example:

Should we leave now? Should we stay? It's been raining for twenty minutes. Maybe it will stop soon.

Should we leave now, **or** should we stay? It's been raining for twenty minutes, **but** maybe it will stop soon.

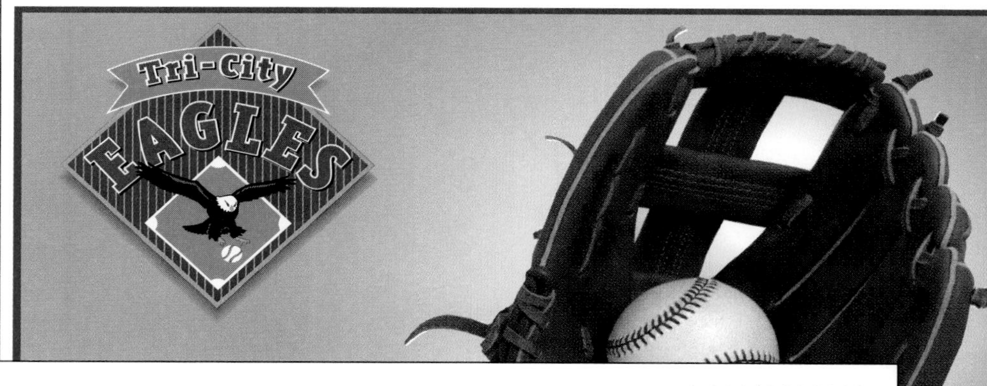

Dear Joey,

The baseball game was very close! My mom is a Tigers fan, but my favorite team is the Eagles. In the bottom of the ninth inning, the score was tied 2-2. The Eagles had one man on base, and Keith Morrow hit a fly into left field. Would it be a home run, or would the Tigers' outfielder catch the ball?

Can you guess? It was a home run, and the Eagles won!

Your friend,
Junji

Joey Hosaka
998 Sunset Lane, Apt. 3D
San Francisco, CA 94610

By joining these two sentences with **or**, the choice is easier to see.

Remember to use a comma before a conjunction in a compound sentence.

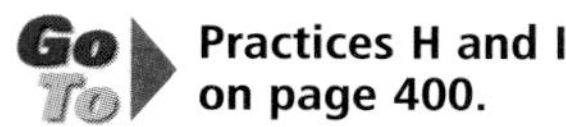
Practices H and I on page 400.

Capital Letters

A word that begins with a capital letter is special in some way.

Example: **The** name of this boat is ***Lucky Seas***.

LUCKY SEAS

Ride on *Lucky Seas!*

Come with us and see big, beautiful whales. The boat leaves every day at 8:00 a.m.

Meet us at pier 9.

- **A capital letter shows where a sentence begins.**
- **When you talk about yourself, use the capital letter *I*.**

Oh, I see the boat.
Soon, you and I will be watching whales!

■ **The name of a person begins with a capital letter.**

Begin all **first and last names** with a capital letter.

Capitalize an **initial** in a name.

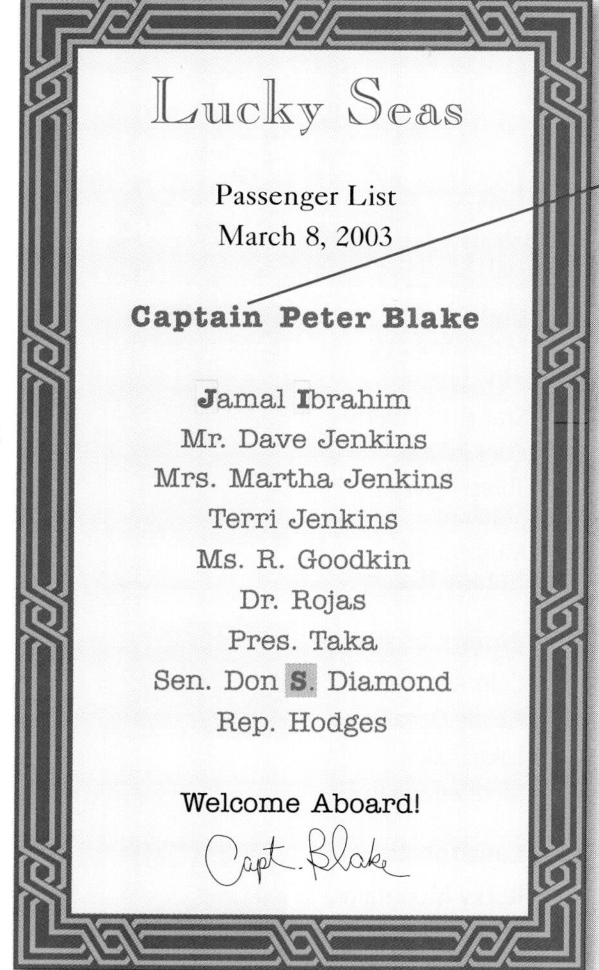

Lucky Seas
Passenger List
March 8, 2003
Captain Peter Blake
Jamal Ibrahim
Mr. Dave Jenkins
Mrs. Martha Jenkins
Terri Jenkins
Ms. R. Goodkin
Dr. Rojas
Pres. Taka
Sen. Don S. Diamond
Rep. Hodges
Welcome Aboard!
Capt. Blake

Capitalize a **title** when it is used with a name.

Sometimes the title is **abbreviated**, or made shorter. Use these abbreviations:

Mr. for a man

Mrs. for a married woman

Ms. for any woman

Dr. for a doctor

Pres. for the president of a country, a company, a club, or an organization

Sen. for a member of the U.S. Senate

Rep. for a member of the U.S. House of Representatives

Capt. for a captain

Watch Out!

▶ **Do not capitalize a title when it is used without a name.**

I'm Mike Hardin. I work with the **captain**.

▶ **Capitalize words like *Mom* and *Dad* when they are used as names.**

Hey, **Mom**! Come meet Mike. Mike, I'd like you to meet **my mom**.

Go To ▶ Practice A on page 400.

Capital Letters, continued

- **The important words in the name of a special place or thing begin with a capital letter.**

Where do you travel on the Lucky Seas?

We go out of San Francisco Bay to the Pacific Ocean.

NAMES OF SPECIAL PLACES AND THINGS

Streets and Roads

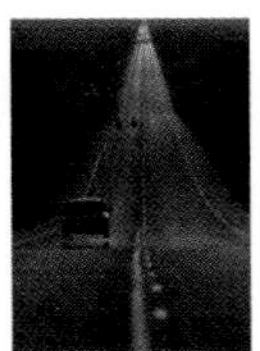

King Boulevard
Avenue M
First Street
Simmons Expressway

Cities

New York City
Houston
Los Angeles

States

New York
Texas
California

Countries

Vietnam
Ecuador
France

Continents

Asia
South America
Australia

Buildings, Monuments, and Ships

Statue of Liberty
Lucky Seas
Three Rivers Stadium
Museum of Natural History

Bodies of Water

Colorado River
Pacific Ocean
Lake Baikal
Mediterranean Sea

Landforms

Rocky Mountains
Sahara Desert
Grand Canyon

Public Spaces

Mesa Verde National Park
Central Park
Arapaho National Forest

Planets and Heavenly Bodies

Earth
Jupiter
Milky Way

Watch Out!

Capitalize an adjective if it comes from the name of a special place.

Mike is from **Canada**.
He is a **Canadian** sailor.

Go To Practice B on page 401.

When you write the **abbreviation**, or short form, of a place name, use a capital letter.

Dear Kim,

Hello from California. We went whale watching today. Did you know some gray whales are over 40 feet long? I really liked it when they came up for air— I could see their spouts. I'll show you some pictures when I get home.

Your friend,
Jamal

Kim Messina
10250 W. Fourth St.
Las Vegas, NV 89015

ABBREVIATED PLACE NAMES

For State Names on Letters and Cards That Are Mailed

AL	Alabama	**MT**	Montana
AK	Alaska	**NE**	Nebraska
AZ	Arizona	**NV**	Nevada
AR	Arkansas	**NH**	New Hampshire
CA	California	**NJ**	New Jersey
CO	Colorado	**NM**	New Mexico
CT	Connecticut	**NY**	New York
DE	Delaware	**NC**	North Carolina
FL	Florida	**ND**	North Dakota
GA	Georgia	**OH**	Ohio
HI	Hawaii	**OK**	Oklahoma
ID	Idaho	**OR**	Oregon
IL	Illinois	**PA**	Pennsylvania
IN	Indiana	**RI**	Rhode Island
IA	Iowa	**SC**	South Carolina
KS	Kansas	**SD**	South Dakota
KY	Kentucky	**TN**	Tennessee
LA	Louisiana	**TX**	Texas
ME	Maine	**UT**	Utah
MD	Maryland	**VT**	Vermont
MA	Massachusetts	**VA**	Virginia
MI	Michigan	**WA**	Washington
MN	Minnesota	**WV**	West Virginia
MS	Mississippi	**WI**	Wisconsin
MO	Missouri	**WY**	Wyoming

For Words Used in Addresses

Ave.	Avenue
Blvd.	Boulevard
Ct.	Court
Dr.	Drive
E.	East
Hwy.	Highway
Ln.	Lane
N.	North
Pl.	Place
Rd.	Road
S.	South
Sq.	Square
St.	Street
W.	West

Capital Letters, continued

- **The first word and all important words in the name of an organization begin with a capital letter.**

NAMES OF ORGANIZATIONS

Clubs
Whale Watcher's Club at Monterey Bay
Girl Scouts of America

World Organizations
International Whaling Commission
United Nations

Sports Teams
Los Angeles Dodgers
Seattle Supersonics

Professional Groups
American Medical Association
Professional Golfers' Association

Political Parties
Democratic Party
Republican Party

Businesses
Sal's Camera Shop
Little Taco House

© 1993 Sea World, Inc.

- **Names of the months, days of the week, and special days and holidays begin with a capital letter.**

If you abbreviate one of these names, begin the abbreviation with a capital letter and end it with a period.

MONTHS AND DAYS

Months of the Year		Days of the Week		Special Days and Holidays
January	Jan.	**Sunday**	Sun.	April Fool's Day
February	Feb.	**Monday**	Mon.	Christmas
March	Mar.	**Tuesday**	Tues.	Earth Day
April	Apr.	**Wednesday**	Wed.	Graduation Day
May	*These months*	**Thursday**	Thurs.	Hanukkah
June	*are never*	**Friday**	Fri.	Kwanzaa
July	*abbreviated.*	**Saturday**	Sat.	Labor Day
August	Aug.			New Year's Day
September	Sept.			Thanksgiving
October	Oct.			
November	Nov.			
December	Dec.			

Watch Out!
The names of seasons do not start with a capital letter.
In spring, the whales go north.
In fall, they go south.

Go To Practice C on page 401.

■ **The important words in a title begin with a capital letter.**

What has a title? Books, magazines, newspapers, and all kinds of written works have titles. So do multimedia works like movies, computer programs, TV shows, and videos. Stories, poems, and songs have titles, too.

Meet a Majestic Sea Mammal

By Sarah O'Neal

Whales are gigantic animals that live in the oceans and seas of the world. Dr. Gregory Pratt knows. He has just published ***The Largest Mammals on the Planet***. In it, he explains that whales look like fish but are really mammals. On a recent segment of the television show ***Nature Hour***, Dr. Pratt said, "Like other mammals, whales have well-developed brains. Unlike fish, whales are warm-blooded and their babies are born alive."

According to Dr. Pratt, the respiratory system of whales clearly makes them mammals. He said, "All mammals have lungs. Whales, therefore, must regularly come to the surface of the water to breathe. But, unlike humans, whales can go for 40 minutes or longer without breathing."

Little words like **a**, **an**, **the**, **in**, **at**, **of**, and **for** are not capitalized unless they are the first word in the **title**.

■ **When a person's exact words appear in print, the first word begins with a capital letter.**

Go To Practice D on page 402.

Punctuation Marks

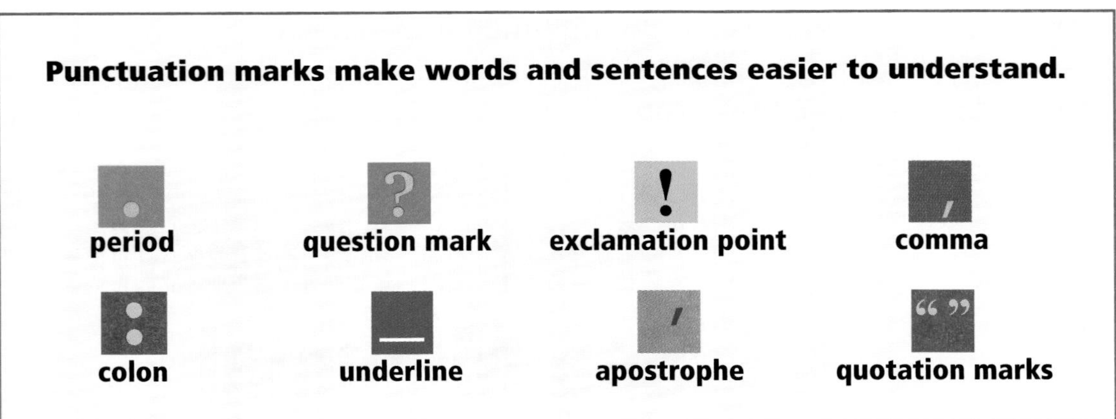

Sentence Punctuation

- **Always use a punctuation mark at the end of a sentence. It gives important information.**

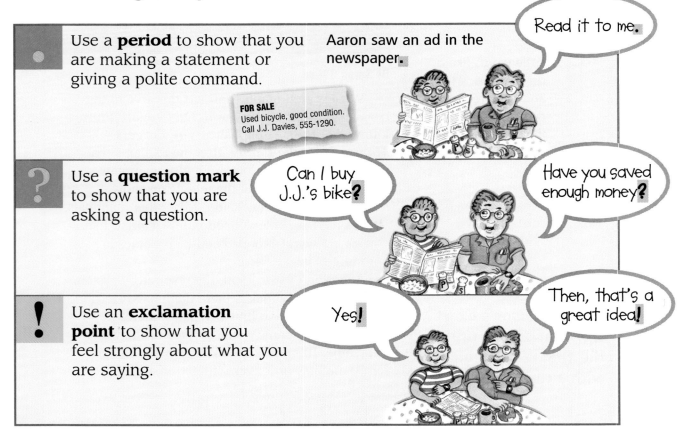

Use a **period** to show that you are making a statement or giving a polite command.

Aaron saw an ad in the newspaper.

Read it to me.

FOR SALE
Used bicycle, good condition.
Call J.J. Davies, 555-1290.

Use a **question mark** to show that you are asking a question.

Can I buy J.J.'s bike?

Have you saved enough money?

Use an **exclamation point** to show that you feel strongly about what you are saying.

Yes!

Then, that's a great idea!

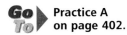

Go To Practice A on page 402.

More Ways to Use a Period

.	Use a **period** after an initial or an abbreviation.	Aaron called J.J. Mrs. Davies answered the phone.
.	Use a **period** to separate dollars and cents. The period is the decimal point.	Mrs. Davies told Aaron the bike cost $55.00 and no less. Aaron had exactly $50.40 and no more.

The Comma

,	Use **commas** to separate three or more items in a series	Aaron needs 4 dollars, 2 quarters, and one dime after all. He could clean the kitchen, the closet, and the bathroom. He could take out the trash, walk some dogs, or sweep the steps.
,	Use **commas** when you write large numbers.	Aaron has taken out the trash 1,000,000 times, so he decides to walk Mrs. Romero's dog. It weighs 1,200 pounds!

Commas have important uses in a letter. How many can you find?

177 North Avenue
New York, NY 10033

October 3, 2003

Dear Mrs. Romero,

I am saving money to buy a bicycle. Can I walk Brute for you? I know that most people pay $.25 to walk a dog, but Brute is big! Can you pay me $5.00?

I will take good care of Brute. I like him even though he is bigger than I am!

Thank you.

Sincerely,

Aaron

Use a comma:

- between the city and the state
- between the date and the year
- after the greeting, or "hello" part, of a friendly letter
- after the closing, or "good-bye" part, of the letter

The Comma, continued

Use **commas** to set off certain words in a sentence.

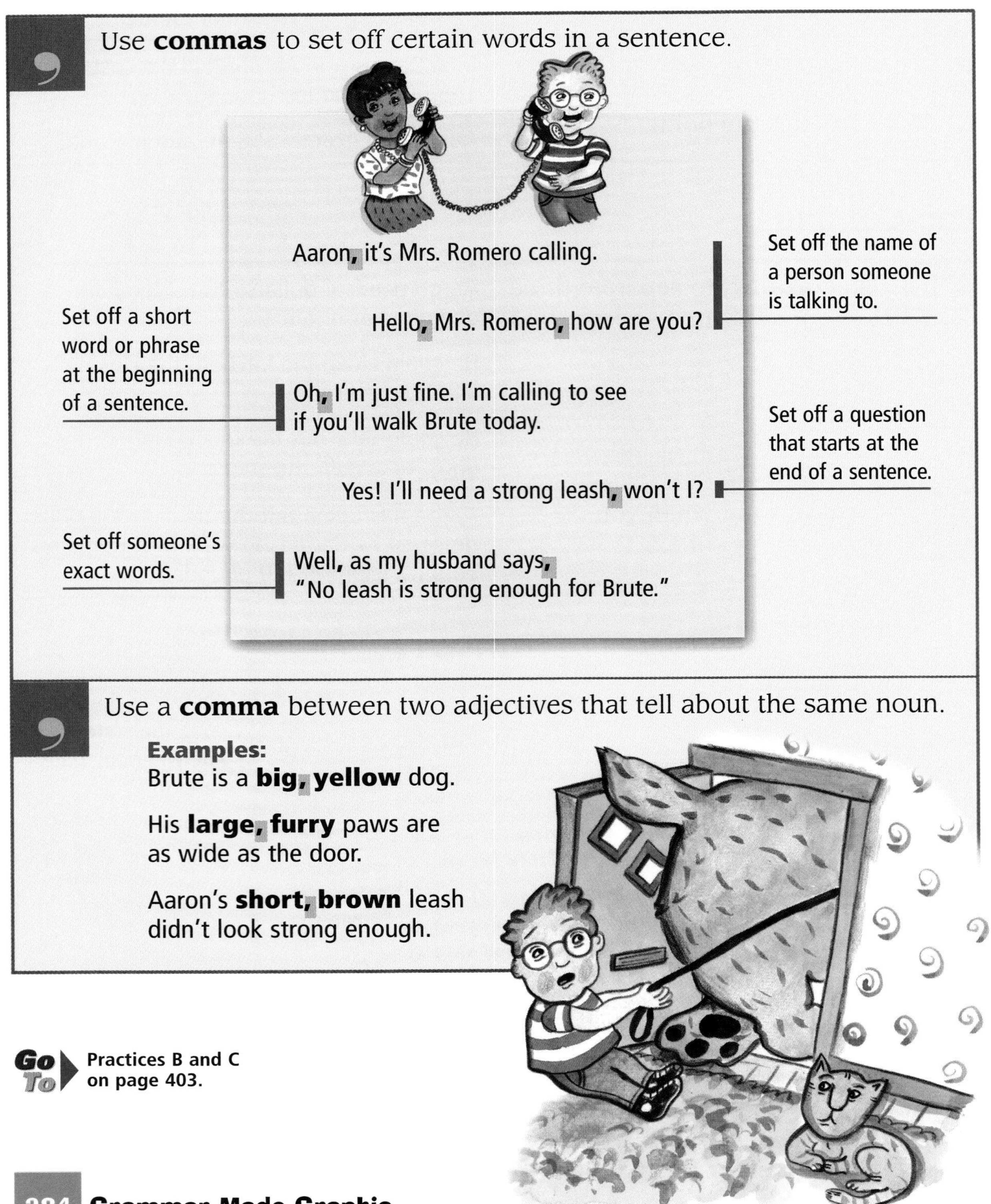

Aaron, it's Mrs. Romero calling.

Hello, Mrs. Romero, how are you?

Set off the name of a person someone is talking to.

Set off a short word or phrase at the beginning of a sentence.

Oh, I'm just fine. I'm calling to see if you'll walk Brute today.

Yes! I'll need a strong leash, won't I?

Set off a question that starts at the end of a sentence.

Set off someone's exact words.

Well, as my husband says, "No leash is strong enough for Brute."

Use a **comma** between two adjectives that tell about the same noun.

Examples:

Brute is a **big, yellow** dog.

His **large, furry** paws are as wide as the door.

Aaron's **short, brown** leash didn't look strong enough.

Go To Practices B and C on page 403.

Use a **comma** before **and**, **but**, or **or** in a compound sentence.

Examples:

Brute was big, **and** Aaron could hardly control him.

Aaron tried to stop Brute, **but** he ran right into Mr. Sayeed's deli.

Boxes either flew out, **or** they got crushed.

Apples went everywhere, **and** a newspaper rack fell down.

Mr. Sayeed was calm, **but** he told Brute he was a bad dog.

179 North Avenue
New York, NY 10033
October 4, 2003

Mr. Omar Sayeed
Sayeed Deli
686 Fifth Street
New York, NY 10033

Dear Mr. Sayeed:

Yesterday, at about 10:30, my neighbor Aaron Jackson took my dog Brute for a walk. Brute is a large dog, and Aaron had some trouble controlling him. Aaron told me that Brute did three bad things:

1. He ate two cartons of apples.
2. He stepped on a customer.
3. He knocked over one newspaper rack.

Aaron said that he apologized to the customer. How much do I owe you for the apples and the rack?

Please accept my apologies. Next time, I will have two boys walk Brute. Or, maybe three!

Sincerely,
Electra Romero
Electra Romero

The Colon

Use a **colon**:

- after the greeting in a business letter
- to separate hours and minutes
- to start a list

The Apostrophe

In a contraction, or shortened form of two words, an **apostrophe** shows that one or more letters have been left out.

	Aaron got $5.00 for walking Brute.
He's = **He is**	**He's** happy now.
I'll = **I will**	"**I'll** go over to see J.J.," said Aaron.
hasn't = **has not**	"I hope he **hasn't** sold the bike."

An **apostrophe** can also show that someone or something owns something.

Use **'s** when one person owns something.	Aaron and his dad look at each building**'s** number. Aaron**'s** heart is pounding.
Use **s'** to show that two or more people own something.	Two boys ride by. The boy**s'** bikes are neat!
If the plural noun does not end in **s**, use **'s**.	A girl rides by. All the children**'s** bikes are neat!

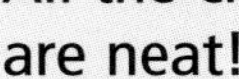

Practice D on page 404.

Underline

If J.J. has sold his bike, I'll look in The Daily News and find another bike for sale.

Underline the titles of books, magazines, and newspapers.

Quotation Marks

Put **quotation marks** around the title of a:

- song, poem, or short story
- magazine article or newspaper article
- chapter from a book

Aaron sang "Let It Be Mine" as he walked up to J.J.'s apartment building.

“ ” Use **quotation marks** around words you copy from a book or other printed material.

The words in the ad were "used bicycle, good condition."

“ ” Use **quotation marks** to show a speaker's exact words.

Aaron knocked on J.J.'s door and said to his dad, "I hope the bike is in really good condition."

"We'll see," said his dad.

Just then a boy opened the door and said, "Hello, I'm J.J. How are you?"

"I'm great," Aaron said. "Can I see your bike? I brought enough money to buy it."

"Sure," J.J. said. "It's a cool bike."

"It sure is," Aaron said happily.

"We'll take it," his dad said. Aaron handed J.J. the money.

"Thank you and enjoy the bike!" J.J. shouted.

"I will! See you later, Dad!" Aaron yelled as he rode off to buy a cookie with the 40¢ he had left.

A new paragraph begins each time the speaker changes.

Practice E on page 404.

Chapter 6
Look It Up!

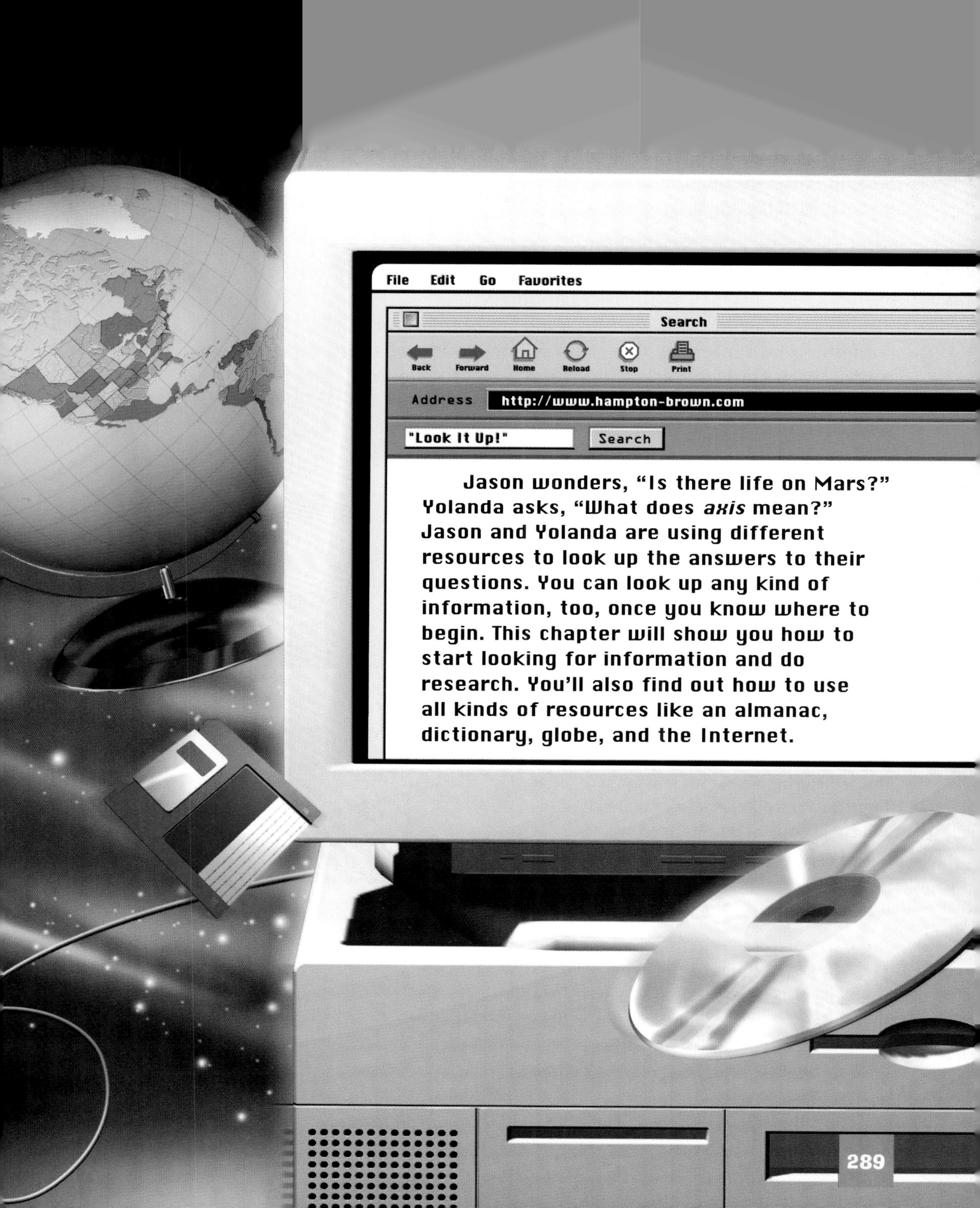

Jason wonders, "Is there life on Mars?" Yolanda asks, "What does *axis* mean?" Jason and Yolanda are using different resources to look up the answers to their questions. You can look up any kind of information, too, once you know where to begin. This chapter will show you how to start looking for information and do research. You'll also find out how to use all kinds of resources like an almanac, dictionary, globe, and the Internet.

The Research Process

When you **research**, you look up information about a topic. You can use the information you find to write a story, article, book, or research report.

STEP 1 Choose a Topic

Think of something you want to learn more about and something that interests you. That will be your research **topic**. Make sure you pick a topic that is not too general. A specific, or smaller, topic is easier to research and to write about. It is also more interesting to read about in a report.

Outer Space
This is a big topic! There are a lot of things in outer space: stars, suns, planets, moons, and black holes. That would be too much to research or write about in one report.

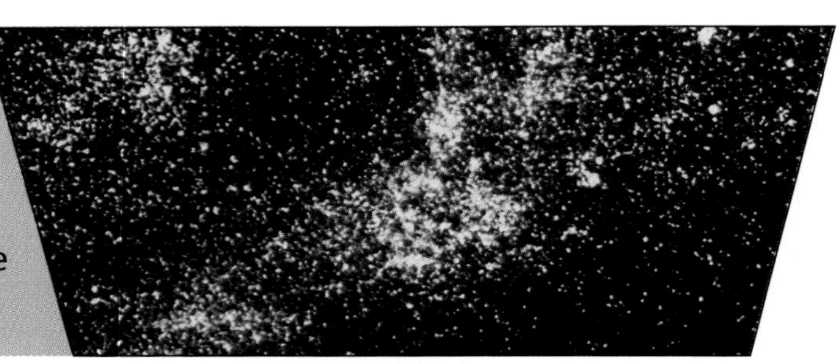

Planets
This topic is better, but it's still too big. There are nine planets in our solar system! You could do a report on the planet Mars. But what is it you want to know about Mars?

Life on Mars
The topic "Life on Mars" is more specific than "Mars." Finding out if Mars has water, plants, animals, or Martians could be VERY interesting!

STEP

2 Decide What to Look Up

What do you already know about your topic? What do you want to know about it? Make a **KWLQ chart** for your research.

KWLQ Chart

Topic: Life on Mars

K What Do I Know?	W What Do I Want to Learn?	L What Did I Learn?	Q What Questions Do I Still Have?
There's life on Earth but no life on the moon. Mars is a planet like Earth. Scientists are studying Mars.	Is there life on Mars? How is our planet similar to Mars? What else do scientists know about Mars? How do they know?	You will fill out these two columns after you do your research.	

Look at the most important words in your questions. Those are **key words** you can look up when you start your research.

STEP
3 Locate Resources

Now that you know what to look up, you can use different **resources** to find information about your topic. Resources can be **experts**, or people who know a lot about a topic. Resources can also be nonfiction books, textbooks, magazines, newspapers, or the Internet. You can find resources all around you.

Expert

Nonfiction Books

Magazines and Newspapers

Encyclopedia

Dictionary

Almanac

Atlas

Internet

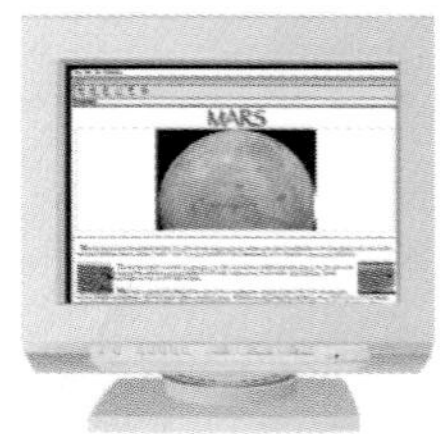

Pages 312–338 for more information on each of these resources.

- Think about your research questions. Some resources may be more helpful than others, depending on what kind of information you need about your topic.
  - Do you need to look up facts or scientific data?
  - Do you want to know about something that happened recently?
  - Are you interested in someone's opinion or experience?
  - Do you want to see pictures?

These questions will help you decide which resources to use.

- Whatever your topic is, try exploring the library first. There you'll discover a world of resources and information!

Go To **The Library** on pages 294–295.

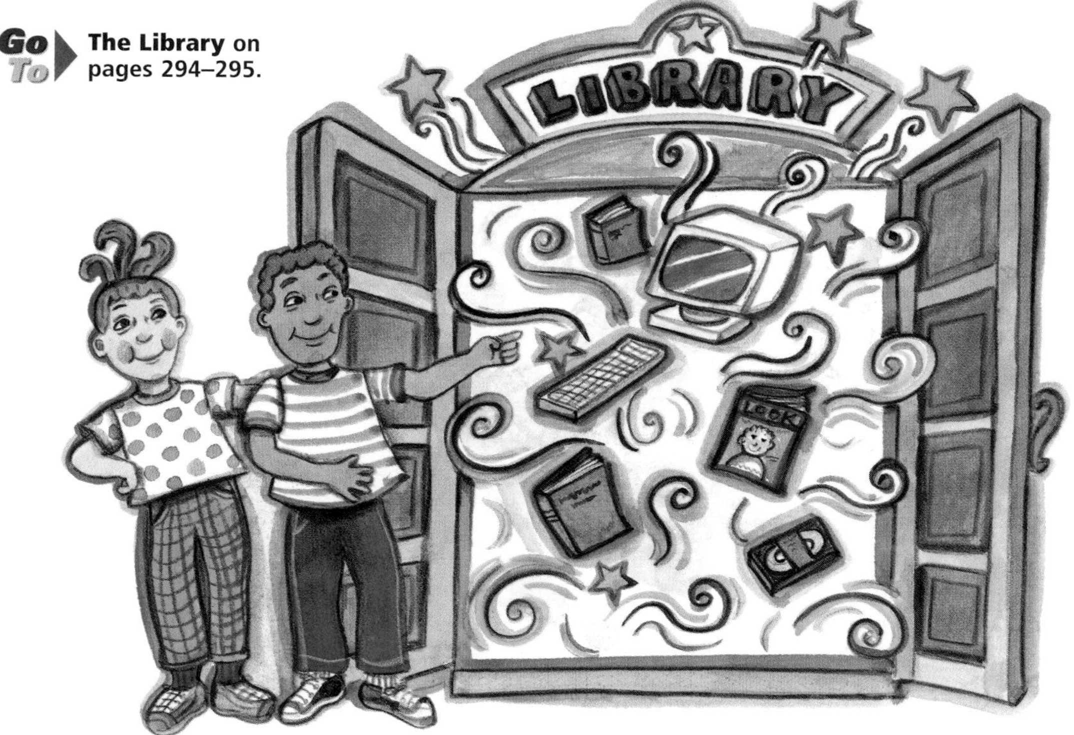

The Library

A **library** is a place full of books and other kinds of resources like videos, magazines, and newspapers. It's organized in a special way so you can find things easily.

Reference Section
The **Reference Section** has lots of special resources. You can't check out reference books like these, but you can make copies of pages or articles.

Atlas

Information Desk
If you can't find what you're looking for, you can ask a **librarian**. The librarian will usually be at the **Information Desk**.

Fiction
One section of the library has all of the **fiction** books. These are stories that are not true. You may find stories here about life on Mars, but they won't be true.

Nonfiction
In the **nonfiction** section, there are books that have **facts** about all kinds of topics.

Children's Room
The **Children's Room** is full of books and magazines especially for kids.

Almanac

Encyclopedia

Dictionary

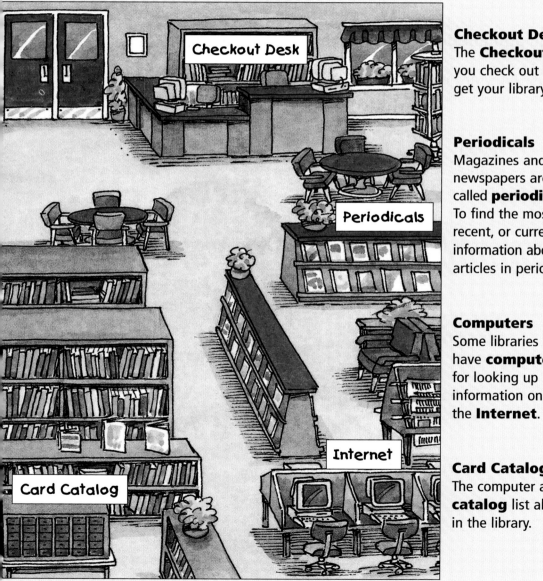

Checkout Desk

The **Checkout Desk** is where you check out books. You can get your library card here, too.

Periodicals

Magazines and newspapers are called **periodicals**. To find the most recent, or current, information about a topic, look for articles in periodicals.

Computers

Some libraries have **computers** for looking up information on the **Internet**.

Card Catalog

The computer and **card catalog** list all the books in the library.

The Resources section on pages 306–338 to find out more about the library and special resources.

The Research Process, continued

STEP

4 Gather Information

When you **gather information**, you find the best resources for your topic. You look up your key words to find facts about your topic. Then you take notes.

How to Find Information Quickly

■ **Use alphabetical order to look up words.**

In many resources, the words, titles, and subjects are listed in **alphabetical order**.

Look at these words. They are in order by the **first** letter of each word.

asteroid
moon
planet
sun

If the word you are looking up has the same first letter as other words in the list, look at the **second** letters.

Mars
Mercury
mission
moon

If the word you are looking up has the same first and second letters as others in the list, look at the **third** letters.

magnetic
map
Mars
mass

■ Skim and scan the text to decide if it is useful.

When you **skim** and **scan**, you look at text quickly to see if it has the information you need. If it does, then you can take the time to read it more carefully. If it doesn't, you can go on to another source.

To Skim:

Read the **title** to see if the article is useful for your topic.

Read the **beginning sentences** and **headings** to find out more about an article's topic.

Skim the **ending**. It often sums up all the ideas in the article.

To Scan:

Look for **key words** or **details** in dark type or italics. If you find key words that go with your topic, you'll probably want to read the article.

PLANETS, STARS, AND SPACE TRAVEL

LOOKING FOR LIFE ELSEWHERE IN THE UNIVERSE

For years scientists have been trying to discover if there is life on other planets in our solar system or life elsewhere in the universe. Some scientists have been looking for evidence based on what is necessary for life on Earth—basics like water and proper temperature.

WHAT SCIENTISTS HAVE LEARNED SO FAR

Mars and Jupiter. In 1996, two teams of scientists examined two meteorites that may have come from **Mars** and found evidence that some form of life may have existed on Mars billions of years ago. In 1997, in photographs of Europa, a moon of **Jupiter**, scientists saw areas with icy ridges and areas without ice. It seemed that underneath the ice there might be water—one of the essentials of life.

New Planets. In 1996, astronomers believed they found several new planets traveling around stars very far away (many light-years away) from our sun. Scientists do not think life exists on these planets, because they are so close to their sun that they would be too hot. But scientists are hoping to find other stars with planets around them that might support life.

AND THE SEARCH CONTINUES

NASA (the National Aeronautics and Space Administration) has a program to look for life on Mars. Ten spacecraft are to be sent to Mars over the next ten years. Some will fly around Mars taking pictures, while others will land on Mars to study the soil and rocks and look for living things. The first two, *Mars Pathfinder* and *Mars Global Surveyor*, launched in 1996, were scheduled to reach Mars in 1997.

Another program that searches for life on other worlds is called **SETI**. SETI (an acronym for Search for Extraterrestrial Intelligence) uses powerful radio telescopes to look for life elsewhere in the universe.

Question: Is there life elsewhere in the universe? **Answer:** No one knows yet.

STEP

4 Gather Information, continued

How to Take Notes

Notes are important words, phrases, and ideas that you write while you are reading and researching. Your notes will help you remember **details**. They'll also help you remember the **source**. The source is where you got the information.

- **Write notes in your own words.**

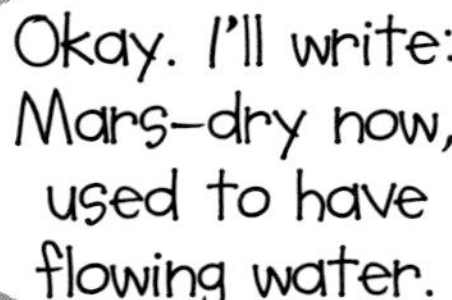

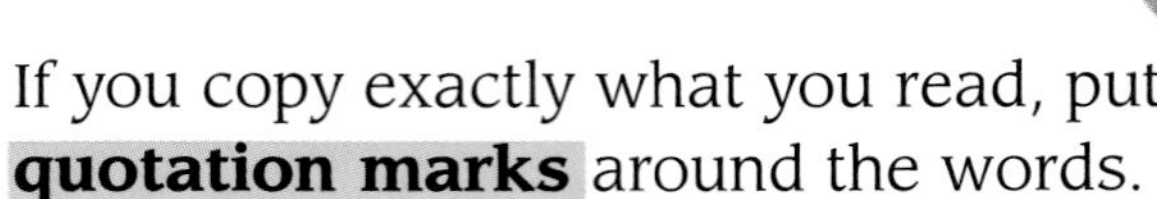

If you copy exactly what you read, put **quotation marks** around the words.

Is there water on Mars?

Mars by Seymour Simon, page 28

— "Mars may look dry as dust, but water once flowed over the surface."

■ **Set up your notecards like these so you can easily put your information in order when you write.**

Notecard for a Book

Include your **research question**.

Write down the **source** so you can remember where you found your facts. List the **title**, **author**, and **page number**.

What do we know about Mars?

Mars by Seymour Simon, page 27

— Viking spacecraft supposed to find out if there's life

— some think experiments showed there isn't

— others believe experiments were the wrong kind; maybe scientists looked in wrong places

List **details** and **facts** in your own words.

Notecard for a Magazine or Newspaper

List the **name**, **date**, **volume**, and **issue number** of your **source**. Also write the name of the article in quotation marks.

What do we know about Mars?

Time for Kids, Sept. 13, 1996 Vol. 2, No. 1

"Next stop: Mars"

— Mars has some features like Earth.

"It has volcanoes and giant canyons."

— hard to prove life, but maybe space missions like Pathfinder can find something

Include your **research question**.

Use **quotation marks for exact words** you copy from a source.

■ **What can you *conclude*, or decide, from your notes? What new questions do you have? Write them.**

We don't know if there's life on Mars now, but was there long ago?

STEP
5 Organize Information

Make an Outline

Follow these steps to turn your notes into an outline. Your outline will then help you write your report.

1 Put all the notecards with the same research question together.

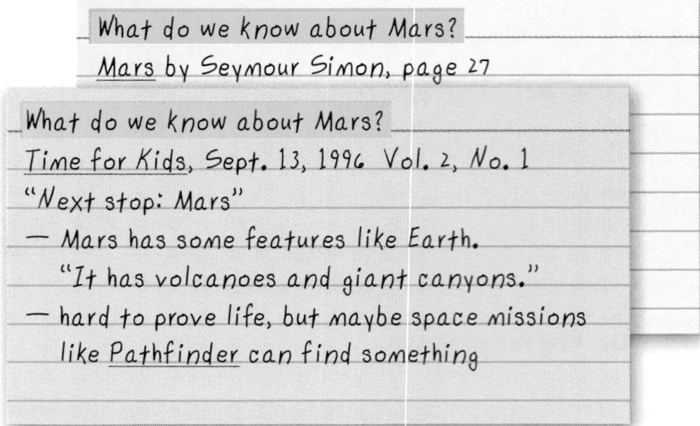

2 Turn your notes into an outline.

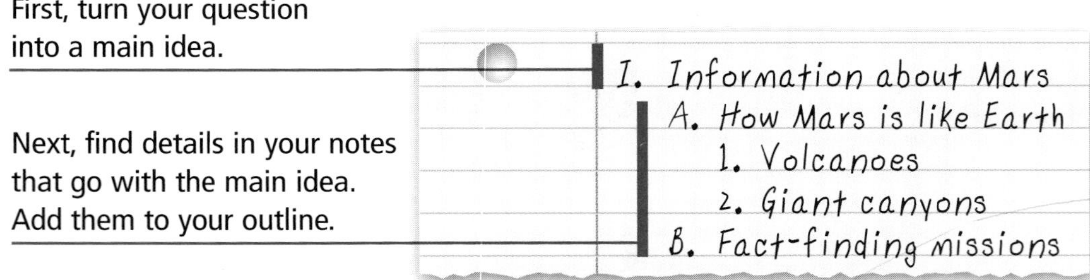

First, turn your question into a main idea.
Next, find details in your notes that go with the main idea. Add them to your outline.
I. Information about Mars
A. How Mars is like Earth
1. Volcanoes
2. Giant canyons
B. Fact-finding missions

3 Write a title for your outline.

Mars: Is Anyone Up There?

Here's an outline for a research report about life on Mars.

The **title** tells what your outline is all about. You can use it again when you write your report.

Each **main idea** follows a Roman numeral.

Each **detail** follows a capital letter. Each **related detail** follows a number.

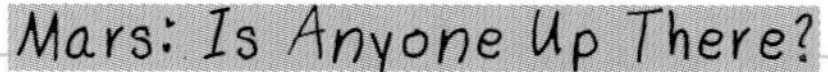

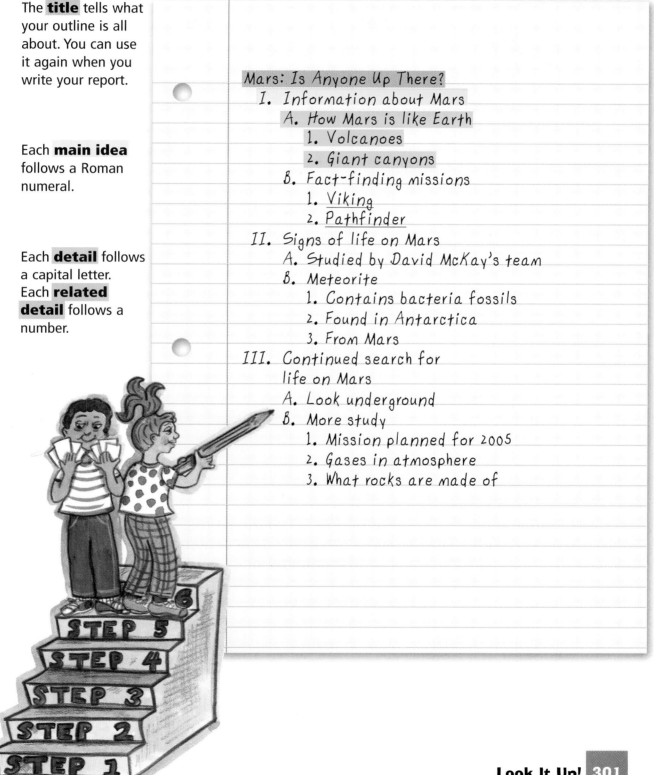

Mars: Is Anyone Up There?

I. Information about Mars
   A. How Mars is like Earth
      1. Volcanoes
      2. Giant canyons
   B. Fact-finding missions
      1. *Viking*
      2. *Pathfinder*

II. Signs of life on Mars
   A. Studied by David McKay's team
   B. Meteorite
      1. Contains bacteria fossils
      2. Found in Antarctica
      3. From Mars

III. Continued search for life on Mars
   A. Look underground
   B. More study
      1. Mission planned for 2005
      2. Gases in atmosphere
      3. What rocks are made of

STEP 6 Write a Research Report

Once you've finished your outline, you're ready to write a **research report**. Turn the main ideas and details from your outline into sentences and paragraphs.

1 Write the title from your outline and an introduction.

The title and introduction should tell what your report is mostly about and should be interesting to your readers.

Outline

Mars: Is Anyone Up There?

Title and Introduction

Mars: Is Anyone Up There?

You've probably seen some pretty creepy outer-space creatures in movies and TV. Are there really living beings up there? People have always wondered if there is life on any other planet, especially Mars.

2 Turn your first main idea into a topic sentence for the next paragraph.

Look at Roman numeral I on your outline. Turn the words into a sentence with a subject and a predicate. That sentence will be the topic sentence for your first paragraph.

Outline

I. Information about Mars

Topic Sentence

We are learning new information about Mars all the time.

3 Turn the details and related details into sentences.

Look at the letters and numbers on your outline. Turn those words into sentences that tell more about the main idea. Add them to your paragraph.

Outline

I. Information about Mars
   A. How Mars is like Earth
      1. Volcanoes
      2. Giant canyons
   B. Fact-finding missions
      1. Viking
      2. Pathfinder

Topic Sentence and Supporting Details

We are learning new information about Mars all the time. We know that Mars is similar to Earth with features like volcanoes and giant canyons, so it's possible that there is life on Mars. There are lots of missions to Mars like the spacecrafts Viking and Pathfinder, so it seems like we might find out soon!

4 Follow steps 2 and 3 to write the other paragraphs for your report.

5 Write a conclusion to sum up your report.

Look back at all the main ideas on your outline. Write a sentence for each main idea to include in the last paragraph of your report. The last paragraph is a summary of the most important information about your topic.

Outline

I. Information about Mars

II. Signs of life on Mars

III. Continued search for life on Mars

Conclusion

Basically, no one knows if there is or isn't life on Mars. It is possible that life does or did exist there. Spacecraft that go to Mars in the future will give us more proof. Hopefully, the mystery will be solved soon.

STEP 6 Write a Research Report, continued

A good **research report** gives facts about a topic in an organized and interesting way.

The **title** and introduction tell what your report is about. They get your reader interested.

The **body** of the report presents the facts you found. Each paragraph goes with one main idea from your outline.

Mars: Is Anyone Up There?

You've probably seen some pretty creepy outer-space creatures in movies and TV. Are there really living beings up there? People have always wondered if there is life on any other planet, especially Mars.

We are learning new information about Mars all the time. We know that Mars is similar to Earth with features like volcanoes and giant canyons, so it's possible that there is life on Mars. There are lots of missions to Mars like the spacecrafts Viking and Pathfinder, so it seems like we might find out soon!

Recently, David McKay and his team of scientists discovered possible signs of ancient Martian life. They found bacteria fossils inside a meteorite that crashed into Antarctica thousands of years ago. They know the meteorite is from Mars because it has the same chemicals in it as the Martian atmosphere. They believe the fossils, which are a lot smaller than the width of a human hair, were alive on Mars from 3 to 4 billion years ago. At that time, there was flowing water on the planet. McKay's team does not think that the bacteria could have gotten into the meteorite after it fell, because the fossils were so far deep in the center of the meteorite.

No one has seen a live Martian, but some scientists feel that we need to keep looking. Since no one has found water on the surface of Mars, maybe Martians live underground where there is water. A mission to look for Martian life and bring soil samples back to Earth is planned for 2005. Until then, scientists will continue to study other aspects of Mars like the gases in its atmosphere and what its rocks are made of.

Each paragraph in the **body** begins with a **topic sentence** that tells a main idea. The other sentences give **details** and **related details**.

A rover explores the surface of Mars.

Basically, no one knows if there is or isn't life on Mars. It is possible that life does or did exist there. Spacecraft that go to Mars in the future will give us more proof. Hopefully, the mystery will be solved soon.

The last paragraph is the **conclusion**. It sums up the report.

The Resources

You can find information in books, periodicals, and videos, on computers, and in many kinds of special resources.

Finding Information in Books

Card Catalog

Some libraries have a set of drawers called a **card catalog**. In the drawers are cards that tell what books are in the library and where to find them. Each card has:

- a **book title** and **author**
- **publishing information**

  Here you will find:

  - the book's edition number. When books are printed all at the same time, they have the same edition number (**1st ed.** means **first edition**).
  - whether the book has a bibliography, or list of other books the author used to write the book (**bibl.** means **bibliography**)
  - the city where the publisher is located and the publisher's name
  - the copyright date (**c** means **copyright**)
  - the number of pages in the book (**p.** means **pages**)
  - if the book is illustrated or has photographs (**ill.** means **illustrated**)
  - how tall the book is (**cm.** means **centimeters**)
- **cross references** to other related subjects

Are we moving to Mars?

J
620.4 Schraff, Anne.
Sch Are we moving to Mars? / Anne Schraff.--
1st ed.--Santa Fe: John Muir Publications.
c1996. 32 p.: ill. (some color); 20 cm.

ISBN 1-56261-310-3.

1. Mars (Planet)--Surface--Juvenile literature.
2. Life on other planets--Juvenile literature.
3. Extraterrestrial (anthropology--Juvenile literature). I. Title.

Each card also has a **call number** that tells you what section of the library the book is in. Call numbers with a **J** mean that the books are in the **J**uvenile, or children's, section of the library.

- **Fiction books** are stories made up by an author. They are arranged on the library shelves in alphabetical order by the author's last name. Their call numbers usually show the first two or three **letters of the author's last name**.

```
J
KIT    Kitamura, Satoshi.
         UFO Diary / Satoshi Kitamura. -
       Farrar, Straus and Giroux, 1991.
       unpaged: color ill. ; 23cm.

         ISBN 0-374-48041-9
```

- **Nonfiction books** contain facts about a subject. They are arranged on the library shelves by **call numbers**. These numbers stand for subject areas from the Dewey Decimal System:

```
        Are we moving to Mars?
J
620.4   Schraff, Anne.
Sch       Are we moving to Mars? / Anne
        1st ed.--Santa Fe: John Muir Pu
        c1996. 32 p.: ill. (some color)

        ISBN 1-56261-310-3.
```

000–099	General Books	500–599	Pure Sciences
100–199	Philosophy	600–699	Technology
200–299	Religion	700–799	The Arts
300–399	Social Sciences	800–899	Literature
400–499	Language	900–999	History and Geography

Biographies are an exception. These nonfiction books give facts about people who really lived. Biographies are grouped on the shelves by the last name of the person the book is about.

Finding Information in Books, continued

The cards in a card catalog are in alphabetical order according to the first word or words on the card. Here are the three kinds of cards you'll find in a card catalog.

Subject Card

The **subject** of a book appears first on a subject card. Only nonfiction books have subject cards.

MARS (PLANET)
J
620.4 Schraff, Anne.
Sch Are we moving to Mars? / Anne Schraff.--
1st ed.--Santa Fe: John Muir Publications.
c1996. 32 p.: ill. (some color); 20 cm.

ISBN 1-56261-310-3.

1. Mars (Planet)--Surface--Juvenile literature.
2. Life on other planets--Juvenile literature.
3. Extraterrestrial (anthropology--Juvenile
literature). I. Title.

Title Card

The **title** of a book appears first on a title card. If the first word is *A* or *The*, look up the next word in alphabetical order.

Are we moving to Mars?
J
620.4 Schraff, Anne.
Sch Are we moving to Mars? / Anne Schraff.--
1st ed.--Santa Fe: John Muir Publications.
c1996. 32 p.: ill. (some color); 20 cm.

ISBN 1-56261-310-3.

1. Mars (Planet)--Surface--Juvenile literature.
2. Life on other planets--Juvenile literature.
3. Extraterrestrial (anthropology--Juvenile
literature). I. Title.

Author Card

The **author's name** appears first on an author card, with the last name first. Look it up in alphabetical order.

J
620.4 Schraff, Anne.
Sch Are we moving to Mars? / Anne Schraff.--
1st ed.--Santa Fe: John Muir Publications.
c1996. 32 p.: ill. (some color); 20 cm.

ISBN 1-56261-310-3.

1. Mars (Planet)--Surface--Juvenile literature.
2. Life on other planets--Juvenile literature.
3. Extraterrestrial (anthropology--Juvenile
literature). I. Title.

Computerized Card Catalog

A **computerized card catalog** is a card catalog on the computer. It's a lot like the paper card catalog, but faster to use because the computer looks up a book for you.

Computerized catalogs are not all the same. Here's one example and the steps you might follow to find *Are We Moving to Mars?* by Anne Schraff.

1 Read the instructions on the computer screen.

The **instructions** will help you find the information you're looking for in the computer.

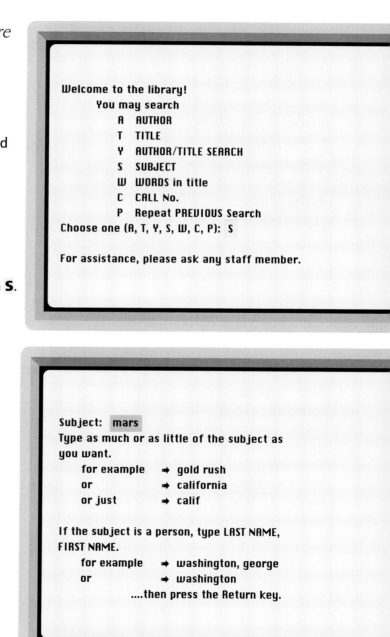

Welcome to the library!
You may search
A AUTHOR
T TITLE
Y AUTHOR/TITLE SEARCH
S SUBJECT
W WORDS in title
C CALL No.
P Repeat PREVIOUS Search
Choose one (A, T, Y, S, W, C, P): S

For assistance, please ask any staff member.

2 Type a letter to start your search.

To search for available information about a **subject**, you would type an **S**.

3 Type in a word or words that name your subject and press the Return key.

For the subject Mars, type in **the planet mars** or just **mars**. It doesn't matter to the computer if you use capital letters or not.

Subject: mars
Type as much or as little of the subject as you want.
for example → gold rush
or → california
or just → calif

If the subject is a person, type LAST NAME, FIRST NAME.
for example → washington, george
or → washington
....then press the Return key.

4 Look at the subjects that come up. Choose the ones you want.

For information about the planet Mars, press 4 on your keyboard.

This number shows how many **entries** there are for a subject. An entry can be a book, a video, or an audiotape.

You can press other keys to go to more entries or to start a new search.

```
You searched for the SUBJECT: mars
78 SUBJECTS found, with 144 entries; SUBJECTS 1-8 are:

1 Mars.....................................................1 entry
2 Mars Mines and Mineral Resources Fiction.................1 entry
3 Mars Planet ➜ See also narrower term SPACE FLIGHT TO ....1 entry
4 Mars Planet..............................................16 entries
5 Mars Colonization Forecasting............................1 entry
6 Mars Planet Drama .......................................1 entry
7 Mars Planet Exploration ➜ See Related Subjects ..........2 entries
8 Mars Planet Exploration .................................5 entries

Please type the NUMBER of the item you want to see, OR
F>Go FORWARD                       A>ANOTHER search by SUBJECT
W>Same search as WORD search       P>PRINT
N>NEW search                       +>ADDITIONAL options
Choose one [1-8, F, W, N, A, P, +]
```

5 Look at the entries that come up. Choose the ones you want.

Read the **titles** and **locations** to see which books are best for you. Press 3 to learn about *Are We Moving to Mars?*

```
You searched for the SUBJECT: mars
16 entries found, entries 1-8 are:

Mars Planet                                              LOCATION
1 Guide to Mars . . . . . . . . . . . . . . . . . . . . .ADULT NON-FICTION
2 The hunt for life on Mars . . . . . . . . . . . . . . .ADULT NON-FICTION
3 Are we moving to Mars? . . . . . . . . . . . . . . . . .YOUTH NON-FICTION
4 The inner planets: new light on the rocky worlds . . .ADULT NON-FICTION
5 Mars and the inner planets . . . . . . . . . . . . . .YOUTH NON-FICTION
6 Mars at last! . . . . . . . . . . . . . . . . . . . . .ADULT NON-FICTION
7 Mars beckons . . . . . . . . . . . . . . . . . . . . .ADULT NON-FICTION
8 Mars, the Red Planet . . . . . . . . . . . . . . . . .YOUTH NON-FICTION

Please type the NUMBER of the item you want to see, OR
F>Go FORWARD                       A>ANOTHER search by SUBJECT
R>RETURN to Browsing               P>PRINT
N>NEW search                       +>ADDITIONAL options
Choose one [1-8, F, R, N, A, P, +]
```

❻ Read the information about the entry you chose.

Would you like to read this book? If so, use the information on the screen to help you find it in the library.

The **location** tells you if the book is in the **J**uvenile or Adult part of the library.

The **call number** will help you find the book on the shelves.

The **status** tells you if the book is currently in the library or if someone has checked it out.

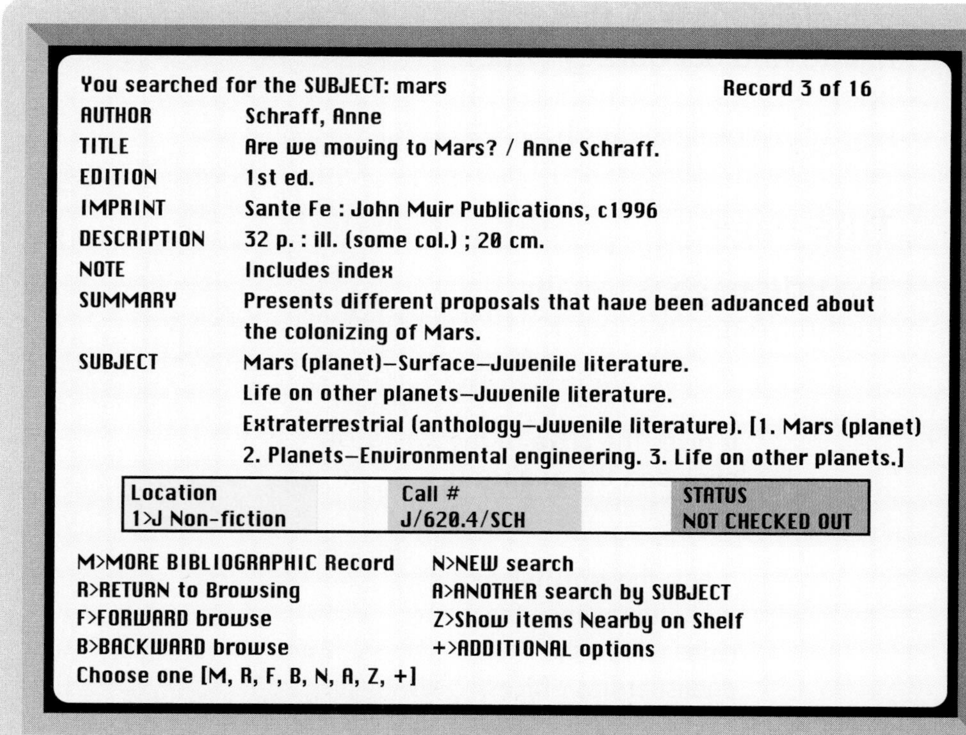

You searched for the SUBJECT: mars Record 3 of 16

AUTHOR	Schraff, Anne
TITLE	Are we moving to Mars? / Anne Schraff.
EDITION	1st ed.
IMPRINT	Sante Fe : John Muir Publications, c1996
DESCRIPTION	32 p. : ill. (some col.) ; 20 cm.
NOTE	Includes index
SUMMARY	Presents different proposals that have been advanced about the colonizing of Mars.
SUBJECT	Mars (planet)–Surface–Juvenile literature. Life on other planets–Juvenile literature. Extraterrestrial (anthology–Juvenile literature). [1. Mars (planet) 2. Planets–Environmental engineering. 3. Life on other planets.]

Location	Call #	STATUS
1>J Non-fiction	J/620.4/SCH	NOT CHECKED OUT

M>MORE BIBLIOGRAPHIC Record N>NEW search
R>RETURN to Browsing A>ANOTHER search by SUBJECT
F>FORWARD browse Z>Show items Nearby on Shelf
B>BACKWARD browse +>ADDITIONAL options
Choose one [M, R, F, B, N, A, Z, +]

❼ Record the call number or press P to print out the information. Use it to look up your book.

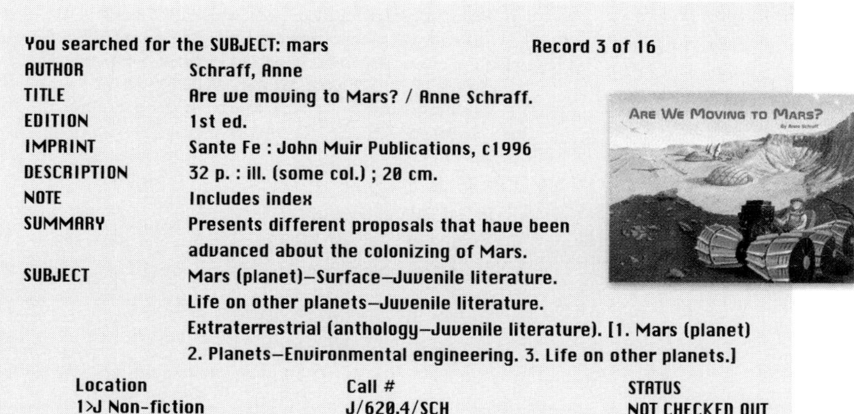

You searched for the SUBJECT: mars Record 3 of 16

AUTHOR	Schraff, Anne
TITLE	Are we moving to Mars? / Anne Schraff.
EDITION	1st ed.
IMPRINT	Sante Fe : John Muir Publications, c1996
DESCRIPTION	32 p. : ill. (some col.) ; 20 cm.
NOTE	Includes index
SUMMARY	Presents different proposals that have been advanced about the colonizing of Mars.
SUBJECT	Mars (planet)–Surface–Juvenile literature. Life on other planets–Juvenile literature. Extraterrestrial (anthology–Juvenile literature). [1. Mars (planet) 2. Planets–Environmental engineering. 3. Life on other planets.]

Location	Call #	STATUS
1>J Non-fiction	J/620.4/SCH	NOT CHECKED OUT

Parts of a Book

The pages at the front and back of a book help you know what the book is about and how it's organized. Look at these pages first to find out quickly if the book has the information you need for your research.

Title Page

The **title page** is usually the first page in a book.

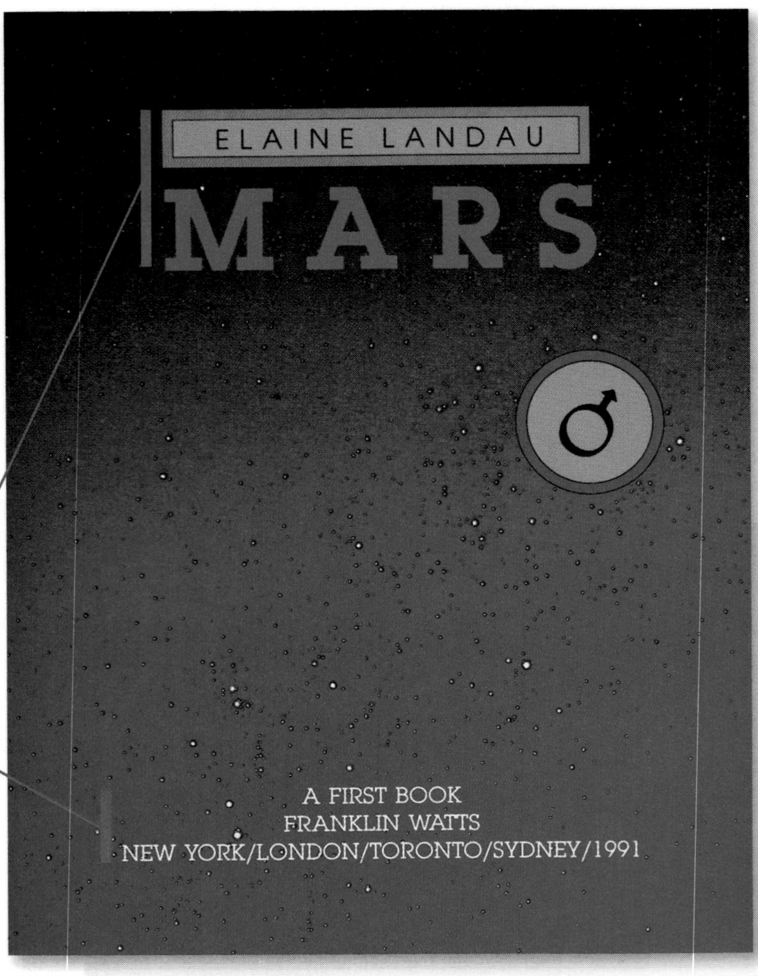

ELAINE LANDAU
MARS
A FIRST BOOK
FRANKLIN WATTS
NEW YORK/LONDON/TORONTO/SYDNEY/1991

It gives the **title** of the book and the **author**.

It tells the **publisher** and often names the cities where the publisher has offices.

Copyright Page

The **copyright** (©) **page** gives the year when the book was published.

Landau, Elaine.
Mars / by Elaine Landau.
p. cm. — (First book)
Includes bibliographical references and index.
Summary: Uses photographs and other recent findings to describe the atmosphere and geographic features of Mars.
ISBN 0-531-20012-4 (lib. bdg.)—ISBN 0-531-15773-3 (pbk.)
1. Mars (Planet)—Juvenile literature. [1. Mars (Planet)]
I. Title. II. Series.
QB641.L36 1991
523.4'3—dc20 90-13097 CIP AC

Copyright © 1991 Elaine Landau
All rights reserved
Printed in the United States of America
6 5 4 3

Check the **copyright** to see how current the information is.

Table of Contents

The **table of contents** is in the front of a book. It shows how many chapters, or parts, are in a book. It tells the page numbers where those chapters begin.

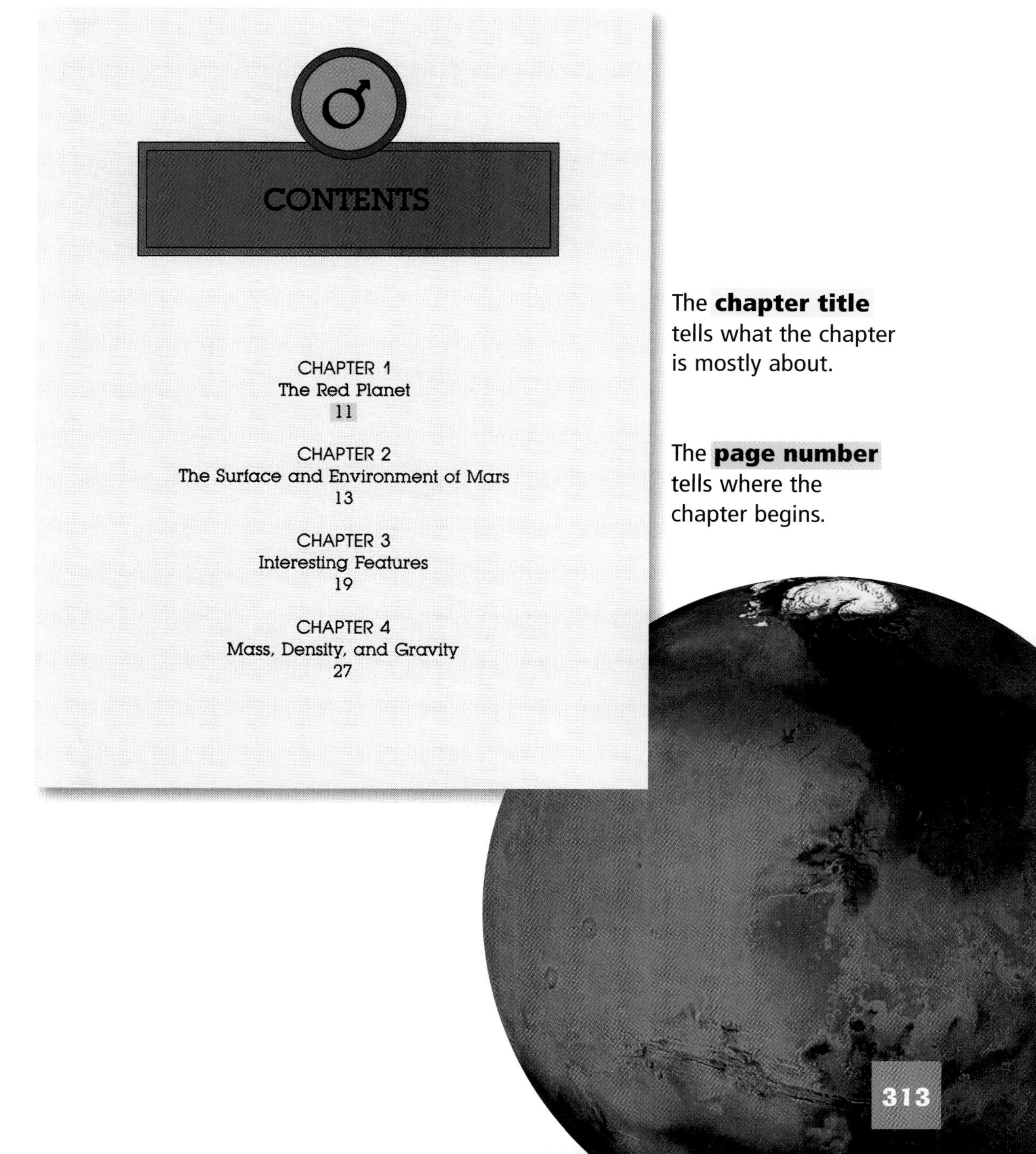

The **chapter title** tells what the chapter is mostly about.

The **page number** tells where the chapter begins.

Index

The **index** is usually in the back of a book. It lists all the subjects in the book in alphabetical order. It gives page numbers where you can find information about those subjects.

Names of people are listed in alphabetical order by their last names.

Related details are often listed for a subject.

INDEX

Sometimes page numbers are in *italics* to show that there is an illustration or photograph on that page.

Some indexes have words in parentheses that explain more about the subject. For example, these pages tell about the moons of Mars.

Glossary

A **glossary** is a short dictionary of important words used in the book. It appears at the back of the book. In a glossary, the words are listed in alphabetical order.

GLOSSARY

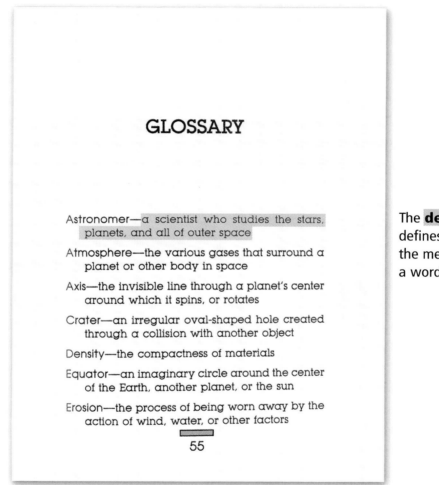

Astronomer—a scientist who studies the stars, planets, and all of outer space

Atmosphere—the various gases that surround a planet or other body in space

Axis—the invisible line through a planet's center around which it spins, or rotates

Crater—an irregular oval-shaped hole created through a collision with another object

Density—the compactness of materials

Equator—an imaginary circle around the center of the Earth, another planet, or the sun

Erosion—the process of being worn away by the action of wind, water, or other factors

55

The **definition** defines, or gives the meaning of, a word.

Finding Information in Special Resources

Almanac

An **almanac** is a book filled with facts about things like inventions, animals, sports, science, movies, and TV. It's rewritten every year, so all the information is very up-to-date.

How to Use an Almanac

1. **Look up your key words in the index.**
2. **Find those pages. Skim and scan to see if the pages have the information you are looking for.**

INDEX

Read the **headings** to help you find the main ideas.

Diagrams and other pictures help explain information.

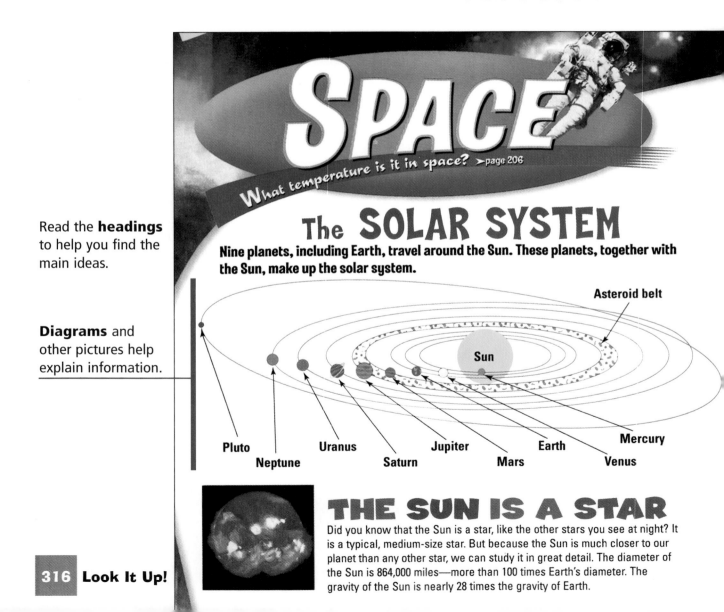

SPACE
What temperature is it in space? ➤page 206

The SOLAR SYSTEM

Nine planets, including Earth, travel around the Sun. These planets, together with the Sun, make up the solar system.

Asteroid belt
Sun
Pluto
Neptune
Uranus
Saturn
Jupiter
Mars
Earth
Venus
Mercury

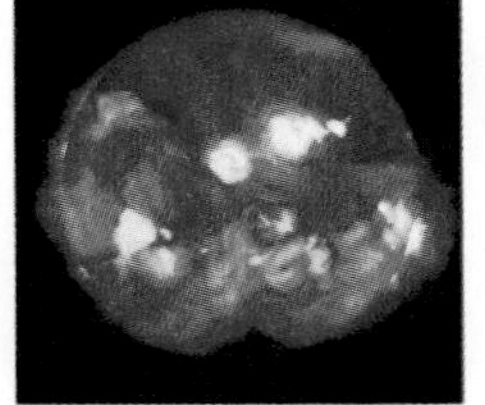

THE SUN IS A STAR

Did you know that the Sun is a star, like the other stars you see at night? It is a typical, medium-size star. But because the Sun is much closer to our planet than any other star, we can study it in great detail. The diameter of the Sun is 864,000 miles—more than 100 times Earth's diameter. The gravity of the Sun is nearly 28 times the gravity of Earth.

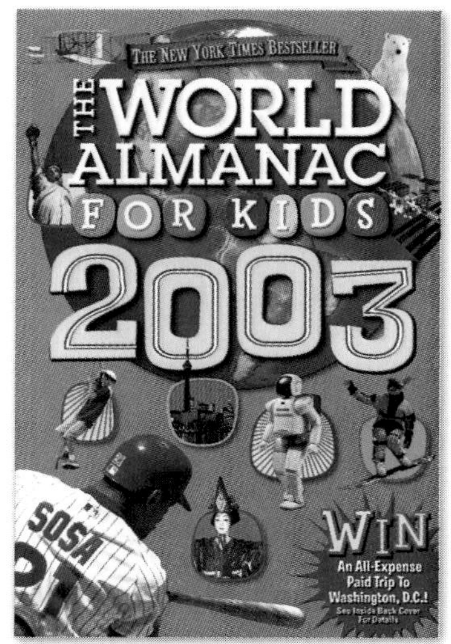

❸ **If the information seems useful for your research, read the pages carefully and take notes.**

SPACE

The Planets

1 MERCURY
Average distance from the Sun: 36 million miles
Diameter: 3,032 miles
Temperature: 333 degrees F
Surface: silicate rock
Time to revolve around the Sun: 88 days
Time to rotate on its axis: 58 days, 15 hours, 30 minutes
Number of moons: 0

DID YOU KNOW? *Four billion years ago a gigantic asteroid hit Mercury, creating a 1,300-mile-wide crater on the surface—so big that the entire state of Texas could fit in it.*

2 VENUS
Average distance from the Sun: 67 million miles
Diameter: 7,521 miles
Temperature: 867 degrees F
Surface: silicate rock
Time to revolve around the Sun: 224.7 days
Time to rotate on its axis: 243 days
Number of moons: 0

DID YOU KNOW? *Even though Venus is farther away from the Sun than Mercury, it is the hottest planet because the high level of carbon dioxide in the atmosphere creates an extreme greenhouse effect, trapping in the Sun's heat.*

3 EARTH
Average distance from the Sun: 93 million miles
Diameter: 7,926 miles
Temperature: 59 degrees F
Surface: water, basalt and granite rock
Time to revolve around the Sun: 365 ¼ days
Time to rotate on its axis: 23 hours, 56 minutes, 4.2 seconds
Number of moons: 1

DID YOU KNOW? *The Earth is moving around the Sun at approximately 67,000 miles an hour.*

4 MARS

Average distance from the Sun: 142 million miles
Diameter: 4,213 miles
Temperature: –81 degrees F
Surface: iron-rich basaltic rock
Time to revolve around the Sun: 687 days
Time to rotate on its axis: 24 hours, 37 minutes, 22 seconds
Number of moons: 2

DID YOU KNOW? *Many features on Mars seem to have been shaped by water, although the only water left on Mars is frozen underneath layers of dust at the north and south poles.*

6 SATURN

Sometimes **tables** and **lists** will give useful information for your report.

Special features like this one give interesting facts.

Atlas and Globe

An **atlas** is a book of maps. A **globe** is a round map that shows the curve of the Earth.

Physical Map

A **physical map** shows features of a place like rivers, forests, mountains, lowlands, coastlines, or oceans.

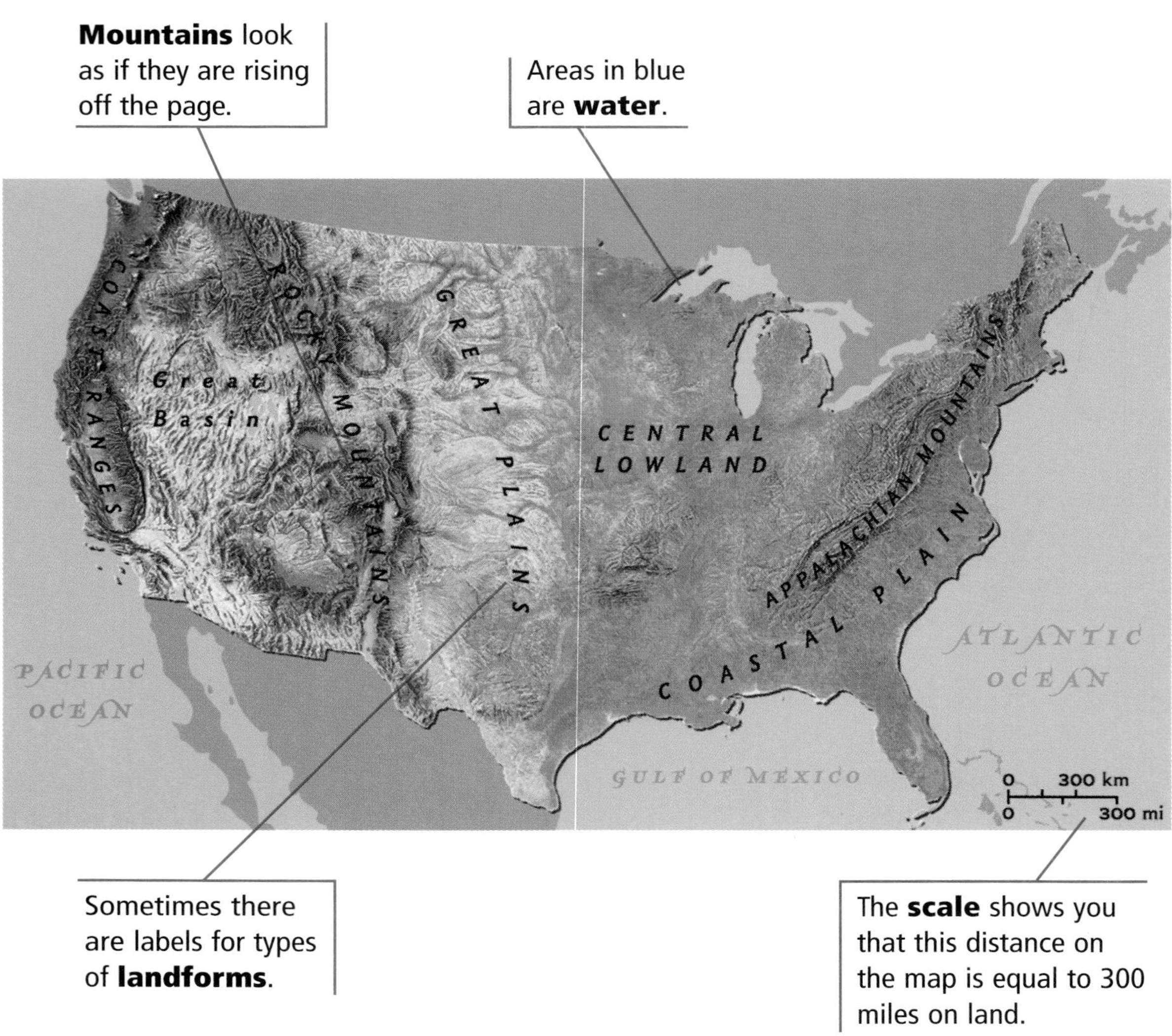

Mountains look as if they are rising off the page.
Areas in blue are **water**.
COAST RANGES
Great Basin
ROCKY MOUNTAINS
GREAT PLAINS
CENTRAL LOWLAND
APPALACHIAN MOUNTAINS
COASTAL PLAIN
PACIFIC OCEAN
ATLANTIC OCEAN
GULF OF MEXICO
0 300 km
0 300 mi
Sometimes there are labels for types of **landforms**.
The **scale** shows you that this distance on the map is equal to 300 miles on land.

Political Map

A **political map** shows the boundaries between countries and states. It also shows the capitals and other major cities.

How to Find a Place on a Political Map

Index

Brunswick	K-6	11
Cape Canaveral	L-6	11
Cape Fear	J-8	11
Cape Fear R.	I-7	11
Carolina Beach	I-8	11
Carrollton	J-4	11

❶ Use alphabetical order to look up the name of the place in the index.

In the index, you'll find the **page number** for the map. You might also find a special code, like **L-6** to help you find the exact **location** of the place on the map.

❷ Look up the map and locate the place.

First turn to the page noted in the index. Then use the code **L-6** to find the place:

- Look for **L** on the side of the map.

Each letter is between two lines of **latitude**. Latitude lines are lines that go from east to west ⟷ around the Earth.

- Look for **6** along the top or bottom of the map.

Each number is between two lines of **longitude**. Longitude lines are lines that go from north to south. ↕

- Find the section where the lettered and numbered spaces meet. Then look for the name of the place.

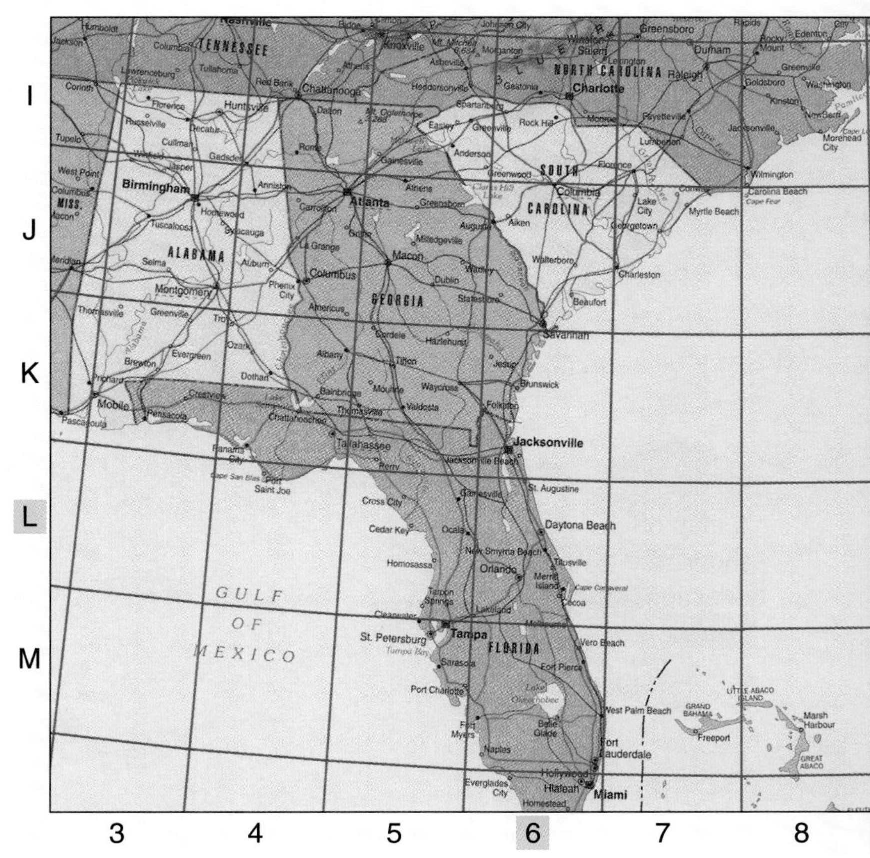

Historical Map

A **historical map** shows when and where certain events happened.

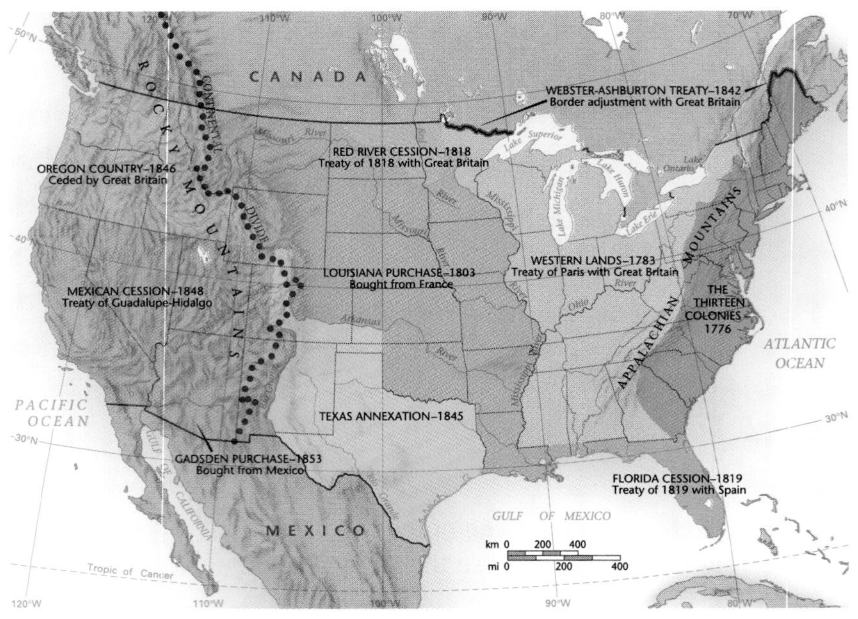

Product Map

A **product map** uses pictures and symbols to show where products come from.

A **legend** shows what each picture stands for.

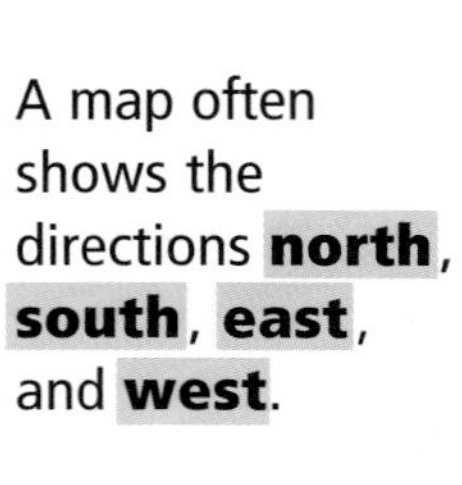

A map often shows the directions **north**, **south**, **east**, and **west**.

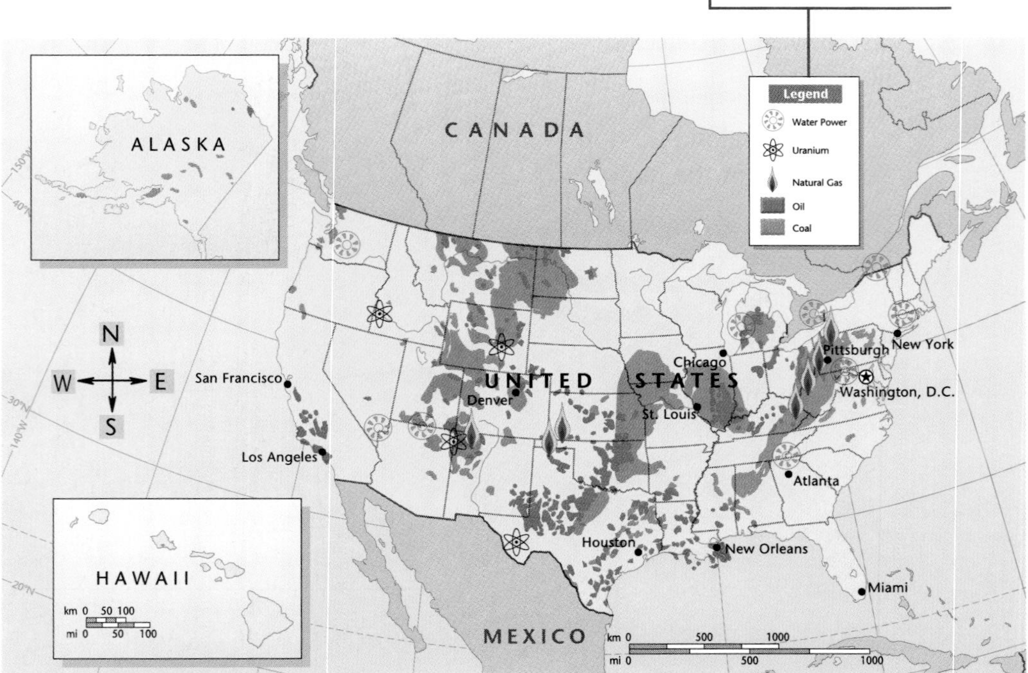

Globe

A **globe** is a small model of the Earth. A globe has a round shape like the Earth does. It gives a better picture of Earth than a flat map does.

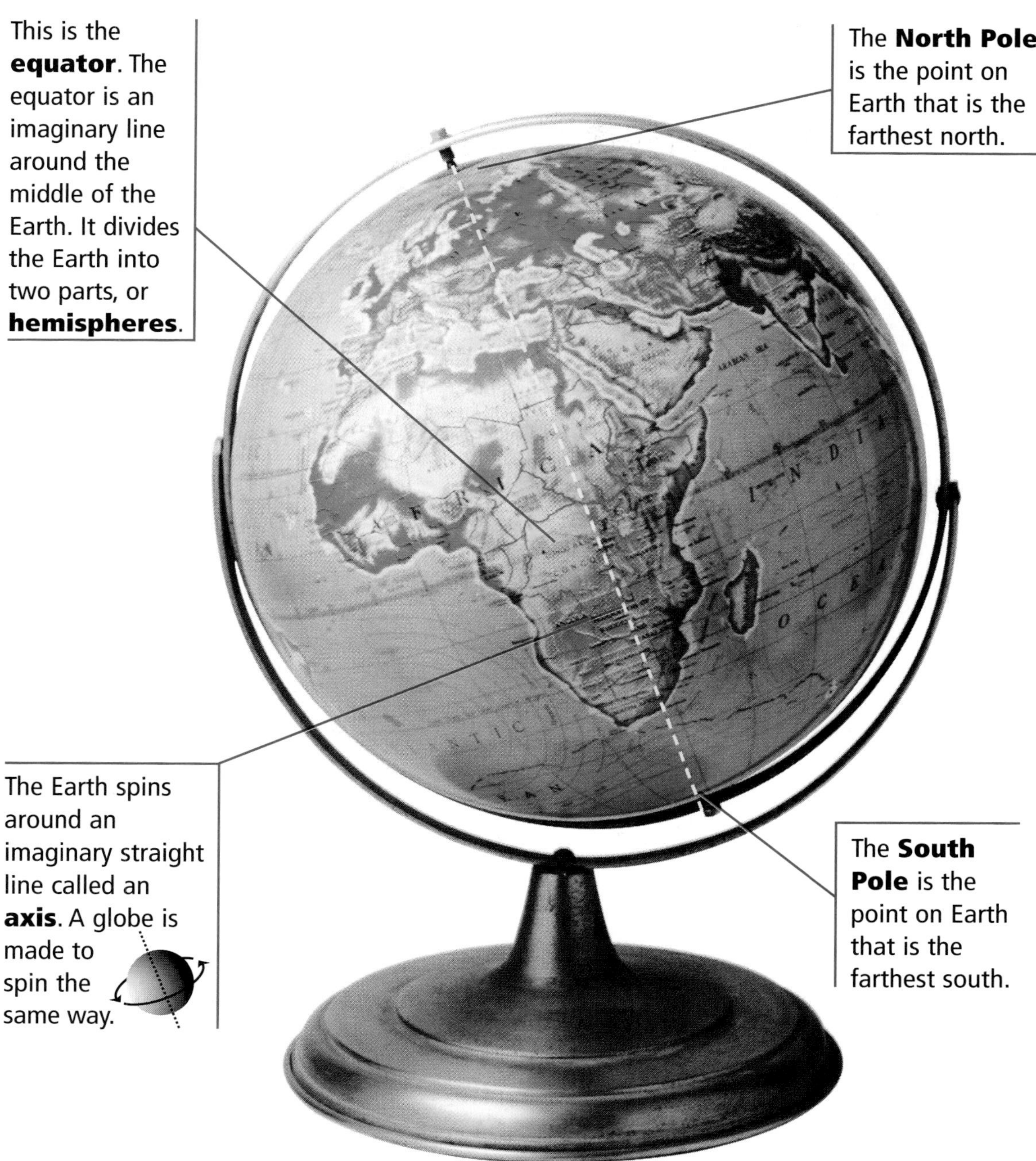

This is the **equator**. The equator is an imaginary line around the middle of the Earth. It divides the Earth into two parts, or **hemispheres**.
The **North Pole** is the point on Earth that is the farthest north.
The Earth spins around an imaginary straight line called an **axis**. A globe is made to spin the same way.
The **South Pole** is the point on Earth that is the farthest south.

Dictionary

A **dictionary** is a book filled with all kinds of information about words. It lists the words in alphabetical order from A to Z.

How to Look Up a Word

1 Look at the beginning letter of your word and turn to the part of the dictionary it would be in.

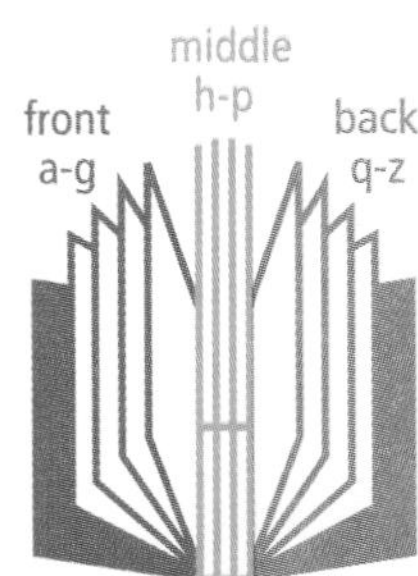

Suppose you want to look up *spacesuit*. Words that begin with *S* are in the back part of a dictionary.

southwards ➤ space shuttle

ward slope of the mountain. Adjective.
south•ward (south′wərd) *adverb; adjective.*

southwards Another spelling of the adverb southward: *They drove **southwards**.* **south•wards** (south′wərdz) *adverb.*

southwest 1. The direction halfway between south and west. 2. The point of the compass showing this direction. 3. A region or place in this direction. 4. **the Southwest.** The region in the south and west of the United States. *Noun.*
○ 1. Toward or in the southwest: *the **southwest** corner of the street.* 2. Coming from the southwest: *a **southwest** wind. Adjective.*
○ Toward the southwest: *The ship sailed **southwest**. Adverb.*
south•west (south′west′) *noun; adjective; adverb.*

souvenir Something kept because it reminds one of a person, place, or event: *I bought a pennant as a **souvenir** of the baseball game.* **sou•ve•nir** (sü′və nîr′ *or* sü′və nîr′) *noun, plural* **souvenirs.**

sovereign A king or queen. *Noun.*
○ 1. Having the greatest power or highest rank or authority: *The king and queen were the **sovereign** rulers of the country.* 2. Not controlled by others; independent: *Mexico is a **sovereign** nation. Adjective.*
sov•er•eign (sov′ər ən *or* sov′rən) *noun, plural* **sovereigns**; *adjective.*

Soviet Union Formerly, a large country in eastern Europe and northern Asia. It was composed of 15 republics and was also called the U.S.S.R. The largest and most important of the 15 republics was Russia.

sow[1] 1. To scatter seeds over the ground; plant: *The farmer will **sow** corn in this field.* 2. To spread or scatter: *The clown **sowed** happiness among the children.*
Other words that sound like this are sew and so.
sow (sō) *verb,* **sowed, sown** *or* **sowed, sowing.**

sow[2] An adult female pig. **sow** (sou) *noun, plural* **sows.**

soybean A seed rich in oil and protein and used as food. Soybeans grow in pods on bushy plants. **soy•bean** (soi′bēn′) *noun, plural* **soybeans.**

space 1. The area in which the whole universe exists. It has no limits. The planet earth is in space. 2. The region beyond the earth's atmosphere; outer space: *The rocket was launched into **space**.* 3. A distance or area between things: *There is not much **space** between our house and theirs.* 4. An area reserved or available for some purpose: *a parking **space**.* 5. A period of time: *Both jets landed in the **space** of ten minutes. Noun.*
○ To put space in between: *The architect **spaced** the houses far apart. Verb.*
space (spās) *noun, plural* **spaces**; *verb,* **spaced, spacing.**

spacecraft A vehicle used for flight in outer space. This is also called a spaceship.
space•craft (spās′kraft′) *noun, plural* **spacecraft.**

space shuttle A spacecraft that carries a crew into space and returns to land on earth. The same

space shuttle

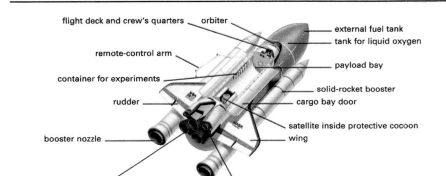

flight deck and crew's quarters
orbiter
external fuel tank
tank for liquid oxygen
remote-control arm
payload bay
container for experiments
solid-rocket booster
rudder
cargo bay door
satellite inside protective cocoon
booster nozzle
wing

2 **Use the guide words to help you find the page your word is on.**

3 **Look down the columns to find your entry word.**

space station ➤ Spanish 

space shuttle can be used again. A space shuttle is also called a shuttle.

space station A spaceship that orbits around the earth like a satellite and on which a crew can live for long periods of time.

spacesuit Special clothing worn by an astronaut in space. A spacesuit covers an astronaut's entire body and has equipment to help the astronaut breathe. **space•suit** (spās′süt′) *noun, plural* **spacesuits.**

Astronauts take spacewalks to repair satellites and vehicles.

spacewalk A period of activity during which an astronaut in space is outside a spacecraft. **space•walk** (spās′wôk′) *noun, plural* **spacewalks.**

spacious Having a lot of space or room; roomy; large. —**spa•cious** *adjective* —**spaciousness** *noun.*

spade¹ A tool used for digging. It has a long handle and a flat blade that can be pressed into the ground with the foot. *Noun.*
○ To dig with a spade: *We spaded the garden and then raked it. Verb.*
spade (spād) *noun, plural* **spades;** *verb,* **spaded, spading.**

spade² 1. A playing card marked with one or more figures shaped like this. 2. **spades.** The suit of cards marked with this figure. **spade** (spād) *noun, plural* **spades.**

spaghetti A kind of pasta that looks like long, thin strings. It is made of a mixture of flour and water. **spa•ghet•ti** (spə get′ē) *noun.*

WORD HISTORY

The word spaghetti comes from an Italian word meaning "strings" or "little cords." Spaghetti looks a bit like strings.

Spain A country in southwest Europe. **Spain** (spān) *noun.*

spamming The sending of the same message to large numbers of e-mail addresses or to many newsgroups at the same time. Spamming is often thought of as impolite behavior on the Internet. **spam•ming** (spa′ming) *noun.*

span 1. The distance or part between two supports: *The span of that bridge is very long.* 2. The full reach or length of anything: *Some people accomplish a great deal in the span of their lives. Noun.*
○ To extend over or across. *Verb.*
span (span) *noun, plural* **spans;** *verb,* **spanned, spanning.**

This bridge spans a wide river.

spaniel Any of various dogs of small to medium size with long, drooping ears, a silky, wavy coat, and short legs. The larger types are used in hunting. **span•iel** (span′yəl) *noun, plural* **spaniels.**

Spanish 1. The people of Spain. The word *Spanish* in this sense is used with a plural verb. 2. The language spoken in Spain. It is also spoken in many countries south of the United States as well as in parts of the U.S. *Noun.*
○ Of or having to do with Spain, its people, or the Spanish language. *Adjective.*
Span•ish (span′ish) *noun; adjective.*

The first **guide word** is *space station* because that word comes first on the page. The second guide word is *Spanish* because that word comes last. Your word will be on the page if it comes between the two guide words in alphabetical order.

Look at the **entry word** *spacesuit*. It's in alphabetical order on the page.

Dictionary, continued

Each **entry** gives you important information about the word.

The **definition** tells you what the word means. If a word has more than one meaning, the definitions are numbered.

An entry may also give the **plural form** or **verb forms** of the word and how to spell them.

as food. Soybeans grow in pods on bushy plants.
soy•bean (soi′bēn′) *noun, plural* **soybeans.**

space 1. The area in which the whole universe exists. It has no limits. The planet earth is in space. 2. The region beyond the earth's atmosphere; outer space: *The rocket was launched into space.* 3. A distance or area between things: *There is not much space between our house and theirs.* 4. An area reserved or available for some purpose: *a parking space.* 5. A period of time: *Both jets landed in the space of ten minutes. Noun.*
○ To put space in between: *The architect spaced the houses far apart. Verb.*
space (spās) *noun, plural* **spaces;** *verb,* **spaced, spacing.**

spacecraft A vehicle used for flight in outer space. This is also called a spaceship.
space•craft (spās′kraft′) *noun, plural* **spacecraft.**

space shuttle A spacecraft that carries a crew into space and returns to land on earth. The same

Some entries have a **sample sentence** to help you know how to use the word.

This information tells you **how to pronounce** the word. You can look up the marks in the **pronunciation key**. The mark **ā** tells you to say the **a** the same way you would say the **a** in **āpe**. The mark **′** tells you to emphasize the first part of the word, **space**.

Pronunciation Key

PRONUNCIATION KEY:

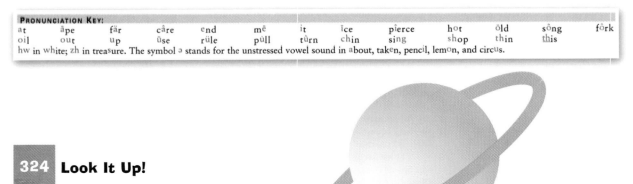

at	āpe	fär	câre	end	mē	it	īce	pîerce	hot	ōld	sông	fôrk
oil	out	up	ūse	rüle	pu̇ll	tûrn	chin	sing	shop	thin	this	

hw in white; zh in treasure. The symbol ə stands for the unstressed vowel sound in about, taken, pencil, lemon, and circus.

All entries include words like *noun*, or its abbreviation *n*, that tell the word's **part of speech**. A word's part of speech shows how the word can be used in a sentence.

Abbreviations for the parts of speech are:

adj	adjective
adv	adverb
conj	conjunction
interj	interjection
n	noun
prep	preposition
pron	pronoun
v	verb

spacesuit Special clothing worn by an astronaut in space. A spacesuit covers an astronaut's entire body and has equipment to help the astronaut breathe. **space•suit** (spās′süt′) *noun, plural* **spacesuits.**

Astronauts take spacewalks to repair satellites and vehicles.

spacewalk A period of activity during which an astronaut in space is outside a spacecraft. **space•walk** (spās′wôk′) *noun, plural* **spacewalks.**

spacious Having a lot of space or room; roomy; large. **—spa•cious** *adjective* **—spaciousness**

Some entries have a **picture** and a **caption**. They give you more information about a word and its meaning.

Encyclopedia

An **encyclopedia** is a set of books. Each book is called a **volume**. Each volume has articles that give facts about many different topics. The volumes and articles in an encyclopedia are arranged in alphabetical order.

How to Find Information in an Encyclopedia

❶ Find the correct volume.

What is the first letter of the word you plan to look up? Find the volume that has articles beginning with that letter.

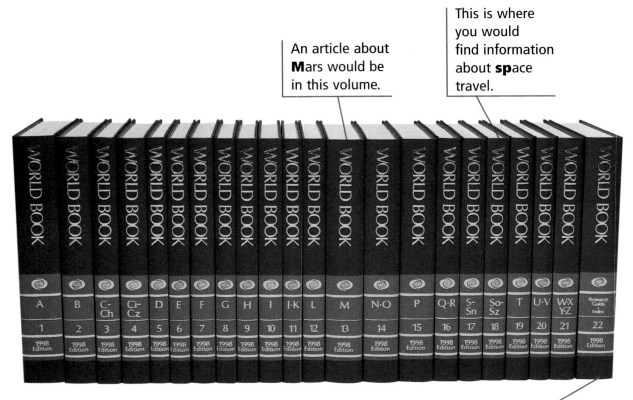

An article about **M**ars would be in this volume.

This is where you would find information about **sp**ace travel.

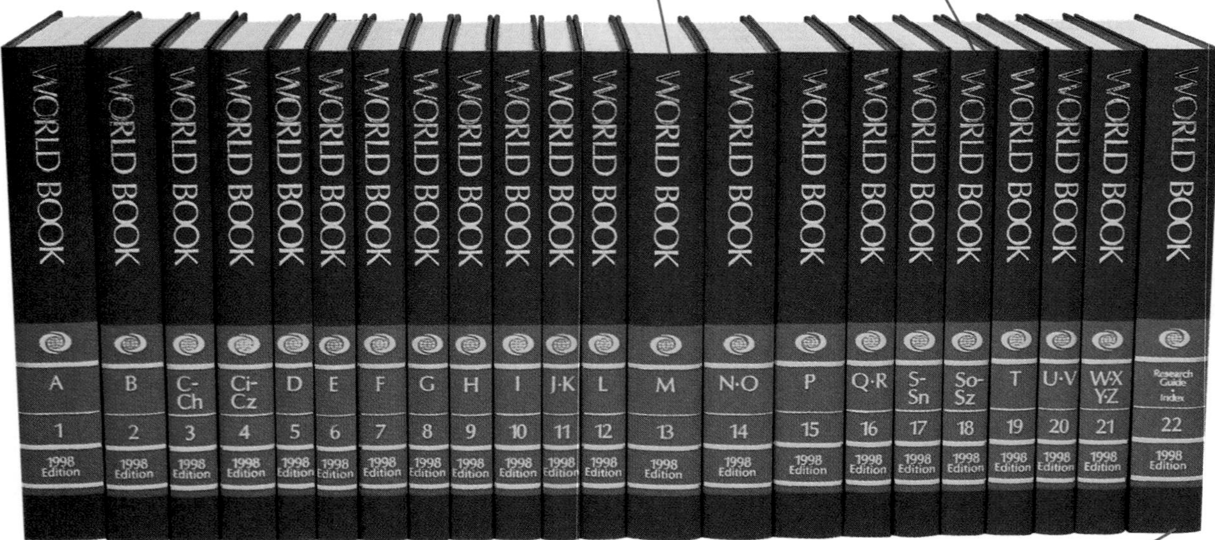

Some encyclopedias are on a computer disk called a **CD-ROM**. You can read the information from the CD-ROM on your computer screen.

Most encyclopedias have a volume called an **index**. The index lists other related subjects to look up.

❷ Use alphabetical order to find the article.

Flip through the pages looking just at the **guide words** to get to the page where the article appears. Then find the article on the page.

❸ Skim and scan the article to see if it has the information you need.

Mars 223

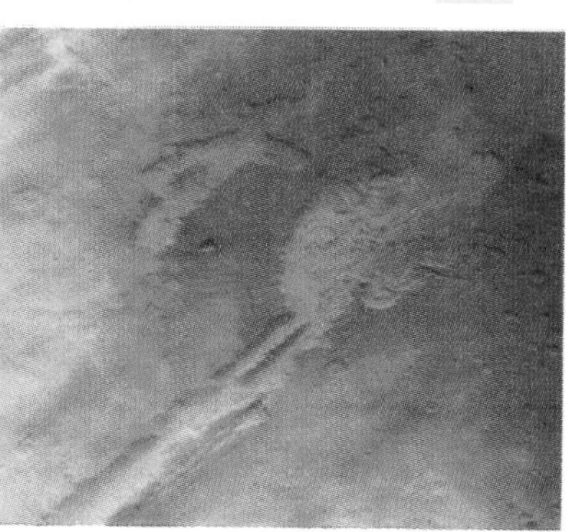

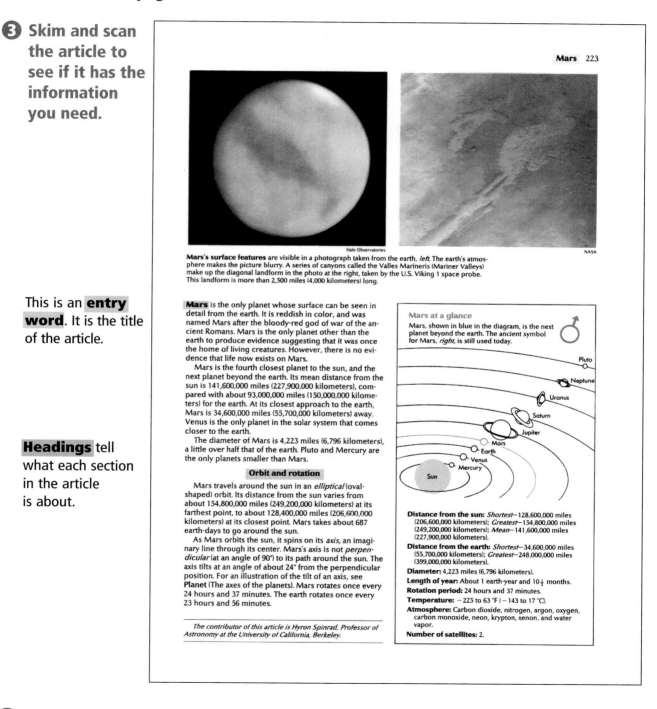

Hale Observatories

NASA

Mars's surface features are visible in a photograph taken from the earth, *left.* The earth's atmosphere makes the picture blurry. A series of canyons called the Valles Marineris (Mariner Valleys) make up the diagonal landform in the photo at the right, taken by the U.S. Viking 1 space probe. This landform is more than 2,500 miles (4,000 kilometers) long.

This is an **entry word**. It is the title of the article.

Mars is the only planet whose surface can be seen in detail from the earth. It is reddish in color, and was named Mars after the bloody-red god of war of the ancient Romans. Mars is the only planet other than the earth to produce evidence suggesting that it was once the home of living creatures. However, there is no evidence that life now exists on Mars.

Mars is the fourth closest planet to the sun, and the next planet beyond the earth. Its mean distance from the sun is 141,600,000 miles (227,900,000 kilometers), compared with about 93,000,000 miles (150,000,000 kilometers) for the earth. At its closest approach to the earth, Mars is 34,600,000 miles (55,700,000 kilometers) away. Venus is the only planet in the solar system that comes closer to the earth.

The diameter of Mars is 4,223 miles (6,796 kilometers), a little over half that of the earth. Pluto and Mercury are the only planets smaller than Mars.

Headings tell what each section in the article is about.

Orbit and rotation

Mars travels around the sun in an *elliptical* (oval-shaped) orbit. Its distance from the sun varies from about 154,800,000 miles (249,200,000 kilometers) at its farthest point, to about 128,400,000 miles (206,600,000 kilometers) at its closest point. Mars takes about 687 earth-days to go around the sun.

As Mars orbits the sun, it spins on its *axis,* an imaginary line through its center. Mars's axis is not *perpendicular* (at an angle of 90°) to its path around the sun. The axis tilts at an angle of about 24° from the perpendicular position. For an illustration of the tilt of an axis, see **Planet** (The axes of the planets). Mars rotates once every 24 hours and 37 minutes. The earth rotates once every 23 hours and 56 minutes.

The contributor of this article is Hyron Spinrad, Professor of Astronomy at the University of California, Berkeley.

Mars at a glance

Mars, shown in blue in the diagram, is the next planet beyond the earth. The ancient symbol for Mars, *right,* is still used today.

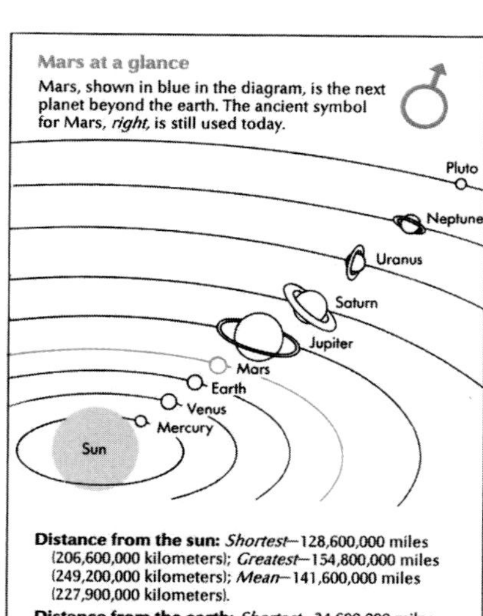

Distance from the sun: *Shortest*—128,600,000 miles (206,600,000 kilometers); *Greatest*—154,800,000 miles (249,200,000 kilometers); *Mean*—141,600,000 miles (227,900,000 kilometers).

Distance from the earth: *Shortest*—34,600,000 miles (55,700,000 kilometers); *Greatest*—248,000,000 miles (399,000,000 kilometers).

Diameter: 4,223 miles (6,796 kilometers).

Length of year: About 1 earth-year and $10\frac{1}{2}$ months.

Rotation period: 24 hours and 37 minutes.

Temperature: −225 to 63 °F (−143 to 17 °C).

Atmosphere: Carbon dioxide, nitrogen, argon, oxygen, carbon monoxide, neon, krypton, xenon, and water vapor.

Number of satellites: 2.

❹ If the article has the information you need, read it and take notes.

Interviewing Experts

An **expert** is someone who knows a lot about a topic. A teacher or librarian can help you identify an expert on your topic. You can also find an expert through the Internet.

How to Conduct an Interview

1 Set up the interview.

Call or write to make an **appointment**, or meeting time. First, identify yourself and tell why you want to talk to the person. Then politely ask for an interview. Be brief. Note the date and time you agree on for the interview.

2 Prepare for the interview.

- Find out as much as you can about the topic and your expert before the interview.
- Write questions.
- Practice your interview with a friend, family member, or teacher.

3 Conduct the interview.

- Make sure you have at least two pencils or pens, plenty of paper, and a tape recorder if possible. Bring extra tapes and batteries.
- Introduce yourself and thank the person for meeting with you.
- If you brought a tape recorder, ask the person for permission to use it.
- Ask your questions. Give the person time to answer. Be a good listener.
- Don't try to write down every word the person says. Write just enough to remember what's important.
- Ask questions if you need to know more.
- At the end of the interview, say thank you. Ask if you can call again in case you need to clarify something.

Interview with Dr. Kwon
Q: Do you think there's life on Mars?
A: Maybe, but unlikely. Possible small life forms like bacteria deep underground.

4 Go over your notes.

- After the interview, rewrite anything you need to make clearer. Add things you remember.
- Note any facts you need to check.
- Write a short note to thank the person you interviewed.

Telephone Directory

Sometimes you need to make a phone call to set up an interview or to get information for a report. You can find the phone numbers you need in the **telephone directory**, or phone book.

White Pages

In the **white pages** you'll find telephone numbers for people and businesses. Names for people are listed in alphabetical order by their last names. Businesses are listed in alphabetical order by the first important word in their name.

Guide words show the first name and last name included on the page.

SANTOS–SETA

Santos Sally 555-1273
Santoso Rini....................................555-8924
Sarma Karan....................................555-5639
Sarma Sanjay 555-0956
Search for Extraterrestrial Intelligence (SETI)
75 Atlantic 555-4563
Seguin G 555-5629
Serrano Aaron 555-1870
Serrano Anthony 51 Porter 555-0446
Serrano E 62 Falconcrest.....................555-0830
Serrano Nera 160 Devon 555-4974
Serrano Q...555-0223
Serre A 555-3856
Serre Francis 555-3847
SERVICE CENTER
199 Townsend 555-5833
Service Deli 111 East St 555-2446
Seta Elizabeth 1462 Zamora 555-9877

Sometimes people or businesses list their **address** as well as their telephone number.

Some businesses will pay to have their name printed in **larger type**. The larger type makes the name stand out from the rest.

Yellow Pages

The **yellow pages** have names and telephone numbers for companies or businesses in your area.

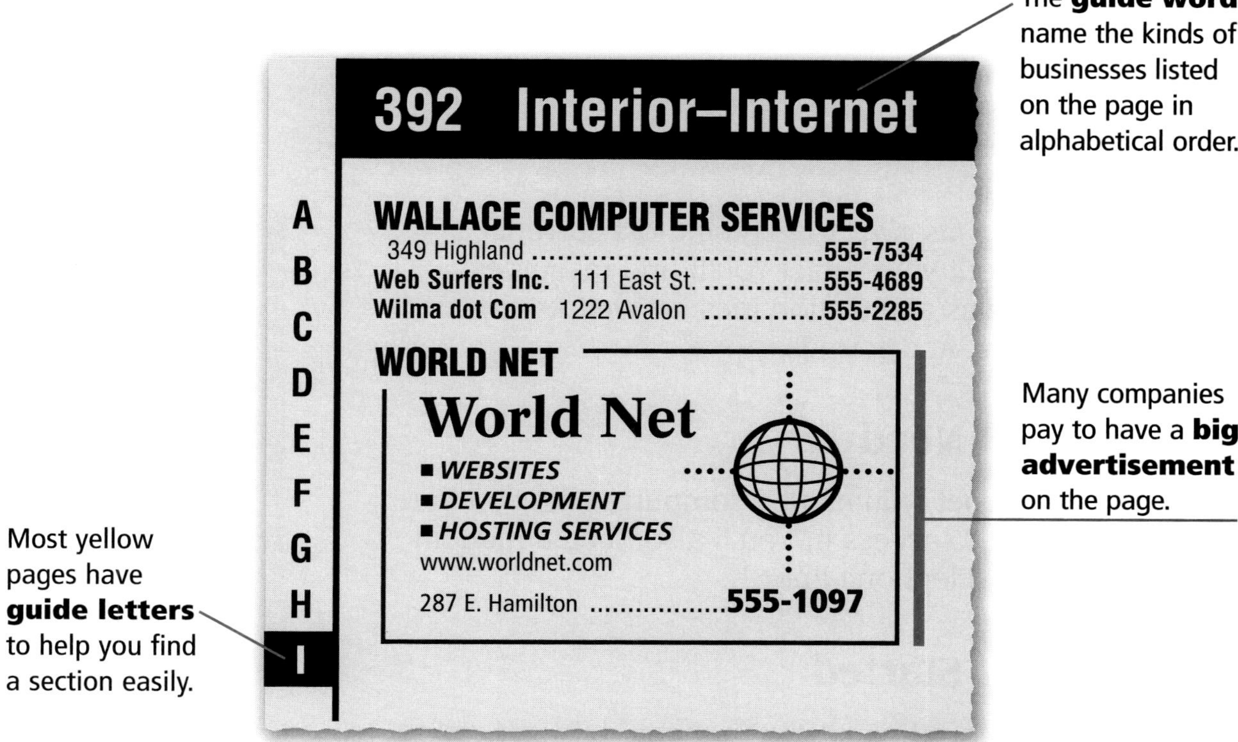

Special Sections

Many telephone directories also have special sections that give information such as

- emergency telephone numbers for the fire and police department
- guidelines for first aid
- names and telephone numbers for government officials
- museums, parks, and other places to visit.

Look in the front pages of the directory to find out more about these special sections.

3. Customer Guide

Emergency Telephone Numbers ....**Section A**
Calling and Service Information ....**Section B**
First Aid and Survival Guide ....**Section C**
Páginas en Español ....**Section D**
Government Offices (Federal and State) ..**Section D**
Downtown Attractions ....**Section E**

Turn to the first page in each section for a complete table of contents.

Finding Information on the Internet

The **Internet** is an international network, or connection, of computers that share information with one another. The **World Wide Web** allows you to find, read, go through, and organize information. The Internet is like a giant library, and the World Wide Web is everything in the library including the books, the librarian, and the computer catalog.

The Internet is a *fast* way to get the most current information about your topic! You'll find resources like encyclopedias and dictionaries, as well as amazing pictures, movies, and sounds.

What You'll Need

To use the Internet, you need a computer with software that allows you to access it. You'll also need a modem connected to a telephone line.

How to Get Started

You can search on the Internet in many different ways. In fact, you'll probably find something new whenever you search on it. Don't be afraid to try something—you never know what you'll find!

Check with your teacher for how to access the Internet from your school. Usually you can just double click on the **icon**, or picture, to get access to the Internet and you're on your way!

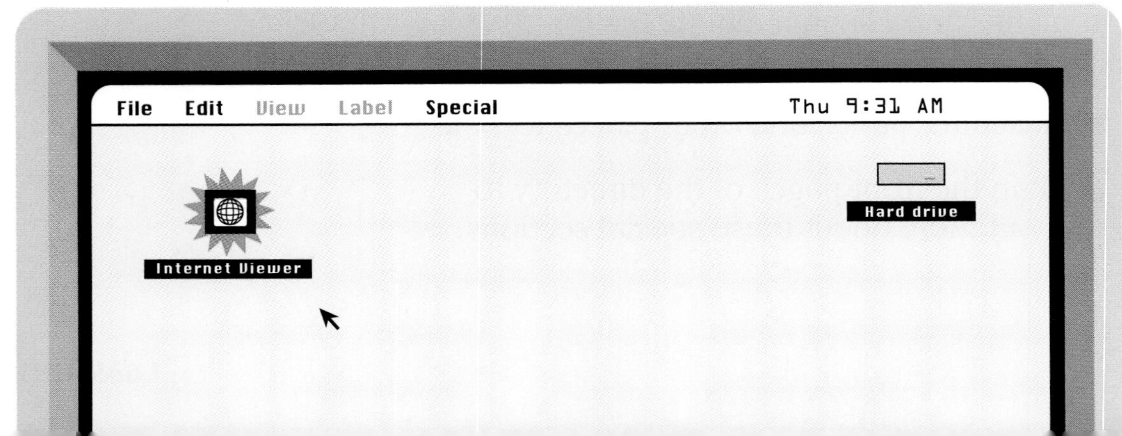

Doing the Research

Once the search page comes up, you can begin the research process. Just follow these steps.

1 Type your subject in the search box and then click on the Search button.

You'll always see a **toolbar** like this one at the top of the screen. Click on the pictures to do things like print the page.

This is where you type in your **subject**.

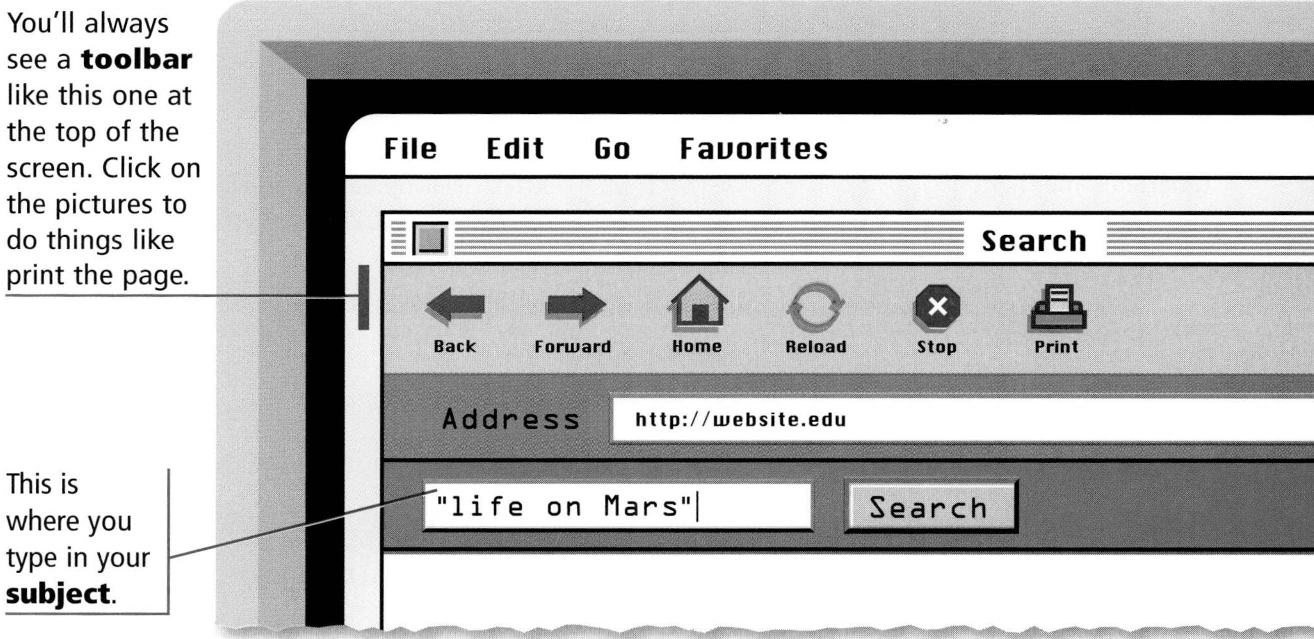

Try different ways to type in your subject. You'll get different results!

- If you type in **Mars**, you'll see all the sites that have the word *Mars* in them. This may give you too many categories and sites to look through!
- If you type in **"life on Mars"**, you'll see all the sites with the exact phrase, or group of words, *life on Mars*.
- If you type in **+Mars +life**, you'll see all the sites with the words *Mars* and *life* in them.

❷ Read the search results.

All underlined, colored words are **links**, or connections, to other sites. They help you get from page to page quickly.

If you want to go directly to a **Web page**, click on a site.

Click on a **category** to see more options for information related to the words you typed.

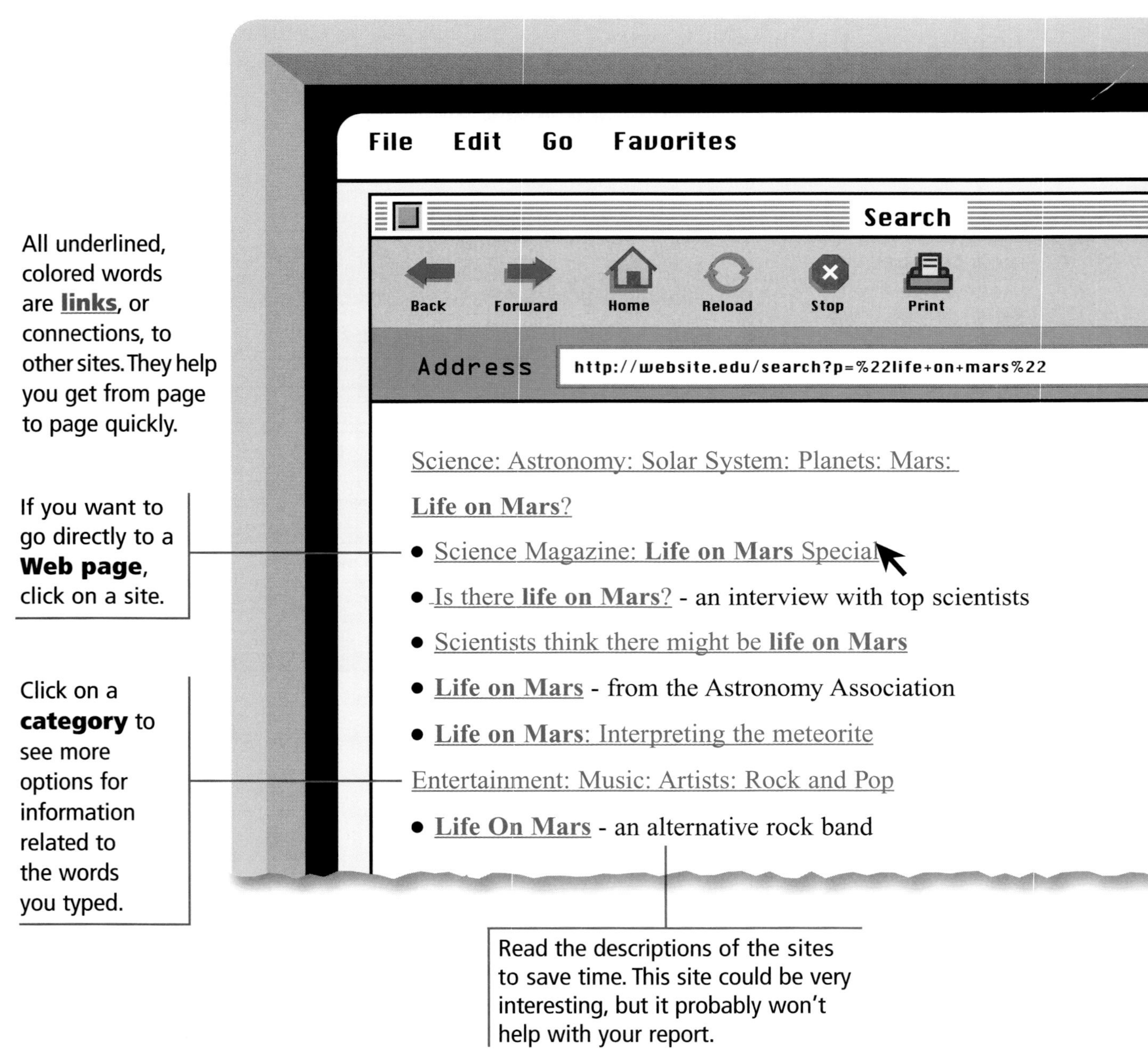

Read the descriptions of the sites to save time. This site could be very interesting, but it probably won't help with your report.

❸ Select a site, and read the article.

You might want to pick a new site or start a new search. If so, click on the **back arrow** to go back a page to the search results.

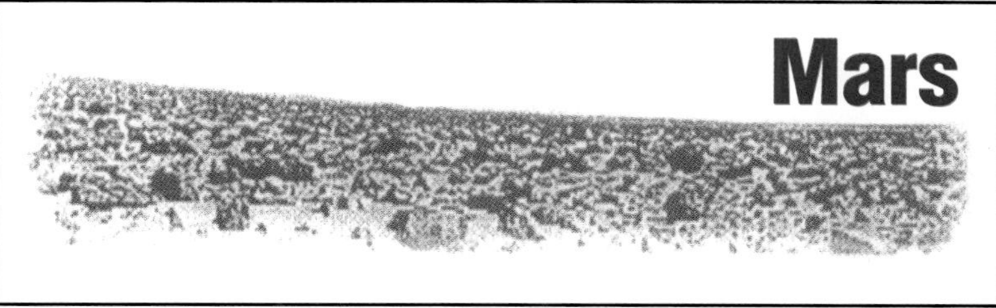

In this special section we bring you all the stories on the Mars probe landing, from New Scientist's award-winning team of reporters. We also offer an extensive archive of articles on NASA's earlier claim that Mars once supported life and a look at the search for life in space, as well as numerous web links. From the August 1996 heady excitement of that announcement--"life on Mars"--to the disappointing revelation--"no, probably not", Planet Science was there.

If you want to go to another Web page, click on a **link**.

MORE ON MARS:

- **Mission to Mars makes do with robots**

The US has formally abandoned its goal of landing astronauts on Mars by 2019. Instead, the new national space policy unveiled last week commits the nation to a permanent robot presence on the Red Planet starting no later than 2000. Human exploration might come later, depending on what the robots find.

MARS LATEST:

13 DEC 97: Hop, skip and jump
A little robot in a lab in Arizona is preparing to take several giant leaps for robotkind. If it reaches Mars in the next century, as its developers hope, it will produce its own fuel and be able to fly, hop and hover over the surface of the Red Planet.

12 NOV 97: In the dark
If life developed on ancient Mars, it got going in almost complete darkness, say scientists in the US and France. The newborn planet was shrouded in dense clouds of frozen carbon dioxide which acted like a mirror, they say, reflecting up to 95 percent of incident lighting. "In its early days, Mars was the white planet rather than the Red Planet".

❹ Print the article if it is helpful for your research. Later on, you can use the article to take notes.

Locating More Resources

If you already know the address of a Web site, you can type it in the address box at the top of the screen. A Web site address is also called the **URL** (Uniform Resource Locator).

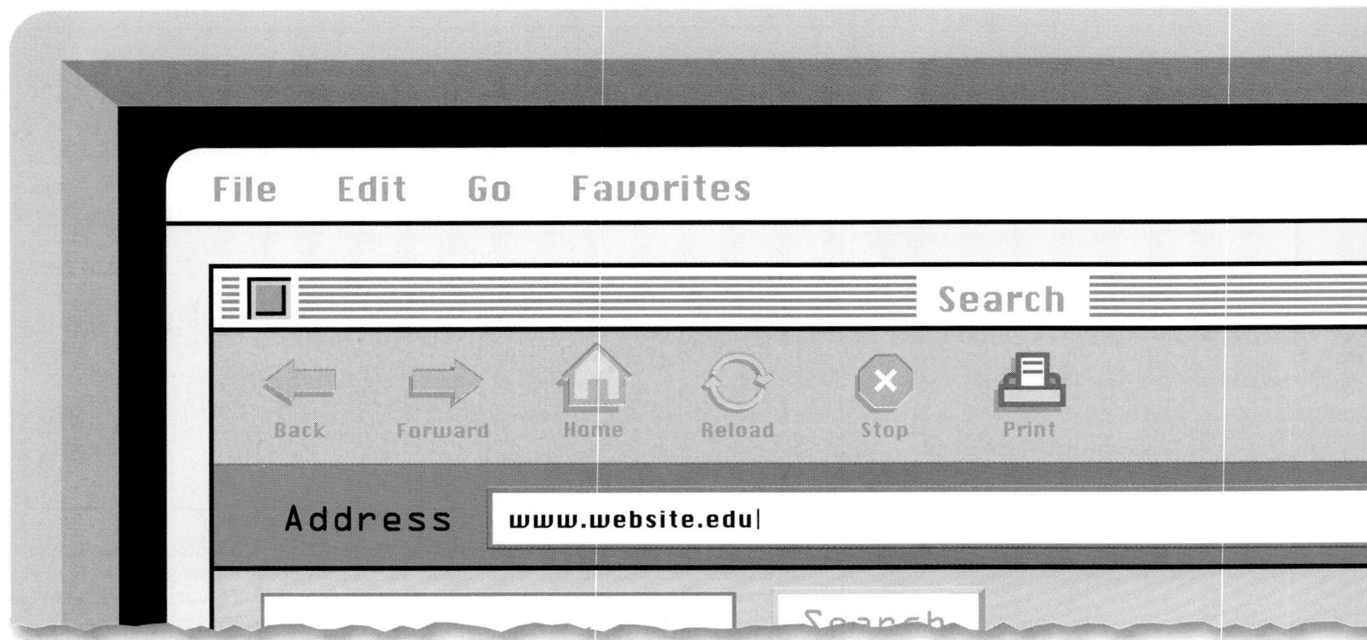

Here are a few good references to try. Because the Internet is always changing, these addresses might change. If you can't find a site, try searching by using its name.

Encyberpedia (Encyclopedia)
www.encyberpedia.com

Encyclopedia Britannica
www.eb.com

Merriam-Webster Dictionary
www.m-w.com

FirstGov for Kids
www.kids.gov

Old Farmer's Almanac
www.almanac.com

One Look Dictionary
www.onelook.com

Ask Jeeves Kids
www.ajkids.com

Yahooligans!
www.yahooligans.com

Keeping Favorite Web Sites

When you find a Web site that you want to come back to, you can tell the computer to "remember" it. It's like putting a bookmark in a book so you can find the page easily again.

1. While you're at the site, click on **Favorites** or **Bookmarks** at the top of the screen.

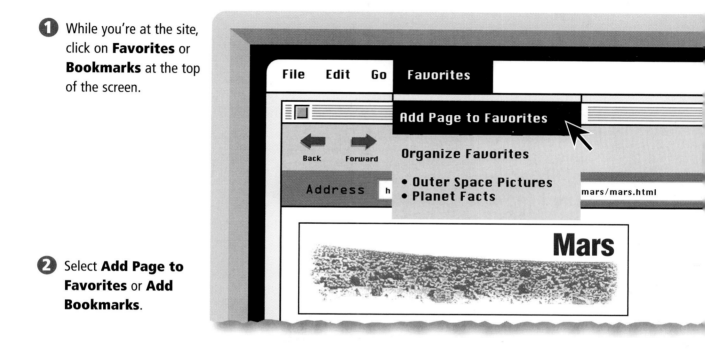

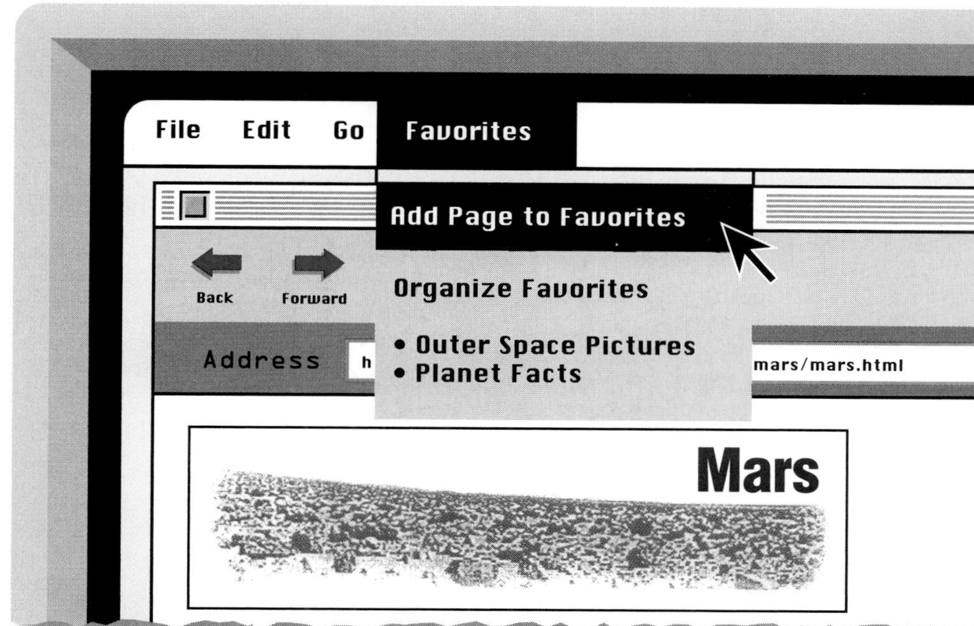

2. Select **Add Page to Favorites** or **Add Bookmarks**.

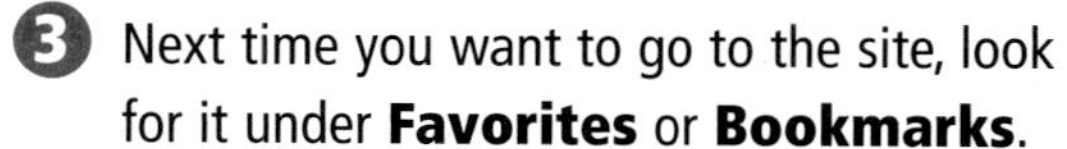

3. Next time you want to go to the site, look for it under **Favorites** or **Bookmarks**.

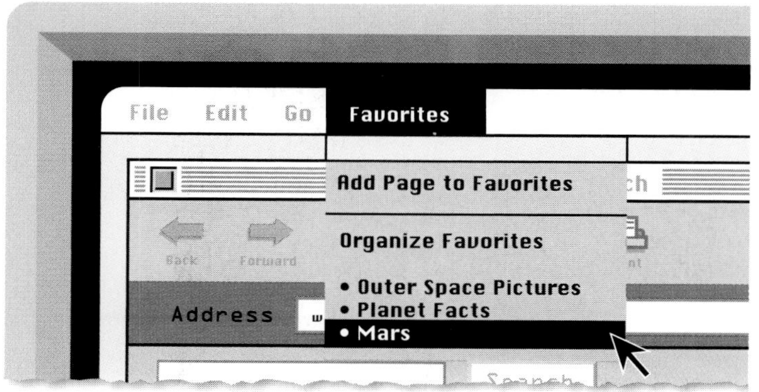

4. Select it, and the Web site will open automatically!

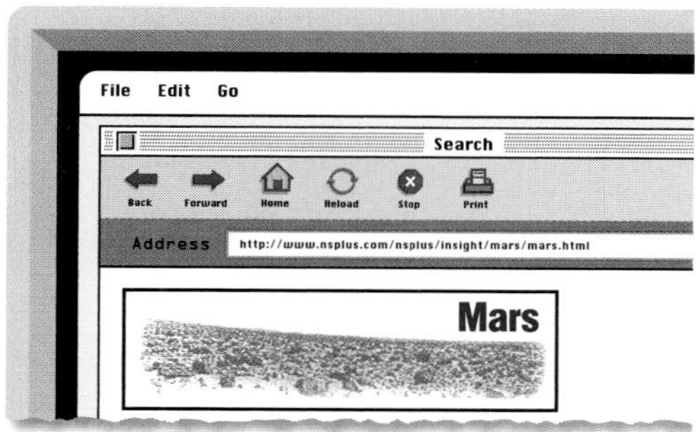

Choosing Data from the Internet

You may find much more information on the Internet than you need. Follow these steps to help you choose data for your research report.

1 Choose your key words carefully.

If your words are too general, the search results might show hundreds or even thousands of sites to choose from. Narrow your search by choosing specific key words.

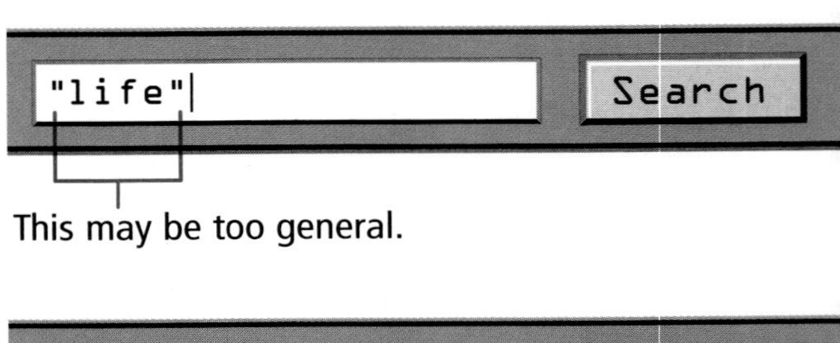

This may be too general.

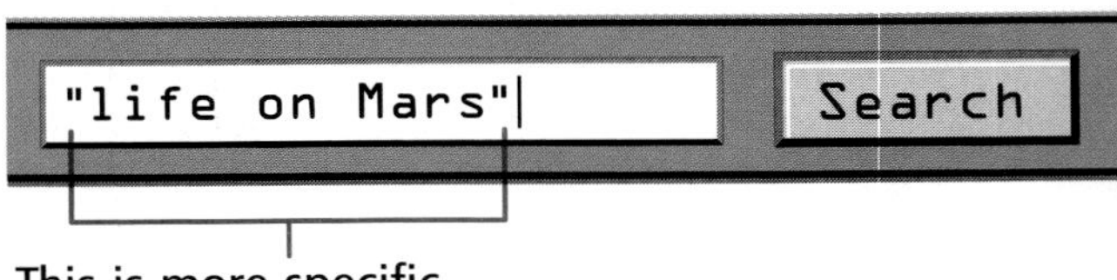

This is more specific.

2 Look back at your research questions.

Skim and scan a Web site to see if it answers at least some of your questions. If it does, save it under "Favorites" or "Bookmarks." You can come back to it later to read more carefully.

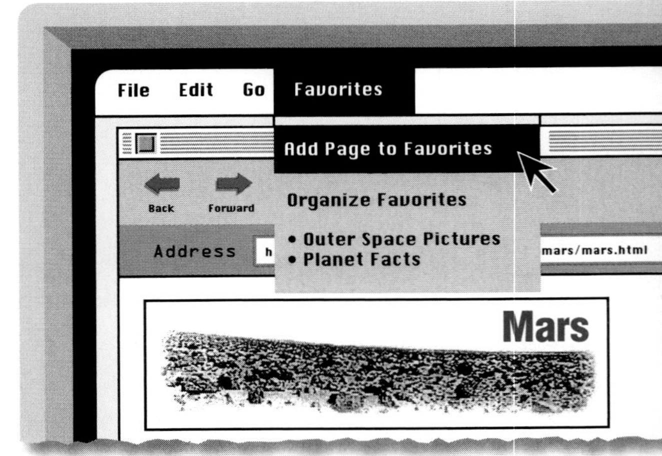

3 Check facts and sources.

Use more than one source to **verify your facts**, or make sure they are true. Try to find the same fact in at least two Web sites or in an encyclopedia. Think about the source, too. A well-known scientific Web site probably has more **reliable**, or true, information than a personal Web site.

Dateline U.S.A.™

New Year's Day

On the international calendar, January 1 is the first day of the calendar year.

- At the beginning of the new year, people often make **resolutions**, or promises to themselves, to stop bad habits like eating too much and to start good habits like exercising. On New Year's Day, people start trying to make their resolutions come true.

- Many people watch parades like the Tournament of Roses Parade in Pasadena, California, or football games like the Cotton Bowl in Texas.

Martin Luther King, Jr., Day

The third Monday in January honors Martin Luther King, Jr., a courageous American. People celebrate by remembering his message of peace and what he did for our country.

- Martin Luther King, Jr., was a minister who helped the sick and needy. He was a leader promoting **nonviolence** during the Civil Rights movement. He and many others helped end laws that were **discriminatory**, or unfair, because they treated different groups of people in different ways.

- In the summer of 1963, Martin Luther King, Jr., gave a famous speech called "I Have a Dream." He said that his dream was for people to judge each other by the "content of their character." He thought people should see each other as individuals and not as groups separated by the color of their skin.

Inauguration Day

Every four years a president is elected to be the leader of the United States. The president's term officially begins on January 20. On that day, people across the nation listen to speeches by the president and invited guests. This ceremony is called an **inauguration**.

The president of the United States lives in the White House.

Who has been president of the United States?

	President	Term
1	George Washington	1789–1797
2	John Adams	1797–1801
3	Thomas Jefferson	1801–1809
4	James Madison	1809–1817
5	James Monroe	1817–1825
6	John Quincy Adams	1825–1829
7	Andrew Jackson	1829–1837
8	Martin Van Buren	1837–1841
9	William H. Harrison	1841
10	John Tyler	1841–1845
11	James Knox Polk	1845–1849
12	Zachary Taylor	1849–1850
13	Millard Fillmore	1850–1853
14	Franklin Pierce	1853–1857
15	James Buchanan	1857–1861
16	Abraham Lincoln	1861–1865
17	Andrew Johnson	1865–1869
18	Ulysses S. Grant	1869–1877
19	Rutherford B. Hayes	1877–1881
20	James A. Garfield	1881
21	Chester A. Arthur	1881–1885
22	Grover Cleveland	1885–1889
23	Benjamin Harrison	1889–1893

	President	Term
24	Grover Cleveland	1893–1897
25	William McKinley	1897–1901
26	Theodore Roosevelt	1901–1909
27	William Howard Taft	1909–1913
28	Woodrow Wilson	1913–1921
29	Warren G. Harding	1921–1923
30	Calvin Coolidge	1923–1929
31	Herbert Hoover	1929–1933
32	Franklin D. Roosevelt	1933–1945
33	Harry S. Truman	1945–1953
34	Dwight D. Eisenhower	1953–1961
35	John F. Kennedy	1961–1963
36	Lyndon B. Johnson	1963–1969
37	Richard M. Nixon	1969–1974
38	Gerald R. Ford	1974–1977
39	Jimmy Carter	1977–1981
40	Ronald Reagan	1981–1989
41	George Bush	1989–1993
42	William Jefferson Clinton	1993–2001
43	George W. Bush	2001–

Chinese New Year

Many Americans celebrate the Chinese New Year, which begins in late January or early February.

- For about two weeks, families wish each other luck, health, happiness, and wealth for the coming year.
- During the celebrations, people set off fireworks and have feasts. They march in big parades, sometimes under a lion's head or a long, colorful dragon. It takes a lot of people to move a dragon down the street!
- The new year is a time of gift-giving, too. Adults give children red envelopes with money inside for good luck.

Where is one of the biggest Chinese New Year parades in the U.S.?

This is Chinatown in San Francisco, California. It has one of the largest Chinese communities in the United States. Thousands of people go to see the Chinese New Year parade every year.

Tet

Tet is another new year's celebration. It occurs on the first three days of the Vietnamese calendar, usually in late January or early February.

- The first visitor to a home on the first morning of Tet is important. If the visitor is kind and honest, the family will have good fortune for the rest of the year.
- Red is considered to be a lucky color, so people eat red food such as dyed watermelon seeds, which stain their hands and mouth.
- People also hang banners on their doors that have greetings like "compliments of the season."

Groundhog Day

An old legend says that a groundhog comes up from its winter nest on February 2.

- If the groundhog sees its own shadow, it means that there will be six more weeks of winter.
- If the groundhog does not see its shadow, it means that spring is about to begin.

Valentine's Day

- On February 14, people exchange cards, or **valentines**, to show they care about each other.
- Many valentines are decorated with red hearts and have messages written on them. Some show Cupid, a boy with wings, whose arrows make people fall in love.

Black History Month

African Americans have made significant contributions in many areas, from science and mathematics to literature and the fine arts. In the month of February, we recognize their contributions and learn more about the experiences of African Americans throughout the history of the United States.

Who are some courageous African Americans who fought for freedom and civil rights in the U.S.?

1841

Frederick Douglass spoke out against slavery.

Until the 1860s, African Americans were slaves, forced to work without pay. Frederick Douglass was born a slave but escaped to New England when he was 21. There Douglass began writing and speaking against slavery. He fought long and hard to stop slavery and to change the way African Americans were treated. ★

1850

Harriet Tubman helped slaves become free.

Harriet Tubman helped over 300 slaves leave the South for freedom in the North. She was a leader for the "Underground Railroad," a group of people who helped slaves by hiding them and moving them north in farm wagons. ★

1861–1865

African Americans fought in the Civil War.

During the Civil War, the Union army fought for the North who wanted to end slavery. About 180,000 African Americans fought with the Union army even though it did not treat them as equals and forced them to serve in all-black regiments. These regiments fought bravely and were important to winning the war and ending slavery. ★

★ 1840s ★ 1850s ★ 1860s

My People

The night is beautiful,
So the faces of my people.

The stars are beautiful,
So the eyes of my people.

Beautiful, also, is the sun.
Beautiful, also, are the souls of my people.

— Langston Hughes

1947

Jackie Robinson joined the Brooklyn Dodgers.

Although many African Americans were playing baseball in the 1940s, they had to play in leagues that were separate from the major leagues. In 1947, Jackie Robinson became the first African American to play on a modern American major league team, the Brooklyn Dodgers. From then on, blacks and whites were able to play baseball in the same leagues.★

1955

Rosa Parks inspired the Civil Rights movement.

Rosa Parks refused to give up her seat on a bus to a white person. Her protest inspired others to act against unfair laws. This was one event that helped get the Civil Rights movement started. **Civil rights** means that all people should be treated equally under the law.★

1967

Thurgood Marshall joined the Supreme Court.

Thurgood Marshall presented the argument for **desegregation** of the public schools. Desegregation meant that African American students could go to the same schools as white children. Later, Marshall became the first African American Supreme Court justice.★

★1940s ★1950s ★1960s

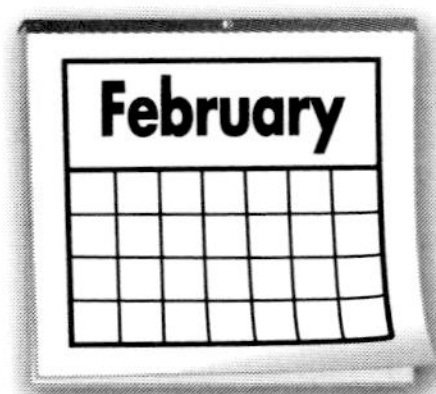

Presidents' Day

On the third Monday in February, Americans honor two great American presidents.

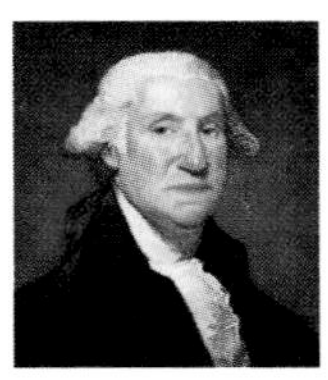

- **George Washington** became the first president of the United States in 1789. He is called the "Father of Our Country."

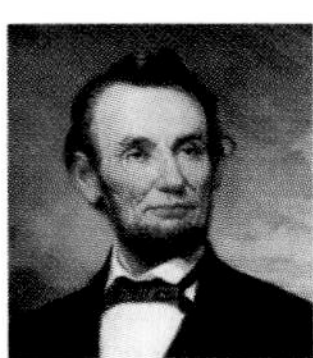

- **Abraham Lincoln,** the sixteenth president, was a great leader during difficult times. He helped to end the Civil War and slavery.

Both presidents were important leaders in the government of the United States.

How does the United States government work?

The Constitution of the United States of America

After the Revolutionary War, the American people needed a plan to help them organize the new government.

In 1787 several important leaders approved the United States **Constitution**. The Constitution is a written document that tells what the main laws of the country are and the powers and duties of each part of the government. It includes the **Bill of Rights** which protects the rights and freedoms of every citizen, such as freedom of religion, freedom of speech, and freedom of the press.

We the People of the United States,
insure domestic Tranquility, provide for the common defence, promote the general
and our Posterity, do ordain and establish this Constitution for the United States of
Article. I.
Section. 1. All legislative Powers herein granted shall be vested in a Congress of the
of Representatives.
Section. 2. The House of Representatives shall be composed of Members chosen every
in each State shall have the Qualifications requisite for Electors of the most numerous Branch of th
No Person shall be a Representative who shall not have attained to the Age of twen
and who shall not, when elected, be an Inhabitant of that State in which he shall be chosen.
Representatives and direct Taxes shall be apportioned among the several States which m
Numbers, which shall be determined by adding to the whole Number of free Persons, including
not taxed, three fifths of all other Persons. The actual Enumeration shall be made within th
and within every subsequent Term of ten Years, in such Manner as they shall by Law direct.
thirty Thousand, but each State shall have at Least one Representative; and until such enum
entitled to chuse three, Massachusetts eight, Rhode Island and Providence Plantations one
eight, Delaware one, Maryland six, Virginia ten, North Carolina five, South Carolina fi
When vacancies happen in the Representation from any State, the Executive Author
The House of Representatives shall chuse their Speaker and other Officers; and shall
Section. 3. The Senate of the United States shall be composed of two Senators from each
Senator shall have one Vote.
Immediately after they shall be assembled in Consequence of the first Election, they
of the Senators of the first Class shall be vacated at the Expiration of the second Year, of the se

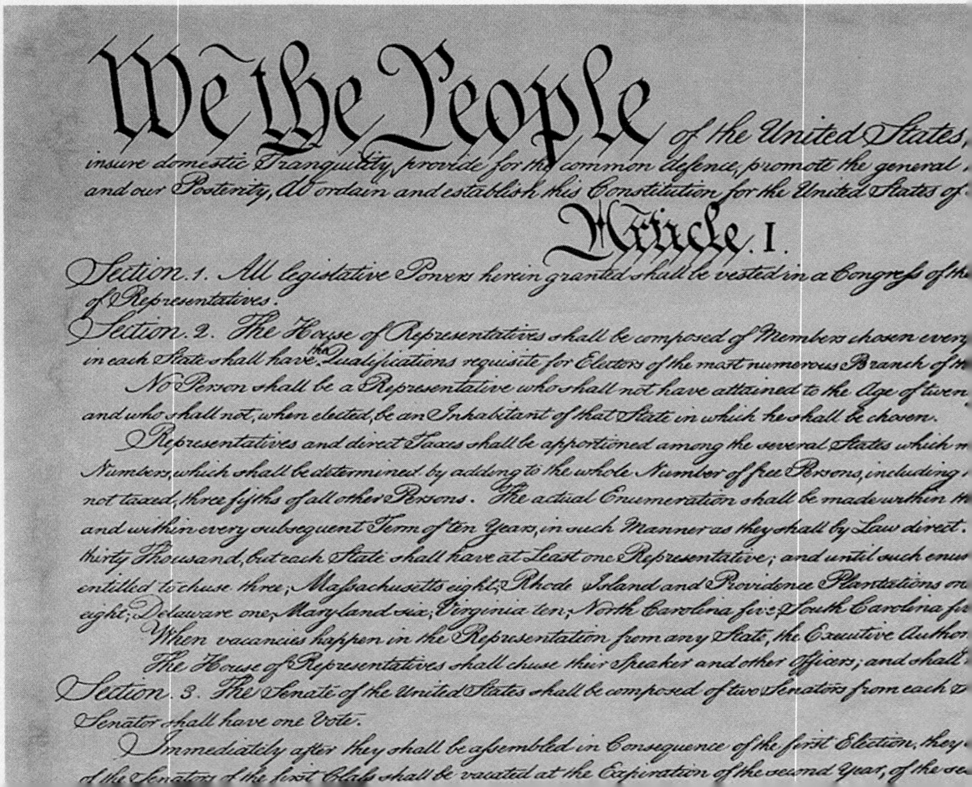

The Three Branches of Our Government

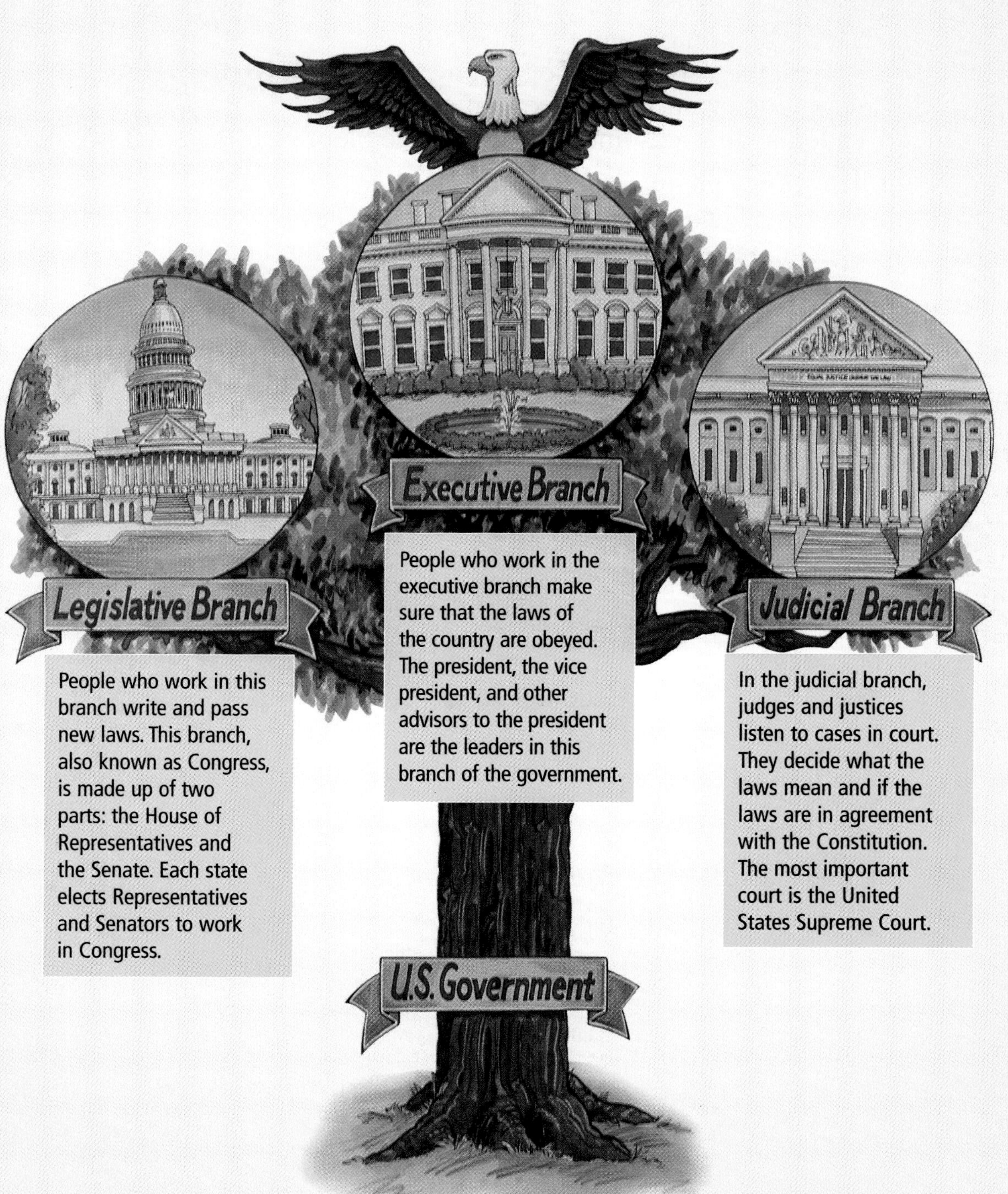

Executive Branch
People who work in the executive branch make sure that the laws of the country are obeyed. The president, the vice president, and other advisors to the president are the leaders in this branch of the government.
Legislative Branch
People who work in this branch write and pass new laws. This branch, also known as Congress, is made up of two parts: the House of Representatives and the Senate. Each state elects Representatives and Senators to work in Congress.
Judicial Branch
In the judicial branch, judges and justices listen to cases in court. They decide what the laws mean and if the laws are in agreement with the Constitution. The most important court is the United States Supreme Court.
U.S. Government

Saint Patrick's Day

On March 17, be sure to wear green! It's a tradition on Saint Patrick's Day. You might also see lots of green decorations, such as three-leaf clovers called shamrocks and tiny elves called leprechauns.

This holiday began as a Catholic holiday in Ireland, a country with lots of green hills and valleys. It was a special day to honor the good works of a man named Saint Patrick. When Irish immigrants came to live in the United States in the 1700s, they brought this tradition with them. It has been celebrated here ever since.

What other groups of people have immigrated to the United States?

When	Who	About How Many
1840–1860	Irish	1,500,000
1840–1880	Germans	4,000,000
1870–1900	Danes, Norwegians, and Swedes	1,500,000
1880–1920	Eastern Europeans	3,500,000
	Austrians, Czechs, Hungarians, and Slovaks	4,000,000
	Italians	4,500,000
1910–1920	Mexicans	700,000
1950–1990	Mexicans	5,000,000
1960–1980	Cubans	700,000
1970–1980	Dominicans, Haitians, and Jamaicans	900,000
	Vietnamese	500,000
1981–2000	Chinese	800,000
	Filipinos	1,100,000

Statue of Liberty

When many immigrants came to the United States, they arrived in New York Harbor. There they were welcomed by this statue, which stands for freedom and opportunity. The Statue of Liberty is still an important symbol today for all Americans.

Easter

Easter is a Christian holiday that occurs between March 22 and April 25. It is also a time when people celebrate new life and the coming of spring.

- Some people wear new suits, dresses, and hats to church on Easter Sunday.
- Children decorate hard-boiled eggs for an imaginary "Easter Bunny" to hide, but it is really the parents who hide the eggs for children to find.

Passover

In March or April, during the Hebrew month of *Nisan*, Jewish families celebrate Passover for eight days. Passover is a time to celebrate freedom for all Jews and people everywhere.

- Right before Passover, families clean house very carefully. This is to get rid of all bread crumbs and food made from flour.
- On the first night, families talk about their history. They also eat a traditional meal called a *Seder* that includes *matzo*, a flat bread, and other special foods.

Ramadan

Ramadan is a Muslim celebration in the ninth month of the Islamic calendar. It lasts almost thirty days.

- At this time, Muslims follow directions from the *Koran*, a holy book, and eat only before sunrise and after sunset.
- Ramadan ends with a festival called *Id al-Fitr,* which means "a festival of happiness and a time of great joy." That's when families exchange gifts and have a large meal, or **feast**.

National Library Week

You can find out anything you want to know in a library. During April, people honor all that libraries have to offer. They might celebrate by going to the library to read books or to listen to favorite stories.

American literature has lots of characters and heroes. Some of the characters are real, while others are made-up. Many of the heroes have become so popular that they are featured in movies and television shows.

Who are some of the well-known characters and people in American literature?

From Cartoon Strips:

Superman

Superman is a comic book super hero who was created by Jerry Siegel and Joe Shuster. Superman is "more powerful than a locomotive" and "able to leap tall buildings in a single bound." When he isn't rescuing someone, he disguises himself as Clark Kent, a reporter for the *Daily Planet* newspaper.

Charlie Brown and Snoopy

Charlie Brown and his dog, Snoopy, are characters in the comic strip "Peanuts" by Charles M. Schulz. Some of their friends are Linus, Lucy, and Peppermint Patty. They all enjoy things like baseball and going to summer camp.

Wonder Woman

William Moulton Marston created Wonder Woman, a quick and strong super hero who had been an Amazonian princess before coming to the United States. She helps others with her magic lasso and can dodge bullets with her magic bracelet. When not fighting off evil, she teaches a message of peace and equality.

From Tall Tales:

John Henry

John Henry built railroad tracks. He was so strong that he could pound steel faster and longer than a steam drill.

Pecos Bill

Pecos Bill was a cowboy who wasn't afraid to do anything. Stories about him tell how he rode a hurricane to shake the rain out of it and rounded up every steer in Texas for his ranch.

From the Wild West:

Annie Oakley

Annie Oakley was so good with a rifle that she could shoot a dime out of the air.

From Literature:

Laura Ingalls

Laura Ingalls Wilder was a real woman who wrote about growing up in the Midwest. She tells about traveling in a covered wagon and living in a log cabin. Her books are called the *Little House* books.

Dorothy

Dorothy is a girl in the series of books about the magical land of Oz, by L. Frank Baum. There she meets creatures like a scarecrow, a tin man, and a lion.

Tom Sawyer and Huckleberry Finn

Tom Sawyer and Huckleberry Finn are two characters in books by Mark Twain. Tom and Huck often get into trouble but always have amazing adventures in their hometown near the Mississippi River.

April Fools' Day

On April 1, don't believe everything you see and hear! On this day, many people play tricks on each other. For example, a friend might tell you that your shoes are untied. When you look down and see that nothing's wrong, your friend will say "April Fools!"

Earth Day

Earth Day is a day to think about and appreciate the Earth. On April 22, people talk about ways to protect our resources and environment. It's important to care about the Earth because people need clean air, water, and land to live a healthy life.

What are some of the special environments to protect in the United States?

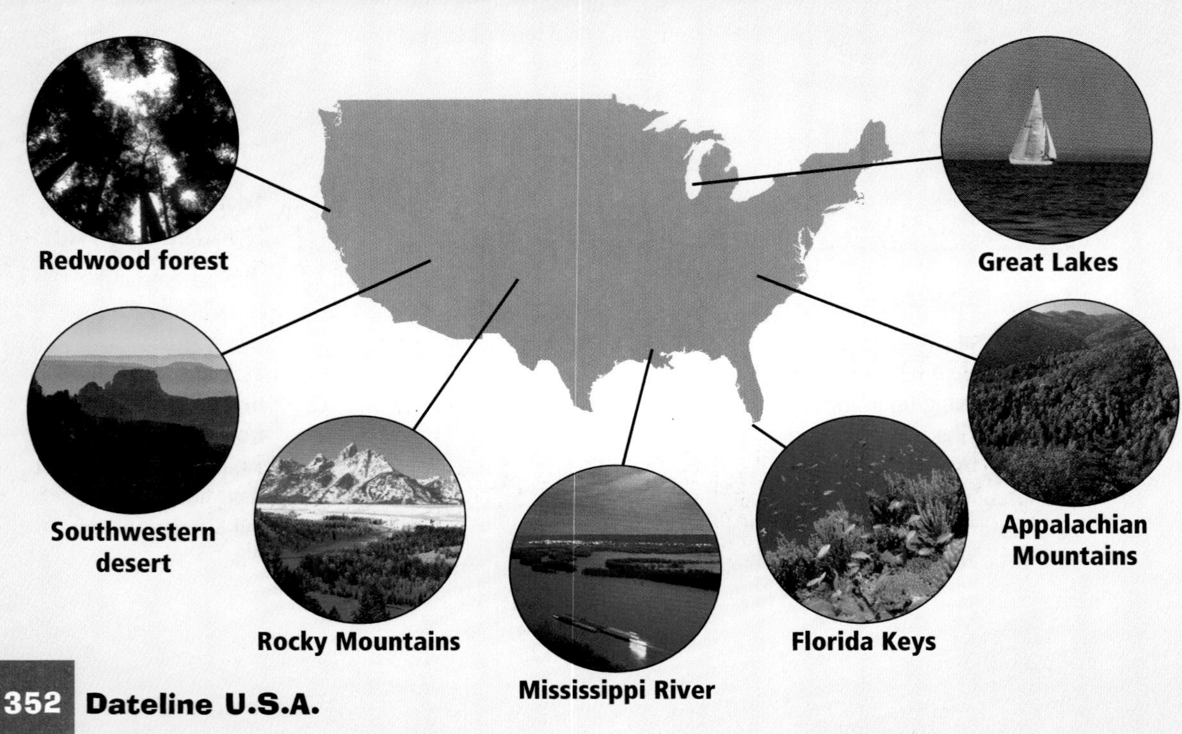

Cinco de Mayo

On May 5, 1862, the Mexican and French armies fought near Puebla, Mexico. The small Mexican army won the battle that day. Every year on May 5, or *cinco de mayo* in Spanish, the people of Mexico celebrate this victory. Mexican immigrants brought this celebration with them when they came to the United States.

Today, people in many U.S. towns celebrate *Cinco de Mayo*. Some people go to carnivals. Others enjoy watching parades and traditional Mexican dancing and listening to Mexican music.

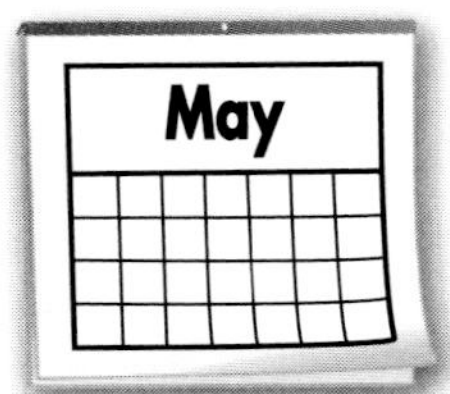

Mother's Day

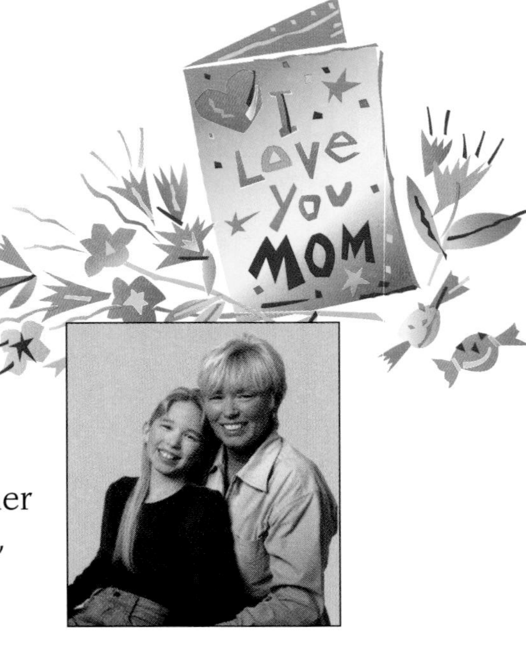

On the second Sunday in May, sons and daughters remind their mothers how much they love them.

- Many people give their moms cards, flowers, or chocolates, and an extra big hug!
- Some people also send greetings to other special women like their grandmothers, aunts, or close female friends.

Memorial Day

Memorial Day began as a way of honoring soldiers who died in the Civil War. Since then, the last Monday in May has become a day to remember all soldiers who have died fighting for the United States.

- On this day, people place flowers or flags on soldiers' graves.
- Some cities have military parades and other special programs.
- Because summer vacation begins on this day in many places, families often celebrate by having outdoor picnics and barbecues.

Flag Day

The United States flag is the most important symbol of our nation. On June 14, Americans pay respect to the flag and all it stands for by displaying it at their homes, schools, and businesses.

- The first flag had thirteen stars and thirteen stripes that stood for the number of original colonies.
- As the United States grew and more territories became states, the flag changed. Today there are still thirteen stripes, but there are fifty stars. Each star stands for a state.

The Flag of 1777

The United States Flag Today

How did the United States grow?

1803
The United States made the Louisiana Purchase.

In the 1700s, the western border of the United States was the Mississippi River. In 1803 the United States bought, or **purchased**, the land on the other side of the Mississippi from the French. This purchase made the United States twice as big! ★

The United States 1803

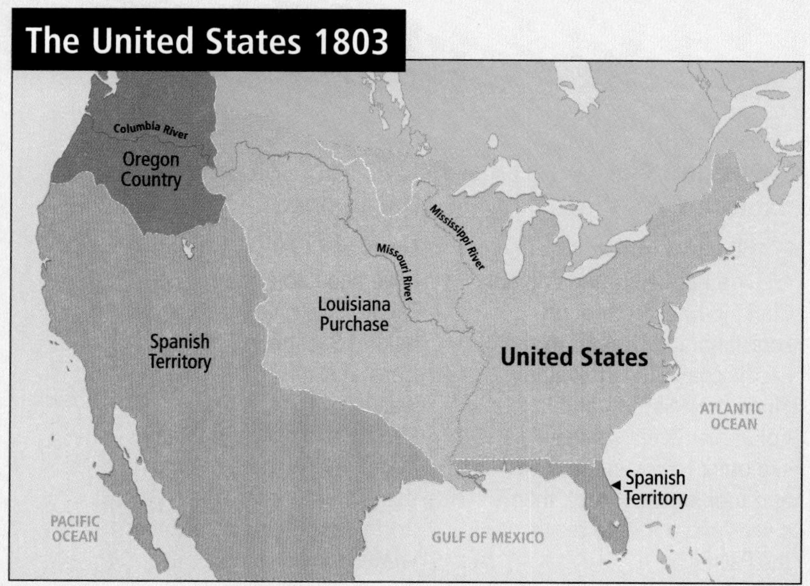

★ 1800s

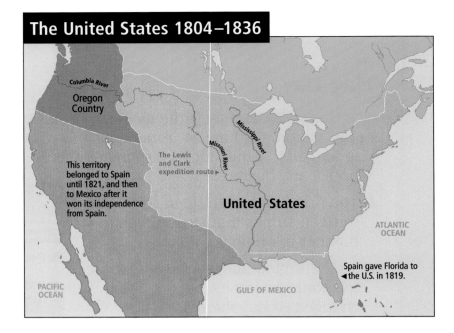

The United States 1804–1836

Columbia River

Oregon Country

Mississippi River

Missouri River

The Lewis and Clark expedition route ▸

This territory belonged to Spain until 1821, and then to Mexico after it won its independence from Spain.

United States

ATLANTIC OCEAN

Spain gave Florida to ◂the U.S. in 1819.

PACIFIC OCEAN

GULF OF MEXICO

1804–1806
Lewis and Clark explored the West.

In 1804, two explorers, Meriwether Lewis and William Clark, journeyed through Louisiana and Oregon to the Pacific coast. They traveled along the Missouri and Columbia Rivers. As they explored, they created maps and took notes. It took them a year and a half to reach the Pacific.★

Sacagawea

Lewis and Clark may not have been able to reach the Pacific Ocean without the help of Sacagawea, their translator and guide. She was a member of the Shoshone tribe. Sacagawea asked her relatives to help the explorers cross the Rocky Mountains before the winter snows came.★

1819
Florida became part of the United States.

Beginning in 1814, General Andrew Jackson lead American troops through Florida. They fought the Spanish until 1819 when the Spanish agreed to give Florida to the United States.★

★1800s

★1820s

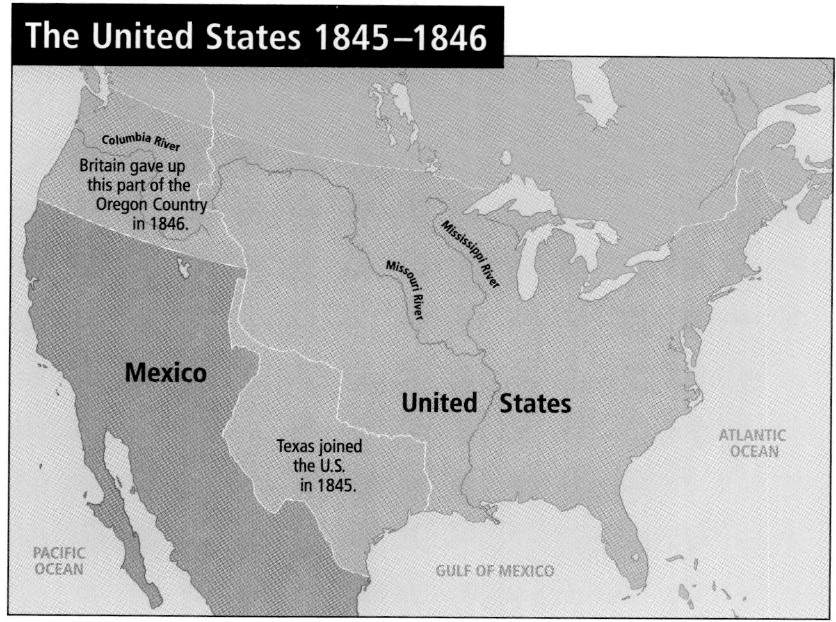

1845
Texas became part of the United States.

So many Americans had moved to Texas that there were more American than Mexican citizens. People started fighting because of this. Sam Houston led a Texan army to victory in the Battle of San Jacinto. Mexico signed the Treaty of Velasco, which made Texas free from Mexico. Almost ten years later, the U.S. Congress offered to **annex**, or unite, Texas with the U.S.★

1846
Britain gave up part of the Oregon Country.

Many people had traveled by covered wagon across the U.S. to settle in the British-controlled Oregon Country. The settlers wanted the country to be a part of the United States. Because Great Britain did not want to go to war, they agreed to give up all the land south of the 49th parallel, which is now the Canadian border.★

★1840s

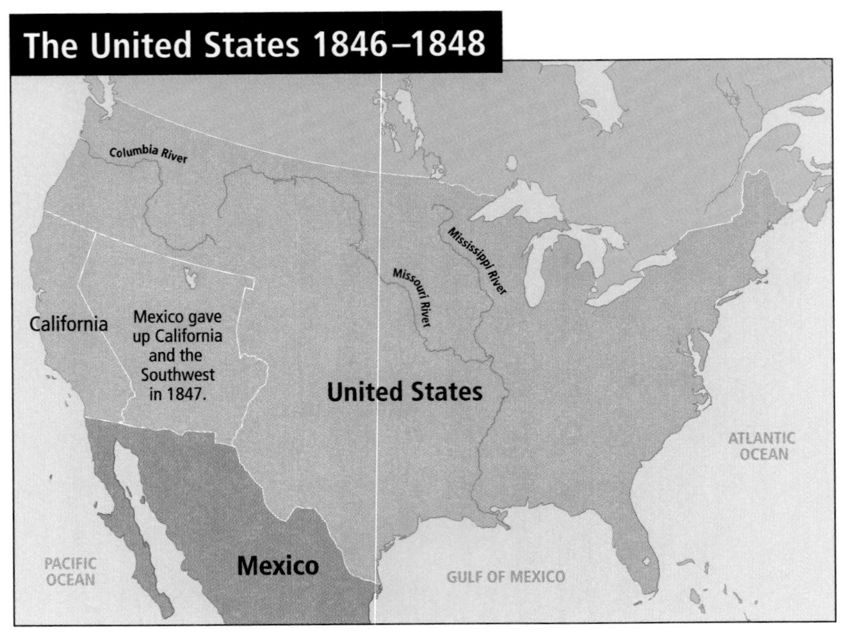

Today's California flag is based on the original flag.

1847
Mexico gave California and the Southwest to the U.S.

American settlers in the Mexican territory of California wanted to be free and become the Bear Flag Republic, named after the flag they designed. The United States sent armies and ships to help them. Mexico surrendered and signed the Treaty of Guadalupe Hidalgo, which gave the United States all of California and the Southwest.★

1848
The California Gold Rush began.

Gold was discovered in California in 1848. As news spread about the discovery, thousands of Americans moved west to pan for gold. They were hoping to get rich. Very few people became rich, but many of them settled in California.★

★1840s

★1850s

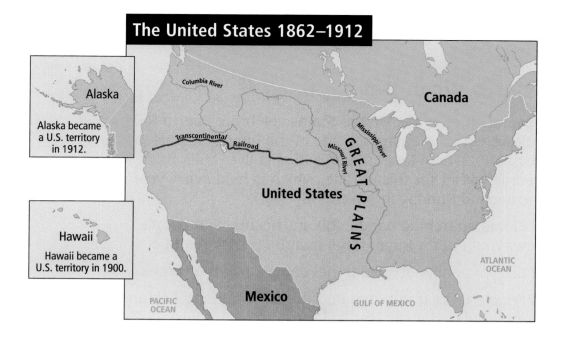

The United States 1862–1912

Alaska

Alaska became a U.S. territory in 1912.

Hawaii

Hawaii became a U.S. territory in 1900.

Columbia River

Canada

Transcontinental Railroad

Mississippi River

Missouri River

GREAT PLAINS

United States

ATLANTIC OCEAN

PACIFIC OCEAN

Mexico

GULF OF MEXICO

1862

Congress gave away free farmland with the Homestead Act.

By the mid-1800s, every part of the United States was settled except the Great Plains. The Homestead Act of 1862 was a law that said anyone who farmed on the Great Plains for five years could keep the land for free. Eventually, hard-working farmers turned the area into "America's breadbasket" and grew most of the food for the rest of the U.S. ★

1869

The first transcontinental railroad was finished.

In 1863, two companies began building railroads. One set of tracks went west from Nebraska; the other went east from California. In 1869, the two tracks joined in Promontory, Utah, to form a transcontinental railroad. This railroad made it possible for millions of people to travel west to establish farms and raise cattle. ★

★1860s

★1870s

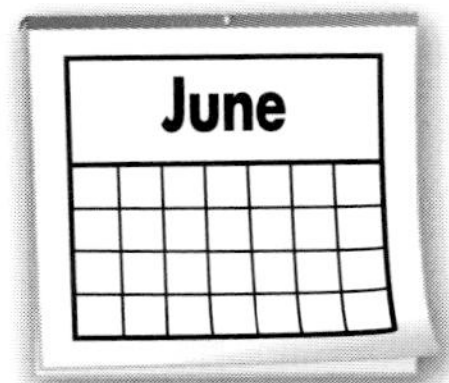

Puerto Rican Day

Several cities in the United States celebrate Puerto Rican culture with a big parade. One of the biggest is in New York City, where lots of Puerto Ricans live. Millions of people gather for this parade, which is held every year on the second Sunday in June.

- Floats, marching bands, folk musicians, and people waving Puerto Rican flags march up Fifth Avenue.
- Lots of people do traditional dances like the rumba.
- People wear traditional Puerto Rican clothing like an embroidered *guayabera*, a long shirt for a man.

Father's Day

The third Sunday in June is a special day for fathers. That's when sons and daughters give their fathers gifts and cards to show their love.

- Father's Day is also a great time for children to go on a picnic, to a baseball game, or any place where they can be with their fathers.
- Often people send "Happy Father's Day" greetings to other men they respect, such as their uncles or grandfathers.

Dragon Boat Festival

In late June, on the fifth day of the fifth month of the Chinese lunar calendar, there are dragon boat races all over the world. These races are part of the Dragon Boat Festival, held in memory of an ancient Chinese poet named Qu Yuan.

When Qu Yuan was punished for saying bad things about his government, he jumped into a river and drowned. Today boat races are held in cities like Boston, New York City, and Honolulu to act out what Qu Yuan's friends did to try to save him.

- Teams use boats that look like dragons. Since dragons are symbols of good luck, the boats are said to spread good luck as they race across the water.
- The teams race each other to a finish line. The team that wins shares the prize money.

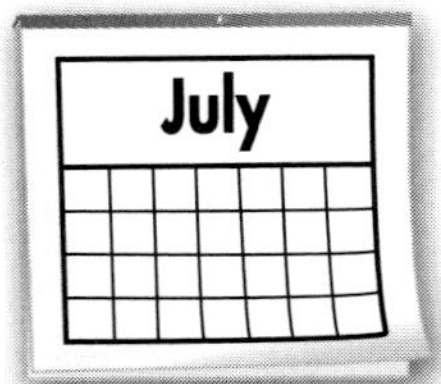

Independence Day

Independence Day is the Fourth of July. On this day, many Americans march in parades, wave the American flag, and watch fireworks at night. They are celebrating the time when America fought for and won its **independence**, or freedom, from Britain.

What events led to America's independence?

1773

The colonists took part in the Boston Tea Party.

In the 1700s, America belonged to Britain. The **colonists**, or the people living in colonial America, got tired of paying unfair British taxes on tea. They dressed as Mohawk Indians and protested by throwing the tea into the ocean. This was one of the events that led to the Revolutionary War.★

1775

The Revolutionary War began.

On April 19, American soldiers fought against the British at Lexington and Concord in the first battle of the Revolutionary War. The soldiers were called "minutemen" because they were ready to fight "at a minute's notice."★

★1770s

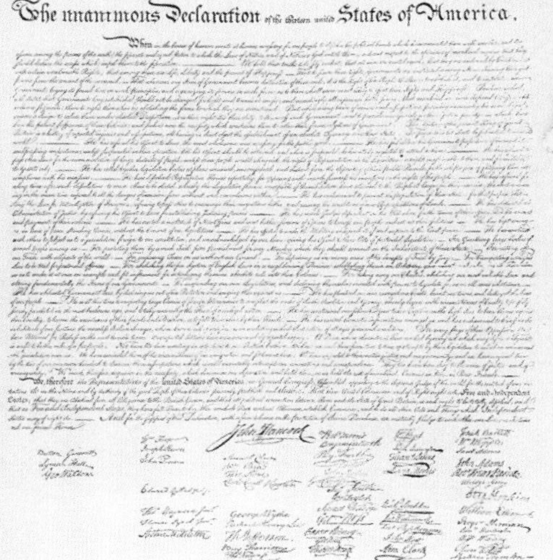

IN CONGRESS, JULY 4, 1776

The unanimous Declaration of the thirteen united States of America.

1776

The Declaration of Independence was signed.

On July 4, 1776, the American colonists signed the Declaration of Independence. This important paper stated that the thirteen American colonies were free from Britain. This meant that the colonies would no longer obey the laws of Great Britain or pay taxes to the British government.★

1781

The British surrendered at Yorktown.

The last major battle of the Revolutionary War was fought in Yorktown, Virginia, in 1781. That's when the British surrendered to American General George Washington.★

1783

The Revolutionary War ended.

Benjamin Franklin, John Adams, John Jay, and Henry Laurens went to Paris to sign a peace treaty with the British.★

★1780s

Anniversary of the First Moon Walk

On July 20, 1969, the world watched as two American astronauts became the first human beings to walk on the moon.

- As astronaut Neil Armstrong stepped from the landing craft *Eagle*, he said, "That's one small step for a man, one giant leap for mankind."
- Armstrong and his partner, Edwin Aldrin, gathered samples of rocks and soil for over two and a half hours. Before they climbed back into the *Eagle*, they put an American flag in the ground.

Who are some other American astronauts? What did they do?

1961
Alan Shepard became the first American in space.

Alan Shepard traveled in space in *Freedom 7* for fifteen minutes.★

1962
John Glenn, Jr., orbited the Earth.

John Glenn, Jr., was the first American to **orbit**, or go around, the Earth. His spacecraft, *Friendship 7*, flew around the Earth three times in a little over four and a half hours.★

1965
Edward H. White II walked in space.

The first American to go outside the spacecraft while in space was Edward H. White II. He was on this spacewalk for 21 minutes.★

1983
Sally Ride became the first American woman in space.

Sally Ride and four other astronauts went on a six-day flight in the space shuttle *Challenger*.★

★1960s ★1970s ★1980s

Native American Powwows

Traditional dancing

On August 12–17, Native Americans get together for the Inter-Tribal Indian Ceremonial at Red Rock State Park in Gallup, New Mexico. This is just one of many powwows held by Native Americans across the United States throughout the year.

A powwow is a gathering of Native Americans to celebrate their culture and heritage.

- Families and friends meet every year for reunions.
- Some groups of people play drums and sing while others tape-record the traditional music. Later, people will use the tapes to practice singing and dancing.
- Family members of all ages compete in dance contests. They can win prizes for traditional, fancy, grass, or jingle-dress dancing.
- There are also special ceremonies. During an **introduction ceremony**, a family dances to introduce their child as a powwow dancer.

Jingle dress

Playing the drums

Labor Day

Americans honor working people on the first Monday in September. Many workers get this day off so they can rest and enjoy the holiday. Labor Day is usually the last day of summer vacation for many students, too! People arrange special events like parades, picnics, and concerts to celebrate the occasion.

Labor Day began during a period of time called the Industrial Revolution. That was a time when people invented many new products, businesses got bigger, more machines made more products, and more people moved to the cities to work in factories.

How did life change during the Industrial Revolution?

1876
Alexander Graham Bell invented the telephone.

Alexander Bell's first telephone was one-way, which meant that only one person could talk while the other listened. Within a year, Bell made a two-way telephone. As people started using this invention, communication became faster and easier for everyone around the world.★

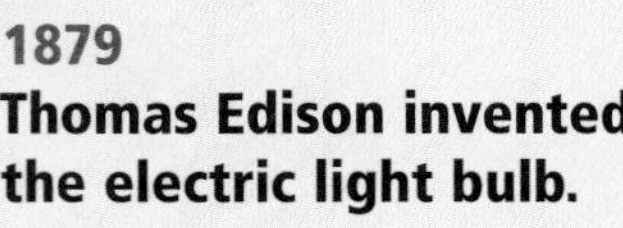

1879
Thomas Edison invented the electric light bulb.

Thomas Edison was one of America's greatest inventors. He is best known for inventing a practical light bulb, but he also invented many other things, including the phonograph. It recorded and replayed sounds. Edison's inventions were so useful that soon everyone had them in their homes.★

1882
Jan Matzeliger invented a shoe machine.

Jan Matzeliger invented the shoe-lasting machine to shape and then attach the top of a shoe to its sole. Shoes cost a lot less because this machine could do what had been done before by hand. ★

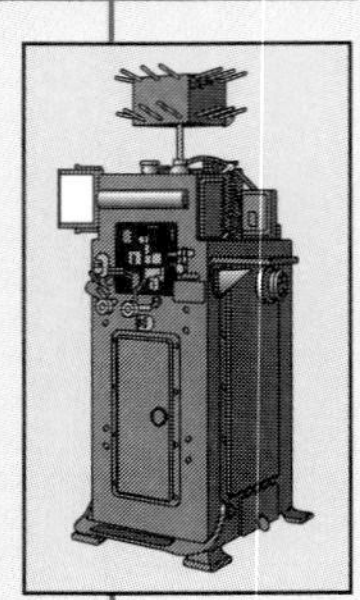

★1870s

★1880s

Expanding Factories and New Inventions

From the mid-1800s to the early 1900s, many people started working in factories. At that time, they had to work twelve to sixteen hours a day for very little money. To improve the unfair working conditions, many workers formed groups called unions. The unions asked factory owners for better pay and safer workplaces.

This was also a time when many Americans thought of new things to make and new ways to do things. From those ideas and inventions, people began to make more and more products, and new companies and businesses were formed.

1886

Samuel Gompers became a labor leader.

Samuel Gompers became an important leader of a large labor union. He worked hard to establish labor laws for all workers, including women and children. These laws led to improvements in working conditions and limited the number of hours people had to work.★

1889

Jane Addams opened Hull House for workers.

During the late 1800s, many immigrants came to the city of Chicago to work. Jane Addams and another social worker created a special center called Hull House to help immigrants learn English and train for new jobs. With Addams's help, immigrants were able to demand fair working conditions.★

1913

Henry Ford started the first modern assembly line.

Henry Ford created the modern assembly line, which made it faster and less expensive to build cars. Workers would do only one job, such as tightening bolts as the cars moved past them on a conveyor belt. Because of the assembly line process, Ford was able to build the first car that many people could afford, the Model T.★

★1890s ★1900s ★1910s

Rosh Hashanah and Yom Kippur

In September or October, in the Hebrew month of *Tishri*, people celebrate the Jewish New Year.

Rosh Hashanah begins on the first day of *Tishri* and usually lasts for two days. *Rosh Hashanah* means "beginning (or head) of the year."

- Jewish people give each other cards, greetings, and good wishes.
- People fix a special treat made of apple slices dipped in honey. The honey stands for hope for a sweet new year!

Yom Kippur is from sunset on the ninth day of *Tishri* until three stars appear in the sky after the tenth day.

- People do not work. Instead, they go to their synagogue to ask forgiveness, and they promise to make the new year a good one.
- In order to concentrate on their religion, people do not eat or drink anything for twenty-four hours. Then they have a festive meal.

Citizenship Day

September 17 is Citizenship Day. It begins a week-long celebration called Constitution Week. People give speeches and display the American flag to show that they are proud to be American citizens.

In 1952, President Harry S. Truman established Citizenship Day to honor the date the United States Constitution was signed in 1787. Then in 1956, Congress established Constitution Week, which lasts from September 17 through September 23. Congress did this because the Constitution is such an important document and symbol of freedom for all Americans.

What are some other symbols of the United States?

The Capitol

This building is located in Washington, D.C., the capital of the United States. It is where people in Congress work together to make laws. The Capitol stands for democracy. That's the kind of government that gives people the right to govern themselves.

The Great Seal of the United States

This **emblem**, or picture, is printed on official documents and on the one-dollar bill. It shows an American bald eagle holding an olive branch and arrows. The olive branch is a symbol of peace. The arrows stand for strength. The paper, or scroll, in the eagle's beak says, *E pluribus unum.* That's Latin for "one (nation) out of many (states)."

Uncle Sam

Uncle Sam is a made-up man who stands for the United States. His name probably came from the initials U.S., the abbreviation for **U**nited **S**tates. You'll see Uncle Sam on posters and cartoons. You might also see him marching in a parade! He'll always be dressed in America's colors: red, white, and blue.

Columbus Day

On the second Monday in October, people remember Christopher Columbus's trip to the Americas in 1492. Columbus was an Italian sea captain who had been looking for a way to sail from Europe to China and India. He landed on an island in the Bahamas on October 12,1492.

- After Columbus, explorers from other countries sailed to the Americas. They were looking for gold, silver, spices, and other valuable things. They also wanted to conquer new lands for their countries.
- Columbus and the other explorers called the land the "New World" because it was new to them. Native Americans had lived in the Americas for thousands of years before the explorers arrived.

Who were some of the explorers?

1492
Christopher Columbus landed in the Bahamas.

Christopher Columbus made four trips to the "New World." He explored the Bahamas, Puerto Rico, Cuba, the Dominican Republic, Jamaica, Trinidad, Venezuela, and Central America.★

1497
John Cabot explored the northeastern American coast.

John Cabot, an Italian sea captain, made two trips to the northeastern American coast. His journeys began the exploration and settlement of North America.★

1513
Juan Ponce de León landed in Florida.

Juan Ponce de León came from Spain. He was the first explorer to land in Florida. Some people say he was seeking the Fountain of Youth, a magical water that would keep him young forever.★

★1490s ★1500s ★1510s

Native North America

There were many different Native American tribes living in North America when the explorers arrived. Each tribe had its own language, culture, and way of life.

Some Native Americans were farmers who stayed in one place. Others were hunters who moved all year long, following the migrations of animals. One thing the tribes had in common was their deep respect for the land and close relationship with nature.

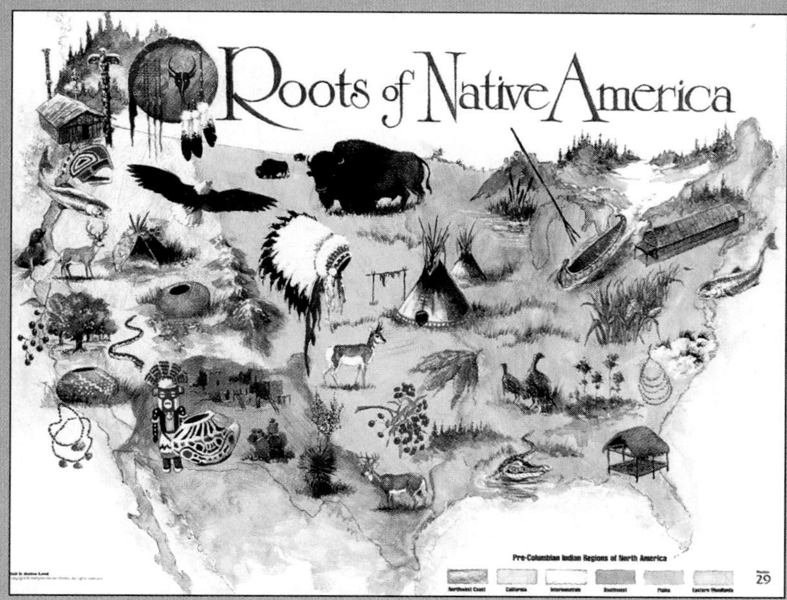

Native Americans taught explorers how to grow and prepare vegetables, like corn and tomatoes. Europeans brought horses, which the Native Americans used to follow and hunt migrating animals.

Sadly, Europeans brought diseases, and many Native Americans died. The explorers also thought they had the right to take whatever land they wanted. Many Native Americans died fighting for their homes.

1540–1542

Francisco de Coronado explored the Southwest.

Francisco Vázquez de Coronado of Spain traveled through much of the Southwest, including the villages of the Zuni tribes.★

1565

Don Pedro Menéndez de Avilés established a fort in Florida.

Don Pedro Menéndez de Avilés also came from Spain. He established a settlement at St. Augustine, Florida, which is now the oldest city in the United States.★

★1540s ★1550s ★1560s

Halloween

On October 31, children and adults celebrate Halloween. It is a time to have fun and be creative.

- People put jack-o'-lanterns on their porches. A jack-o'-lantern is a hollow pumpkin with a face carved in it.
- Lots of children dress in costumes and masks and go to different houses in their neighborhoods. The children knock on the door and, when someone opens it, they say, "Trick or treat!" Then they get candy or other treats.
- Some families have Halloween parties instead of going out. One popular game at this kind of party is Bobbing for Apples. A large tub is filled with water, and then apples are put in the water. Two players kneel next to the tub. Each player tries to bite an apple and take it out of the water without using his or her hands.

Day of the Dead

On November 1 and 2, for the Day of the Dead, people remember friends and relatives who have died.

- Families create an **altar**, or a memorial table, at home. These altars are decorated with candles, flowers, fruits, chocolate, and photographs of people who have died.
- People make skeleton figures and papier-mâché masks that look like skulls. People wear the masks as they walk to a cemetery to honor those who have died.

Veterans Day

On November 11, Americans honor veterans who have fought in wars for the United States. All over the country there are parades and speeches to thank veterans for their service to the United States and its people.

At the end of World War I, President Woodrow Wilson named November 11 Armistice Day. An **armistice** is an agreement between countries to stop fighting a war. It was a day to celebrate peace and the end of that war. Later on, the name was changed to Veterans Day to honor veterans of all American wars.

What happened during World Wars I and II?

1914–1918
World War I

World War I was the first war involving countries from all over the world. Germany, Austria, Hungary, and Turkey formed a group called the Central Powers. They fought against Britain, France, the United States, and Russia, who were called the Allied Powers. The Allies won the war in 1918.★

1939–1945
World War II

In the late 1930s, **dictators** in Germany, Italy, and Japan (the Axis Powers) used their armies to invade neighboring countries. A dictator is a ruler who has complete control over a country. Britain and France (the Allied forces) declared war on Germany. The United States joined the war in 1941, when the Japanese attacked Pearl Harbor, Hawaii, by surprise. Germany and Japan surrendered in 1945.★

★1910s ★1920s ★1930s ★1940s

Thanksgiving

The fourth Thursday in November is a very special day for Americans. Thanksgiving is a day when people give thanks for all the good things in their lives.

- Families and friends gather together for a large meal. Some traditional Thanksgiving dishes are baked turkey, sweet potatoes, cranberry sauce, and pumpkin pie.
- Before eating, someone may give thanks for the food on the table and for being together.

The celebration of Thanksgiving began when settlers arrived in North America. The first Thanksgiving meal took place when some of those settlers gave thanks for a good harvest after a difficult winter.

When did English settlers arrive in North America? What was their life like?

1585

The first English settlers arrived in North America.

The settlers arrived on what is now Roanoke Island off the coast of North Carolina. They tried to start a colony there, but living in an unfamiliar place was too hard so they returned to England.★

1607

Jamestown became the first permanent English colony.

The settlers in colonies such as Jamestown survived because they learned how to make their own supplies and grow their own food. At first the settlers lived in homes in holes in the ground with bark roofs. Later, they used lumber to build wooden houses. They learned how to fish and dig for clams on the beaches. They hunted for deer, geese, ducks, and wild turkeys in the woods. Many settlers became farmers and grew corn, potatoes, beans, wheat, rye, and oats.★

★1580s ★1590s ★1600s

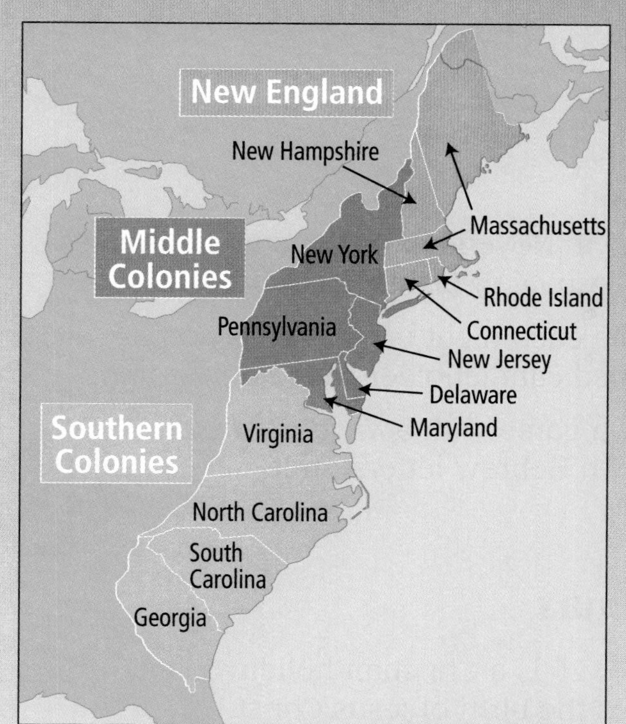

The Thirteen Original Colonies

The settlers sold things to each other and to other countries such as England. Settlers in New England sold fur and lumber. People in the Middle Colonies made glass, leather, and iron tools. Farmers in the Southern Colonies sold tobacco, which people said was worth its weight in silver.

1620

The Pilgrims wrote the Mayflower Compact.

Many of the settlers wanted to govern themselves. The Pilgrims who settled in Massachusetts wrote and signed the Mayflower Compact, an agreement to make and follow fair and equal laws. The United States government is based on some of the same ideas that these settlers had.★

1621

The event that is now called Thanksgiving was celebrated in the Plymouth Colony.

In 1621, the Pilgrims in Plymouth Colony had survived a very difficult winter because a member of a Native American tribe, the Wampanoag, had taught them to fish, hunt, and plant corn. To celebrate their first harvest, the settlers had a three-day celebration and invited the Wampanoag.★

1630

The Massachusetts Bay Company formed.

In England in the 1600s, people called Puritans formed the Massachusetts Bay Company. That company sent lots of families to New England. The Puritans took everything they would need, such as farm animals, tools, and clothing. They first settled in Boston, Massachusetts.★

★1620s

★1630s

Hanukkah

For eight days starting in November or December, families celebrate the Jewish Festival of Lights, or *Hanukkah*.

- People light a candle each night of the holiday on a special nine-branched candleholder called a *menorah*.
- Children often play a game with a *dreidl*. A *dreidl* is a spinning top with Hebrew letters on it.

Christmas

December 25 is a Christian holiday that celebrates the birth of Jesus Christ.

- During the Christmas season, many people like to sing songs called Christmas carols.
- Families and friends give each other gifts and often put them under decorated trees. Children believe that if they are good, a character named Santa Claus will bring them gifts.

Kwanzaa

African Americans celebrate Kwanzaa from December 26 through January 1.

- On each day, someone lights a candle in a *kinara*, a special candleholder. Each candle represents a value such as unity or creativity.
- Families have a feast called *karamu*. During *karamu*, people wear traditional African clothes, play music, and dance.

New Year's Eve

On the international calendar, December 31 is the last day of the year. On this day, many people stay up until midnight. That's when the new year officially begins. At midnight, they throw confetti, blow horns, and wish each other "Happy New Year!"

If you want to be part of a great New Year's Eve celebration, where should you go?

Go to New York City!

One of the biggest New Year's Eve celebrations in the United States takes place in Times Square. A ball of lights slowly drops from the top of a tower just before midnight. When the ball reaches the bottom, at exactly midnight, thousands of people cheer loudly to welcome the new year.

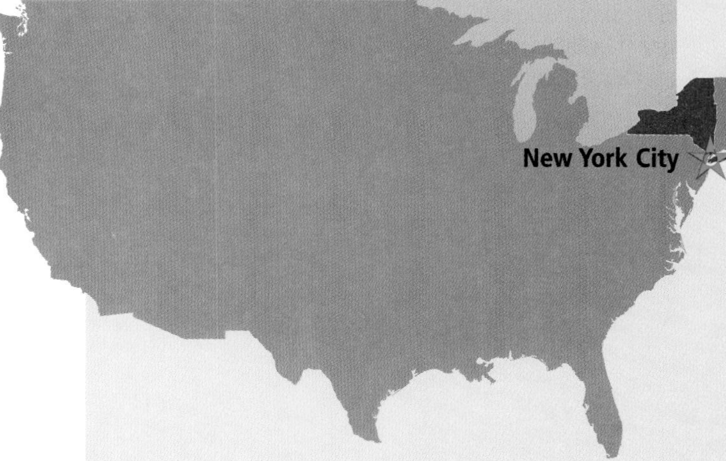

Facts

- More than 8 million people live in New York City. It is the most populated city in the United States.
- The Empire State Building, one of the tallest skyscrapers in the world, is in this city.
- Many of the world's largest banks are here, too. That's why New York City is often called the "financial center of the world"... and it's a great place to celebrate the new year.

U.S.A. Time Line

Up to the 1400s

Native America

Native Americans lived in America thousands of years before the first Europeans arrived. Each Native American tribe had its own language, culture, and way of life.★

1500s

Europeans Explore North America

From the late 1400s through the 1600s, many explorers sailed to America from Europe. They came to find land and claim it for their countries.★

1600s

Settlers Form Colonies

Groups of European settlers such as the Puritans and the Pilgrims moved to America to build villages and towns called colonies. The colonists sold products to each other and to other countries.★

1700s

American Revolution

By the 1760s, there were thirteen colonies that belonged to Britain. The colonists fought to be free because they wanted their own laws. They won their independence in 1783.★

1800s

Westward Expansion

At first, most of the people settled in the East, but starting in the 1800s, the U.S. bought and fought for more land. Soon people called *pioneers* moved into the open spaces in the Midwest and the West.★

Civil War

The people in the northern and southern parts of the United States led very different lifestyles. They disagreed so strongly about slavery and their ways of life that they fought the Civil War. The war and slavery ended in 1865 when the North won the Civil War.★

Industrial Revolution

From the 1860s to the 1900s, many companies started using machines to make products faster. It was also a time when new inventions like the light bulb and the telephone made people's lives easier.★

Becoming a World Leader

By the 1900s, the U.S. was greatly respected for its fine products and ability to defend itself. It had become a strong influence in the world.★

World War I (1914–1918)

The Great Depression

When many people lost money in the stock market crash of 1929, they were left without homes or jobs. A horrible drought, in an area of the Midwest that became known as the Dust Bowl, made things even worse. The depression lasted for many years.★

World War II (1941–1945)

Civil Rights Movement

Beginning in the 1960s, many Americans marched and demonstrated for equal rights for black Americans. Several laws were passed that helped stop discrimination.★

Exploring Outer Space

In the 1960s, American astronauts began journeys into outer space. The space program continues today as the astronauts help build an international laboratory in space and plan new missions.★

Information Age

Today many Americans use computers to give and receive information. With technology such as electronic mail, the Internet, and cellular phones, people around the world are able to quickly and easily communicate with each other.★

Grammar Practice

Sentences

A. Choose an ending from the box to finish each sentence. Write the sentence.

mighty arms!	he do?
a strong man.	is Paul Bunyan.
amaze you!	he?
appearance.	famous lumberjack.

1. **statement** The statue shows ______________
2. **exclamation** Wow, he has ______________
3. **question** Who is ______________
4. **statement** His name ______________
5. **command** Describe his ______________
6. **question** What did ______________
7. **command** Listen to the story of this ______________
8. **exclamation** The story of Paul Bunyan will ______________

B. Make up questions about this picture. Write them down. Then trade papers with a partner and answer the questions.

1. Is ___________?
2. Who ___________?
3. When ___________?
4. Can ___________?
5. Why ___________?
6. How ___________?
7. Are ___________?
8. Will ___________?
9. What ___________?
10. Does ___________?

C. Work with a partner to add a subject. Write the sentences.

1. _____ worked with Paul Bunyan.
   subject | predicate
2. _____ was a lumberjack.
   subject | predicate
3. _____ cleared trees from the land.
   subject | predicate
4. _____ watched Paul Bunyan.
   subject | predicate

D. Work with a partner to add a predicate. Write the sentences.

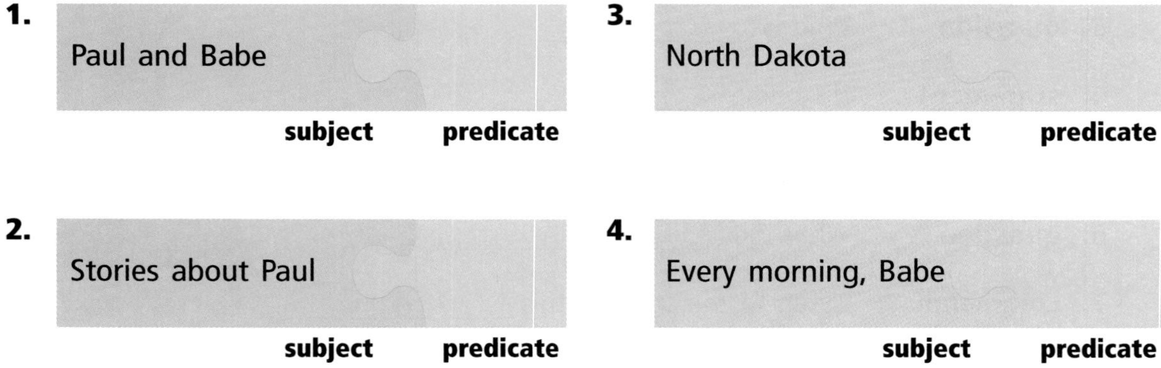

E. Make each sentence you wrote in C and D into a question.

Example: Did your grandfather work with Paul Bunyan?

F. Make each sentence you wrote in C and D into a negative sentence.

Example: My grandfather did **not** work with Paul Bunyan.

G. Choose *and, but,* or *or* to join each pair of sentences. Write the compound sentences.

1. There were no more trees to cut down in North Dakota. Paul Bunyan wanted to keep working. **but / or**

2. Paul could stay in North Dakota and be bored. He could go west to find more trees. **but / or**

3. Paul and Babe decided to go west. They said good-bye to their friends. **but / and**

4. On the way, Paul's sharp pole made the Grand Canyon. Babe's footsteps made paths through the Cascade Mountains. **or / and**

5. At first, the West was full of trees. Paul and Babe cut them down quickly. **but / or**

6. Now Paul and Babe could quit working. They could go to find more trees. **or / and**

Nouns

A. Write these sentences. Add the correct noun.

Gold Room	room	Galveston	corner
man	Broadway	James M. Brown	museum

1. Luisa went on a tour of this house in ___________.
2. Its address is 2328 ___________.
3. It is on the ___________ of the street.
4. The house is now a ___________ in Galveston.
5. Luisa read about the ___________ who built Ashton Villa.
6. His name was ___________.
7. One room in Ashton Villa is named the ___________.
8. Luisa thought it was the most beautiful ___________ in the house.

B. Write the plural of each noun. Then copy the paragraph and add the new words.

1. beach
2. shell
3. child
4. city
5. roof
6. half
7. wave
8. foot

Galveston is one of the best _______ to visit. It has many places that are fun for parents and their _______. People can visit the sandy _______. They can pick up colorful _______, too. One beach is Stewart Beach. It is behind a seawall that is 17 _______ high. At this beach, kids can play in the _______, or they can fly kites over the _______ of nearby homes. Some visitors walk through a life-size maze called "Amaze'N Texas." At the end, they make sure that both _______ of their group made it through!

C. Write these sentences, using the red word. Make the red word plural if you need to.

kind	**1.** There are many ___________ of vehicles to see in Galveston.
equipment	**2.** People go to Seawolf Park to see military ___________ such as a real World War II submarine.
information	**3.** At the Lone Star Flight Museum there is ___________ on more than 40 restored planes.
lunch	**4.** Some people ride the Galveston Island Trolley car to the beach. There, they eat the ___________ they've packed in bags or baskets.
time	**5.** Others ride on the *Colonel* paddle boat and imagine going back in ___________ to the 1800s.
water	**6.** Many people tour the Tall Ship *Elissa,* which sits in the ___________ in the Galveston port.
group	**7.** The displays in the Railroad Museum are popular with ___________ of people who visit the city.
lunch	**8.** These visitors often eat ______________ at the Santa Fe Choo Choo Diner there.

D. Write these sentences. Add the correct word.

1. Look at **these / a** pictures I took at Moody Gardens.

walking stick

2. I went to **the / some** Rainforest Pyramid there.
3. Inside there is **a / some** special place to watch caterpillars turn into butterflies.
4. I got to watch **a / some** butterflies form!

5. This picture shows **some / an** insect called a walking stick.
6. I spent over **an / a** hour looking at all the insects.
7. **That / An** walking stick was my favorite insect in the Rainforest Pyramid.
8. This is a picture of **a / an** macaw I saw sitting in a tree.
9. **The / Some** macaw was very colorful.
10. It was very safe in **a / the** tall trees.

macaw

11. **Those / That** trees were over 55 feet tall!

bat

12. **An / This** picture shows one of the bats.
13. Later, I saw **a / the** fruit bat, too.
14. I had **a / an** interesting day at Moody Gardens!

E. Write this paragraph. Decide if you need to add *the* where there is a blank.

In ____ April, we went to Galveston's Grand KIDS Festival. There were lots of arts and crafts booths. My favorite booth was ____ Swedish woodcarving one. ____ woman at ____ booth even spoke ____ Swedish! We ate lots of food, including burritos from ____ Rita's Tacos. On the way home, we stopped at ____ Stewart Beach and went ____ swimming.

F. Write these sentences. Add the correct possessive noun.

1. __Luisa Rafael's / Luisa Rafaels'__ house is near the water.
2. In the front yard is her __dads' / dad's__ boat.
3. Today, her family is going on a fishing trip near one of __Galvestons' / Galveston's__ jetties.
4. All of the family is going, including __Luisa's / Luisas'__ two older brothers.
5. Catching crabs is her __brothers' / brother's__ favorite thing to do.
6. The boys have learned how to take crabs off their lines so that they don't get pinched by the __crab's / crabs'__ claws!
7. Luisa likes to fish for trout with her __mom's / moms'__ fishing pole.
8. She drops the line into the __bays' / bay's__ warm water.
9. The fish start nibbling at the bait on the __hook's / hooks'__ sharp point.
10. At the end of the day, the __boys' / boy's__ bucket is full of crabs.
11. The five fish Luisa caught flop around on the __boat's / boats'__ deck.
12. For dinner tonight, the Rafaels will be eating the __world's / worlds'__ best seafood!

G. Write the paragraph. Replace the underlined words with specific nouns about a city you know.

Take a stroll down the street. Delicious smells come from the café. You can almost taste the food. Pause to look in the store windows. Look at all the things displayed there. Listen, can you hear music playing? It's coming from the shop. Have fun visiting this city!

H. Write a paragraph about a place you have visited. Use specific nouns.

Pronouns

Lisa

Jasmine

Tom

A. Write these sentences. Add the correct pronoun.

One	More than One
I you he, she, it	we you they

One	More than One
me you him, her, it	us you them

1. One day at practice, a bee buzzed by Lisa. "It might sting **me / he** ," she said.
2. "Just stand still," Tom said to **she / her** .
3. Lisa stood very still, but the bee kept buzzing near **him / her** .
4. **I / It** buzzed around her ears and her eyes.
5. Jasmine said, "**Her / You** will be okay in a minute."
6. Then the bee left as fast as **you / it** came!
7. "Whew," said Lisa. "**He / I** really don't like bees."
8. "But **it / they** are not as scary as snakes," said Jasmine.
9. "Snakes?" asked Tom. "**We / They** aren't scary at all!"
10. "Are you sure **you / I** aren't afraid of snakes?" the girls asked.
11. "**I / She** am sure," said Tom.
12. The girls didn't believe **him / we** .
13. "**We / Us** will see," they said to each other.
14. The girls knew a little snake was crawling toward **they / them** .
15. Tom jumped. **He / She** was scared!
16. "That snake is coming right at **we / us** !" yelled Tom.
17. "Just stand still," Lisa said to **he / him** .
18. "**You / Him** will be okay in a minute," Jasmine said.

Lisa

Juan

Tom

Jasmine

Coach

B. Write these sentences. Add the correct pronoun.

1. Tom and his friends were at **their / theirs** soccer practice. Tom and Lisa found a backpack.
2. They asked Juan, "Is this backpack **yours / your**?"
3. Juan said, "No. Ask Jasmine. Maybe it's **hers / theirs**."
4. "I've got **my / mine**," Jasmine said.
5. "Coach! Someone left a backpack on the field. Our friends say it isn't **their / theirs**."
6. "Oh! That's **my / yours** backpack," said the coach. "I've been looking everywhere for it!"

One	More than One
my	**our**
your	**your**
his, her, its	**their**

One	More than One
mine	**ours**
yours	**yours**
his, hers	**theirs**

C. Write these sentences. Add the correct pronoun.

1. Oh good, **anything / someone** brought juice.
2. Has **anyone / something** seen my soda?
3. **Everything / Somebody** put a napkin over it!
4.  Did **everyone / someone** get enough to eat?

D. Write this paragraph. Add a pronoun from the box for each blank.

he	him	his
it	us	their

Mr. Brown is our soccer coach. All of the Bobcat players like _______. We have to practice hard, but Mr. Brown is always fair. _______ lets everyone have a chance to play during the games. When we win a game, he celebrates with _______. He and his wife had a party for us after we beat the Eagles. They invited all the players and the fans to _______ house. It was fun! Sometimes Mr. Brown loses things. One time he lost _______ lucky cap. We found _______ right there in his pocket!

E. Write a paragraph about your favorite coach or teacher.

Adjectives

A. Write these sentences. Add the correct adjective from the box.

hungry
one
ripe
sharp

1. Just __________ berry isn't enough for the toucan.
2. This __________ bird gobbles up all the berries.
3. The toucan uses its __________ beak to pick them from the tree.
4. It loves berries and other kinds of __________ fruit.

---

noisy
hot
top
hollow

5. The toucan is always squawking. It is very __________!
6. The toucan lives in the __________ rainforest.
7. Its nest is in a __________ trunk of a tree.
8. The toucan likes to sit on the __________ branches of a tree.

B. Write these sentences. Add the correct adjective.

1. There are **many / much** different kinds of flowers in the rainforest.
2. Some flowers are very colorful, but others have **only a little / only a few** color.
3. The hibiscus does not have **many / much** smell, but it is very colorful.
4. The water lily has **much / many** petals. It smells like butterscotch and pineapple.
5. **Many / Much** people do not like the horrible smell of the arum lily.
6. Some orchids have **several / not much** spots on their petals.
7. Most orchids have **only a little / only a few** leaves on them.
8. The different flowers add so **much / many** beauty to the rainforest.

C. Write these sentences. Add *-er* or *-est* to the red adjective to make a comparison.

wet 1. Monkeys and sloths both live in the __________ place in the world. Yet, these animals have many differences.

slow 2. Of the two animals, the sloth is __________.

small 3. A sloth's tail is __________ than a monkey's tail.

big 4. A monkey has one of the __________ and most useful tails in the animal world.

large 5. A sloth has __________ claws than a monkey.

hungry 6. A monkey eats all day and is always __________ than a sloth.

quiet 7. The sloth doesn't make much noise; it is __________ than a monkey.

noisy 8. A monkey is one of the __________ animals in the rainforest!

sloth

D. Write these sentences. Add the correct word.

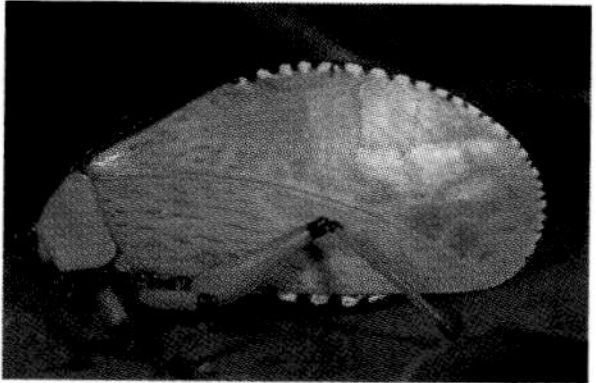
katydid

1. Ms. Steinberg's class went to the rainforest exhibit. They talked about what they liked the __more / most__.
2. Nina said the jaguar had a __good / best__ disguise.
3. Toshiro thought that the katydid's disguise was __better / more better__ than the jaguar's.

walking stick

4. They both agreed that the walking stick had the __better / best__ disguise of all.
5. Rita thought that the spotted, brown snake was the __some / most__ frightening snake.
6. Tony felt that the long, green snake was __some / more__ frightening than the brown one.
7. Everyone agreed that the sloth was the __less / least__ active animal there!

toucan

8. The toucan was pretty __bad / worse__ at keeping quiet.
9. The monkey was __worse / worst__, though!
10. Everyone said that their __little / least__ favorite thing was going home!

E. Write this paragraph. Add an adjective for each blank.

monkey

Our zoo has a _______ rainforest exhibit. Inside, the air feels _______. There are _______ vines hanging from the trees. _______ spiders crawl on the ground. You can see _______ butterflies fluttering through the air. Hanging from the branches are _______ monkeys. In the background, you can hear a _______ waterfall. This exhibit is _______!

F. Write a description of an animal that lives in the rainforest. Use adjectives to help your readers picture the animal clearly.

Verbs

A. Write each sentence and add the verb.

1. At first the sky ________ clear.
2. Then the clouds ________ in.
3. They ________ almost black.
4. Something ________ across the sky.

is
flashes
roll
look

---

5. It ________ lightning!
6. I ________ the loud thunder.
7. Then the rain ________ from the sky.
8. The raindrops ________ very cold and wet.

is
are
falls
hear

B. Write each sentence and add the verb.
Then circle each helping verb.

1. The weather reporter says it __________ warmer today.
2. We __________ our T-shirts and shorts.
3. The weather __________.

can wear
is changing
will turn

---

4. The flowers __________ now.
5. The birds __________.
6. Spring __________!

might return
has arrived
should bloom

C. Write each sentence in Exercise B again.
Add the word *not*.

D. Write each sentence, using a contraction for the underlined words.

1. Tomorrow we are going to do weather projects.
2. I would like to make something to measure the amount of rain.
3. It should not be hard to do.
4. First I will cut off the top of a plastic bottle.
5. Then I am going to mark the sides of the bottle.
6. It will not work unless I put the bottle outside!
7. I cannot forget to empty the bottle after it rains.
8. Otherwise, the measurement would not be right the next time it rains.

E. Write each sentence and add the verb.

1. In winter, the sun **rise / rises** later in the morning.
2. The sky **get / gets** dark early, too.
3. Some people **want / wants** winter to end.
4. They **like / likes** the long days of summer.
5. I **prefer / prefers** winter, though.
6. To me, cold air **seem / seems** fresher than hot air.
7. My sister **think / thinks** winter is the best, too.
8. She **play / plays** in the snow with our dog Sam.
9. He **run / runs** through the deep snow drifts.
10. We **laugh / laughs** at Sam when he chases snowflakes!

F. Add *-ed* to each red verb to make it tell about an action that happened in the past. Then use the verb to write each sentence.

visit	**1.**	A TV weather reporter __________ our class yesterday.
stay	**2.**	She __________ for two hours.
show	**3.**	She __________ us different thermometers.
measure	**4.**	Everyone __________ the air temperature.
study	**5.**	Then we __________ a poster with different clouds on it.
try	**6.**	We __________ to draw pictures of each kind.
create	**7.**	The reporter __________ a cloud inside a jar.
clap	**8.**	The whole class __________. It was amazing!
play	**9.**	Before the reporter left, we __________ a guessing game about the weather.
learn	**10.**	We __________ that it is hard to predict the weather!
thank	**11.**	We __________ the reporter for coming to our class.
plan	**12.**	We also __________ a time for her to come back again.

G. Write each sentence. Change the underlined verb to make it tell about an action that happened in the past. Use the chart on page 263 to help you.

1. In the morning, Mr. Cruz <u>sees</u> dark clouds.
2. He <u>finds</u> the weather report in the newspaper.
3. The forecast <u>is</u> for a sunny day.
4. Mr. Cruz <u>does</u> not believe it.
5. He <u>takes</u> his umbrella just in case.
6. The sky <u>gets</u> very dark at about 4:00 p.m.
7. Mr. Cruz <u>hears</u> thunder.
8. Before long, there <u>are</u> raindrops coming down.
9. On his way home, Mr. Cruz <u>keeps</u> his umbrella over his head.
10. He finally <u>runs</u> for a taxi to get out of the rain.

H. Write each sentence. Change the underlined verb to make it tell about an action that happened in the past.

1. Lihn <u>listens</u> to a story about a snowy day.
2. She <u>thinks</u> about snow.
3. She <u>finds</u> a picture of snow.
4. It <u>looks</u> so white and pretty.
5. Lihn <u>wonders</u> about snowflakes.
6. She <u>writes</u> a poem about snow.
7. In her poem, Lihn <u>says</u> that snow is cold and wet.
8. She <u>names</u> her poem, "Does Snow Feel Soft?"
9. She <u>brings</u> her poem to her teacher.
10. "Does Snow Feel Soft?" <u>makes</u> the teacher smile.

I. Write this paragraph to tell about an action that will happen in the future.

will bring	is going to
am going to	are going to go

Tomorrow ____________ be hot. It will be the first day of summer. We ____________ to the lake. Mom and Dad ____________ their rafts, but I ____________ swim.

J. Write each sentence. Change the underlined verb to form the present-perfect tense. Use the chart on page 265 to help you.

1. The weather <u>feels</u> much warmer this week.
2. It <u>stops</u> raining.
3. The clouds <u>go</u> away.
4. I <u>hear</u> birds chirping.
5. Eggs <u>start</u> to hatch in their nests.
6. I <u>store</u> my warm sweaters, coats, and boots.
7. Summer <u>begins</u> at last.
8. It <u>makes</u> people happy.

K. Write each sentence. Use the red verb to form the past-perfect tense. Use the chart on page 265 to help you.

arrive **1.** We ________ at school when it started to rain again.

bring **2.** Ezra was happy because he ________ his jacket.

take **3.** Tanya was smiling because she _______ her umbrella.

see **4.** They _______ the weather report for today.

expect **5.** I __________ the weather to be sunny, but it was raining.

ride **6.** I was not happy, because I ________ my bike!

L. Write the paragraph. Replace each underlined verb with a verb that is more colorful.

The hot sun was directly overhead. Freddie went to the pool. Some people were in the wading pool. Freddie looked at the water. He got into the pool. "Aaah, I'm finally cool," he said.

M. Write a paragraph about something you did when the weather was hot, cold, wet, or dry. Use colorful verbs.

Adverbs

A. Write these sentences. Add the correct word.

1. The gymnasts are practicing **everywhere / nowhere** in the gym.
2. Beto always performs **good / well** on the mat.
3. Today he jumped **higher / highest** than he had ever jumped before!
4. Beto's muscles are getting **real / really** strong.
5. Mariah tumbled **smooth / smoothly** on the balance beam.
6. Then she stood **perfect / perfectly** still.
7. She stepped more **quick / quickly** than usual across the beam, too.
8. The gymnasts improve when they practice **often / most often** .

Mariah

Beto

B. Write a paragraph about a sport. Use adverbs to describe how the players move and act.

Prepositions

C. Where is the red dot? Write the correct answer.

1. The red dot is **under / in front of** the line.
2. The red dot is **off / in** the box.
3. The red dot is **inside / outside** the box.
4. The red dot is going **around / through** the tunnel.

D. Make more drawings of the line and the red dot. Trade papers with a partner and tell where the red dot is.

E. Write each sentence. Use the correct preposition.

1. My brother Tito and I were excited about the kite-flying contest **on / in** March.
2. It was **on / in** the first Saturday in March.
3. **During / After** breakfast that morning, we hurried to Grant Park.
4. The contest did not begin **until / on** noon.
5. Tito and I wanted to practice **on / before** the contest.
6. We got our kite ready **at / in** 11:00 o'clock.
7. Tito flew the kite **after / from** 11:00 to 12:00.
8. The wind blew nicely all morning **before / in** the start of the contest.
9. **During / At** 12:00 o'clock, there was hardly any wind at all!
10. Our kite did not fly high **during / on** the contest, but we did win the "best design" award!

F. Write this paragraph. Add a phrase from the box for each blank.

around the kite	with a blue head	in his hand
for his birthday	to the beach	into the air

Daniel's uncle gave him a kite that looks like a red bird ________. It was a gift ________. Daniel and his uncle took the kite over ________. His uncle tossed the kite ________ while Daniel held the string ________. The sea gulls circled ________ because they were very interested in the strange, new bird!

G. Write a paragraph about a kite or something else that flies. Include prepositions to tell about time, location, and direction.

Conjunctions

H. Write these paragraphs. Use conjunctions from the box to combine some sentences.

and	but	or

1. Jungi never misses an Eagles' baseball game. He'll go to the stadium. He'll watch the game on TV. The Eagles lost their last game. They won all the games before that.

2. Robert Pérez is Jungi's favorite player. Robert is the pitcher. He is one of the best in the league. Robert could not play in the last game. Jungi thinks that is why the Eagles lost.

I. Write a paragraph about a team you like. Use the words *and, but,* and *or* at least once.

Capital Letters

A. Write each sentence. Use capital letters correctly.

1. Today i am going on a whale-watching trip.
2. My friend richard yee will join me.
3. His mother, mrs. yee, might come, too.
4. Mr. ernie vega owns the boat.
5. His helper is Alice c. Beck.
6. she is a scientist who studies whales.
7. we will learn about whales from dr. Beck.
8. dr. Beck and i will watch for whales from the top of the boat.
9. last time Mr. Vega was the first to see a whale.
10. This time i hope that i am!

B. Write these sentences. Use capital letters correctly.

1. I know the captain of a whale-watching boat in boston.
2. He lives on hanover avenue.
3. It's near christopher columbus park.
4. The boat is called *deep dreamer.*
5. The captain has sailed all over the atlantic and pacific oceans.
6. He used to work for a british company.
7. He often sailed around the tip of africa.
8. He has even been to the great barrier reef.
9. In fact, he has sailed most of earth's oceans.
10. Now he doesn't go far from the massachusetts coast.

C. Write this letter. Use abbreviations for the underlined words.

472 Lincoln Avenue
Chicago, Illinois 60643
Friday, October 24, 2003

Captain Boris Davidov
9 East 15th Street
Boston, Massachusetts 02101

Dear Captain Davidov,

My family and I wanted to go on a whale-watching trip next weekend: Saturday, November 1, or Sunday, November 2. Do you have room on your boat for four people on one of those days?

Sincerely,
Claude Delors

D. Write each sentence. Use capital letters correctly.

1. The boy scouts are planning a whale-watching trip.
2. They're going during the first weekend in september.
3. It will be labor day weekend.
4. The scoutmaster told the boys, "we might see some gray whales."
5. He showed them a video called the great whales.
6. It was made by the national geographic society.
7. He also read them an article called "protecting the gray whales."
8. The boys could hardly wait for that saturday.

Punctuation

A. Write each sentence. Add the correct punctuation at the end of what each person says.

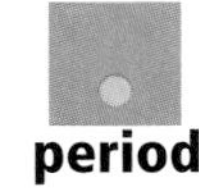

period

question mark

exclamation point

Aaron

1. Please show me the newspaper

Dad

2. Would you like to see the ads
3. Here is an ad for a used bike

Aaron

4. Wow, it sounds great
5. What is the price

Dad

6. Call the number to find out

Aaron

7. How much can I spend
8. I've been dreaming about a bike forever

B. Write each sentence. Add commas where they are needed.

Aaron

1. Mrs. Romero it's Aaron calling.
2. I wanted you to know that I can walk Brute Friday Saturday or Sunday.

Mrs. Romero

3. Oh Saturday should be fine!
4. But, wait, your school fair is Saturday isn't it?

Aaron

5. As Dad always says "You have to be flexible."
6. I'm willing to take your big gentle dog for a walk anytime.

Mrs. Romero

7. I have 1000000 things to do on Saturday anyway.
8. Plus, Sunday is supposed to be a warm sunny day.

Aaron

9. OK I'll take Brute on Sunday.
10. I'll see you Sunday Mrs. Romero.

C. Write this friendly letter. Add commas where they belong.

251 Ramos Drive
Tucson AZ 85737
April 3 2003

Dear Mr. and Mrs. Sanchez

My mother said that you are looking for helpers for your garage sale. Can I help you set up? I can also help sell things. Please let me know if you want my help. Thank you.

Your neighbor
Jaime

D. Write this business letter. Add commas, colons, and apostrophes where they are needed.

comma

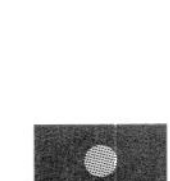
colon

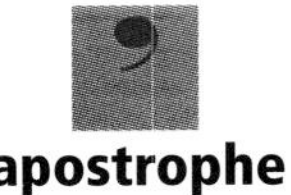
apostrophe

248 Ramos Drive
Tucson AZ 85737
June 12 2003

Ms. Ella Jefferson
ABC Publishers
12 Brown Avenue
Sunset NJ 07109

Dear Ms. Jefferson

I read your book *Kids Make Money* and I learned a lot from it. I tried these ideas walking my neighbors dog helping at garage sales and delivering newspapers every morning from 530 to 700. I would like to buy your other book *Kids Make More Money* but I cant find it. Can you please tell me where its sold?

Sincerely yours

Jaime Santiago

Jaime Santiago

E. Write each sentence. Add quotation marks and underlining where they are needed.

underline

quotation marks

1. How can I earn some money? Aaron asked his dad.
2. His dad had seen a sign that said, Teenagers Wanted for Garage Clean-up.
3. His dad also told him to look in the magazine Dollars.
4. There was an ad for delivering the Times-Press newspaper.
5. There was also an article called Kids Can Run a Business.
6. It talked about a book called Earning Money After School.
7. The chapter called How to Quickly Earn $5 sounded interesting.
8. Aaron asked his dad, Can I borrow some money to buy this book?

Index

A

B

C

D

E

F

G

H

I

J

K

L

M

Q

R

S

T

U

V

W

Acknowledgments, continued:

P161: Cover from THE WOMAN WHO OUTSHONE THE SUN reprinted with the permission of the publisher, Children's Book Press, San Francisco, CA.

P166: Adapted from DEAR AMERICA: THE WINTER OF RED SNOW: THE REVOLUTIONARY WAR DIARY OF ABIGAIL JANE STEWART, VALLEY FORGE, PENNSYLVANIA, 1777 by Kristiana Gregory. Copyright © 1996 by Kristiana Gregory. Reprinted by permission Scholastic Inc. DEAR AMERICA is a trademark of Scholastic Inc.

P167: Excerpt from JUMANJI by Chris Van Allsburg. Copyright © 1981 by Chris Van Allsburg. Reprinted by permission of Houghton Mifflin Co. All rights reserved.

P168: "The World's Fastest Car" © 1997 Time Inc. Reprinted by permission. Photo from Reuters/Stringer/Archive Photos.

P170: From PAUL BUNYAN by Steven Kellogg. Copyright © 1984 by Steven Kellogg by permission of Morrow Jr. Books, a division of William Morrow and Company, Inc.

P193: Cover from DORY STORY. Text copyright © 2000 by Jerry Pallotta. Illustrations copyright © 2000 by David Biedrzycki. All rights reserved. Used with permission by Charlesbridge Publishing, Inc.

P202: Cover from BACKYARD BIRDSONG Compact Disk. Text copyright © 1991 by Richard K. Walton and Robert W. Lawson. Illustrations copyright © 1982 from FIELD GUIDE TO THE BIRDS COLORING BOOK by Houghton Mifflin Company. Reprinted by permission of Houghton Mifflin Company. All rights reserved.

P268: "Icy," from STORIES TO BEGIN ON by Rhoda W. Bacmeister. Copyright © 1940 by E.P. Dutton, renewed © 1968 by Rhoda W. Bacmeister. Used by permission of Dutton Children's Books, a division of Penguin Putnam Inc.

P280: Endangered Species poster © 1993 Sea World, Inc.

P292, **p307**, and **p311:** ARE WE MOVING TO MARS? by Anne Schraff. Copyright © 1996 by John Muir Publications, Santa Fe, NM 87505.

P292 and **p295:** TIME FOR KIDS © 1996 Time Inc. Reprinted by permission.

P292, **p295**, and **pp326-327:** From THE WORLD BOOK ENCYCLOPEDIA. © 1998 World Book, Inc. By permission of the publisher.

P288, p292, **p295**, and **p316-317:** Cover and pp. 200-201, WORLD ALMANAC FOR KIDS 2003. Copyright © 2003 by World Almanac Education Group, Inc. Used by permission of World Almanac Educational Group, Inc.

P288, p292, p294, and **p319:** Cover and map from WORLD ATLAS. © 1998 by Rand McNally R.L. #98-5-90.

P294 and **p307:** Cover illustration from UFO DIARY by Satoshi Kitamura. Copyright © 1989 by Satoshi Kitamura. Reprinted by permission of Farrar, Straus & Giroux, Inc.

P297: Reprinted with permission from THE WORLD ALMANAC FOR KIDS 1998. Copyright © 1997 PRIMEDIA Reference Inc. All rights reserved.

P305: Photo of Mars rover, courtesy of Jet Propulsion Laboratory (California Institute of Technology)/NASA.

Pp309-311: Computerized card catalog used by permission of Innovative Interfaces, Inc., Emeryville, CA.

P318: Map, NGS Maps/NGS Image Sales

P320: Maps by GeoSystems from BUILD OUR NATION in WE THE PEOPLE by Hartoonian, et al. Copyright © 1997 by Houghton Mifflin Company. Reprinted by permission of Houghton Mifflin Company. All rights reserved.

P335, **p337**, and **p338:** "Mars" downloaded from NEW SCIENTIST web site http://www.newscientist.com. Produced 1998 by Reed Elsevier Group, RBI Limited, London. Used by permission.

P345: From COLLECTED POEMS by Langston Hughes. Copyright © 1994 by the Estate of Langston Hughes. Reprinted by permission of Alfred A. Knopf Inc.

P350: PEANUTS © United Features Syndicate, Inc.

P350: Superman is a trademark of DC Comics © 1998. All rights reserved. Used with permission.

P350: Wonder Woman is a trademark of DC Comics © 1998. All rights reserved. Used with permission.

P351: Cover illustration from THE WIZARD OF OZ by L. Frank Baum. Published by Apple Classics, an imprint of Scholastic Inc. Cover copyright © by Scholastic Inc. Reprinted by permission.

P351: Jacket art by Garth Williams. Jacket design by Charles Krelloff. Jacket copyright 1994 by HarperCollins Publishers. Little House is a trademark of HarperCollins Publishers, used by permission of HarperCollins.

P375: Plimoth Plantation photo courtesy of Plimoth Plantation, Plymouth, Massachusetts.

Illustrations:

Winifred Barnum Newman: p124 (Stone Soup), p125 (Cinderella), p154 (The Legend of the Chinese Zodiac), p356 (Sacagawea).

Lisa Berret: p25 (suitcase), p27 (dartboard), p30 (ice cubes, pancakes, bird, feather, peas), p35 (paring apple), p44 (More Words That Tell When), p47 (lighthouse), p48 (reversible coat), p51 (girl with toy train), p56 (pancakes).

Doug Bekke: p148 (alligator), p149 (crocodile), p252 (rainforest animals), p253 (More Ways to Tell "How Many" or "How Much"), p254 (birds), p255 (monkeys), p262 (Galileo's Thermometer), pp390-391 (monkeys).

Annie Bissett: p157 (Oak).

Liz Callen: p126 (get well card).

Chi Chung: p263 (bird, desert scene).

Lynne Cravath: p50 (Suffixes, continued), p52 (unhappy girl), p200 (Videos), p202 (Multimedia Presentation), pp204-205 (Practice Your Presentation), p205 (Give Your Presentation, Conclude Your Presentation), p266 (bird nest, flowers), p267 (boy watering flowers).

Darius Detwiler: p351 (John Henry, Pecos Bill).

Stephen Durke: cover, p4 (letter I), p5 (lightbulb), p6 (envelope and letter), p7 (notepad, pencil and sharpener), p9 (exclamation point), p10 (computer and CD), pp12-13 (background), pp68-69 (background), pp90-91 (background), p93 (book cover), pp190-191 (background), pp230-231 (background), pp288-289 (background).

Ray Godfrey: p42 (clocks), p73 (Scientific Diagram), p77 (Line Graph), p85 (volcano erupting).

Peter Grosshauser: p267 (spade, flower border).

Pauline Howard: p45 (Weight).

Beatrice Lebreton: p126 (Kwanzaa card), p366 (Jan Matzeliger).

Claude Martinot: p72 (kites), p80 (apartment building), p82 (spider), p87 (sewing materials), p88 (first place ribbon), p120 (Directions), p151 (hearts), p343 (Tet, Groundhog Day, Valentine's Day), p348 (Saint Patrick's Day), p349 (Passover), p354 (Mother's Day card), p361 (gift), p372 (Halloween), p376 (Christmas), p377 (confetti).

Paul Mirocha: p144 (glass of water with ruler, flower pot), p258 (Verbs).

Barry Mullins: p371 (Roots of Native America).

Russel Nemec: p43 (Times of the Day), p342, p352, pp355-359, and p375 (maps), p366 (shoe lasting machine), p377 (map).

Barbara Johansen Newman: p31 (Sound Words), pp36-39 (Synonyms and Antonyms), pp58-61 (Words Used in Special Ways), p171 (night light, kids with shoes, boy eating cherries, oyster), p225 (sheep), p276 (Capital Letters), pp282-287 (Punctuation Marks), p291 (Decide What to Look Up), p293 (kids at library), p296 and p298 (Gather Information), p301 (Organize Information), p302 and p305 (Write a Research Report), p397 (warm boy), p402 (Aaron, Dad), p403 (Aaron, Dad, Mrs. Romero).

Donna Perrone: p232 (covered statue), p234 and p245 (Paul Bunyan Statue), p236 (book cover), p237 and p381 (Babe the Blue Ox), p240 (kites), p242 (display table), p243 (umbrellas), p245 (restaurant table, Parrot Café).

Thom Ricks: p351 (Tom Sawyer and Huckleberry Finn).

Mary Rojas: p24 (compass), p126 (birthday card), p158 (Haiku), p159 (Today is Very Boring).

Roni Shepherd: p24 (fair), p179 (girl Rollerblading), p222 (Late and Later), p227 (Spell Long Words), pp228-229 (Words That Sound Alike), p396 (birds singing), p397 (kids in school).

Robbie Short: pp294-295 (library), p347 (The Three Branches of Our Government).

Kris Wiltse: p139 (Daedalus and Icarus).

Elizabeth Wolf: p21 (basketball court), p78 (basketball), p164 (Parts of a Story), pp246-250 (Pronouns), pp269-270 (Adverbs), p274 (Interjections), p387 (Lisa, Jasmine, Tom), p388 (Lisa, Juan, Tom, Jasmine, Coach, juice, soda, napkin, girl), p398 (girl on balance beam, boy jumping).

Lane Yerkes: p25 (corn growing).

Photographs:

Alicia Sternberg: p41 (tame cat).

Animals Animals/Earth Scenes: p46 (jellyfish, © Segars, Herb), p190 (blue jay, © Daybreak Imagery; cardinal, © Shirk, David L.), p254 (parrot, © John Chellman; toucan, © Michael Dick; motmot, © Paul Freed), p255 (motmot, © Ruth Cole), p256 (jaguar, © John Chellman; jaguar lying down, © Partridge Productions), p257 (katydid, © Michael Fogden; stick insect, © C. McLaughlin; katydid on leaf, © Patti Murray), p279 (whale, © Donna Ikenberry), p385 and p391 (walking stick, © C. McLaughlin), p391 (katydid, © Patti Murray; toucan, © Michael Dick).

Batista Moon Studio: p292, p295, and p326 (encyclopedias), p306 (card catalog).

Bruce Coleman, Inc.: p140 (puffin, © John Shaw), p226 (fox, © Rolf Kofle).

California State Archives: p358 (Bear Flag Republic).

Cartesia: p23 (U.S. map), p29 (U.S. map), p239 (Texas map), p319 (U.S. map).

Corbis: (all © Corbis) p23 (tree trunk, © DigitalStock), p24 (sports fans, © Tom & Dee Ann McCarthy), p27 (sheep pen, © Robert French/The Stock Market; pitcher, © DigitalStock), p29 (astronaut, © DigitalStock), p30 (blonde girl and friends, ©DigitalStock), p32 (bee, © DigitalStock), p35 (sea, © DigitalStock), p40 (kids exiting school, © Tom Stewart; finish line, © Pete Saloutos), p41 (wild cat, © DigitalStock), p44 (fall leaves, winter snow, spring flowers, © DigitalStock), p47 (rainbow, © DigitalStock), p54 (congress, © Bettman), p55 (UN Headquarters, © Joseph Sohm; ChromoSohm Inc.), p57 (couch, © PBNJ Productions), p62 (woman with car, © David Woods/The Stock Market), p64 (boy reading, © Gabe Palmer/The Stock Market), p65 (family eating, girl with dictionary, © Jose Luis Pelaez, Inc./The Stock Market), p74 (flag cake, © Charles Gold/The Stock Market), p77 (snowboarder, © Duomo), p85 (volcano, © DigitalStock), p108 (Haitian school, © Philip Gould), p122 (manitees, © DigitalStock), p127 (city, © DigitalStock), p136 (boy, © DigitalStock), p141 (boy and puffling, © Richard T. Nowitz), p145 (coast, © DigitalStock), p156 (lightning, © DigitalStock), p190 (finch, © Darrell Gulin), p214 (Sally Ride, © Bettman, p252 (tree frog, © DigitalStock), p253 and 390 (sloth, © Norbert Wu/The Stock Market), p255 (hummingbird, macaw, © DigitalStock), p259 (clouds, © DigitalStock), p261 (lightning, © DigitalStock), p278 (boulevard, Statue of Liberty, city, coast, Earth, © DigitalStock), p339 and 348 (Statue of Liberty, © DigitalStock), p352 (Redwood Forest, Southwestern desert, Rocky Mountains, Appalachian Mountains, © Digital Stock), p354 (Memorial Day, © DigitalStock), p369 (The Capitol, © DigitalStock), p371 (Francisco De Coronado), p373 (Veterans Day, © DigitalStock), p385 (macaw, © DigitalStock), p392 (lightning).

Corel: p252 (Florida Keys).

Culver Pictures, Inc.: p346 (George Washington).

Digital Studios: p6 (stamps), p15 (clock, hanger), p16 (penny, watch, pencil), p18 (hot soup, soft cotton), p19 (carrot, radio), p24 (fan), p25 (corn, strawberry jam, key), p26 (lamp), p27 (juice pitcher), p28 (vegetables on scale, hand with hammer, hand wearing ring), p30 (hat), p32 (flour products), p33 (four, one), p40 (cork floating and sinking), p41 (empty and full glass, broken and fixed vase), p42 (watch, sundial, stopwatch, hourglass, clock, alarm clock, timer), p45 (ruler, teaspoon, tablespoon, cup, pint, quart, gallon), p46 (backpack, fingernail, flashlight, bathtub), p47 (seashell, shoelaces, sweatshirt, motorcycle), p48 (vase, pencil, pencil sharpener), p49 (useful and useless umbrella, forward and backward truck), p53 (recycled glass, vase), p63, p92, p142, p215, and p329 (pencil), p66 (milk pouring into glass), p67 (highlighter), p79, p128, p131, p175, and p211 (pencil), p86 and p92 (pen), p92 (notebook), p126, p127, p275, and p279 (blue jay stamp), p127 (envelope), p127 (stamps), p128, p144, p169, and p329 (notepad), p131 and p175 (journal), p134 (pen), p137 (stamp), p139, p154, p167, and p181 (open book), p146 (stamps), pp162-163 (fossils), p169 (spiral notebook), p174 (Rollerblades, helmet, knee pads, elbow pads), p175 (Rollerblades), p178 (Rollerblades, helmet), p226 (lamp), p272 and p399 (fish kite), p273 (How To Make a Fish Kite), p346 (Constitution), p369 (Great Seal), p395 (umbrella).

Digital Vision: p290 (outer space), p292, p295 and 328 (Mars).

Elizabeth Garza Williams: p12 (boy and girl), pp18-19 (girl seeing, feeling, smelling, hearing, and tasting apple), p20 (Feeling Words), p21 and p78 (boy), p22 (formal greeting), p26 (kids in line), p29 (mother and son at table), p30 (cold boy, girl singing, girl with balloon), p32 (girl eating sandwich, girl smelling flower, girl with glasses), p46 (bookshelf), p51 (team cooperating), p54 (girl writing), p55 (boy with small shirt, boy being measured, kids with grown-up), p62 (kids talking), p65 (boy writing), p68 (girl writing), p90 (Put it in Writing), pp100-101 (Revising), pp109-111 (head shot of boy), p134 (girl writing), p135 (girl with video game), p150 (boy drawing), p190 (girl preparing speech), p192 (boy demonstrating, bird feeder), p193 (girl speaking, boy with book), p194 (boy with chart, news report), p196 (girl with bird feeder), p198 (bird feeder and supplies), p201 (girl with T.V./video cart), p210 (right-handed manuscript and cursive, left-handed manuscript and cursive), pp220-221 (Spelling Tips), p223 (girls jogging, boy studying), p224 (hand writing), p227 (hand with magnet), p230 (boy), p233 (kids and park worker), p234 (park worker showing statue to kids), p235 (kids typing), p238 (girl reading, boy reading, park worker), p239 (girl riding bike, boy running), p240 (kids holding kites), p242 (man with shirt and girl), p243 (man and woman with girl), p244 (kids with flight museum shirts), p244 (man and girl with caps), p246 (Future Tense Verbs), p288 (Look it Up), p292 (expert), p328 (Interviewing Experts), p330 (boy with phone book).

Galveston Island Convention & Visitor's Bureau: p239 (family, Ashton Villa, Tall Ship Elissa), p283 (Ashton Villa).

Getty Images, Inc.: (all © Getty Images) p15 (window, present, © PhotoDisc; starfish, © Artville), p16 (runner, © PhotoDisc), p17 (basket, © PhotoDisc), p18 (apple, sunset, clouds, basketball, worm © PhotoDisc; chalk, grapes, pepper © Artville) p19 (celery, orange, herbs, broccoli, eggplant, pretzel, lemon, orange slices © Artville), p23 (speaker, dog barking, bat, © PhotoDisc; farm, © Artville), p24 (sailboat, © PhotoDisc), p25 (inner tube,

Continued on page 416.

© Grant V. Faint/The Image Bank), p26 (cookie, girl writing, © PhotoDisc), p27 (tomatoes, © Artville), p28 (boy pointing, eye, © PhotoDisc), p29 (pumpkin on scale, goldfish, © PhotoDisc), p30 (gold, © Artville), p32 (paddle, flower, © PhotoDisc), p33 (penny, clock, © Artville; ribbon, © PhotoDisc), p35 (pear, © Artville; walk through woods, © PhotoDisc), p40 (whole pizza and pizza slice, © Artville; male, female, runners at start © PhotoDisc; winning team, © Peter Correz/Stone), p41 (elephant, beautiful landscape, © PhotoDisc), p42 (flamingos, © PhotoDisc), p44 (girls on beach, © PhotoDisc), p46 (backyard, © Geostock/ PhotoDisc; basketball, © PhotoDisc), p47 (sunflower, © PhotoDisc; pineapple, popcorn, © Artville), p48 (runner, © PhotoDisc), p51 (automobile, © Artville), p52 (shoes, marbles, © PhotoDisc), p53 (replacing test tube, globes © PhotoDisc; pizza, © Artville), p55 (baby, © PhotoDisc), p56 (sandwich, peanuts, © Artville), p57 (string beans, faucet, © PhotoDisc), p62 (ice, waitress, © PhotoDisc), p64 (hand with CD, boy practicing violin, © PhotoDisc), p66 (girl recycling, © PhotoDisc), p67 (man turning pot, © PhotoDisc), p71 (moon over field, © FPG International), p75, (sombrero, hot dogs, hamburger, © Artville), p92 (eraser, © Artville), p129 (Wynton Marsalis, © Deborah Feingold/ Archive Photos), p131 (girl writing, © PhotoDisc), p137 (eggplant, chilis, lime, coconut, pineapple, © Artville), p138 (mushrooms, pineapple, corn, avacado, pepper, jalapeño, garlic, eggplant, sugarcane, chilis, grapes, exotic fruit, shrimp bowl, burrito, salad, coconut, © Artville), p147 (gift, © Artville), p151 (girl writing, © PhotoDisc), p152 (audience, © Ron Chapple/Taxi), p156 (peach, pear, pepper, pineapple, © Artville), p172 (disk, boy on computer, © PhotoDisc; notebooks, © Artville), p177 (person skating, © PhotoDisc), p187 (girl with Rollerblades, © PhotoDisc), p192 (CD, videotape, slide projector, © PhotoDisc), p194 (storm on T.V., © PhotoDisc), p219 (girl writing, © PhotoDisc), p225 (sunset and girls on beach, © PhotoDisc), p226 (fly, © Artville; stones, puppies © PhotoDisc), p241 (footballs, © Artville), p251 (soccerball, © Artville), p265 (raincloud,© PhotoDisc), p275 (baseball mitt and glove,© Artville), p278 (mountains, © PhotoDisc), p292 (newspaper, © David Buffington/ PhotoDisc), p332 (internet, © Jason Reed/ PhotoDisc), p339 (hotdog, quarter, penny, baseball, © Artville), p341 (White House, © Peter Gridley/FPG International), p344 (soldiers, © Matthey Brady/Archive Photos), p345 (Langston Hughes, Rosa Parks © Georg Dabrowski/ Archive Photos; Jackie Robinson, © FPG International; Thurgood Marshall, © Hulton Archive; baseball, gavel, © PhotoDisc), p349 (Easter Egg basket, © Artville), p351 (Annie Oakley, © Hulton Getty), p352 (Mississippi River, Great Lakes, © Artville), p354 (mother and daughter, © PhotoDisc), p358 (gold miners, © Hulton Archive; gold bars, © Artville), p366 (first telephone, Alexander Graham Bell, electric lightbulb, Thomas Edison, © Hulton Archive), p367 (factory, Henry Ford, Model T © Hulton Archive), p370 (John Cabot, © Hulton Archive), p372 (Day of the Dead, © Artville), p373 (World War I, © Hulton Getty), p376 (dreidl, © PhotoDisc), p377 (New Year's in New York, © Jerry Driendl/FPG International), p378 (Thomas Edison, electric lightbulb, © Hulton Archive), p385 (bat, © PhotoDisc).

Houseboat Magazine: p46 (houseboat).

Image Club/Object Gear: p14 and p48 (mask), p17 (Ukrainian eggs), p201 (videotape), p363 and p378 (Liberty Bell, © PhotoDisc).

Image Quest: p63 (cowboy with cattle), p65 (flying geese).

Index Stock Imagery: p108 (Haiti, © Michele Burgess).

Janine Boylan: p119 (Vietnam market).

Library of Congress: p357 (Sam Houston, © F Davignon), p374 (English settlers, Jamestown).

Lunar Planetary Institute: pp328-329 (Mars landscape).

Lawrence Migdale: p25 (parade float), p340 (New Year's Day parade, © David Young-Wolff), p353 (Cinco de Mayo), p365 (playing the drums), p376 (Kwanzaa).

Metaphotos: p18 and p41 (ants), p19 (trash can, mustard), p49 (spider), p56 and p138 (soda), p67 (flag), p138 (coffee), p150 (oil can), p363 (flag and fireworks).

NASA: p11, p364 and p379 (Challenger), p89 (Dr. Franklin Chang-Díaz), p313 (Mars), p364 (Alan Shepard, John Glenn, Jr., Sally Ride).

National Archives: p373 (World War II).

New Century Graphics: p41 (clean and dirty towel), p53 (mushrooms), p92 (printer and computer), p98 (computer), p110 (scanner), p111 (printer), p189 (binder, accordian file, folders), p191 (radio), p202 (radio), p226 (dress), p321 (globe).

Newell Colour: p290 and pp314-315 (Mars terrain).

Norbert Wu Photography: p281 (whale).

North Wind Picture Archives: p344 (Frederick Douglass and Harriet Tubman), p356 (Lewis and Clark, Andrew Jackson), p357 and p378 (covered wagon), p359 (Homesteaders, Transcontinental Railroad), p362 (Boston Tea Party, Revolutionary War), p363 (Yorktown, Declaration of Independence), p367 (Samuel Gompers, Jane Addams), p370 (Christopher Columbus, Juan Ponce de León), p371 (Don Pedro Menéndez de Avilés), p375, p378 (Mayflower Compact).

PhotoEdit, Inc.: p22 (informal greeting, © David Young-Wolff), p27 (man working at plant, © Amy C. Etra), p33 (telling secrets, © Myrleen Ferguson); p52 (car speeding, © Spencer Grant), p54 (voting booth, © Dennis MacDonald), p57 (drinking fountain, © David Young-Wolff), p67 (book return, © Tom Prettyman), p87 (kids forming pyramid, © Richard Hutchings), p118 (friends, © Jeff Greenberg), p132 (girl feeding dog, © David Young-Wolff), p143 (girl writing, © Michelle Bridwell), p147 (girl shopping, © Michael Newman), p224 (crossing guard, © Richard Hutchings), p260 and p394 (weather reporter, © Tom McCarthy), p342 (Chinese New Year dragon, © David Young-Wolff), p360 (Puerto Rican Day, © Robert Brenner), p361 (father and son, © Myrleen Ferguson; dragon boats, © James Shaffer), p365 (traditional dancing, © Tony Freeman, Jingle dress © Deborah Davis), p368 (apples and honey, © Bill Aron), p369 (Uncle Sam, © Bonnie Kamin).

Stockbyte: p14 (dolls), p15 (egg), p18 (medal), p19 (flower, perfume, drums), p24, p47 and p309 (keyboard), p34 (boots), p41 (butterflies), p46 (headphones), p47 (toothbrush, videocassette), p48 (baker), p49 (butterfly), p51, p113, and p165 (bicycle), p86 (basketball), p88 (girl smiling), p109 (fax machine), p128 (cassette recorder), p181 (baby), p226 (brush), p364 (astronaut on moon).

SuperStock, Inc.: p63 (grandmother on phone), p138 (family at café), p142 (boy on phone), p340 and p379 (Martin Luther King, Jr.), p346 (Abraham Lincoln, © The Huntington Library).

The Image Works: p41 (ugly landscape, © John Eastcott and Eva Momatiuk).

Uniphoto: p27 (planting seeds, © T. Stephen Thompson), p40 (woman giving gift, © Michael R. Keller; kids entering school, © Paul Conklin), p64 (bus stop, © Bob Daemmrich), p66 (neighbors meeting, © Howard Grey).

English At Your Command!
Development Team

Design and Production: Helen Aguirre-Greenwood, Andrea Carter, Darius Detwiler, Jeri Gibson, Raymond Ortiz Godfrey, Susan Scheuer, Curtis Spitler, Alicia Sternberg, Andrea Pastrano-Tamez, Edward Tamez, Teri Wilson, Command P, Zeitgraph, Inc.

Editorial: Janine Boylan, Julie Cason, Roseann Erwin, Frederick Ignacio, Dawn Liseth, Sheron Long, Stephen Newitt, C. M. Antoinette Nichols, Heather Peacock, Sharon Ursino, Andrea Weiss, and Ink, Inc.

Permissions: Barbara Mathewson.

California in Depth

California in Depth

A STEREOSCOPIC HISTORY

Jim Crain

CHRONICLE BOOKS
SAN FRANCISCO

Library of Congress Cataloging-in-Publication Data:
Crain, Jim.
California in depth: a stereoscopic history / by Jim Crain.
p. cm.
Includes bibliographical references and index.
ISBN 0-8118-0423-2
1. California—History—Pictorial works.
2. Photography, Stereoscopic. I. Title.
F862.C72 1994 93-44431
979.4—dc20 CIP

Designed by Terril Neely
Printed in Singapore.

Distributed in Canada by Raincoast Books,
112 East Third Ave., Vancouver, B.C. V5T 1C8

10 9 8 7 6 5 4 3 2 1

Chronicle Books
275 Fifth Street
San Francisco, CA 94103

Picture Credits

(T-top, C-center, B-bottom)

I wish to thank the following collectors and institutions for the use of their stereoviews:

The Bancroft Library, University of California, Berkeley: 17T, 30B, 31T, 49C, 60B, 93B, 101, 106B
California Historical Society: 49B, 64T
California Museum of Photography, University of California, Riverside: 49T
California State Library: 16T, 39B, 44, 46B, 55B, 63B, 66, 67B, 70B, 81C, 88, 89B, 90B, 92T, 109T, 109B
John Carpenter: 64B
Bill Eloe: 10, 24T
Ken Harrison: 77T
The Huntington Library: 26T, 38T, 40T, 40C, 41T, 41C, 54T
Kansas State Historical Society: 21B
Bill Lee: 22B, 45B
Library of Congress: 102
Missouri Historical Society: 21T
Montana Historical Society: 25T
Larry Moskovitz: 18T, 26B, 53, 54C, 105T, 111
Russell Norton: 47T, 106T
Richard Osborne: 47B, 56B, 96
Peter Palmquist: 16B, 17C, 31B, 34, 46T, 46C, 48B, 61B, 62T, 67C, 72T, 72B, 81T, 86B, 91T, 92B, 94T, 94B, 97B, 105B
Mary Etta Segerstrom: 32T
The Society of California Pioneers: 29B, 31C, 33T, 48C
Barry Swackhamer: 24B, 37, 38C, 39T, 40B, 41B, 42, 76B
Utah State Historical Society: 25B
Leonard Walle: 17B, 22T, 23T, 82T, 83C, 84B, 91C, 98, 100T, 108T, 108B
The Yosemite Museum, National Park Service: 61C, 62C, 62B, 94C, 100B
Author's collection: 6, 18C, 18B, 23B, 24C, 29T, 30T, 30C, 32B, 33B, 36, 38B, 45T, 48T, 50T, 50C, 50B, 54B, 55T, 55C, 56T, 59T, 59C, 59B, 60T, 61T, 63T, 67T, 68T, 68B, 69T, 69C, 69B, 70T, 70C, 71T, 71B, 75T, 75B, 76T, 77C, 77B, 78T, 78C, 78B, 81B, 82B, 83T, 83B, 84T, 85T, 85B, 86T, 89T, 89C, 90T, 91B, 92C, 93T, 97T, 99T, 99B, 107T, 107B, 110

Other guidance and assistance was provided by Bob Chandler, Wells Fargo History Room; John Dennis, National Stereoscopic Association; and Mead Kibbey, Sacramento. Special thanks to Peter Palmquist for photographic reproduction and generous advice and consultation.

Contents

Copyright 1894, by B. W. Kilburn.
9533. Into the Jaws of death we go without a thought.
California Midwinter Exposition.

The entrance to Dante's Inferno, an amusement exhibit at the California Midwinter exposition in Golden Gate Park, San Francisco, 1894. Pictured full-size.

Preface

Collecting can be a real passion. I nibbled at the idea throughout my youth as interests came and went. First, it was arrowheads. They lay there in the dirt on our ranch, free for the finding, and they made great souvenirs of a romantic era. Then came model cars; I built them, and I collected them. Coins were fascinating, too. I can remember the albums with those empty spaces I knew I would never fill, but the compulsion and preoccupation to collect one thing or another urged me on.

The year 1977 was a turning point. I had set out to find some historical illustrations of California for use in a book. At one local history library I was handed a box of stereoviews and a stereoscope. As I placed each of the double-image cards in the viewer I became mesmerized by the wealth of information that appeared before me—in full 3-D. After a short time I realized I was on a journey into another era. History had always been one of my interests, and this was like stepping back in time and being swallowed by each tiny image as it suddenly filled my entire range of vision and became a window-sized view of the past. I recall one card in which hydraulic miners, only a few inches in front of my face, were directing their high-powered streams of water at far-off hillsides in an effort to dislodge gold. In another, a stagecoach loaded with passengers was rounding a bend, heading straight toward me. That first encounter with the stereoscope, with the fascination of looking history square in the eye, was nothing less than a magic carpet ride through nineteenth-century California.

I spent the next several weeks contemplating what I had seen. It became clear that whatever motive I lacked before in amassing a comprehensive collection of anything, I should now set my sights on stereoviews. At a neighborhood antique shop I found an old stereoscope; the velvet lining on its hood was frayed and worn, but the lenses were good. The shopkeeper suggested a couple of sources for cards, and I was off to my first antique show.

One of the things I remembered from my coin collecting days was that pristine examples become the most prized collectibles. That advice seemed especially appropriate when searching for stereoviews. It did not take long for me to realize these relics do not weather well over time when subjected to careless handling and improper storage conditions. Rummaging through what cards I could find in search of fine, collectible views proved to be a real Easter egg hunt. But dejection turned to euphoria each time I stumbled across a stereoview of superior content that had managed to survive a century or more in excellent condition. Without fading and damage, these artifacts take on lives of their own as miniature works of art.

Before long I was prowling photographica trade fairs, where I found table after table of antique photos. Evening telephone auctions provided additional opportunities to acquire stereoviews. The bidding sometimes crept into the wee hours while I chased a particularly desirable Indian portrait or a gleaming locomotive. Joining the National Stereoscopic Association put me in touch with an entire network of avid, astute, and knowledgeable collectors equally intent on finding and preserving these magical cards. The thrill of the chase was heightened by each new rumor of a long-dormant collection about to surface. Major finds by fellow enthusiasts often led to spirited trading sessions. I knew I had arrived in the big leagues when I began to receive calls from out of the blue, "I have my parents' collection. Would you be interested?" Absolutely!

Now, after fifteen years of assembling the very best stereoviews I could find, I have a select collection of about three thousand cards. I missed the era when these small relics of history were cheap and plentiful at flea markets and thrift stores; nevertheless, I continue to be fascinated by the views I have acquired. One is a portrait of John Sutter, the California pioneer who owned the mill where gold was first discovered. The view was made toward the end of his life after he retired to Lititz, Pennsylvania, in the 1870s. The local photographer there was out taking pictures of churches and resorts around town when he stopped by the Sutter residence and made the only known stereoscopic portrait of this famous Californian.

I have also collected self-portraits of photographers proudly posed with their stereo cameras, as well as views of small California towns that bit the dust over a century ago. One favorite series was taken by Carleton Watkins in 1863 and shows early logging activity around Mendocino. These were printed on rarely used glass mounts. When the stereoscope is held to the light, the transparency reveals a full-quality image.

Some of the rewards of studying stereoviews in depth are the intriguing revelations that still lie hidden within their images. I have spent hours with a loupe probing every detail of these cards for clues. Only recently I discovered, in one stereoview, the previously unrecognized faces of the artist Albert Bierstadt and western geologist Clarence King posed together during their travels in Yosemite in 1872.

Looking at stereoviews is a unique way of looking at history. Through the stereoscope I have witnessed events that vividly depict the development of a great state. I have also come face-to-face with John Muir and Mark Twain and other heroic figures that helped shape the image of California. This book is an opportunity to pass along some of the great cards I have encountered in collecting and researching various facets of California history that were photographed in stereo. I am most grateful to fellow collectors and institutions for allowing access to their excellent collections in order to show some of the finest examples of stereographic art.

Jim Crain

Introduction

Everyone loves an illusion. Our ability to see things in depth, in the third dimension, is something we live with every day and take for granted. Only when the perception of depth is re-created as an illusion through another medium—in a movie or a video game or on a printed page—does it take on an added fascination. Many of us from recent generations are familiar with putting on special glasses to view 3-D comics. But drawing the perception of depth from a printed illustration is nothing new. As early as the 1850s, photographers using twin-lensed cameras made stereoscopic photographs that took the Victorian public by storm. These pictures, mounted on card stock, came to be known as stereographs. Oliver Wendell Holmes was an early critic who became obsessed with the new marvels. He avidly collected and promoted stereographs and created the most practical version of the stereoscope. Today stereographs are most commonly called stereoviews. The stereoview is composed of two small, almost identical images mounted side by side. The images are recorded by a stereo camera, whose dual lenses are spaced approximately the same distance apart as the eyes. Each lens sees the subject from the same vantage point as each eye. When placed in a viewer, the two images merge into one to create a realistic, three-dimensional glimpse of each scene. In these views, one is able to see the depth and breadth of the landscape and the spatial relationship of foreground to background. Holmes described the realism that he saw through the stereoscope:

> The first effect of looking at a good photograph through the stereoscope is a surprise such as no painting ever produced. The mind feels its way into the very depths of the picture. The scraggy branches of a tree in the foreground run out at us as if they would scratch our eyes out.

Stereoviews were a natural consequence of the newfangled invention called photography, which was announced to the world in 1839 by a Frenchman, Louis J. M. Daguerre. Building on the research of others, he perfected the first practical method of making a photograph. The result was aptly called a daguerreotype, an image on a sensitized, silver-plated copper sheet. Each image was one of a kind because the process did not have a "negative" for duplicating copies. Although the first daguerreotypes were single images, stereo-daguerreotypes made their debut in 1851. They were rather expensive and used primarily for portraiture. By the mid-1850s the "wet-plate glass negative" process came into use and revolutionized the business of mass producing paper images. It was the breakthrough photographers needed in order to make stereoviews the format of choice.

It was apparently in 1859 that outdoor subjects in the West were first photographed in stereo. The Lander Expedition obtained about fifty views during its foray into the Rockies. That same year Charles Weed took views in San Francisco and Sacramento then ventured into Yosemite to take the first stereoviews there. Artists preceded photographers throughout the West, but their vision was quite different. They had a tendency to embellish and romanticize their subjects and to invent what they wanted to see instead of recording life as they saw it. Their landscapes at times bore little resemblance to the actual features they were intended to represent. By contrast, the photographers, with their ability to record reality in detail, surpassed artists in documenting life on the frontier. Our vision of California and the early West owes much to the stereophotographers who used their primitive magic boxes to freeze the everyday pursuits of emigrants turning the wilderness into a productive land.

Well over a century ago stereophotography was an important news-gathering and entertainment medium. A stereoscope in the parlor was equivalent to a television set in the den today and served precisely the same purpose. Family members and friends gathered for evening sessions of viewing captivating three-dimensional scenes that brought the realities of events, places, and personalities directly into the home. The latest stereoviews taken on Civil War battlefields, at the "joining of the rails" in Utah, or in the aftermath of the San Francisco earthquake provided viewing as popular as today's televised news segments. The development of the West unfolded in the stereoscope as onlookers saw Mormon emigrants heading west to rebuild their lives. They saw almost mile-by-mile construction of the railroad as it spread its tentacles across the country. And they witnessed the graphic documentation procured by stereophotographers who accompanied expeditions and surveys to record the geology, wagon routes, and Indian culture west of the Mississippi. Enthusiasts of the stereoscope not only gaped at the West's natural glories but were shocked by grisly hangings as frontier justice was caught on camera. Mountains of bones from the senseless slaughter of buffalo, as seen in 3-D, undoubtedly had an awakening impact on Americans and their vision of the West. The photographic images on stereocards also allowed citizens to see, for the first time, precise and realistic likenesses of their presidents and heroes in an era when primitive printing processes allowed only the use of engravings in the printed media. Between 1860 and 1900, millions of fascinating and informative stereoviews were sold for entertainment and educational purposes. After the turn of the century, interest waned, and the stereoscope was eventually replaced by advanced do-it-yourself cameras and its more modern counterparts: movies and television.

Stereoviews have great historical value today because of their highly documentary nature, giving us an important visual record of American life and social interests in the nineteenth century. Unlike larger "art" photos with carefully selected subjects and viewpoints, stereoviews were used to record just about everything the photographers saw, from the pretty and the ugly to the spectacular and the mundane. The journalistic fidelity shows us facets of life that do not appear in paintings and other artwork of the era. Artists had their own agenda—drama and beauty—and their canvases were sold to wealthy patrons. Stereophotographers, by contrast, created a medium for the masses, and captured what the public wanted to see. They made their best sales in scenic landscapes and views of main streets geared for tourists and armchair travelers. But historians and collectors today are more fascinated by their legacy of Indian portraits, pictures of technological constructions and disasters, and scenes of war and western expeditions—the stuff history books are made of.

California was the perfect setting for the practice of stereophotography. It was the end of the line and the ultimate goal in the progressive march across the country in search of new frontiers and new lives. The gold rush of 1849 drew hordes westward on a giant treasure hunt, a human migration of unprecedented magnitude, creating an urgent and unquenchable demand for knowledge of this distant place. In the years following the gold rush potential emigrants wanted to know what lay ahead—Was the country hospitable? What did it have to offer? What did the towns look like? Were people actually leading normal lives? After 1860, photographs, and particularly stereoviews, played a major role in communicating the endless opportunities that lay waiting in the West. Stereo was the most commonly used format in photography between 1860 and the turn of the century. The views were relatively cheap and could be obtained in quantities and series on almost any topic. No other region of the country offered a better variety of subject matter than that which was recorded by the photographers who came to California. A large number of practitioners arrived to stake out their territories from San Diego to Yreka, with camera-toting itinerants filling the gaps. No single photographer could capture the extent of California's development; however, their collective vision produced a wealth of documentation that not only satisfied the Easterners' thirst but preserved the colorful history of the Golden State.

Enthusiasts of the stereoscope not only gaped at the West's natural glories but were shocked by grisly hangings as frontier justice was caught on camera. No. 916. San Antonio justice. (Photo by William H. Jackson, Denver, Colorado, c. 1881.)

The Photographers

The craft of making a photograph in the 1860s required a feat of dexterity, and California was blessed with an enterprising breed of photographers skilled in their profession. Their talent had been applied primarily to portraiture, which was the bread and butter of established galleries caught up in the dog-eat-dog competition for customers. Photography was a business that went through economic downturns just like other businesses during the 1860s and 1870s. Survival depended on offering the newest processes, the most stylish poses, and first-class printing techniques.

As the mania for stereophotography swept across the country, photographers recognized a trend that meant big money. The most ambitious, consequently, armed themselves with stereo cameras and traveled to the places that provided them with the most salable scenes of wonder and curiosity—Yosemite, the Big Trees, the hot spring spas, and the unique California attractions that were of interest to tourists and would-be travelers.

Making photographs in the studio had its difficulties, but accomplishing the same on the road compounded the problems many times over. First, the photographer needed a vehicle to get from place to place. If he was involved in long hauls he had a wagon, usually a delivery-type wagon, outfitted to carry the hundreds of pounds of equipment needed to take pictures and to serve as a darkroom. If the session required going where the wagon could not go, a portable "darktent" was included, which was set up near the work site.

An infinite amount of patience, dedication, and expertise was essential for stereophotographers who chose to work away from their studios. Taking a photograph in the 1860s and 1870s was far from the point-and-shoot technology of today. The "wet-plate" era of photography required the cameraman to slip into the confines of a darkened tent and evenly coat a glass plate with collodion, a syrupy solution that spread over the plate as it was rocked from side to side. The plate was next dipped in a sensitizing bath, placed in a lightproof holder, and quickly taken to an already focused camera. The plate was exposed by uncapping the lens, then hurriedly carried back to the tent and laboriously developed, fixed, and washed. The entire process could take half an hour. Blowing sand, gnats, bad weather, and a lack of water added to the hazards of coating and developing the negatives. Once the plate was in the camera, even a gentle breeze could cause movement in the trees and, because of the long exposure time, create a blurred image. Reaching desirable viewpoints meant toting chemicals, tripods, boxes of plates, fresh water, portable darktent, and cumbersome cameras up and down mountains on the backs of packhorses and mules. It was not uncommon for the animals to be swept downstream while fording a swift current, or to fall on a steep trail, crushing the plates. A number of photographers chose to work only in the stereo format, possibly for the ease of dealing with smaller cameras and less burdensome equipment.

Overall, stereophotography was a documentary medium, but several photographers developed keen artistic sensibilities that made their record of a developing state all the more successful. The finest California stereoviews were produced by the following practitioners.

Charles Leander Weed (1824–1903) was at the forefront of stereophotography in California, having made the first outdoor stereoviews in San Francisco, Sacramento, and Yosemite in 1859. He never issued stereocards under his own imprint, but he did provide negatives to publishers Lawrence & Houseworth and E. Anthony & Company.

Carleton Eugene Watkins (1829–1916) was the most prolific photographer. His early stereo work, sometimes printed on glass mounts, began in Yosemite in 1861 and extended throughout the West well into the 1880s. He documented the greatest variety of subjects, places, and events. Although an excellent photographer, he was a terrible businessman, and during the hard times of the mid-1870s he lost most of his life's work to a competitor, I. W. Taber. Watkins returned to photograph many of his favorite places and issued a "Watkins's New Series" of stereoviews.

Eadweard Muybridge (1830–1904) rivals Watkins in his artistic endeavors, and the two are regarded as California's finest photographers. Most of his stereoviews were published by Bradley & Rulofson, but his earliest work was self-published under the name "Helios." He photographed some unusual subjects in stereo (the Modoc War, San Quentin prison, the people of Guatemala) before making a major contribution in motion studies that led to the development of moving pictures.

Alfred A. Hart (1816–1908) was the official photographer for the Central Pacific Railroad, issuing 364 captioned stereoviews of the construction plus many variants. (See "Building the Pacific Railroad.") Watkins obtained Hart's negatives about 1870 and republished the cards using Hart's numbers and captions.

John James Reilly (1838–1894) got his start making stereoviews at Niagara Falls before settling in Marysville. He photographed throughout central California but is best known for his views of Yosemite and custom portraits of tourists who visited there.

Martin Mason Hazeltine (1827–1903) marketed stereoviews of central California under his own name, but large numbers of his uncredited views also show up on the mounts of John P. Soule, Kilburn Brothers, and Thomas Houseworth, as well as J. G. Parks of Montreal and Ferrier & Soulier of Paris.

Lawrence & Houseworth and subsequently **Thomas Houseworth & Company** published an extensive inventory of subjects made by uncredited photographers—Hart, Hazeltine, Muybridge, Weed, and possibly others.

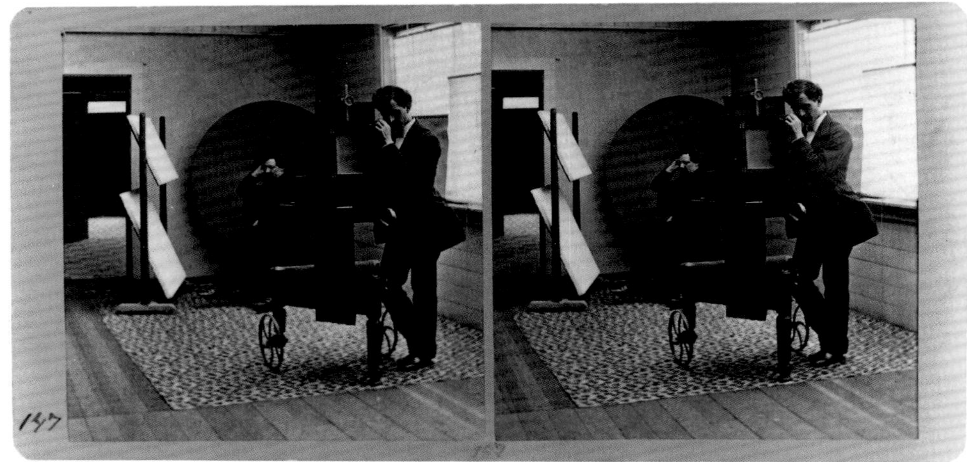

Out of the Studio

T. H. Rea, sitting, and H. Rauscher, of Santa Rosa, were typical of photographers churning out portraiture of local citizens. But, recognizing the need for a broader inventory, they packed up their gear and went into the countryside to take stereoviews of the Russian River area and the logging activities around Guerneville, as well as street scenes in Santa Rosa and surrounding towns.

While other photographers were hauling their glass plates out of the wilderness to make paper stereoviews back home in the studio, J. J. Reilly created the best of both worlds. As a traveling photographer, he simply set up his studio in Yosemite and did a thriving business taking custom stereo-portraits of groups only a few feet from his door. The plates were quickly processed, and stereoviews were made in time for the tourists to carry them home.

In the Field

Carleton Watkins's wagon was typical of a photographer's conveyance for getting equipment from place to place. For extremely long hauls throughout the West, Watkins made arrangements with the railroads to transport the wagon on a specially constructed flatcar in return for photographic services. The vehicle had a white canvas covering that was used during the summer to reflect the heat.

726—Photographer's first glimpse of the Yo Semite Valley, California.

Charles Pond, from Buffalo, New York, came west to make many stereoviews around Northern California. Here he sets out with the most vital piece of photographic equipment, the stereo camera, to capitalize on the wonders of Yosemite. Stereoviews of Yosemite were much in demand back east.

Eadweard Muybridge collectively called his photographic gear "The Flying Studio." The darktent was barely large enough for him to move around in while coating and developing the glass negatives. A small yellow window allowed enough filtered light to see what he was doing. Some photographers improvised their portable darkrooms. Mrs. E. W. Withington, of Ione, fashioned her long, black skirts into a perfectly usable tent in an emergency.

114. The Flying Studio.

Self-portraits

For all the documentation the photographers provided us, they left few portraits of themselves.

In later years, Carleton Watkins's daughter recalled that her father did not care to have his picture taken, but he did make this one, posing as a miner, for his children (c. 1883).

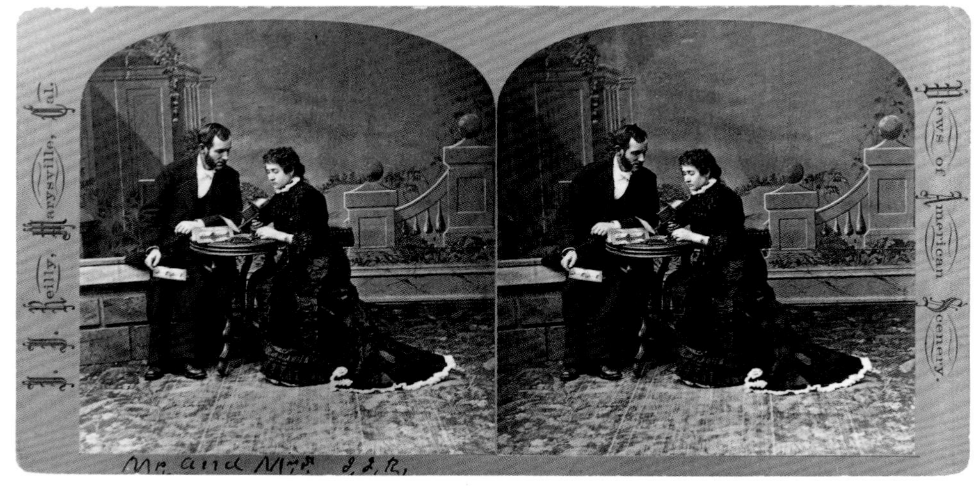

J. J. Reilly and his wife, Jennie, peruse stereoviews in his studio, about 1881. The simple handwritten notation reading, "Mr. and Mrs. J. J. R.," in lieu of a printed caption, indicates this self-portrait was probably intended as a memento for family or friends. It is the only copy known to exist.

Eadweard Muybridge's wry humor is evident in this 1870 view as he pretends to nap in the art gallery at Woodward's Gardens. The paintings were mostly copies of European masters. Perhaps his pose is a commentary on the art. Four years later a different side of Muybridge emerged when he murdered his wife's lover. The jury acquitted him on a plea of temporary insanity.

The Trail to California

Neither the trek to California nor the decision to make it were easy ones for the pioneers. But life became increasingly difficult in the East. Early in the nineteenth century several depressions wrecked the economy, and the agrarian society was rapidly overrunning the available land. Black slavery presented an issue that many people found repugnant. Moving on to such slave-free states as California solved that dilemma. As early as 1840 other assets of California and the West came into the limelight and emphasized the unrestricted opportunities that lay waiting for those who were adventuresome enough to seek them out. The new territory embodied the spirit of national expansion with its millions of acres of fertile land, a wealth of precious minerals, unlimited timber resources, and abundant game. Explorers determined that the territory along the Pacific Coast was the most desirable for new settlements. California, especially, seemed to have it all; the big obstacle was getting there.

For many easterners it was risky business to pull up roots and head west on a journey fraught with endless hardships. The trip would have to be a long haul, all the way across the bleakness of the Great Plains and the Rocky Mountains to the lush Pacific. Apparently, the gamble was worth it. About half of the emigrants chose to board clipper ships and steamers that took them around the tip of South America then north along the coast to San Francisco. The other half struck out across the wilderness by way of the Overland Route, also known as the Oregon-California Trail. Banding together in groups, they faced the rigors of uncharted terrain, drenching prairie storms, and shortages of food and water. Dreaded cholera epidemics took their toll. The misery was compounded by the hardships of living in a wagon for six months and the perils of traveling through a generally inhospitable land. But California, Oregon, and the Salt Lake Valley were irresistible, and the discovery of gold made California a particularly enticing destination. The emigrants' determination prevailed as some two hundred thousand made their way to California by wagon between 1841 and 1860.

Setting Out

Emigrants bound for the West congregated at one of several westernmost towns on the edge of civilization to join together for the long cross-country haul. Steamboats transported many pioneers to the jump-off communities of Westport, Independence, and St. Joseph, Missouri, as well as Fort Leavenworth, Kansas, and Council Bluffs, Iowa. Everything needed for the trip could be bought in St. Louis, and the levee teemed with newly arrived pioneers ready to purchase tools, supplies, and wagons. (Photo by Boehl & Koenig, St. Louis, c. 1867–72.)

Most of the wagon trains preceded the era of stereophotography, but we do get a taste of what the processions were like as early as 1859, when the first stereoviews were made in the West. This view was taken by a photographer with the Lander Expedition in that year as the party was leaving St. Joseph to survey new wagon routes through the Rockies. Although the emigrants depicted here were headed for the gold rush in the Pike's Peak region of Colorado, they were not unlike those in the convoys that made the long haul to California. One difference on the longer trip may have been the use of oxen, instead of mules, because of their endurance.

92 Ford on the Little Blue River, Kansas.

Emigrants on the Move

Emigrants had to time their departure carefully, leaving shortly after the spring rains stopped, giving grass along the rivers time to reach sufficient height to provide forage for the livestock. Swollen rivers sometimes created delays, as did bad weather, food shortages, uncleared trails, and a multitude of unforeseen obstacles. The goal was to cross the Sierra Nevada before the snows started to fall in October, otherwise the wagon parties would be stranded for the winter without food and fuel. (Anonymous photographer, Lander Expedition, 1859.)

After leaving the jump-off towns, the pioneers headed northwest along the corridor valleys of the Platte and North Platte rivers to the present-day location of Casper, Wyoming. They continued west along the Sweetwater River to South Pass, which marked the easiest crossing of the Rockies. From there some caravans chose a route southwestward to the Great Salt Lake then west to the Humboldt River. Others continued on the main trail to Fort Hall on the Snake River in Idaho then southwest to the Humboldt. The Humboldt River was the lifeline through the barren, desolate stretches of Utah Territory (now Nevada) before reaching the Sierra Nevada range in California. (Photo by C. W. Carter, Salt Lake City, c. 1867.)

Indians along the Overland Route were not always the threat that legend has portrayed them to be. It was extremely rare for a circled wagon train to be attacked; the Indians simply knew better than to go against such odds. Most problems resulted from small bands sneaking into corrals at night and stealing livestock. The few serious incidents that occurred undoubtedly established a respectful level of fear among the emigrants.

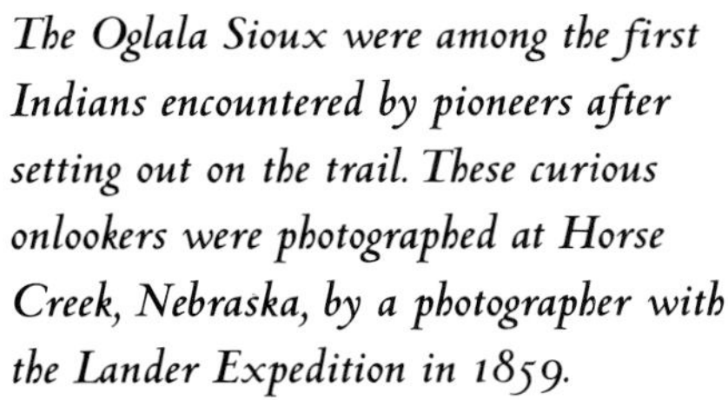

The Oglala Sioux were among the first Indians encountered by pioneers after setting out on the trail. These curious onlookers were photographed at Horse Creek, Nebraska, by a photographer with the Lander Expedition in 1859.

These Indians, photographed about 1870, could be representative of some of the tribes the pioneers came in contact with. It shows Chief Washakie's camp of Shoshones near South Pass, Wyoming, not far off the wagon route. Washakie's band was a peaceful tribe who aided settlers in crossing their territory. When supplies ran low, the wagon masters found them to be useful trading partners who would gladly accept tobacco and whiskey in return for buffalo meat, fish, and other edibles.

Passing the Landmarks

VIEWS IN THE ROCKY MOUNTAINS.
Prof. F. V. HAYDEN, in charge.
Dep't of Interior, U.S. Geological Survey of the Territories.
W. H. JACKSON, Photographer, Washington, D. C.
126.—Independence Rock. From East.

The pioneers were delighted by the sight of each anticipated landmark that marked their progress along the trail. They had a number of unusual geological formations to look forward to on the journey west. Independence Rock, in Wyoming, was a broad, flattened dome of granite that bordered the wagon road. The name was a result of the pioneers' itinerary, which usually placed them at the rock around the Fourth of July. It was a favorite campsite, and travelers took time to paint and chisel their names on the surface.

On the route through Echo Canyon, in Utah, emigrants skirted Pulpit Rock perched above the banks of the Weber River. Brigham Young purportedly climbed atop the natural pulpit to urge his Mormon followers onward. The rock was demolished in this century when a super highway was built through the canyon.

C. Bierstadt, Photographer
Niagara Falls N.Y.
1269. Pulpit Rock in Echo Canon, U.P.R.R.

Emigrants had all the reason in the world to associate the Devil with the unexplainable formations they saw. Devil's Slide, on the approach to the Great Salt Lake, was one of the strangest they encountered. Two parallel walls of rock project vertically from the hillside, resembling a giant slide to the river below. Wagons passed by here in the early days of the trail before a more practical route bypassed Weber Canyon. (Photo by Andrew J. Russell.)

Survival

The weather, sickness, and potential Indian problems were constant threats to the pioneers' safety. Survival also meant a daily food supply. They carried as many basic staples as they could: flour, salt, sugar, coffee, dried fruit, and with luck a milk cow. Meat, however, had to be obtained along the trail. Small game was usually present, but once they reached the Great Plains the men went scouting for buffalo. Aside from fresh steaks, they yielded strips of meat that were hung on the sides of the wagons to dry as "jerky." Buffalo "chips" were often the only source of fuel for campfires on the treeless prairies. (Photo by F. Jay Haynes, c. 1882.)

When the first wagons rolled, there were very few outposts as sources of supplies. Fort Laramie and Fort Bridger, in Wyoming, and Fort Hall, in Idaho, were the primary trading posts run by fur trappers. After 1849 more settlements appeared along the way. By 1860 the wagon route more or less coincided with the Overland stagecoach route and the Pony Express Trail. A Salt Lake City photographer, C. R. Savage, accompanied one emigrant train in 1866 while returning from the East with photo supplies. The wagon party posed for this group portrait. Before setting out, travelers were advised to hang together for security, otherwise stragglers could be harassed by Indians. Savage wrote of his concerns about lingering alone behind the wagons to take pictures and his fear of being "gobbled up by a few stray rascals who are always on the look-out for a weak party."

666. MORMON EMIGRANT CAMP.

End of the Journey

These Mormon emigrants, on schedule, have camped at Lake Tahoe on the last leg of their journey. Failing to cross the California mountains before the winter snows fell was a major threat that spurred the pioneers onward. The wagon train carrying the Donner party, in 1846, did not make it. Selecting an ill-advised route across Utah, they took twenty-one days to hack their way through thirty-six miles of an untested "shortcut." By the time they reached Truckee Lake (now Donner Lake) an early snowfall forced them to entrench for the winter. Thirty-five of the eighty-two members perished before rescue parties from Sutter's Fort reached the emaciated survivors.

Most wagon trains made it safely over the mountains to the Sacramento Valley. From there the pioneers chose a number of destinations; Sutter's Fort at Sacramento was one of the earliest. Some traveled north to settle the towns of Oroville, Marysville, and Shasta City. Others headed south to Sonora and the southern mines. Placerville (right), was centered in the gold rush region and became an eagerly awaited destination after 1848. The last stanza of the song "Sweet Betsey from Pike" expresses the pioneers' relief at finally arriving there:

608. Main Street, from the Cary House.

> They suddenly stopped on a very high hill,
> With wonder looked down upon old Placerville;
> Ike sighed when he said, and he cast his eyes down,
> "Sweet Betsey, my darling, we've got to Hangtown."

Native Californians

California did not produce any Sitting Bulls or Geronimos as ferocious as those men who earnestly defended their territories in the mountain and plains states against the encroachment of homesteaders and miners. By the time white settlers began to come to California, many Indians had already been subjected to Spanish attempts to Christianize them and change their way of life in an effort to colonize along the West Coast. Also, California was, for the most part, a land richly endowed with wild game, water, food, and sources of building materials. The various tribes, therefore, did not develop the hostile characteristics of other western tribes forced to compete against one another for the land's meager resources.

In spite of the relative peace among themselves, native Californians did not fare so well with the arrival of the pioneers. The Spanish mission system was a failure and detrimental to the lives of coastal tribes. The later invasion of gold-seekers brought a new animosity that made life intolerable for those in the interior areas. Indian lands were confiscated, hunting grounds spoiled, and peaceful villages pillaged without excuse. Although a few were employed for gold panning, the miners found the Indians' presence an obstacle to their search for gold and used them for target practice. The population of native Californians had dwindled substantially by 1870.

Photography arrived too late to give us a picture of Indian life in California prior to the gold rush migration. With a few exceptions (see "The Modoc War"), early stereoviews from the 1860s and 1870s show California's natives to be a rather friendly and peaceful people coexisting with settlers in a changing world. Stereoviews also show California's Indians as having a different look from other western tribesmen of the same era. No native Californians appear in finely feathered headdresses, hand-stitched buffalo skins, or the decorated regalia of plains Indians. Nor did they have the fierce look of southwestern warriors clad only in loincloths. Earlier contact with the Spanish missionaries and interaction with settlers and miners gave California's Indians access to modern skills and a certain amount of education. Manufactured clothing was obtained by bartering, working at various jobs, and salvaging cast-offs.

The Mission Indians

As early as 1769 Spain sent Father Junipero Serra to establish a network of missions along the coast of California as a means of warding off settlement by the Russians and the English. Serra's goal was to convert the local Indians to Christianity and teach them the skills needed to fit into Spanish colonial life. The mission system was plagued with operational problems from the beginning, however. Compounding the difficulties were the Indians' loss of their familiar customs, mistreatment at the hands of their stewards, and lack of immunity to white men's diseases. Converts died by the thousands. The mission experiment failed and was eventually abandoned as Spain lost its foothold on California.

This 136-year-old Indian was photographed at San Antonio Mission, near Jolon, about 1880. That would mark his birth date as 1744, twenty-five years before the first California mission was established at San Diego in 1769. The old-timer undoubtedly witnessed many changes brought about by Spanish efforts to impose an agrarian way of life on the coastal tribes.

Indigenous Structures

California's Indians had more diverse styles of dwelling than in any other region of the country. Depending on tribe and location, habitats were constructed as conical huts of redwood or cedar bark, semi-subterranean earth lodges, domes of woven thatch and brush, wickiups of tule matting over willow poles, rectangular plank houses, and other variations.

The acorn cache was an ingenious construction for storing a family's supply of acorns through the winter. Slender poles supported an interior basket of woven branches lined with wormwood to ward off insects. The exterior was thatched with cedar boughs held in place by strands of grapevine.

The sweat house was the men's communal area, a sauna-type structure where they bathed, loitered, gossiped, and sought relief from certain ills. A good sweat, followed by a dip in a nearby stream, removed the human scent from hunters before they set out to stalk game.

Daily Chores

Acorns were a basic food source. They were pulverized then leached of bitter tannin on a shallow, hard-packed basin of sand. The process produced a daily meal of mush and baked bread patties.

Women basket makers kept very busy, and they excelled at their craft. Their woven utensils were indispensable for all sorts of domestic purposes: seed gathering, winnowing, cooking, carrying, drying, and storage. Novel designs made excellent baby cradles, fish traps, hats, dippers, bowls, and drinking cups.

Hunting was the man's job, and he went after everything from fish to fowl and elk to insects. The resourceful Indians utilized game to the fullest. Rabbit skins made excellent carrying sacks, and deer skins were stitched together for clothing. Antlers were used for a variety of tools, while bones were carved into fishhooks and whistles.

Cultural Legacies

Rituals were practiced by all California Indians, and dances were an important part of their ceremonies. Their rites related to death, marriage, puberty, religion, healing, harvests, and the acquisition of wealth, among others. These Miwok dancers were photographed in Sonora by either Daniel Sewell or Thomas Wells in the late 1860s.

There are numerous occurrences of Indian "rock art" in eastern California. Incised petroglyphs, or pictographs, are regarded by scholars as acts of artistic expression related to hunting and food-gathering practices. The "pictured rocks" shown here were carved into a broad expanse of granite near Donner Lake. A. A. Hart photographed the markings about 1868 while taking stereoviews along the route of the Central Pacific Railroad, which was under construction at the time.

Practically nothing is known about Chief Pokotucket except for the caption on this stereoview, which reads, "the Indian Chief who first led the Americans into Yo-Semite." This could indicate he was the guide who led Major James Savage and his followers into Yosemite in 1851. They were the first white men to set foot in the valley. The chief's noble, weathered face earned the attention of the photographer, and the tag line may be the only testimony to Pokotucket's claim to fame.

Sierra Nevada Mountains.
M. M. Hazeltine, Artist.
POKOTUCKET, the Indian Chief who first led the Americans into Yo-Semite.

These Miwok women in Yosemite have donned their finest calico dresses to pose for Eadweard Muybridge in 1872. Years after the intrusion of settlers destroyed the Miwok way of life, remnants of the tribe still lived in the valley. They were the chief source of the labor needed to handle the burgeoning tourist traffic, which grew steadily stronger after the area was made a state park in 1864. The Miwoks' presence, dances, and ancestral pursuits contributed to the tourists' experience there. The women did all sorts of domestic chores, such as laundry, sewing, and basket weaving for the hotels and visitors. Men sold fish and venison to the innkeepers and worked as guides and trail builders.

Of all the writers in the nineteenth century, Helen Hunt Jackson perhaps did the most to bring the plight of the Indian to the attention of the public. Her first book about the cause, *A Century of Dishonor* (1881), documented the government's record of broken promises and reprehensible treatment of Native Americans.

The book did not fully achieve the impact Jackson expected, so she turned to fiction. The result was *Ramona* (1884), a classic Western novel. She drew from her extensive research into conditions of California's "mission Indians" and wove a romantic tale of love and sacrifice set amid the colorful era of the Spanish ranchos.

The scene above is from an outdoor pageant based on the book and held annually in Hemet, California. It pictures Ramona, half-Indian, half-Scottish, and Alessandro, a full-blooded Indian, who proclaim their love for each other, then are hounded from place to place by marauding white settlers, who seize their land and eventually kill Alessandro. (Warner's "Stereoscopic" Views, San Bernardino, c. 1925.)

Jackson hoped to expose the government's denial of Indian rights and arouse sympathy in the minds of Americans in the same way that Harriet Beecher Stowe used Uncle Tom's Cabin *to further the cause of the slave. The book did awaken public sentiment and led to some well-intentioned reformist legislation. But the widely read novel had a second impact. It so vividly depicted the lure of the missions and the noble era of Spanish aristocracy that it gave a tremendous boost to tourism in California.*

Building the Pacific Railroad

The completion of the Transcontinental Railroad in 1869 ranks as one of the great technological accomplishments in American history and a vital link in bridging the continent. Construction was preceded by years of exploratory surveys, bickering over preferred routes, power struggles, and the inevitable scandals. The sheer folly of laying track across mountain ranges, alkali deserts, and Indian country required an epic determination.

Workers eventually began laying the Central Pacific tracks eastward from Sacramento and raced to join the rails with the Union Pacific crews working westward from Omaha. They met and celebrated the laying of the last rail and the driving of the final spike at Promontory, Utah, on May 10, 1869. For the first time opposite ends of the country were united by the means that would allow California and the West to prosper beyond their wildest dreams.

The Central Pacific Railroad hired Alfred A. Hart as its official photographer to record progress on the California end. Andrew J. Russell was his counterpart with the Union Pacific. Hart used only a stereo camera to document for posterity the construction and scenery along the Central Pacific route through California and Nevada to its linkup with the Union Pacific in Utah. In his stereoviews, Hart achieved some stunning visual effects in close-ups of construction, views over the sides of cliff-hugging roadbeds, and shots of the remarkably fascinating locomotives.

No. 56. Rounding Cape Horn—road to Iowa Hill from the river. (All photos by Alfred A. Hart.)

The locomotive A. A. Sargent, *named for a California congressman, sits on Front Street in Sacramento only a few blocks from the businesses owned by the Big Four. After months of preparatory work and scrambling for funds, the first rails were laid from here on January 8, 1863.*

CENTRAL PACIFIC RAILROAD CALIFORNIA.

214. J Street, from the Levee.

The Start

The idea of a railroad connecting the east and west coasts had been kicked around as early as 1838, when Congress ridiculed the proposal for being as silly as building a railroad to the moon. In the West, Theodore Judah became the outspoken promoter of this elusive dream, which earned him the name "Crazy Judah." As chief engineer, he had already built the Sacramento Valley Railroad connecting Sacramento and Folsom in 1856. It was the first passenger line west of the Rockies. During the 1850s Congress failed to act decisively on Judah's request to create a Pacific Railroad Act. To drum up support, he set out on his own to define the most viable route through the Sierra Nevada and to raise the capital for surveys and preliminary construction. He eventually persuaded four prominent Sacramento businessmen, Leland Stanford, Charles Crocker, Collis P. Huntington, and Mark Hopkins (later known as the "Big Four") to back the enterprise. Together with other interested parties, they formed the Central Pacific Railroad of California in 1861.

The Civil War was raging at the time, and further lobbying convinced legislators in Washington that a transcontinental railroad was not only vital in binding California to the Union but also essential for military control of the state. Construction was finally authorized when the Pacific Railroad Act was passed by Congress and signed into law by President Lincoln in July 1862.

Mighty Locomotives

1. Locomotive "Gov. Stanford."

The Gov. Stanford *came disassembled with the first equipment that arrived from the East by sailing ship via a long journey around the tip of South America. The engine was named in honor of Leland Stanford, president of the C. P. R. R. and governor of California at the time.*

The Arctic, *towing passenger cars, brought interested parties to the railhead at Dixie Cut, near Blue Canyon. This cut and others were hand-carved, mostly by Chinese laborers. The V-shaped channel at Bloomer Cut was chiseled through incredibly hard cemented gravel. It was eight hundred feet long and sixty-three feet high, the most difficult on the route.*

60. Train in Dixie Cut. Gold Run Station, Placer County.

182 "Oneonta," at Cisco.

The Oneonta *was named for C. P. Huntington's hometown in New York state. It sits on a siding at Cisco, the busiest little town between Sacramento and Reno. Cisco became a vital supply point and staging ground while they dug the summit tunnels through the Sierra.*

Long Ravine was one of the greatest obstacles on the challenging stretch between Colfax and Emigrant Gap. A large work force was required to prepare foundations and erect the huge combination trestle and bridge span that stretched 1,050 feet in length and 120 feet high.

CENTRAL PACIFIC RAILROAD
CALIFORNIA.
41. Long Ravine Bridge, near Colfax. Length 1,050 feet.

Some crossings were conquered by creating filled embankments, such as the one at Heath's Ravine, in lieu of building bridges. This was a monumental task for workers using only horse-drawn carts and wheelbarrows. Culverts, as much as 185 feet long, allowed water to drain through.

The Construction

The locomotive Conness *was among the engines constantly ferrying massive amounts of materials to the construction crews. Once unloaded, the locomotives were revolved on this semi-portable turntable, eliminating the need to build turnaround track at each new point of the railhead.*

The camera looks out from Tunnel No. 10, one of fifteen required to maintain a negotiable grade through the mountains. Blasting powder and pickaxes were used to bore these holes through solid granite, sometimes gaining only a few inches each day. Nitroglycerine was used on one tunnel, No. 6, but was abandoned after it proved too difficult to handle.

Snows wreaked havoc with the work crews during severe winters. Avalanches were notorious for destroying portions of completed track as well as sweeping away human lives. To keep construction trains running, and later the regular trains, the railroad had no choice but to build a patchwork of wooden snow sheds over a forty-mile distance through the highest elevations.

The Workers

The Chinese were the backbone of the work force. They proved to be hardworking, reliable, and easily trained in every facet of the construction. Over twelve thousand were eventually hired. Without them, progress might never have attained the speed it did in reaching the Utah terminus. The movable headquarters of the construction superintendent, James Strowbridge, is parked beside this Chinese tent town.

Constructing the railroad was not just a matter of laying track. These workers in the quarry at Rocklin are cutting and shaping granite lintels for use in culverts, trestle footings, bridge abutments, and even the roundhouses at Rocklin and Truckee.

The two railroad crews raced to lay track as quickly as possible to receive government subsidies for each mile constructed. When the Union Pacific gang put down seven miles in one day, Charles Crocker boasted that the Central Pacific crew could lay ten. The vice president of the U. P. wagered ten thousand dollars that it could not be done. After a well-planned operation and a grueling day's work by the crew, Crocker won the bet, and the record stands to this day.

CENTRAL PACIFIC RAILROAD.
UTAH.
357 The Rival Monarchs.
Scene at Promontory Point, May 10th, 1869.

At the moment Hart made this picture from the top of the Union Pacific locomotive, Russell was busy taking a similar photo from the top of the Central Pacific engine. Savage is seen with his camera and tripod at the left, in front of the distant row of onlookers.

Laying the Last Rail

As construction crews approached each other in the Utah desert, Congress resolved that the two railroads should meet and connect at Promontory Summit. The Central Pacific got there first, arriving on April 30, 1869. The Union Pacific finished its work around May 8. To celebrate the occasion, a ceremony to lay the last rail was carried out on May 10. Leland Stanford represented the Big Four and used a silver-headed mallet to pound a golden spike that bound the final rail to the cross-tie. At that moment the event was telegraphed to major cities in the East and West, where bells rang, cannons fired, and people rejoiced in the streets.

Three photographers were on hand to witness the occasion, Alfred Hart, Andrew Russell, and Charles Savage. All three made stereoviews of the participants and the locomotives as they came together to pose for the event. These are some of the most important and dramatic photographs in American history.

The Daily Grind

The work ethic was alive and well as emigrants to California settled into making the frontier state a productive place to continue their lives. They brought with them a social blueprint and prior skills that they collectively applied with all the resourcefulness of intrepid adventurers transforming a wilderness into a prosperous land. Settlers in California may have had an easier time building their dream than in other parts of the country. The abundance of natural resources had been the drawing card to begin with.

Stereophotographers demonstrated a fascination with the occupational endeavors of Californians and recorded many laborers pursuing their livelihoods with tools of the trade in hand. Watkins photographed whalers, fruit pickers, beekeepers, and early oil-well crews. Muybridge took stereoviews of pioneer wine makers, Japanese acrobats, and even San Quentin convicts building yachts, wagons, and furniture. Their cameras also witnessed the new technology of an approaching machine age.

California was one whopping territory that had to be mapped in its entirety. These men are part of Lt. George M. Wheeler's survey party in Yosemite in 1878. One leans on his transit, while another tows an odometer strapped to a lone wagon wheel.

The Town-Builders

CALIFORNIA.
1190. Street View in Mendocino City. Post Office
In the foreground.

The first task of the newcomers was to set about establishing a frontier necessity—a town—a base for supplies and services and the nucleus of a social structure. Mendocino was one of many towns spawned by the proximity of an abundant resource—in this case, lumber. Other communities resulted from mining frenzies or the presence of railroad construction camps, waterways, or natural travel routes. (Photographer unknown, published by Lawrence & Houseworth, c. 1866.)

Merchants and citizens gathered on Mill Street in Grass Valley to accommodate the photographer. The town was established early in the gold rush era and survived the fading excitement due to continually productive quartz mines nearby. Note that the townsmen successfully "paved" the street with wooden planks. (Photographer unknown, published by Lawrence & Houseworth, c. 1865.)

The gold rush created a rash of new towns and escalated growth in the old ones. Much lumber was required to fill the needs of newcomers. Loggers, undaunted by the size of giant redwoods, harvested a California resource that was as good as gold.

With a growing population, mechanization was important to the burgeoning agriculture business in the 1880s. The noisy, straw-burning steam thresher was a sight to behold as the monster machine, pulled by teams of mules or horses, inched its way through the wheat fields.

After the Transcontinental Railroad was completed, workers set about constructing a network of lines within the state. Rail travel was a boon to businessmen, tourists, and ordinary travelers eager to avoid the rough ride in a stagecoach. Chinese workers played a major role in the building of western railroads.

Technology on Display

The mechanical marvels of the machine age were modern, efficient devices that instilled pride in their keepers. Among the fanciest and most ornate machines were the vitally important fire engines. In San Francisco, the Monumental Fire Company received this gleaming steam-powered pumper on a trial basis. It is shown here on display at the Mechanics' Institute. It was touted by its builder in New York as being sufficiently light to be hand-drawn by volunteers, thereby avoiding costly stabling of horses.

Inventors were hard at work perfecting their ingenious, newfangled creations. Frederich Marriott, a financier and editor of the San Francisco Newsletter, *spent twelve years developing his unmanned, steam-powered prototype of the* Avitor *for the Aerial Steam Navigation Company. It was the first lighter-than-air hydrogen-filled craft of its kind in the United States. Marriott launched the dirigible July 2, 1869, at a San Mateo racetrack. Men on the ground held onto the balloon with ropes while it reached a hefty five miles per hour. Unfortunately, a carelessly discarded match brought about its demise.*

Odd Jobs

Mercury was a vital element in separating gold particles from crushed ore and was heavily used by miners in the Mother Lode. The mercury mines at New Almaden, just south of San Jose, produced major amounts of the stuff. In 1863 Watkins photographed the entire complex and its workers, including this gentleman weighing the quicksilver.

Ferryboat captains saved travelers time and effort by shortening routes. The steamer Solano *was a connecting link in the Central Pacific Railroad, ferrying entire trains across the Sacramento River between Benicia and Port Costa.*

Women had busy hands in their multitalented roles as housekeepers. As seamstresses they stitched everything from socks to quilts in a never-ending cycle of wear and tear. These women gathered at William A. Bell's photo gallery in Santa Cruz for a group portrait of their sewing circle. A sewing "bee" not only eased the grind of household chores but gave women a social outlet.

Getting educated was as much a part of the daily grind for students as harvesting redwoods was for the menfolk. From grade school through college, education meant "change" and the opportunity for a better life ahead. These youngsters, around the turn of the century, received their geography lessons through the stereoscope. (Unknown photographer, published by Keystone View Company.)

Dr. A. A. O'Neil conducts an anatomy class in Toland Hall on the University of California campus. Eadweard Muybridge took some of the earliest photos of the new facilities in April 1874, six months after its relocation to the Berkeley countryside.

Young ladies gather for a class portrait under the trees at Mills Seminary (now Mills College) in Oakland. Mills was the first women's college west of the Rockies and relocated to this site from Benicia in 1871.

When the Work Was Done

After the work was finished, there was time to play, time to relax the mind and spirit from the hard work required to fulfill daily chores.

TOP: *The traveling circus was an American tradition; some were large, some small, but the entertainment was always riveting. Dan Castello's Overland Circus was the first to make a cross-country tour by train. It opened a three-day run in Sacramento on July 20, 1869, only weeks after the completion of the Transcontinental Railroad.*

CENTER: *A good parade gave the whole town an opportunity to express community pride through a turnout of civic groups, marching bands, and decorated floats. This procession on Sonora's main street in 1900 pauses to allow an anonymous photographer to take a picture.*

BOTTOM: *A day at the track was a popular pastime at the forty racecourses that were operating in California by the turn of the century. Men enjoyed the thrill of a good race, and it was an opportunity to gossip with neighbors, make new friends, and cultivate new customers.*

After the Gold Rush

Photography was still in its infancy during the California gold rush of 1849. Daguerreotypes are the only surviving photographs showing the earliest miners at work, and none of those are in the stereo format. By the time photography advanced to the point that paper prints could be mass-produced as stereoviews, it was the early 1860s, and the process of mining for gold had undergone changes. The surface gold had been gobbled up, and the working of shallow deposits with gold pans and primitive washing equipment became increasingly unproductive. More advanced machinery, techniques, and skills were employed to root out underlying deposits and squeeze the precious metal from the ores.

Publishers Lawrence & Houseworth, of San Francisco, issued the most significant number of stereoviews showing every aspect of the devices and methods used by the miners during the 1860s. The actual photographer of these few selected mining scenes is unknown, but the series exemplifies the documentary nature of stereoviews as a historical record.

The first participants in the gold rush merely bent over and picked up shiny pieces of metal gleaming through the shallow water of sandbars and ledges. Poking around with a good stick uncovered more. But most of the gold was in the form of tiny flakes, or "dust." To retrieve this, a miner used a shovel and a special tin pan to find the specks. The pan was swirled to wash water over silt, thereby separating it from the heavier gold, which sank to the bottom. This was a time-consuming process.

The prospectors naturally sought faster and more productive ways of separating gold from the earth. The "rocker," also called a "cradle," was a three-foot-long box with a hopper on top. The hopper was loaded with sediment and gravel, water was poured over the mixture, then the entire contraption was rocked from side to side. The water drained through the perforated bottom of the hopper onto a canvas apron and out the open end of the box, leaving gold-bearing sediment caught on a series of riffles nailed to the bottom of the box.

Still, the miners, in all their urgency, developed more efficient ways to wash large quantities of earth on a grand scale. During the 1860s, mining companies were created that had sufficient capital to obtain and construct the machinery that would make mining a major industry.

PLACER MINING.
317 and 319 Montgomery Street, S. F.
991. THE DALY CLAIM—Columbia, Tuolumne County.

Placer Mining

Placer mining had a vital connection with natural waterways. This is where the gold ended up after the base material in which it was embedded decomposed. The rivers acted like natural sluices; the heavier gold settled in crevices or sandbars and sometimes sank dozens of feet below the surface.

ABOVE: *Columbia Gulch, outside the town of Columbia, was an example of a rich placer find. As much as sixty feet of topsoil was displaced to get at the gold-bearing sediment. A tremendous setup of flumes and hoisting wheels was constructed to bring water to the site and lift the gouged-out earth to the surface. The gulch became an eerie chasm of exposed rock outcroppings and mounds of gravel tailings.*

CALIFORNIA.
1009. Placer Mining—Columbia, Tuolumne County.
Interior of the Dump-box.

ABOVE: *After the miners, working deep in the bowels of the gulch, filled each ore car with potential gold-bearing material, the car was hauled up the inclined track to the top of the dump-box by means of a primitive turbine engine called the Friedenburr Water Wheel.*

LEFT: *The ore in the car was dumped into the interior of the dump-box. Water from a flume poured into the back of the box and washed the earth into sluices where the gold was trapped for retrieval.*

Hydraulic Mining

Washing the earth with water was the universal method of getting at rich deposits of gold. Hydraulic miners had to transport water over great distances from far-off lakes and rivers. They built elaborate trestlelike flumes, sometimes fifty to one hundred feet high.

From the flumes, water was channeled into pipes that gradually reduced in size to build up water pressure. At the end of each pipe was a hose and nozzle. It was much like a fire hose, only the stream of water was considerably more powerful. At full force the gushing torrent could cut a man down if he got in the way.

The terrible force was used to cut down hills and mountains, washing the soil with a rapidity that put shovels and wheelbarrows to shame. The process itself was a shame. Hydraulic mining was eventually outlawed because it destroyed the landscape and its silted runoff clogged streambeds in the lowlands.

HYDRAULIC MINING.
THOMAS HOUSEWORTH & CO.
SAN FRANCISCO.
1404. Hydraulic Mining near French Corral. Piping the Bank, (near view.) Nevada County.

Quartz Mining

The last-ditch effort to wrench the remaining gold from the soil lay with the "hard-rock" miners. They traced ancient river channels deep into the earth where rich veins were embedded in strata of gravel and quartz that rested on layers of bedrock. Vertical shafts were driven hundreds of feet below the surface to allow miners to reach these deposits. Solid quartz ores were raised to the surface in ore cars then smashed into powder by half-ton stamps. The gold was then separated by use of chemicals, such as mercury, that readily amalgamated with the gold.

The most successful quartz mining district in California was in Nevada County, particularly around Grass Valley. The Rocky Bar Mine was one of several that contributed to a long and steady flow of productivity that prevented the community from becoming just another ghost town.

This elaborate engine at the Gould & Curry Mill in Virginia City, Nevada, was not unlike machinery in the huge stamp mills in California. Steam-powered engines were used to operate pumps that kept the shafts dry and hoists that raised and lowered men and ore. They also powered the deafening stamps, sometimes a hundred or more, that pulverized the ore.

In the Valley of the Yosemite

The first white men entered Yosemite Valley in 1851 and gazed upon one of the grand marvels of the American landscape. On both sides of the glacier-carved canyon were sheer granite cliffs, tapering spires, and shimmering rock domes that towered above grassy meadows. Snow-fed waterfalls crashed from great heights, spilling into the Merced River. Yosemite was immediately recognized as a unique setting, and this newly discovered Eden was destined to become the ultimate symbol of paradise on earth. Throughout the rest of the nineteenth century, most people knew Yosemite only by its wonders in the stereoscope. An extremely arduous trek to the ice-sculpted canyon placed the landscape out of reach of all but the most determined travelers. Even from the nearby town of Merced, the valley was still a two-day, hair-raising ride by stagecoach over dusty, rocky trails that tested one's endurance and resolve.

As for stereophotographers, nothing could keep them away. Yosemite was a mecca for these picture makers and became a staple subject in their catalogs of views. The majestic wilderness setting was photographed and rephotographed from every conceivable angle, and the images found their way into parlors across the country and abroad.

Some extremely fine Yosemite photos of a larger format, taken by C. E. Watkins, found their way into the offices of Washington politicians in 1864. The legislators were so impressed by the incomparable scenery that a bill designed to preserve the area was prepared and placed on President Lincoln's desk for his signature. In the midst of the Civil War, and in a bold and foresighted move for that day and age, he signed the legislation that set aside "The Yo Semite" as a state "grant," a place for the public good, for all time. It was the seed and the inspiration for the National Parks program that followed and in which Yosemite was included in 1890.

By the 1880s there were several routes that led to Yosemite. One of these found tourists disembarking a steamer at Stockton then boarding a Southern Pacific train at nearby Lathrop for the journey to Merced. After a night's rest at El Capitan Hotel, the travelers took a stagecoach east to Mariposa.

Mariposa was and remains one of the gateway towns to Yosemite. It was from here that localites began to explore the valley in 1851 in the course of rounding up marauding Indians. Tourists continued by stage over Chowchilla Mountain to Clark's Station, later known as Wawona, on the southerly approach to the valley.

Wawona was an important stopping point for visitors traveling the southern route. Galen Clark built the first hostelry there. In 1875 it was taken over by the Washburn brothers, and they built the now-famous Wawona Hotel. The strategic location was only a stone's throw from the incomparable Mariposa Grove of Big Trees. Travelers were advised to spend a day among the giant sequoias before continuing to the valley.

Descent into Eden

The stage road north from Wawona roughly paralleled today's route into the valley. At Inspiration Point tourists got their first glimpse of the magnificent landscape they had traveled so far to see. Stage drivers halted for a few minutes to allow passengers to absorb the beauty laid out before them.

After descending the steep, rutted path to the valley floor, the stage passed most of the prominent landmarks, Bridal Veil Falls, Cathedral Rocks, El Capitan, Sentinel Dome, and The Three Brothers. James Hutchings described the experience in his book In the Heart of the Sierras *(1886):*

> Once within the encompassing walls of the glorious Valley, and the broad shadows of its mighty cliffs are thrown over us like some mystic mantle, fatigued as we may be, every jutting mountain, every pointed crag, every leaping waterfall, has a weird yet captivating charm, that makes us feel as though we were entering some fictitious dreamland.

As impressed as they were, the weary tourists would explore the landmarks later. Their first priorities were hot baths and hot meals at their choice of several hotels.

On the Line of the O. R. & N. Co.
M. M. Hazeltine, Baker City, Oregon.
YOSEMITE VALLEY CAL.

James Hutchings may have been a better promoter than hotel keeper. He was a Yosemite pioneer who, in 1855, led the first tourist party into the valley. He owned the Hutchings Hotel, and although it was not the most accommodating, his widely read articles and guidebooks may have established name recognition with visitors.

George Leidig built his two-story hotel in 1869, but it was Mrs. Leidig whom the guidebooks commended for the fine dining room. Outside, guests could sit on the porches and enjoy an impressive, head-on view of Yosemite Falls.

J. C. Smith's Cosmopolitan Hotel, constructed in 1870, had it all, a combination saloon, bathhouse, barber shop, hotel, and dining room. It boasted a first-class billiard parlor. Every little detail of comfort and amenity was provided, for which the tourists gladly paid extra.

Nature's Glories

Yosemite Falls, in springtime, greeted tourists with the roar of its thundering torrent plunging to the valley floor. Guides led parties to the base of the falls, where they experienced, with mist in their faces, the up-close power and beauty of the spectacle. The Falls was the most memorable feature of the valley and the preferred setting for visitors, such as these horsemen, who wanted stereoview portraits.

At every turn the tourists found a new picture of beauty as the spiritual mystique of the valley unfolded. Sunlight and shadows on the lofty rock monuments created soothing reflections in the still waters of the Merced River.

Mirror Lake was not only one of the spots most visited by tourists but also a favorite hangout for artists and photographers. The tranquil lake, with the reflection of Mount Watkins mirrored on the surface, was one of the most serene and beautiful settings in the valley.

Half Dome

Half Dome (also called South Dome), is the second largest exposed granite monolith in the world; only El Capitan on the north side of the valley is larger. The northern face of the dome has eroded to a near-vertical surface over millions of years. Some believe this was caused by the grinding effect of ancient glaciers that plowed through the valley; others attribute it to the natural exfoliation of granite, or a combination of both. Whatever the cause, the towering promontory has become Yosemite Valley's symbolic landmark. (Photo by M. M. Hazeltine, showing C. L. Pond sitting beside his camera, c. 1871.)

The noted geologist J. D. Whitney once proclaimed Half Dome to be unclimbable. The first man to prove him wrong was George Anderson, a blacksmith in the valley. He scaled the rocky promontory over its arching backside on October 12, 1875. He was soon followed by four Englishmen vacationing in the valley. (The four "dudes" are easily spotted in this stereoview taken by Watkins.) All the climbers conquered the last four hundred feet of the glassy slick dome by means of a system of ropes tied to eyebolts hammered into holes in the rock.

Famous Visitors

In 1865, at the end of the Civil War, Speaker of the House Schuyler Colfax (third from left, middle row) and a party of prominent politicians and newspapermen made a tour of western states to investigate their natural and scenic resources. After touring the Nevada mining districts and the assets of Oregon and Washington, the party reached Yosemite in August. It was a grand encampment with the added attendance of Frederick Law Olmsted, co-designer of New York City's Central Park, and William Ashburner of the Geological Survey. Olmsted presented the group with a report about the government's right to set aside such scenic attractions as Yosemite for the public's enjoyment. Carleton Watkins had the honor of photographing this first excursion party of dignitaries to visit the valley.

Yosemite attracted many other famous personalities, such as Horace Greeley, Richard Henry Dana, Ralph Waldo Emerson, Susan B. Anthony, and former president Ulysses S. Grant. One surprising visitor in June of 1870 was P. T. Barnum, America's chief entrepreneur of amazing oddities. Even Barnum (seated, second from left) must have been struck with wonder at the incomparable scenery of Yosemite.

BOYD
12

San Francisco

San Francisco has always been a special place on a special site since its early beginnings around 1836 as a sleepy village called Yerba Buena. At the time, it languished as a makeshift town on the leeward side of the bay along what would be Montgomery Street today. But when gold was discovered in California in 1848, San Francisco quickly came alive, and its strategic port location transformed it into an instant boomtown and a major hub for commerce and trade. Everything of significance on the West Coast seemed to be happening in San Francisco, and its gold rush roots made it one of the most exciting cities in the world.

Along with the gold-seekers came the photographers. Richard Carr is the first practitioner known to have opened a daguerreotype gallery in 1849. Ten years later, Charles Weed took the first stereoviews of the city, making a fine panoramic series of buildings and the bay. The city of the Golden Gate, sprinkled on the hilly terrain, was as photogenic as any metropolis that existed, and the photographers that established their galleries there made certain that no streetscape went unrecorded. Over time, San Francisco would appear in stereoviews as one of the most photographed and best-documented cities on earth.

WATKINS' PACIFIC COAST.
429 Montgomery Street, San Francisco
Broadway street from Kearny—looking East.
1383
Entered according to Act of Congress, in the year 1867, by C. E. WATKINS, in the Clerk's Office of the District Court of the United States for the Northern District of California.

Early engineers had a plan to level Telegraph Hill. They did not succeed, but they did gnaw away at the edges, in this case to flatten a right-of-way for Broadway.

Image of the City

Today, just the name, San Francisco, conjures up visions of bustling wharves, the rattle of cable cars, and quaint Victorian homes clinging to steep hills.

TOP: *Broadway Wharf, about 1865, was one of several piers showing activity that could match any port in the world. Sailing ships arrived from all over the globe, and steamers carried passengers to and from Sacramento and Stockton.*

CENTER: *Andrew Hallidie watched with dismay as horses pulling streetcars fell on the steep, slippery hills, suffering serious injuries. In 1873 the inventive engineer put into use an ingenious system that allowed cars to grip onto a continuously running cable buried beneath the street. A small dummy car was often attached for riders who preferred the open air.*

BOTTOM: *The steepest hills, Nob, Russian, and Telegraph, have given San Francisco much of its charm. Most residents shunned these aeries until the invention of the cable car made them more accessible.*

The "Palace"

The "Palace" was the brainchild of William Ralston, San Francisco's preeminent millionaire banker, who had his hand in countless entrepreneurial ventures, especially Nevada mining stocks. By the mid-1870s most of his schemes had turned into disastrous, cash-eating speculations. But Ralston felt sure his luck would change if he built the grandest, most opulent hotel in the world, a monumental centerpiece that would boost San Francisco's status as a world financial center. In the same year the Palace opened, Ralston's empire collapsed. On the day following "Black Friday," when Nevada mining stocks crashed, Ralston, up to his ears in debt, went for his usual swim in the bay—and drowned. It was never determined whether his death was suicide or an accident. The Palace, however, remained a source of civic pride, which even the earthquake of 1906 could not diminish.

A one-legged news vendor hawks his papers on Montgomery Street as the Palace Hotel looms in the background. At left are the photographic galleries of C. E. Watkins, I. W. Taber, T. H. Boyd, and Thomas Houseworth.

Lloyd Tevis (center), president of Wells Fargo & Company, confers with fellow financiers on the upper balcony of the Great Court. The Palace was a social center that played host to a parade of wheeler-dealers, presidents, kings, and celebrities.

Woodward's Gardens

Robert Woodward used the profits from his successful hotel, the What Cheer House, to build a home and lavishly landscaped gardens among the barren sand hills at Mission and Fourteenth streets. Those who peeked over the fence hungered to visit his art museum, statuary, grottoes, waterfalls, and collection of tamed and stuffed animals.

After much pestering by the citizenry, Woodward opened the grounds to the public in 1866,. and Woodward's Gardens became San Francisco's "Disneyland." The townspeople were treated to traveling sideshows and a theater, a bandstand, a skating rink, a seal pond, and a museum of peculiar stuff that would have amazed P. T. Barnum.

The zoo held an assortment of exotic animals and the first saltwater aquarium in the country. Kids had a field day riding camels and the whirling "rotary boat." Balloon ascensions were special events that astonished the entire crowd. (Photo by C. E. Watkins, published by I. W. Taber.)

Nob Hill Mansions

No. 104 Residence of C. Crocker Nob Hill, San Francisco, Cal.

San Francisco was a haven for entrepreneurs who made their fortunes in gold, silver, lumber, and real estate. The most expressive statement of their wealth was the opulence of their homes. On California Street, atop Nob Hill, Charles Crocker and his fellow railroad barons built their grandiose mansions that rivaled some of the finest palaces in Europe.

Leland Stanford's Italianate home had an art gallery, library, music room, and billiard room, each furnished in the most exquisite detail with carved wood, marble, tapestries, and ornamentation. In the center was a great rotunda flanked by granite columns and adorned with ceiling frescoes painted by prominent Italian artists.

San Franciscans looked upon the Mark Hopkins residence as something of an absurdity. It was a never-ending concoction of Gothic detailing that epitomized the excesses of the "nouveau riche." All these lavish monuments, among others, went up in smoke during the earthquake of 1906.

At the Beach

Since 1863 a succession of Cliff Houses have perched on the precipitous, rocky bluff overlooking Seal Rocks and the Pacific Ocean. The first was a modest one-story building on a magical site. Tourists and townsfolk loved to make the buggy ride to the ocean to watch the barking sea lions and ships passing through the Golden Gate. Occasionally, visitors were treated to the sight of tightrope walkers making their way out to Seal Rocks on cables stretched from the Cliff House.

– Rawlings –
On the Beach at Cliff House,
San Francisco, Cal.

The third and grandest of the Cliff Houses was built in 1896 and resembled a huge French chateau. Its owner, Adolph Sutro, made his fortune in the Comstock mines of Nevada and owned a mansion on the crag above the Cliff House site. Although the gingerbread palace survived the 1906 earthquake with minor damage, it burned to the ground in a fiery spectacle in 1907.

The Chinese people have been a vibrant part of San Francisco's culture since they first poured into the city during gold rush days, congregating in a community of their own. Despite the racism and prejudice directed at them, they were excellent workers. Even in the early years Chinatown was an adventure for tourists. It was a fascinating taste of Old China, a mysterious place of strange customs, exotic shops, and colorful sidewalk groceries selling the most peculiar edibles. The Chinese themselves, dressed in baggy pantaloons and wearing pigtails, added to the picturesque flavor of the neighborhood.

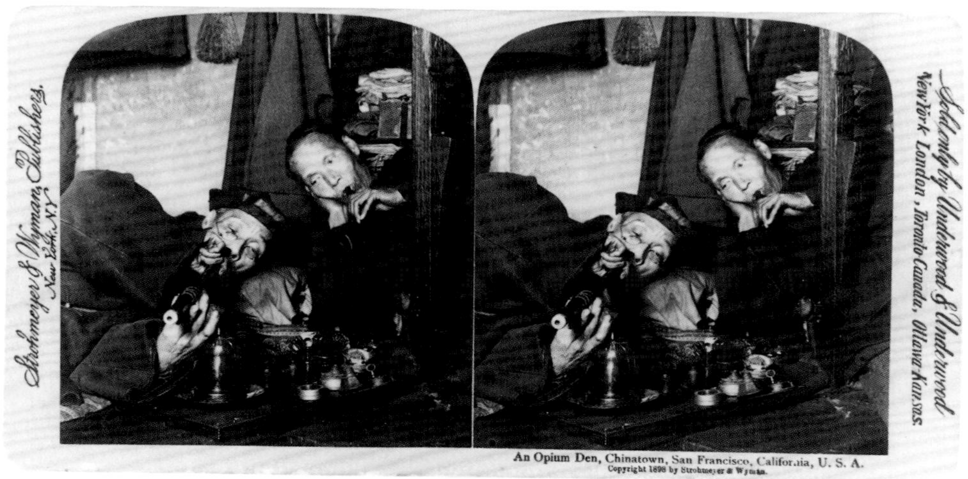

Underneath the facade were two classes, upper and lower, with the poor living in a world of squalor as thirty thousand Chinese crammed themselves into twelve square blocks. Male tourists, attracted to the seedier side of life, enlisted guides for nighttime tours through gambling saloons, brothels, and opium dens where the sweet smoke filled the air.

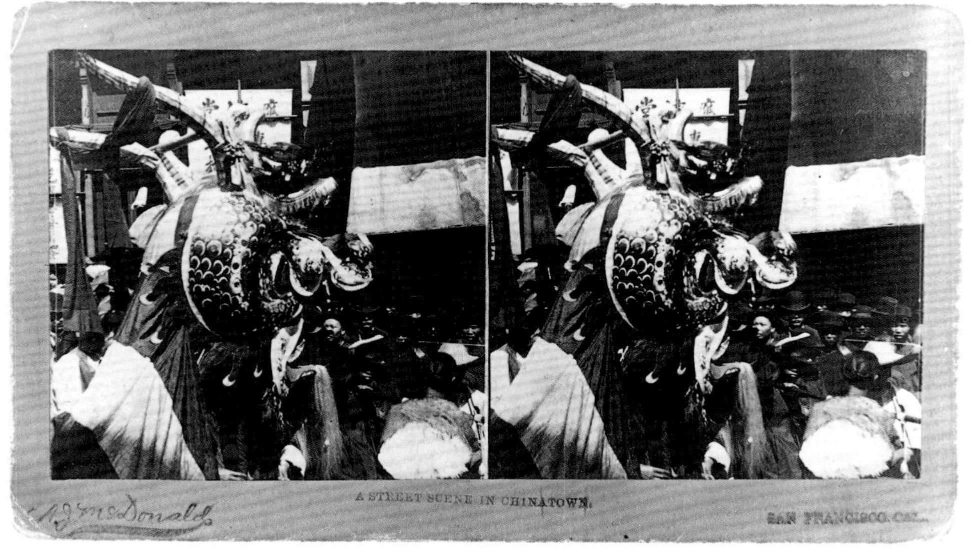

The image that lingered longest in the early tourists' memories were the colorful New Year's parades that surged through the streets to the sounds of firecrackers and drums. Since the 1860s the parade has been capped by a brilliant, undulating dragon manipulated by a score of young men.

Bonanza Road

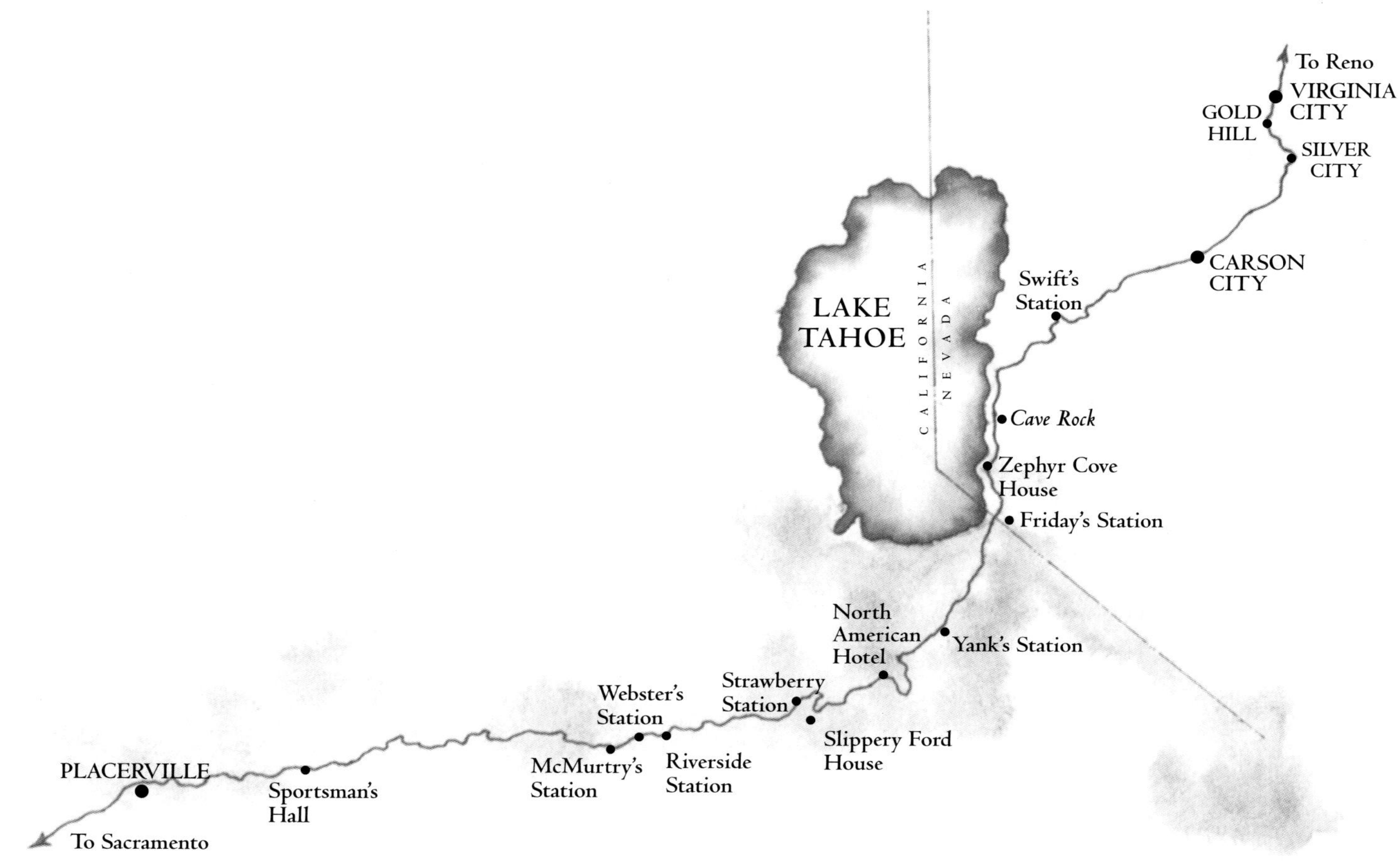

During the 1860s, photographers working for the stereo-publishing firm of Lawrence and Houseworth recorded the bustling freighting scene along the route between Placerville, California, and Carson City in Nevada's Washoe Valley. This was "Bonanza Road," the road to Washoe. Backbreaking work and private capital transformed a primitive wilderness trail into a practical, yet rugged road traversing the Sierra Nevada. This was the vital lifeline from the Sacramento Valley to the rich Washoe mining district in western Nevada. Every conceivable commodity needed for day-to-day living and working was hauled over the mountains in an almost endless stream of wagons. To accommodate the teamsters, nearly one hundred way stations sprang up along the route, providing bed and board. They had colorful names like Sportsman's Hall, Slippery Ford House, and Strawberry Station.

The Pony Express added to the colorful history of the route. Seven stations between Placerville and Carson City served as rider remount or relay points during the short life of the venture, from April 1860 to October 1861. The Pioneer and California Company stage lines carried passengers over the road.

The stereoviews illustrated here were taken about 1864 or 1865 during the peak of the freighting period. The steady flow of wagons continued until the Central Pacific Railroad, farther north, was completed between Donner Lake and Reno in 1869. Traffic on "the road" faded fast after that.

East from Placerville

Sportsman's Hall was only twelve miles from Placerville and a favorite breakfast stop for teamsters and travelers. During the Pony Express era, it was the only station between Sacramento and the Nevada border where a change of riders was made.

CALIFORNIA.
614. Webster's Station and Sugar Loaf Mountain.

Webster's Station was also known as Sugar Loaf House for the towering Sugar Loaf Mountain behind it. These three loaded wagons, coupled together and pulled by a dozen mules, were typical of the outfits carrying supplies to Nevada. Both the Pony Express riders and the Pioneer Stage Line switched to fresh horses here.

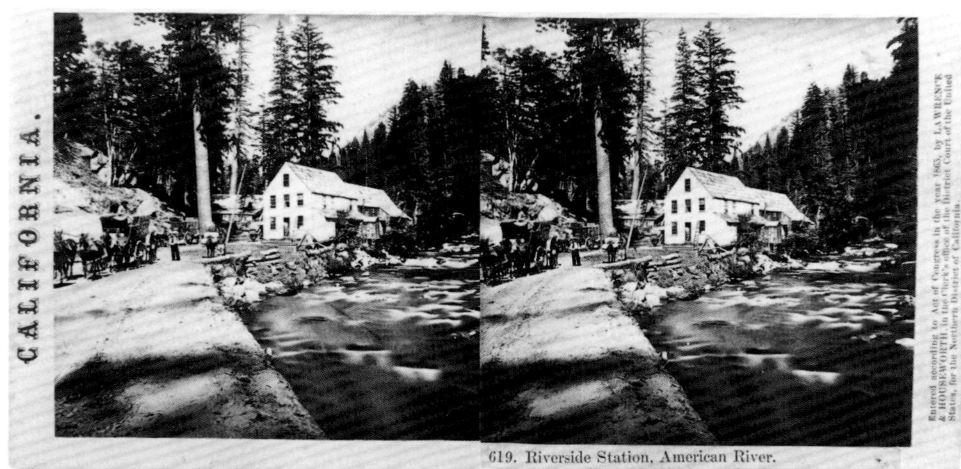
CALIFORNIA.
Entered according to Act of Congress in the year 1865, by LAWRENCE & HOUSEWORTH, in the Clerk's office of the District Court of the United States, for the Northern District of California.
619. Riverside Station, American River.

Feeding the Teams

Riverside Station, perched on the edge of the American River, was located about a mile east of Kyburz. Freighters fed and rested their mule teams here before starting the long haul toward the summit.

CALIFORNIA.
By Thomas Houseworth & Co.
Entered according to Act of Congress, in the year 1866, by LAWRENCE & HOUSEWORTH, in the Clerk's Office of the District Court of the United States, for the Northern District of California.
621. Feeding the Teams. Scene on the Placerville route.

This scene of activity was taken behind Riverside Station during a rest stop. The teamsters have parked their wagons loaded with mining gear while the mules feast on hay. The preference for mules over oxen was a controversial one. Oxen were cheap and foraged on grass along the trail but were much slower than mules. Mules quintupled the price, and hay had to be carried with the rest of the cargo. In the long run, the speed of mules usually won out on the Placerville route.

Over the Sierra Nevada

Two Concord coaches, belonging to the Pioneer Line, await departure at Strawberry Station. The stagecoach line reportedly carried twenty-five thousand passengers over the route in 1861. Hank Monk was a legendary stage driver on the route. He was well known for his boozing, practical jokes, and hair-raising rides down the mountain to Placerville.

CALIFORNIA.
637. Teams passing through the Snow, on the
Road leading down into Lake Valley, from Summit of Sierra Nevada.

Heavy snows in the Sierra Nevada prevented freighting during the winter months. But the wagons rolled again in the spring as soon as the road-keepers carved a path through the snowbanks. These wagons have cleared the summit of the mountains, headed east.

CALIFORNIA.
642. Yank's Station. Valley of Lake Tahoe.

After descending into Lake Tahoe Valley, the teamsters arrived at Yank's Station. It was a sizable, bustling place with livery stables, a cooperage, a general store, a couple of saloons, and the best dining room on the route. The location is called Meyers today.

Arriving at the Mines

Various pieces of "the road" were maintained and operated on a toll basis. "Friday" Burke and his partner were responsible for their franchise. On a good day as much as $1,500 in tolls were collected at Friday's Station. Remnants of the station still remain, sitting only a short distance from the casinos on the Nevada side of the state line.

NEVADA.
676. Cave Rock, Lake Tahoe. View from the Road.

Part of the route at Cave Rock, on the eastern shore of Lake Tahoe, had to be shored up with granite foundations to create a narrow, one-way section of roadbed. These apparently empty wagons are returning from Nevada heading down into the valley.

Gold Hill, Nevada, was one of several destinations in the Washoe mining district where freighters delivered their loads of machinery and supplies needed to carry out the mining of gold and silver. The big cannons at Fort Homestead, overlooking the town, were fired on important occasions and gave the Union loyalists a sense of security during the Civil War.

The Modoc War

In 1873 the United States Army sent a thousand troops to Northern California to subdue a rebellious band of fifty-two Modoc Indians entrenched in the lava flows around Tule Lake. The conflict had built up over decades. The Modocs, like many other Native Americans, had found themselves displaced by the early encroachment of white settlers and miners who destroyed their hunting grounds, their aboriginal culture, and their economic way of life. The dwindling tribe was forced into marauding for survival. Over time, the Modocs recognized that immigration would not cease and fully resigned themselves to the prospect of a peaceful life on a reservation. After years of unfulfilled promises and treaties broken by the government, the Modocs were denied a reservation of their own and were forced onto the reservation of their traditional foes, the Klamath Indians in Oregon. Captain Jack, a quasi-leader of the Modocs, and his followers found life unbearable among the Klamaths, whom they found to be hostile, thieving people. After several attempts to co-exist there, with little help from the government, Jack and his people fled the reservation and returned to their ancestral homeland on Lost River near the California-Oregon border. Pressure from neighboring white settlers prodded the government to try and return the Modocs to Oregon. Jack refused to go, and the warfare that followed cost the army eighty-three lives before the Modocs were finally flushed from the rugged terrain, tracked down, and captured.

Eadweard Muybridge was the more prominent of the two photographers who photographed the topography, participants, and encampments of the war; Louis Heller, from nearby Yreka, was the other. Although no pictures were taken of the actual fighting, Muybridge returned to San Francisco with more than fifty stereoview negatives that illustrate the conflict.

Hostilities Begin

In November 1872, the army attempted to round up the Modocs by raiding their camp at Lost River. The Modocs escaped and withdrew to the lava beds on the south side of Tule Lake, in California, killing a number of civilians along the way. They secreted themselves in a jumbled landscape of lava outcroppings and twisted rock formations riddled with an interconnected network of caves. This seemingly impregnable fortress came to be known as "Captain Jack's Stronghold."

Gen. Edward Canby, a Civil War hero and the military commander in the northwest, quickly moved troops into the area around the lava beds to protect settlers and ranchers from the Modocs.

On January 17, 1873, the army felt confident that its 330 men were sufficient to launch an attack on the stronghold and rapidly remove the Modocs back to the Klamath reservation. Due to a heavy ground fog, a lack of understanding of the terrain, and a general ineptness on the part of the army, the maneuver resulted in nine deaths and twenty-eight wounded soldiers before the troops retreated. No Modoc lives were lost.

General Canby Is Killed

After several attempts at peace negotiations with Jack and his followers, Canby sent Toby Riddle, wife of his interpreter, to Jack's hideout to relay terms of amnesty and safety for all who would turn themselves in. Toby (standing at center) reported back that some Modocs were ready to give up, but the more vocal members would not allow it. Toby warned Canby of an overheard threat that if he attended the next peace conference he would be killed.

Canby scoffed at the threat and assumed that the Modocs were more interested in peace. The small peace party met alone with Jack and his men on April 11, 1873. Jack reiterated his long-standing request for a homeland in the lava beds area and tried to elicit Canby's promise in return for peace. Canby was sympathetic to the plight of the Modocs but did not have the authority to grant such a promise. Suddenly, according to a prearranged plan, the Indians killed Canby and a second member of the commission, then fled. Jack hoped this would scare away the other soldiers forever. Instead, this blunder sealed the fate of the Modocs.

The Modoc War.
Illustrated by MUYBRIDGE, Published by BRADLEY & RULOFSON.
1624—Toby, (the Squaw who warned General Canby of his impending fate), and four Old Modoc Squaws.
1601—The Peace Commission Tent, and Stone on which Gen. Canby was sitting when shot by Capt. Jack.

The Scouts Arrive

The nation had generally been sympathetic toward the Modocs and their cause but now was outraged by Canby's death. President Grant ordered that "utter extermination" was justified if necessary to bring the Modocs under control. More troops were sent to the field.

Warm Springs Indians, natural enemies of the Modocs, had been enlisted earlier by Canby as scouts and for use in combat. He had felt it was best to let Indians fight Indians. The scouts arrived two days after his death.

Donald McKay, a Warm Springs Indian himself, was a veteran Indian fighter who had assisted the army many times. He was chosen to lead the scouts. He was not particularly liked by the rest of his band, but they accepted his leadership in order not to lose out on the government pay.

More Battles

Two more raids on the Modoc stronghold again failed to subdue the handful of Indians, even though heavy artillery was used. The massacre of troops patrolling with Captains Thomas and Wright cost the bewildered army another twenty-six lives. Not a single Modoc had even been spotted during the attack.

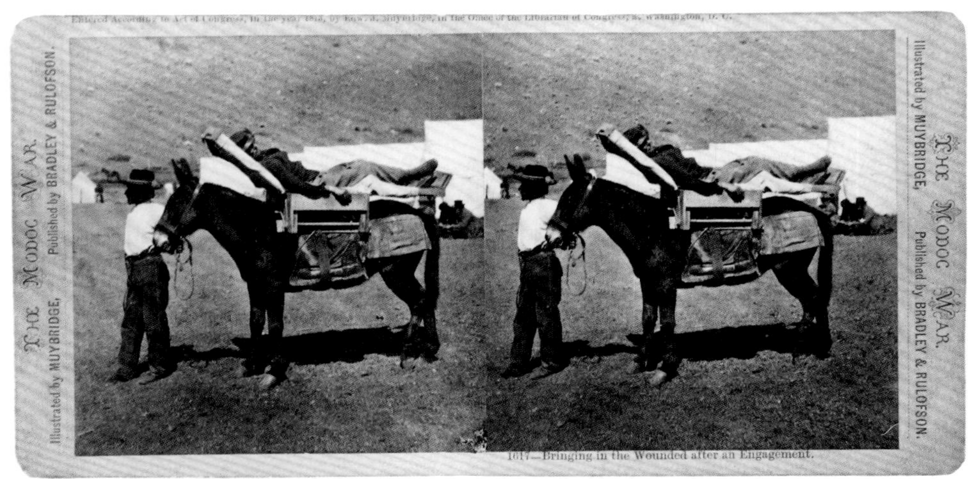

Removing the wounded from the rocky battlefield was such torture to the injured that a specially designed reclining chair was devised to strap on the back of a mule.

As the war dragged on, the American press clamored for an end to the Modocs. Several newspapers sent reporters to the scene to record the activities. This newsman, preparing a dispatch, is believed to be William McKay, a correspondent with the San Francisco Bulletin. *His reports, and others, were sent via the transcontinental telegraph and gave the rest of the country almost instant access to news from the front.*

The photographer Muybridge was not allowed to get near the actual warfare, so he staged a few scenes to simulate combat. In this photo he posed one of the government's Indian scouts as "A Modoc Brave on the War Path." Several of the stereoviews were used as a basis for engravings in Harper's Weekly.

Rout of the Indians

Col. Jefferson C. Davis (no relation to the Confederate president) arrived to replace Canby in late April (seated second from left, front row). He found a demoralized army of men who seemed unable to cope with the Modoc's guerrilla warfare. The time-tested strategies of Civil War battles proved worthless against the Indians.

Davis needed a victory badly. He sent Capt. H. C. Hasbrouck, the Indian scouts, and a company of cavalry to search for Jack in the lava beds. Jack spotted their encampment first and made a surprise attack. This time the soldiers held their ground and fought hard against the snipers. As the Modocs retreated, they were blocked by the scouts. Jack and his ragged band fled the area, abandoning their horses and supplies. The tables had turned, and in a short time, the tired, hungry Modocs began turning themselves in.

On June 1, 1873, Jack finally surrendered, and the only Indian war fought within the state of California came to a close. After a military trial, Jack and three associates were hanged for the murder of Canby. Two were imprisoned on Alcatraz Island, and the rest were exiled to a reservation in Indian Territory (Oklahoma). By the time the conflict ended, public sentiment had again swung in favor of the Modocs for their heroism in taking on the U.S. Army to defend their right to a homeland. The government was persuaded to go easy on remaining members of the tribe. Today, a few descendants still live in eastern Oklahoma.

The Tourists

What tourists saw through the stereoscope undoubtedly enticed them into the countryside to visit the actual sites that intrigued them. California was endowed with pleasurable wonders, from hot spring spas and coastal forests to secluded mountain retreats in the High Sierra. The tourists, in turn, became the subjects in the stereoviews, some peering through curtains of steam at The Geysers, others gathering on the gigantic stump of a mammoth tree.

Photographers found a healthy commercial enterprise in making on-the-spot stereoviews of tourists who wanted to document their excursions. The cards made perfect souvenirs, just like picture postcards and snapshots today. Photographers found it advantageous to use people in the foreground to enhance the sensation of depth. Also, by relating people to the landscape, for scale and human interest, they further sanctioned the traditional "picturesque" quality of a scene as long practiced by artists.

"Dressing" for the outdoors was undoubtedly the fashionable thing to do at resorts. Women were stylish, men dapper, and hats were always worn by both sexes.

The train approaching Colfax has halted so travelers can stretch their legs at Cape Horn. The completion of the Transcontinental Railroad brought a new dimension to cross-country tourist travel. Railroads organized tours and promoted vacation spots in their advertising in order to boost the use of rail service. Stereoviews became a major ingredient in drawing easterners to the romantic West. Views of all the greatest attractions were sold at train stations along the way.

No. 223 Overland Train Coming Round Cape Horn, C. P. R. R. Cal.

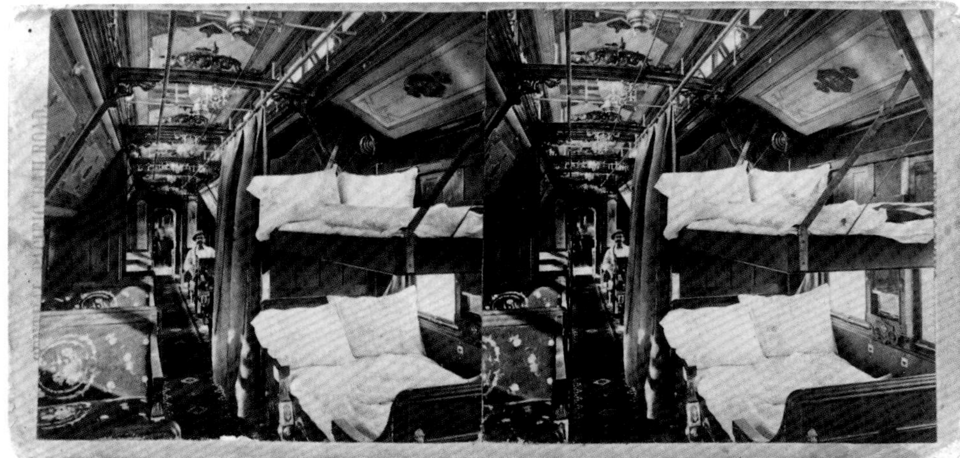

The trains from New York took about seven days to reach San Francisco. To attract customers, the ornate Silver Palace cars were made as accommodating as possible. Travelers in the bunk facilities achieved some semblance of privacy by drawing the curtains, but they still had to contend with heat and cold and the rattling, lurching movements of the train. (Photo by Alfred Hart.)

Several steamers, such as the Antelope, *the* Chrysopolis, *and the* Julia, *carried tourists from San Francisco to Stockton, where they boarded trains and stagecoaches for various routes to Yosemite and Calaveras Big Trees. Riding the big side-wheelers was an experience in itself. The steamers plowed swiftly up the Sacramento and San Joaquin rivers as the clunking of paddle wheels echoed in the passengers' ears. (Photographer unknown, published by Lawrence & Houseworth, c. 1865.)*

CALIFORNIA
JULIA
1027. Steamer Julia at the Levee, Stockton; San Joaquin Co.

Big Trees

Skeptical tourists traveled to the Calaveras Big Trees to see for themselves the incredible things they had heard about the size of giant sequoias. They were not disappointed. The discoverer of the grove in 1852, A. T. Dowd, had reported the find to his campmates, but they laughed at his tale until they were finally led to the site. When a section of one tree was displayed in New York in 1854, the exhibit flopped because it was perceived as just a California hoax.

The Mammoth Grove Hotel was host to a steady drove of visitors who came to walk among the towering giants and climb in and out of the hollow tunnels of their fallen comrades.

Farther south, on the northern approach to Yosemite, was the Tuolumne Grove, which gained much attention due to its easier access and proximity to popular Yosemite Valley. The grove was smaller and the trees less stately than those in the Calaveras Grove; nevertheless, tourists loved to drive through the "Dead Giant," where they posed for pictures aboard a carriage parked in the hollowed cavity.

The Geysers

Tourists were attracted to "The Geysers" by advertisements that compared its amenities to Saratoga, Baden-Baden, and other great spas of the day. On arrival, the guests may have been somewhat disappointed in the small hotel with paper-thin walls and a lack of finely appointed bathhouses. But The Geysers and its therapeutic waters, one hundred miles north of San Francisco, did become one of California's most visited attractions.

The 1870s and 1880s were busy times for the spa once Clark Foss began his stage runs from Calistoga and Healdsburg. The legendary "whip" was almost as well known as The Geysers, and he earned a tribute in Robert Louis Stevenson's book of essays about the area, Silverado Squatters *(1904).*

The Geysers was not a typical spa, and no spouting geysers actually existed. The main attraction was the eerie chasm where the ground boiled and bubbled and spit at visitors through ancient fissures. Such curiosities as The Tea Kettle, Devil's Kitchen, and Witches' Cauldron oozed sounds and smells that overwhelmed the tourists' senses.

Lake Tahoe

Tahoe is an Indian word meaning "Big Water," and the early tourists were definitely awed by the expanse of blue twenty-two miles long and ten miles wide. Stagecoaches brought visitors from the railhead at Truckee to Tahoe City, where a few first-class hotels, such as Tahoe House, put up guests in style.

Vacationers occupied their time with buggy rides along the shore, trout fishing, exploring waterfalls, and boarding steamers for cruises on the lake. The Governor Stanford *is moored at the Customs House wharf at Tahoe City, awaiting passengers.*

One natural oddity on the south shore was a favorite posing spot for visitors. A freakish burl, growing in the forks of a cedar tree, had the eerie likeness of a "hoary headed old sinner." Yank Clement, owner of the nearby hotel, dubbed the old gent "Nick of the Woods." Some guests thought the contorted growth looked a lot like Yank himself.

The Hotel del Monte was a self-promotion of the Southern Pacific Railroad to increase the resort value of its large land holdings on the Monterey Peninsula. The hotel opened in 1880 as a fashionable playground for San Francisco's well-heeled elite, who, predictably, made use of the railroad to get there.

Only one of the grand wooden resort hotels that once dotted the California coast still exists—the Hotel del Coronado—completed in 1888 on a jackrabbit-infested peninsula across the bay from San Diego. It was designed as a stately centerpiece for a huge land development scheme. Like other large western resorts, it became popular with the Atlantic coast populace, who were becoming jaded by eastern spas and hotels and also sought out the mild winters of Southern California.

Recording the Visit

WATKINS' PACIFIC COAST.
429 Montgomery Street, San Francisco.
Entered according to Act of Congress, in the year 1867, by C. E. WATKINS, in the Clerk's Office of the District Court of the United States for the Northern District of California.
1577. In the Devil's Pulpit, Geysers.
Napa County, Cal.

The tourists were not satisfied with merely purchasing stereoviews of the sites they visited. If possible, they wanted actual evidence to show that they had traveled to and participated in the grand experience of nature's realm. Photographers were often on hand to oblige. The caption, "In the Devil's Pulpit," gives testimony that these anonymous vacationers did indeed visit The Geysers.

Gustav Fagersteen (standing at right) was a German immigrant who set up shop during the summers in Yosemite Valley in the 1880s. He was responsible for a vivid legacy of tourists' portraits. The sign on his wagon, which served as a portable darkroom, reads "Yosemite or Bust."

By the 1890s, cameras had become so simplified that even amateurs could chronicle their pastimes. These tourists with a California camera club carried a variety of folding cameras to the Mariposa Grove in Yosemite, where this stereoview was taken.

History-Makers

The first stereoviews taken in California were stereo-daguerreotype portraits of gallery patrons. These were housed in fancy folding cases with built-in stereo lenses patented by John F. Mascher in 1853. The Mascher cases were made available by a few San Francisco photographers in that year. Although expensive compared to standard portraits, the stereo-cased images were nevertheless popular at first because of the novelty of 3-D. The daguerreotype era, however, was not long-lived, and the process was soon replaced by more advanced photographic techniques using paper prints mounted on card stock.

Stereoviews did not become an accepted format for portraits. Instead customers wanted single-image *cartes de visites* (2½ by 4 inches) and cabinet cards (4¼ by 6½ inches), which were easily stored in albums or placed in small tabletop frames. But stereophotographers never lost interest in capturing the antics of famous figures—presidents, statesmen, heroes, writers, actors—the people making the headlines. The movers and shakers of the late nineteenth century were as fascinating as places or events, and their stereo likenesses were commercially successful. Some posed in studios, others in the arena of their profession. Whatever the setting, customers were delighted at the experience of seeing their favorite personalities "in depth."

Lotta Crabtree started her career as an uninhibited child entertainer in Grass Valley during the gold rush era. She proceeded to become the highest paid actress of her day by appearing in theaters around the world. In 1875 she generously donated Lotta's Fountain to the city of San Francisco.

John Augustus Sutter, a native of Germany, was among the earliest and most influential of California's pioneers. He established Sutter's Fort as a successful trading post on his Mexican land grant at New Helvetia, now called Sacramento. Sutter set out to make his fortune providing one of the most precious of frontier commodities—lumber. But in 1848, his right-hand man, James Marshall, found yellow specks of metal in the tailrace of Sutter's sawmill at Coloma. When word got out, the great gold rush was on. Sutter's workers ran off to the diggings, and miners continually pillaged his mill for boards to use in their sluices. Sutter never recovered from the problems caused by the gold-seekers, and creditors forced him into bankruptcy. He eventually retired to Pennsylvania embittered and impoverished. He once commented on the irony that had it not been for the discovery of gold, he would have been a rich man.

At the age of forty-two, Galen Clark came to the invigorating mountain air of Yosemite to restore his tuberculosis-ridden lungs after being given only a short time to live. He was the first settler in the Wawona area, and for several years his log cabin was the only way station on the southern route into the valley. In 1866, two years after Yosemite was made a state grant, Clark was appointed its "Guardian." Throughout the rest of his life he became an inseparable part of the park's history. And the mountain air must have agreed with him. He died at the ripe old age of ninety-six.

Seth Kinman was one of California's most colorful characters. He was an avid huntsman drawn to the West by the gold rush in 1849. In short order he found that digging for gold was hard work and that a better living could be made providing the miners with meat.

He eventually settled in the remote Humboldt Bay region of Northern California in 1852, where the sparse population and unruly Indians made life appealing only to the hardiest of pioneers. He was attracted by the abundance of wild game and became the provider of fresh meat to the town of Eureka and newly established Fort Humboldt.

J. Carbutt, Photographer, Chicago, Illinois.
196.—Seth Kinman, The California Trapper.

Kinman was a one-man killing machine, bagging hundreds of elk and grizzlies during his lifetime. A by-product of his skill was a huge pile of elk antlers that he fashioned into elaborate chairs by intertwining pairs of horns. He became famous as the provider of these unique chairs to four presidents, including Abraham Lincoln.

Clad entirely in buckskins, Kinman, with his long white hair, stood out like a sore thumb wherever he went. His lively fiddle playing, frontier tales, and flintlock rifle, called "Old Cotton Bale," made him the center of attention. On trips to eastern cities he was the most photographed person in town. In later years Kinman operated small museums and toured the country showing off his lifelong accumulation of Indian souvenirs, curiosities, guns, chairs, and a variety of handmade treasures. Among the artifacts he toted from place to place were a fiddle made from a mule's skull and a stuffed grizzly bear on wheels.

Gold Rush Storytellers

The gold rush era itself was a gold mine of material for writers. Easterners hungered for stories about the frenzied search for wealth in the West. Samuel Clemens helped fill the bill. He started as a reporter on the Territorial Enterprise, *in Virginia City, Nevada, where he first used the pseudonym Mark Twain. But in 1864, his involvement in a dueling incident forced him to flee the state, and he moved on to a position with the* Call *in San Francisco. There he rubbed elbows with the city's literati, and his most productive acquaintance was Bret Harte, editor of* The Californian. *Harte was instrumental in polishing Twain's writing style to capture the essence of frontier humor. The experience led to such successes as* The Celebrated Jumping Frog of Calaveras County *and* Roughing It.

Bret Harte established his own place in the bohemian literary world of 1860s San Francisco. He became a master of short stories for the Overland Monthly, *dwelling on the colorful and robust tales rooted in the gold rush era of California.* The Outcasts of Poker Flat, The Luck of Roaring Camp, *and* Plain Language from Truthful James *captured the pathos, morality, and humor of mythical life in the mining camps.*

The Artists

Albert Bierstadt developed an uncanny ability to capture the awe-inspiring drama of western landscapes. He was, perhaps, the most famous artist to visit California, and Yosemite became his favorite subject. The view at left is one of two that Eadweard Muybridge made of Bierstadt as he sketched local Indians in the valley. Muybridge made a third stereoview of Bierstadt posing with the geologist Clarence King in the high country. The interests of the three men—artist, photographer, and geologist—were quite intertwined in the summer of 1872 as they explored the magnificent landscape together. The Yosemite stereoviews taken by Muybridge had a tremendous impact on Bierstadt's work. He used them to derive the same illusionistic, three-dimensional qualities in his paintings.

Thomas Hill (right) is the artist most closely associated with Yosemite. He was a prolific painter who, for years, sold his canvases at studios in the valley and adjacent to the Wawona Hotel.

Hill's lifelong friend Virgil Williams (left) came to San Francisco to paint copies of the works of old masters to hang in the art museum at Woodward's Gardens. He eventually became a respected artist in his own right—his subject, California landscapes. (Photo by C. E. Watkins, 1865.)

San Francisco's Emperor

In 1853, Joshua Norton's get-rich plan was foolproof. As an established and successful entrepreneur, he would simply buy up the scheduled shiploads of rice arriving in San Francisco, corner the market, and wait for prices to rise. The plan went awry when unanticipated shipments arrived, and his own stockpiles became worthless. Norton was devastated at the loss of his wealth, and his mind eventually snapped. For years he roamed the city on foot and bicycle as the self-proclaimed "Norton I, Emperor of the United States and Protector of Mexico." To affirm his rank he created his own military-style costume consisting of a tall plumed hat, a saber, and a navy blue coat with epaulettes and brass buttons.

Only San Francisco could indulge a character such as Norton. The citizenry took a sympathetic attitude toward the penniless old gent and accepted his worthless promissory notes in return for meals and drinks. He traveled by train at no charge and was guest of the house on frequent trips to the theater. Two scruffy, rat-killing mongrels, Bummer and Lazarus, were always at his side. At times Norton issued proclamations, one of which directed the Central Pacific Railroad to build suspension bridges spanning the bay. When Norton died, in 1880, leading merchants chipped in to ensure that he received a funeral befitting an emperor.

This portrait of John Muir (right) and Teddy Roosevelt on Glacier Point was taken by a photographer with the Keystone View Company during the president's visit to Yosemite in 1903. Although half of this stereoview has been published many times as a single image, it is presented here for the first time in full stereo.

John Muir—On the Rocks

John Muir was obsessed with preserving the American wilderness. Mountaineering was his religion, and he practiced it diligently as he traveled to every corner of the globe. Yosemite became Muir's favorite stamping ground from his first visit in 1868. He did not just study the unique landscape, he immersed himself in it. He rode avalanches and climbed to the top of tall pines to take in the "wild music" of mountain storms. He reveled in the excitement of Yosemite's earthquakes and devised ways to study their movements. There were times when he almost got himself killed—attempting to peer into the winter ice cone at the base of Yosemite Falls and clambering around in places where no man should go. In 1892, as a co-founder and first president of the Sierra Club, Muir established a viable means for advancing public awareness of the importance of preserving the wild places that invigorate people's lives.

THE FRENCH RESIDENTS COMMEMORATE A CENTURY OF LIBERTY
WASHINGTON
LAFAYETTE
1876
IMPORTERS OF
PUTNAM

Front-Page Events

The importance of photographers as witnesses to history is well illustrated by their lasting photographs of passing events. Matthew Brady started it all when he sent his cameramen to record from beginning to end the event of all events—the Civil War. Because the exposure times of their lenses were just too slow for action shots, the photographers were unable to capture actual battle scenes. But they did come away with a wealth of documentary material showing every facet of the conflict—troop movements, embattlements, captured rebels, architectural ruins, corpses littering the battlefields, as well as the general misery of war. They showed for the first time that the camera could be more than just a studio contraption for memorializing the faces of American families, immigrants, and celebrities.

Since the Civil War, photojournalists have dragged their cameras to the scenes of events to capture those sudden fleeting glimpses of moments in time. The stereo camera was particularly suited for this. It was the lightest and most portable of the primitive cameras and was the only type of camera present to record certain events. The resulting wealth of stereoviews is a godsend to historians. The camera has an awesome power to convince, and that power is further validated by the stereoscopic effect.

Sacramento, sitting squarely on the banks of the Sacramento River, had a history of floods. Big ones in 1850 and 1851 prodded townsfolk to raise the level of the streets two feet and to shore up weakened levees. Still, the rains that fell in December 1861 and January 1862 created the worst disaster yet for the capital city. Again the waters rose, higher than ever, creating considerable damage and prompting newspapermen to proclaim Sacramento a "doomed city." Citizens were undeterred and once more pursued the herculean task of raising the level of the streets and buildings another eight feet over the next decade.

"Sacramento During the Flood." K Street east from Fourth Street, No. 9. (Published by Lawrence & Houseworth.)

Fortunately the destruction of the flood of 1862 was recorded in stereo by at least one photographer, Charles L. Weed. Weed had previously taken a few stereoviews of the waterfront and streets in 1859. Together these are the earliest stereoviews of Sacramento.

"Sacramento During the Flood." Fifth Street south from L Street, No. 12. (Published by Lawrence & Houseworth.)

Lincoln Obsequies

Portrait taken in Matthew Brady's gallery, Washington, D.C., 1861.

On April 9, 1865, General Lee surrendered his confederate forces to General Grant at Appomattox, and the Civil War came to an end. With this eventful moment in American history, the burden of the nation was lifted from the shoulders of President Abraham Lincoln. He was free to set about realizing the fulfillment of his greatest dream—the equality of all people. But the dream was shattered only five days later when his assassin, John Wilkes Booth, fired a bullet into Lincoln's head at Ford's Theater.

As the president's body lay in state in the nation's capital, word was telegraphed to mayors of cities across the land that obsequies would be held simultaneously at 12:00 noon on Wednesday, April 19.

In San Francisco the outpouring of grief from the citizenry typified the nation's mourning for its respected leader. Businessmen closed their establishments, draped their buildings in black bunting, and lowered all flags to half-staff. At exactly twelve noon on Wednesday, an endless procession of San Franciscans and civic groups marched silently on foot through the streets from Washington Square, across Market Street, and back to the Mechanics' Pavilion on Stockton for the final eulogies. In the midst of the procession was a large catafalque drawn by six gray horses. The black-canopied base supported a ceremonial sarcophagus bearing the name "Lincoln" in simple gilt letters.

Wreck of the Viscata

On March 7, 1868, the British vessel *Viscata* was swept ashore at Baker Beach, near Fort Point, en route for the open sea. It was loaded with wheat and bound for Liverpool. After getting caught in a severe backcurrent, the pilot, Captain Jolliff, struggled in vain to arrest the ship's course by dropping one of the anchors, but the cable snapped like a thread. Even though the economy-minded owners had not provided a steam tug for the *Viscata,* the pilot nevertheless should have made a routine departure from the bay. Jolliff's license was lifted for having strayed from his course and having failed to make use of a second anchor. It was not the first ship he had lost. He had grounded the *Oliver Cutts* on the rocks off Alcatraz Island only a few weeks earlier.

The Viscata *was quite a spectacle. It foundered like a beached whale for three weeks while various attempts to pull it free failed. Newspapers touted the best routes by which curious onlookers could get to the scene, and the steamer* Goliath *took sightseers on Sunday excursions to the site. Workers managed to unload most of the wheat by way of chutes, and soon after, waves pummeled the* Viscata *until its sides broke apart and timbers scattered over the beach. C. E. Watkins was the only photographer who took pictures of the vessel over several days at various stages of its deterioration.*

CALIFORNIA.
ILLUSTRATED BY HELIOS' FLYING STUDIO.
453—Mill at Haywood after eathquake, 21st October, 1868.

Earthquake of 1868

The big quake of 1906 was not the first to wreak havoc upon the Bay Area. At 7:53 A.M. on October 21, 1868, the most severe shock to date struck the area, its epicenter near Hayward. It lasted for almost a minute and has been estimated at 7.0 on the Richter scale.

San Franciscans thought Judgment Day had arrived as they were jostled from their beds. A considerable amount of damage was reported by the newspapers, mostly roofs caving in, chimneys toppling, and brick firewalls buckling. Some of the accounts were a bit amusing; the Eureka Dairy, on Stockton Street, had the cream on its milk pans so stirred up that it was useless. A team of horses belonging to the Union Bakery ran off with the delivery wagon, leaving a trail of bread scattered over several blocks. People were seen moving their chairs into the middle of the streets, where they waited for the aftershocks.

The Daily Morning Chronicle *suggested this was the severest earthquake that San Francisco would likely ever experience. But it was merely a portent of things to come.*

The summer of 1876 was an eventful one in American history. Custer's cavalry was massacred at the Little Big Horn, the Jesse James gang made its last major raid on a Minnesota bank, and Bill Hickok was shot dead during a poker game in Deadwood. These distractions in the seemingly wild and woolly West, however, did not deter Americans from celebrating the country's first one hundred years of progress. The big event for showing off the nation's technology was the Centennial Exhibition held in Philadelphia, where the Declaration of Independence was signed in 1776. But other cities planned extravaganzas, and San Francisco was not to be outdone.

San Franciscans gaily decorated their buildings in flags and bunting and prepared for three days of unrestrained festivities. A fifty-foot-high triumphal arch was erected by the French population at Kearny and Sutter streets and proved to be the grandest of the city's decorations. A Master Mariners' Regatta, torchlight parade, and Carnival Ball were among the events.

A naval "bombardment" at the Presidio was scheduled to show off the military's firepower between shore batteries and warships. An improvised ironclad monitor, actually an old scow with a false wooden turret, was rigged with explosives to create a spectacular blast when fired upon by artillery from Alcatraz and offshore vessels. None of the rounds hit their mark, and in a rather inglorious ending, a crew was finally dispatched to set off the old tub.

"FREE-VIEWING"

"Free-viewing" is the art of focusing the eyes to see stereocards in 3-D without the aid of a mechanical viewer. Collectors strive to accomplish this for the freedom of viewing cards when a stereoscope is not available. Some people find free-viewing impossible to master; their eyes may be too close together or their patience may wear thin, but for those who stick with it, the results can be intriguing. Most of the stereoviews in this book have been reduced from their actual length of 7 inches to 5 inches, which makes free-viewing easier to accomplish.

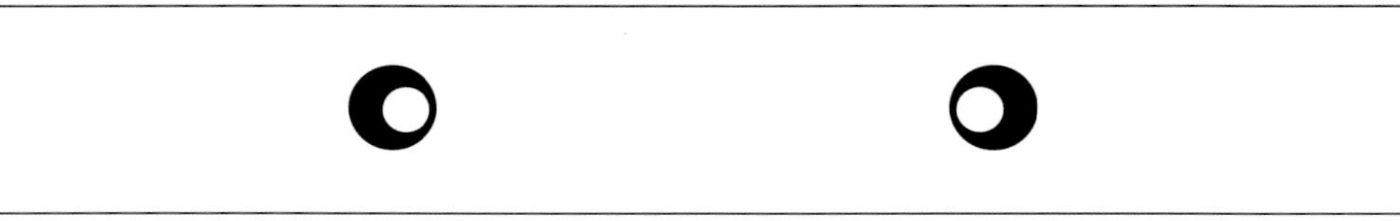

One of the easier free-viewing techniques involves making a card to lay on the page above each illustration as a guide for prefocusing the eyes. Make a photocopy or a replica of the card above containing two precise dots spaced the same distance apart as the centers of the two stereo images. Lay the card flat on the page directly above a stereoview illustration. Stare at a point between the two dots as if you were looking *through* the card at a point in the distance. If the two dots merge into one dot in the center, with a dot appearing in peripheral vision on each side, then you have accomplished parallel fusion; that is, your lines of sight are parallel rather than converging. The right eye is now looking at the right image, and the left eye is looking at the left image. Without blinking, lower your eyes onto the stereoview illustration. If you can hold that position, then the stereoview should appear in amazing 3-D. It will take some practice to hold the eyes in parallel fusion. Free-viewing is simply an alternative to using the enclosed viewer.

For Further Reading

Lawrence & Houseworth/Thomas Houseworth & Company: A Unique View of the West 1860-1886, by Peter E. Palmquist. Columbus, Ohio: National Stereoscopic Association, 1980. The text gives an insight into the early business of stereo production on the West Coast and the volume of work created by these pioneer publishers.

Points of View: The Stereograph in America, a Cultural History, edited by Edward W. Earle. Rochester, New York: Visual Studies Workshop, 1979. The results of a seminar and workshop concentrating on the stereograph as a primary source of visual history.

Return to Eldorado: A Century of California Stereographs from the Collection of Peter Palmquist. Riverside: California Museum of Photography, University of California, 1986. An exhibition catalog featuring examples from a major collection of California stereoviews and an essay on stereoscopy by Peter Palmquist.

Stereoviews: An Illustrated History and Price Guide, by John Waldsmith. Radnor, Pennsylvania: Wallace-Homestead Book Company, 1991. The first complete book on stereophotography for collectors at all levels. Includes a history of stereoviews, biographies of leading photographers and publishers, list of dealers, and tips on collecting cards and organizing information.

The World of Stereographs, by William C. Darrah. Self-published, Gettysburg, Pennsylvania, 1977. The Bible for stereoview collectors, librarians, and historians. Surveys stereoviews on the basis of historical, geographical, and topical points of view with information about worldwide stereophotographers.

The National Stereoscopic Association is a nonprofit organization that brings stereo buffs together to promote the history, appreciation, and collecting of stereoviews. *Stereo World* magazine is published six times yearly with articles of original research devoted to all aspects of stereoscopy from antique to modern. It is also the best source for stereoview dealers, mail auctions, and photo show announcements. The highlight of NSA activities is the annual convention, held in a different city each year with three days of seminars, presentations, and exhibits and a trade fair, an auction, and photographic excursions to local attractions. Membership information is available (with SASE) from N. S. A., P. O. Box 14801, Columbus, Ohio 43214.

The Monster Crab on display at Woodward's Gardens, San Francisco. (Photo by Eadweard Muybridge, c. 1867.)

Index